BUILDERS OF EMPIRE

BUILDERS OF EMPIRE

FREEMASONS AND

BRITISH IMPERIALISM,

1717–1927

JESSICA L. HARLAND-JACOBS

The University of North Carolina Press

Chapel Hill

Designed by Amy Ruth Buchanan
Set in Carter & Cone Galliard by Keystone Typesetting, Inc.
Manufactured in the United States of America. The paper in this book
meets the guidelines for permanence and durability of the Committee
on Production Guidelines for Book Longevity of the Council
on Library Resources.

*Frontispiece: The Duke of Connaught, English Grand Master, leading
a Masonic procession, Bulawayo, Rhodesia, 1910 (copyright, and reproduced
by permission of, the United Grand Lodge of England).*

Library of Congress Cataloging-in-Publication Data

Harland-Jacobs, Jessica.

Builders of empire : Freemasons and British imperialism, 1717–1927 /
Jessica L. Harland-Jacobs.

p. cm.

Includes bibliographical references and index.

ISBN-13: 978-0-8078-3088-8 (cloth : alk. paper)

1. Freemasonry — Great Britain — History. 2. Imperialism — History.
3. Great Britain — Colonies — History. I. Title.

HS595.S5.H37 2007

366'.109410903 — dc22   2006020060

Portions of this book appeared previously, in somewhat different form, as
" 'Hands Across the Sea': The Masonic Network, British Imperialism, and
the North Atlantic World," *Geographical Review* 89 (April 1999): 237–53,
used here by permission of the American Geographic Society, and "All in
the Family: Freemasonry and the British Empire in the Mid-Nineteenth
Century," *Journal of British Studies* 42 (October 2003): 448–82, used here
by permission of the University of Chicago Press.

11 10 09 08 07   5 4 3 2 1

To

MATT,

ALEXANDRA,

and

JEREMY

CONTENTS

ILLUSTRATIONS, MAP,
AND TABLES

ILLUSTRATIONS

ACKNOWLEDGMENTS

This book began many years ago with a question I posed at the end of a compelling lecture on the United Irish Rebellion of 1798. The lecturer, Jim Smyth (who is cited frequently in Chapter 3), was conducting a Cambridge summer course on Irish history in which he briefly discussed the role of Masonic lodges as vectors of revolution in the 1790s. After class, I asked for more details. To be sure, I had picked up passing references to the Masons in conversations and the media, but I had no inkling of who they were, what they did, and what their history was. Smyth informed me that the Masons were an eighteenth-century fraternity that had played a very significant yet understudied role in Irish history. A couple of weeks later, on the plane ride home from the UK, I was engrossed in reading for the first time Kipling's novel *Kim*. There they were again! Kim O'Hara, the orphaned child of an Irish soldier (and Mason) who had died in India, escapes life in a Masonic orphanage to travel around India with an itinerant holy man. Feeling like some sort of conspiracy was beginning to engulf me, I decided to look further into the matter of Freemasonry and empire during my first semester in graduate school. I have been intrigued ever since.

This project first took shape under the keen direction of several excellent scholars at Duke University. Although John Cell initially expressed skepticism about how a non-Mason, and a woman at that, could gain access to the records of a secretive fraternity, he soon became convinced of the value and feasibility of the project and offered me sincere encouragement and effective guidance. He taught me a tremendous amount about researching, conceptualizing, writing, and teaching the history of the British Empire, particularly by setting an example for me to follow. My only regret in this whole enterprise is that he is not here to see the finished product. I also owe much to John Thompson, Susan Thorne, Kären Wigen, Peter Wood, Jan Ewald, and Cynthia Herrup. I admire each of them greatly and appreciate the role each played in shaping me into a historian. Daniel Baugh and the late Nan Karwan-Cutting at Cornell University were formative influences during an earlier phase in my life and also have my profound respect and appreciation.

I would like to thank the Center for European Studies at Columbia University, the Government of Canada, Duke University, and the University of Florida for providing funding at various stages of this project.

Cell's skepticism about my getting access to sources was understandable, but, as I soon learned, easily answered. Every step along the way, I have benefited from the openness and helpfulness of members of the brotherhood as well as Masonic archivists and librarians. I would like to thank the Grand Lodge of Canada in Ontario and the Grand Lodge of Nova Scotia for allowing me to work in their libraries. Bill Krueger at the Iowa Masonic Library was extremely helpful during my visit to Cedar Rapids and in subsequently sending many a book for me to consult from afar. Over the length of this project I have worked my way through three librarians at Freemasons' Hall in London: John Ashby, Rebecca Coombs, and Martin Cherry. Each provided a different kind of assistance at a different stage of the project, but each played a crucial role, enabling me to take full advantage of their remarkable library and archives. I am especially indebted to Martin Cherry for his help in procuring many of the images that bring this text to life and promptly answering last-minute inquiries. To the director of the library, Diane Clements, and the jovial staff of book fetchers and tour guides, I extend my heartfelt thanks for welcoming me over the course of three visits. The staff at Freemasons' Hall, Dublin, especially Alexandra Ward and Rebecca Hayes, was equally eager to assist and instrumental in helping me complete this project. Irish Masonic historian Keith Cochrane supplied me with a copy of his highly useful CD-ROM, *Irish Masonic Records*, for which I am very grateful.

I consulted the collections of several institutions outside the world of Masonic archives (a full list appears in the bibliography). I extend my thanks to the staffs of all these libraries and archives, especially that of the British Library (including the Oriental and India Office Collections). Terry Barringer, at the Royal Commonwealth Society Collection, provided me with an especially memorable experience when she took me into the bowels of the Cambridge University Library and opened before my eyes the full lodge chest of the Royal Colonial Institute Lodge (founded 1912).

I have benefited from the astute feedback of colleagues working in British history and in the history of Freemasonry. Fellow panelists and commentators at numerous conferences helped send this project in new directions. Doug Peers had many helpful suggestions as I worked to transform the dissertation into a book. Dane Kennedy did the same and also helped me refine my arguments about Freemasonry's relationship to the Enlightenment. Margaret Jacob has taken a strong interest in my work over the years and offered helpful advice about publishing. The book measurably improved as a result of the careful attention of two readers for the University of North Carolina Press. John Mackenzie provided encouragement as well as critical assessment; I am especially grateful for his urging me to look further into the history of Freemasonry in South Africa. Steven C. Bullock was an incredibly thorough and insightful reader. Even a brief perusal of my endnotes reveals my enormous debt to his research and ideas.

Chuck Grench at UNC Press was enthusiastic about this project from the moment I first presented it to him. He was masterful at coordinating and offering feedback while also allowing this project to remain very much my own. Working with Katy O'Brien, Ron Maner, Eric Schramm, and a number of other individuals at the press has been a privilege and a pleasure. Their professionalism, efficiency, and responsiveness are unmatched.

At the University of Florida, I am indebted to a very supportive department and a number of individuals who are not only my colleagues but also my friends and fellow travelers. My thanks to Swapna Banerjee, Rori Blum, Nina Caputo, Matt Jacobs, Angel Kwolek-Folland, Charlie Montgomery, Leah Rosenberg, and Luise White for reading various parts of the manuscript. I feel especially grateful for the keen insight and unwavering support of Sheryl Kroen, who gave so freely of her time and played a crucial role in the main revision of the book. Her ability to see arguments and assist in their formulation, as well as her generosity of spirit, are truly remarkable. Matt Gallman, Bill Link, Howard Louthan, Joe Spillane, Brian Ward, and Jenny Ward provided valuable assistance once I entered the publishing stage of this project.

Thanks to Catherine Phipps, Jon and Beverly Sensbach, Peggy and Tom Grimm, and Grace Kang and Jonathan Helton for their invaluable friendship. Thanks also to my extended family for their interest in this project—for sending pictures of Masonic halls around the country and newspaper clippings about matters Masonic. Through the years Randall, Dana, Jory, and Marc Harland and Julie, Dave, Douglas, and Bradley Rouse have provided welcome breaks from working and writing; they will certainly breathe a collective sigh of relief now that "BAB" is finally finished. My parents, Edgar and Beverly Harland, have spent countless hours taking care of their grandchildren and made it easier for me to have both a family and a career. I also thank my father for reading almost every word I have ever written and his expeditions on my behalf to Davis Library at the University of North Carolina, Chapel Hill. I thank my mother for having high expectations and for encouraging me as a writer for as long as I can remember.

My most profound debt is to Matt Jacobs, who skillfully balances the demands of critic, husband, and friend. He offered astute commentary on endless drafts of this book and enriched the project in inestimable ways. My accomplishments owe much to his encouragement, help, and unfailing confidence in me, no matter the endeavor. Alexandra Jacobs, age six, and Jeremy Jacobs, age three, have never known me without this book. Alexandra's insatiable curiosity seems amazingly to extend even to the writing and publishing of books. Jeremy's humorous observations on life have offered welcome comic relief. Together they have helped me renew my appreciation for many of life's most important pleasures (like playing with puppies, building Lego, and reading Richard Scarry). I am grateful to them for regularly pulling me out of the past and keeping me squarely anchored in the present. I dedicate this book to the three of them as meager compensation for their forbearance, their support, and, most of all, their love.

BUILDERS OF EMPIRE

INTRODUCTION

The Ancient and Honourable Fraternity
of Free and Accepted Masons

In 1827 a letter from a police magistrate in the young colony of New South Wales arrived at the offices of the Grand Lodge of English Freemasonry. The magistrate's name was John Stephen. The son of an English judge, he had migrated to Sydney less than a year before sending the letter. In the intervening months, he told Masonic officials in the metropole, he had familiarized himself with "the state of Masonry in this distant part of the World." Stephen expressed both concern and optimism. He was worried about what he saw as an overabundance of Irish lodges in the colony as well as the lack of a centralized authority to shepherd those who wanted to affiliate with English lodges. But he was sanguine about the prospects for Freemasonry in the settlements, which were rapidly expanding with the "almost daily" influx of free emigrants. In the letter, this rather ordinary colonist proceeded to make two keen observations about the role of Freemasonry in the burgeoning British Empire of the early nineteenth century. First he observed that "the greater part of the free community have been admitted as Masons in England from the prevailing notion of the *necessity* of being so on becoming Travellers." By this point Masonry had earned a well-deserved reputation for being an institution that offered its members a passport to countless benefits available in all parts of the empire and, indeed, throughout the world. Second, Stephen realized that this brotherhood had a role to play in strengthening the British Empire. The growth of Freemasonry in the Australian colonies would serve to create "an eternal bond of unity which will more closely connect this colony with England than any other that can possibly be devised." Though Stephen was writing about a particular part of the empire at a particular moment, his observations about Freemasonry's value to colonists and the empire are applicable across time and space.[1]

The fraternity to which this early-nineteenth-century police magistrate belonged — the Ancient and Honourable Fraternity of Free and Accepted Masons — had formally emerged in London in 1717, though its roots extend back to mid-seventeenth-century Scotland and England. During the mid-eighteenth century, the brotherhood became a global institution. One by one, lodges took root throughout the British Isles, Europe, Britain's Atlantic empire, and the wider world. Freemasonry expanded as the empire expanded, and the main centers of Masonic activity abroad paralleled the main centers of the eighteenth-century empire: the Caribbean, British North America, and South Asia. By 1752 the Grand Lodges of England, Ireland, and Scotland had warranted lodges in Bengal, Gibraltar, Pennsylvania, Massachusetts, Georgia, South Carolina, New Hampshire, the Caribbean, Nova Scotia, New York, Newfoundland, Turkey, Rhode Island, and Connecticut. Provincial grand masters were appointed for the East Indies, the North American colonies, Montserrat, Antigua, Barbados, and Jamaica. In the subsequent half-century the British set up lodges in Madras, several additional American colonies, Bombay, Quebec, Bermuda, Honduras, Upper Canada, New Brunswick, Gambia, Prince Edward Island, Ghana, and New South Wales. This period also witnessed British Freemasonry's export to areas outside the formal empire: Dutch Guiana and the Cape, Sumatra, China, Florida, Ceylon, and Argentina. Meanwhile, Freemasonry had spread to Europe and then, in its various national guises, into the empires of France, the Netherlands, Spain, and Portugal.

The primary mechanism responsible for the building of this expansive network of lodges was the regimental lodge. By the early nineteenth century, every regiment in the British army boasted at least one lodge that accompanied it on its imperial sojourns. Freemasons in the army helped plant permanent lodges among civilian populations in colonies of all types. Exposed to Freemasonry in the British Isles, nineteenth-century emigrants also directly exported the brotherhood by requesting warrants to set up their own lodges in their new homes in North America, Australasia, and southern Africa. As in the eighteenth century, the metropolitan grand lodges continued to establish provincial grand lodges wherever the brotherhood took root or was expected to flourish. The three mechanisms — regimental lodges, the processes of migration, and provincial

TABLE 1. British Overseas Lodges (including military lodges)

	English	Scottish	Irish
1850	222	12[a]	53
1859	293	46	64[b]
1875	369	—	76[c]
1886	541	208	76
1890	432	175	74
1900	469	218	50
1930	704	321	65

Sources: Grand Lodge of Scotland Proceedings; Laurie, History of Free Masonry; Freemasons' Calendar and Pocket Book (London, 1850, 1859, 1886, 1890, 1900, 1930); Irish Freemasons' Calendar and Directory (Dublin, 1850, 1856, 1876, 1886, 1890, 1900, 1930); FC 111, 2869 (4 January 1930): 4–5.

Note: The decrease in English lodges between 1886 and 1890 is attributable to the founding of independent grand lodges in New South Wales and Victoria. See Table 6.

a. 1836
b. 1856
c. 1876

grand lodges — combined to effect the proliferation of a vast network of lodges that connected men across the formal and informal empires. Freemasonry spread so effectively that by the late 1880s the Grand Master of Scotland could justifiably claim: "Wherever our flag has gone, we are able to say there has Masonry gone, and we have been able to found lodges for those who have left our shores to found fresh empires."[2] In fact, over 820 British lodges were at work throughout the empire by this point; this figure does not include the hundreds of lodges under the semi-independent grand lodges in Canada, Australia, New Zealand, and South Africa (see Tables 1–3).

Wherever they happened to be, British Freemasons called on what one nineteenth-century member aptly described as Masonry's "vast chain extending round the whole globe."[3] Merchants and colonial administrators, soldiers and officers, and ordinary colonists of all types joined the brotherhood because membership offered a passport to convivial society, moral and spiritual refinement, material assistance, and social advancement in all parts of the empire. By fulfilling a variety of needs — ranging from homosocial association to easing

TABLE 2. Lodges in India (including Ceylon and Burma)

	English	Scottish	Irish
1859	56	7	1[a]
1886	109	34	4
1890	113	37	4
1900	138	43	3
1930	229	78	14

Note: These figures are subsets of the figures in Table 1.

a. 1856

men's transition from one colonial society to another — belonging to the fraternity made life easier for Britons who ran, defended, and lived in the empire. Its appeal extended to men in the highest echelons of the British imperial world, men like Benjamin Franklin, Joseph Brant, Prince Edward (Duke of Kent), Lord Hastings, Lord Durham, Lord Dalhousie, Lord Kitchener, Lord Wolseley, and the Duke of Connaught. It had a strong presence in the official institutions of empire, especially the army, the monarchy, and the colonial service. Freemasonry, it appears, was central to the building and cohesion of the empire. Observing this fundamentally reciprocal relationship between Freemasonry and imperialism, former Secretary of State for the Colonies and high-ranking Masonic official Lord Carnarvon proclaimed: "Following closely in the wake of colonisation, wherever the hut of the settler has been built, or the flag of conquest waved, there Masonry has soon equal dominion. . . . It has reflected . . . and consolidated the British Empire."[4] This book tells the story of British imperial Freemasonry and, in the process, offers some new ways to think about the history of imperialism.

Like the empire it helped to constitute, Freemasonry — and the conceptions of brotherhood it promoted — underwent significant changes in the period examined here. From its beginnings the institution identified closely with the ideals of Enlightenment cosmopolitanism: universal brotherhood, sociability, toleration, and benevolence. The only stated requirement for membership was belief in the existence of a supreme being, described generically in the lodge as

TABLE 3. Lodges in the Caribbean

	English	Scottish	Irish
1859	35	14	2[a]
1886	29	21	2
1890	29	21	2
1900	28	14	2
1930	27	21	3

Note: These figures are subsets of the figures in Table 1.

a. 1856

the Great Architect of the Universe (GAOTU). Thus, the institution claimed to admit men of any religious, political, national, or racial background. As one eighteenth-century Masonic orator put it, Masonry "teacheth Men of every Nation, of every different Faith, and of every Rank in Life, overlooking the Prejudices and Distinctions, which Education or Fortune may have established, to embrace one another like Brethren, and to give the Soul to Harmony and Love."[5] To preserve a tolerant environment, the rules of the order forbade the discussion of politics and religion within the lodge.

Examining the fate of Freemasonry's inclusive promise in the diverse historical circumstances presented by the British Empire is the central hinge upon which this story unfolds. The British Empire of the eighteenth century provided fertile ground for the building and functioning of an extensive Masonic network (Chapter 1). In this period, the fraternity remained a relatively fluid and inclusive institution that did, at times, live up to its ideology of cosmopolitan brotherhood. Although dominated by white Protestant men, eighteenth-century British Masonry did have room in its lodges for Jews and Muslims, African Americans and South Asians, and other "others." Women, however, were never admitted into Masonic fellowship; Freemasonry's cosmopolitanism was by definition fraternal (Chapter 2). Eighteenth-century Masonry also included men of a diverse range of political opinions who both supported and challenged the Whig oligarchy running Hanoverian Britain and its growing empire (Chapter 3).

As Britain withstood the age of revolution and emerged victorious from the Napoleonic Wars, Masonry underwent a major transformation that reflected the strengthening currents of nationalism, capitalism, and imperialism. Like their eighteenth-century brethren, nineteenth-century Freemasons continued to champion Masonry's ideology of openness, but in practice the brotherhood abandoned, to a great degree, its cosmopolitan and radical pasts. Reacting against Freemasonry's elasticity during the previous century, grand lodge officials fought and won a struggle to gain control over the brotherhood by consciously identifying the brotherhood with loyalty to the state. Meanwhile, as the Catholic Church waged a sustained campaign against worldwide Freemasonry, the brotherhood became a primarily Protestant institution (Chapter 4). In the colonies, Masonry's long-established associations with men of prominence (such as military officers and colonial governors) made it attractive to rising men who sought status and power to accompany their wealth. Local lodges were willing to admit some men of humble origins, but colonial Masons made every effort to ensure the respectability of the brotherhood by regulating the membership, conducting elaborate public ceremonials, and keeping leadership positions in the hands of the most respectable brethren. The brotherhood was thus instrumental in the making of a colonial middle class and defining its boundaries at the very moment its male constituents were entering into power-sharing arrangements with traditional elites (Chapter 5). The brotherhood that was initially open to all men was, after the age of revolution, dominated by loyalist, Protestant, respectable white men. It thus reflected and contributed to the "fundamental reordering of the Empire" as the old Atlantic empire transformed into the so-called "Second British Empire" of the nineteenth century.[6]

By the last third of the nineteenth century, the Masonic brotherhood had become an unquestioning ally of the British imperial state. It took part in various efforts to shore up the empire in the face of internal and external pressures during the age of high imperialism. Imperial proconsuls like Kitchener, Wolseley, and Connaught considered Freemasonry a valuable ally not only as they governed and defended the empire but also as they pursued the imperialist mission of making the empire a source of national strength. In places like Canada, Australia, and New Zealand, the brotherhood helped turn men into ardent citizens of the empire who contributed their energy, money, and even their lives to the imperial cause (Chapter 7). Meanwhile, outside the settlement colonies, indigenous men of various religious and racial backgrounds had begun seeking admission into Masonry. The empire became a practical testing ground of Freemasons' commitment to their ideology of cosmopolitan brotherhood in an age of increasingly racialized attitudes. British Freemasons on the imperial periphery ultimately and reluctantly admitted native elites but they did so only because they believed it would help strengthen the empire (Chapter 6). As it turned out, many indigenous elites were attracted to Masonry because of its ideology of cosmopolitan brotherhood, an ideology that could be used as much to undermine as to uphold British imperialism (Conclusion).

Telling the story of British imperial Freemasonry — of an Enlightenment brotherhood that intersected with imperialism and was transformed as a result — requires us to journey far and wide. Like many of the individuals examined in these pages, we will travel from the metropole out into the empire and back to the British Isles. Time and again, the history of Freemasonry demonstrates the great extent to which metropole and colony were mutually constitutive spaces, parts of an "imperial social formation" comprised of distinctive yet interacting domestic and imperial contexts.[7] The "metropole," for our purposes, consists of England, Wales, Scotland, and Ireland. Though historians of Masonry have focused on specific "national" contexts within the British Isles, the brotherhood was in fact a British institution that should be approached adopting the perspectives and assumptions of "British history."[8] Occupying an ambiguous place in between metropole and empire, Ireland is especially crucial to the story of British imperial Freemasonry. First, the Irish Grand Lodge devised most of the administrative mechanisms that facilitated Masonry's spread abroad. Second, the activities of Irish Masons in London spurred the creation of a rival English grand lodge, known as "the Ancients," with enormous consequences for Masonry in both the British Isles and the empire. Third, events in Ireland at the turn of the nineteenth century precisely illustrate the shift toward loyalism traced in the middle of the book. Finally — as we see in John Stephen's letter quoted above — Irish Masons in the colonies often met with resistance from the English "brethren" who accused the Irish of lacking respectability and being troublemakers. As a result, Irish Masons in places like Upper Canada and New South Wales spearheaded movements to set up independent grand lodges in the colonies. Thus, the very complexity that causes many historians to avoid Ireland presents in fact a fascinating entrée into the history of British imperialism.[9]

Relating the story of British imperial Freemasonry also requires a comparably expansive approach to the empire. Like much of the so-called "new imperial history," this study examines Britain's relationship with India and the tropical colonies. But it does not sacrifice the settlement colonies in the process. In fact, the brotherhood flourished in the colonies of North America, Australia, New Zealand, and South Africa, where emigrants planted new Britains overseas.

Fully incorporating the Dominions is important for more than the basic reason that Masonry was popular among colonists in these parts; it also has significant methodological payoff. Simultaneously examining developments in the metropole, the dependent empire, and the settlement colonies provides opportunities to ask questions of a comparative nature. For example, how did metropolitan authorities react to concurrent developments in Canada and India? Moreover, it allows us to appreciate Linda Colley's observation "that imperial history is vitally about connexity, the identification and investigation of the manifold connections that existed over time between different sectors of the world and different peoples."[10] So, building on the same question, how did the fact that Masonry's network connected men in Britain, Canada, and India affect concurrent developments in all three places? In these ways, the history of Freemasonry demands that we reclaim the settlement colonies from the historiographical margins to which they have been consigned.[11]

While this history of Freemasonry thus builds on and pushes forward recent work in British history and the new imperial history, it is also conceived as an exercise in world history. Tracking a discrete, identifiable institution across the wide chronological and geographical expanse of the British Empire presents a viable way to "do history" outside the restrictive framework of the nation state, an analytic category whose weight has overwhelmed the historical profession for too long.[12] Notably, this did not start out as a world history project. But the primary sources quickly threw up issues that required attention to the concerns and methodologies of this burgeoning subfield, such as the emergence of commercial networks, the playing out of imperial rivalries, and the movement of people around the world. The world of British Masonry encompassed not only the various elements of Britain's empire — the British Isles, the settlement colonies, India, and the crown colonies — but also parts of the world over which Britain did not claim sovereignty. With British lodges operating throughout Europe, in the empires of European rivals, and in Britain's spheres of commercial influence known as the "informal empire," the British Masonic network stretched to international dimensions. Moreover, Masonry provided a space for men of different nations to meet, even in times of intense national rivalry. The first Masonic meeting to take place in New South Wales, for example, occurred among French naval officers of the Baudin expedition and British officers of the New South Wales Corps in 1802, in the midst of a race to map and thus claim the southern regions of the Australian continent. I have therefore found that simultaneously overlaying the lenses of national, imperial, and transnational history significantly enhances our view of Freemasonry.

Despite Freemasonry's well-established presence in the British Empire and the wider world, historians of imperialism have yet to investigate the brotherhood. In 1969 John M. Roberts published an article entitled "Freemasonry: Possibilities of a Neglected Topic" in the *English Historical Review* in which he urged historians to attend to Freemasonry's rich documentary record in their investigations of eighteenth-century English society and culture. Though he correctly identified Masonic lodges as important "cultural agencies" that functioned "as generators and transmitters of ideas and symbols, and as sources of attitudes and images," Roberts was focused on the English rather than the British or imperial contexts. Ronald Hyam was the first imperial historian to take note of Freemasonry seven years later when he observed in *Britain's Imperial Century* (which has subsequently undergone a second and third edition) that Freemasonry's "function in spreading British cultural influences has . . . been seriously underrated" and urged historians to investigate Freemasonry's role in the empire.[13] In spite of such calls, there is, as yet, no literature for imperial Britain comparable to the sophisticated work on Freemasonry in continental Europe, the thirteen colonies and the nineteenth-century United States, and Russia.[14] The only imperial historian to make Freemasonry a focus of his analysis is Paul J. Rich. Rich has written on the connection between Freemasonry, public schools, and ritualism. Drawing on Gramsci's concept of hegemony, he argues that the British used ritualism as an effective "instrument of control" in extending their power overseas. Freemasonry, according to Rich, was part of the "secret curriculum" of public schools that molded pupils into imperial proconsuls and gave them access to "the ultimate old boy network."[15] Though this work is suggestive regarding the multifaceted nature of imperial power, it treats Masonry in a superficial manner and is insufficiently attuned to specific historical contexts.

Meanwhile, none of the scholars who have examined Freemasonry in Europe and America has studied the brotherhood for what it can tell us about imperialism. Steven C. Bullock's early chapters in *Revolutionary Brotherhood* come the closest, but he is more concerned with the brotherhood's role in colonial North America's transition to democracy than with examining Freemasonry as an imperial institution. And, surprisingly for investigations of a brotherhood that came to span the globe, the existing historiography of Freemasonry displays a distinct lack of transnational perspective. We now know a great deal about the history of the brotherhood in specific national contexts (with Margaret Jacob's study of Freemasonry in Britain, France, and the Netherlands being the most broadly conceived). But the topic's promise for doing connective and comparative history is as yet unrealized. Even the recently published volume edited by William Weisberger, *Freemasonry on Both Sides of the Atlantic*, looks at just that—case studies of Freemasonry in nations on both sides of a body of water that seemed to serve as more of a barrier than a bridge.[16]

The time is ripe, therefore, to see what Freemasonry can reveal to us about British imperialism and, in the process, the "connexity" that resulted from global networks of institutions, commerce, and people. Specifically, my analysis of Freemasonry across two centuries and multiple geographic sites bears on five interconnected themes that run through this study: globalization, supranational institutions and identities, imperial power, masculinity, and fraternalism.

My first emphasis is on the role of cultural institutions in *globalization*, the process by which diverse peoples and distant places have become increasingly interconnected over time. Current obsessions with the significance of globalization in our own times—whether celebratory or admonitory—have tended to obscure the fact that the roots of the phenomenon reach back far in time. The relative absence of historians in current debates has meant that most analyses of globalization are presentist and based on problematic assumptions about its historical trajectory. Urging historians to engage with one another, as well as social scientists, about globalization is the central point of *Globalization in World History*, a provocative volume edited by historian A. G. Hopkins (2002). In his own chapter, "The History of Globalization—and the Globalization of History," Hopkins expresses surprise that historians have been so delinquent in recognizing potential areas of research in the history of globalization. He encourages them to take advantage of a "sizable opportunity . . . to make a systematic and effective contribution to this wide-ranging and highly topical debate." For Hopkins, the opportunity is not limited to what historians can contribute to the globalization debate, "to comment on the claims made for and against the novelty of globalization." It also involves historians' openness to "use current preoccupations with the changing shape of the world order to frame new questions about history."[17]

Hopkins and his fellow contributors to the *Globalization in World History* volume are certainly right to identify empires as "powerful agents of globalization." Imperialism, in its various formal and informal guises, and its frequent bedfellow, capitalism, have arguably been the most powerful connective forces in world history. Although not central participants in the globalization debate, historians have long studied the role of imperial states and the commercial networks their citizens created in bringing together diverse peoples and places in complex relationships of exploitation and interdependence. In so doing, they have focused primarily on the economic and political dimensions of globalization. But its cultural aspects, as Tony Ballantyne points out in the Hopkins volume, have yet to be subjected to rigorous historical analysis.[18]

Examining the history of Freemasonry, I argue, presents an excellent way to evaluate the contribution of cultural institutions to the historical process of globalization. Freemasons established one of the first global institutional networks that not only linked farflung Britons to one another but also brought Britons into contact with other European imperialists as well as indigenous men throughout the formal and informal empires. An analysis of Freemasonry makes it possible to identify various characteristics that enable institutions to function on a worldwide basis and promote globalization. These include a well-established administrative structure with a central hub; a set of mechanisms to effect the proliferation of the institution's network; an ability to adapt to diverse circumstances while maintaining discrete, identifiable institutional features; evidence of geographic "extensity"; ways for members to identify and communicate with one another, even if they are strangers; usefulness to members; and finally an ideology that promotes awareness of the wider world.[19] That such an institutional network was functioning in the second half of the eighteenth century suggests that the period between 1750 and 1815 was a crucial phase in globalization.[20] We should therefore seek the history of globalization not only in the trading networks and empires of the early modern period, and the vast migration streams and commodity flows of the twentieth century, but also in the cultural institutions that connected men across the global landscape of the eighteenth and nineteenth centuries.

Freemasonry's remarkable success in building a global network points to the second concern of this book, namely the formation and operation of *supranational identities*. Identity has become a central preoccupation of scholars in recent years. A primary reason for its popularity is its broadness and flexibility as a concept. Scholars seeking to use class, gender, *and* race as interacting categories of analysis take some comfort in being able to encompass their ambitious agenda under the rubric of "studying identities." But the very broadness and flexibility that make it attractive also require those claiming to study identity to define their understanding of it. Here, I use the term to describe the continuously ongoing process by which people define, within limits determined by the circumstances in which they live, their communities of belonging. For example, people who are born into slavery are defined by their circumstances as slaves but have some say in deciding with which other communities they identify, such as to which religious systems they decide to subscribe. Identities, as historians like Kathleen Wilson and Catherine Hall have so masterfully demonstrated, are not fixed or static, not based on essential characteristics that possess transcendent power. Rather, they are always contingent, tentative, and in flux, shifting according to the configuration of specific historical circumstances. People's identities are multiple and at times even contradictory.[21] Their complex nature results from the fact that they are made up of so many axes, including age, gender, sexuality, race, ethnicity, nationality, religion, language community, occupation, and class. Identities are constructed and expressed through discourses that reveal the "inchoate interdependence" of these and other categories. Finally, as "the product of both agency and coercion," identities signify relations of power.[22]

Thanks to the fact that so many scholars have directed their attention to identities and identity formation in recent years, we have increasingly nuanced understandings of how men and women defined themselves in terms of class, gender, race, and nation. The literature on the interaction of gender, nation, and race in the context of imperialism is especially sophisticated. But sustained analyses of supranational identities and the institutions that promote them are relatively rare, both within and outside the discipline of history. A supranational identity results when people define a community of belonging that extends beyond their national place of origin. Supranational identities may be ideological (e.g., Communism), religious (e.g., Catholicism), or political (e.g., Pan-Africanism). They take other forms, such as the ones investigated here: universalism, fraternalism, cosmopolitanism, and imperial citizenship. Supranational identities do not necessarily supersede or conflict with national identities. Rather, they interact in complex ways with national identities, and can often serve to solidify them, particularly when intimately connected with an imperial mission.

Third, I use the history of this brotherhood to explore the complex dynamics of *power* in Britain and the empire. We still have much to learn about the varied forms and faces of imperial power, about the ways colonizers deployed their power and how subject populations responded to it. As Dane Kennedy explains, "While imperial historians have attended to the issue of power since the inception of their field of study, and while their inquiries have given rise to a sophisticated body of work that traces the exercise of power from coercion to collaboration, the fact remains that the circumstances that allowed relatively small contingents of Europeans to acquire and maintain authority over vastly larger numbers of Asians, Africans, and others represent one of the most persistent conundrums to arise from the study of Western imperialism."[23] One reason for this is the fact that most studies have focused on the obvious agents of imperial power—the army and the navy, the crown, Parliament, colonial governments, trading companies and other mercantile interests, and technology. We must, of course, appreciate the role of these crucial imperial agents that served as the primary bases of British overseas power. But we can achieve a more complete and nuanced understanding of imperial power if we also turn our attention to institutions and agents that exercised a more subtle influence. An overlooked informal institution of empire building, Freemasonry contributed in important ways to the establishment, maintenance, and extension of imperial power. First, it was instrumental in lubricating the aforementioned administrative, military, and commercial networks on which Britain's power was based. Belonging to the brotherhood helped colonial officials, military personnel, and merchants move through the empire, adjust to difficult environments, secure promotions and profits—in short, do their jobs.[24] Freemasonry also eased the passage of ordinary migrants who extended Britain's influence by establishing overseas settlement colonies. The Masonic hall was at times the first and only community structure in new settlements on the empire's frontiers. As the settlement colonies matured, the brotherhood continued to solidify the empire by assisting rising men in their bids to become local power brokers, thereby helping to constitute colonial elites in the mid-nineteenth century. And during the age of high imperialism, from the 1870s through the First World War, the institution encouraged its members to give their energy, money, and even their lives to uphold the imperial power and prestige of the "motherland."

Examining Masonry enables us to explore another dimension of British overseas power: the use of ritual, ceremony, and symbolism to project the impression of invincibility and permanence. Effective imperial power involves more than the deployment of brute force. It is also about performance. Remarking on this aspect of British power, historian A. J. Stockwell notes that "contemporary apologists for the British empire, therefore, used ceremonial set-pieces and images of its institutions to justify its existence, soften its impact, or disguise its weakness, and to mollify its subjects, counter its critics, or discipline its practitioners." Other scholars have explored the performative dimensions of British power. Looking at the ways in which mid-nineteenth-century colonial governors used ceremonies to display their authority, political scientist Mark Francis argues that "in colonial society ceremonial procedure was of equal importance to policy or efficiency." According to Paul Rich, "the ability to enforce politics by force was limited. The British used ceremonies as a substitute for gunboats."[25] Finally, in a much more sophisticated and contextualized argument, David Cannadine has identified imperial pomp (evident in ceremonies, architecture, imperial honors, and chivalric orders) as the primary means through which the British built and expressed a culture of ornamentalism that underpinned the empire.

Yet arguing that the ceremonial dimensions of imperial power were more significant than raw military force is in some ways a fruitless exercise. Effective imperial power needs both force and impression; they work in tandem.[26] Closer attention to the world of Freemasonry reveals this dynamic at work.[27] At the same time that lodges were traveling with army regiments as they moved around the empire enforcing Britain's will, Freemasons were also engaged as the shock troops of imperial ceremony. Their ceremonial role was not confined to the privacy of the lodge. Though assumed to be draped in mystery and intrigue, Freemasonry was during the period examined in this book as much a public institution as an esoteric club. Everywhere one went in the empire, one could witness Freemasons marching in processions, occupying prominent places in official ceremonies to greet or bid farewell to imperial officials, and observing milestones in the life of the monarch. And everywhere they laid foundation stones — of churches, legislative buildings, Masonic halls, hospitals, commercial exchanges, markets, hotels, theaters, monuments, private houses, colleges, bridges, orphanages, courts, jails, canals, lighthouses, libraries, and schools. In these elaborately staged public appearances, Masons put their fine regalia and tools on display, deposited the coins of the realm, and anointed the architecture of empire with the symbols of their order.[28] In so doing, these builders of empire helped construct imperial edifices as well as the impression that Britain's presence was a permanent feature of the colonial landscape.

Through a combination of force and impression, the British sought not only to get their way but also to convince their subjects that British rule was in their best interests. At this point, the point of hegemony, British power was at its height. British Masons thought that their brotherhood could help accomplish the objective of securing the consent of elite indigenous men to British rule. A central argument for admitting Hindus, in fact, was the belief that the lodge might serve as a factory for building collaborators who were invested in and loyal to the empire.[29] The enthusiasm with which elite Indian men joined Freemasonry suggests that Masonry did indeed contribute to this process. But indigenes had many different responses to imperial rule, responses that are much harder to gauge than the intentions of the powerful. What looked like collaboration might also have elements of manipulation. An indigenous man might join the brotherhood to endear himself to the British, but he might also use the brotherhood's ideology of cosmopolitan fraternalism to challenge the "rule of colonial difference" that underlay imperial power and to demand equality with his British "brothers." After all, Freemasonry, a highly elastic institution, had a history of being put to subversive ends in the tumultuous world of the eighteenth-century British Atlantic. It could certainly play a similar role in the era of colonial nationalism. In sum, this history elucidates how an institution that helped extend imperial power (in its material, ceremonial, and hegemonic forms) might also be used to contest the legitimacy of that authority.

Studying the history of an exclusively male institution also lends itself to an exploration of *masculinities*, which is my fourth theme. The book pushes forward the project of demonstrating "the critical ways in which the construction, practice, and experience of Empire for both colonizer and colonized was always and everywhere gendered, that is to say, influenced in every way by people's understanding of sexual difference and its effects, and by the roles of men and women in the world."[30] Work on women, gender, and empire is increasingly sophisticated. But "the gendered study of men" and exclusively male institutions is still in its infancy.[31] To be sure, several scholars have written on Victorian ideas about manliness and the all-male environments, such as the public school, that promoted them.[32] Yet, as John Tosh points out, much of the work on manliness has been "quite innocent of gender."[33] Like the historians who have studied public schools and athletic clubs, I examine a predominantly male environment that excluded women, but women are by no means excluded from my analysis. Rather, the case of Freemasonry clearly demonstrates the fundamentally *relational* quality of all masculinities.[34] Any thorough examination of masculinity must explore how men's roles and responsibilities, expectations of men, and even men's interactions with other men were always regulated with women in mind.

Masonry allows us to look at the relational nature of masculinities by exploring the significance of homosociality to imperialism. The empire itself was a predominantly masculine environment, especially before the mid-nineteenth century. For many administrators, traders, soldiers, and especially sailors, their interactions with other Britons took place within "a culture of singular masculinity."[35] What difference did the operation of all-male institutions like Freemasonry within an already predominantly male environment make to men and to women?[36] For the men, the homosocial spaces afforded by Masonry presented opportunities for building close relationships with fellow Britons in the empire. The relative absence of women in many parts of the empire necessitated men turn to one another for support. In this way, Freemasonry operated as a surrogate family that helped meet a range of material, recreational, and psychological needs. But if some men joined Masonry because of an absence of women, many others took part because of their presence. Recent scholarship has demonstrated that the empire was not as exclusively a masculine environment as was once assumed. Though certainly outnumbered by men, British women did help constitute the empire-building population as the wives, companions, or dependent relations of military personnel, colonial administrators, missionaries, and colonists. And all along, of course, British men engaged in relations of varying degrees of coercion with indigenous women. Operating parallel to this heterosocial and heterosexual world was a vibrant homosocial world, off limits to women (regardless of their race or status) and jealously guarded by its denizens. Imperial men, it seems, needed homosocial refuges when women were in their midst, even if these women were vastly outnumbered and clearly occupying positions of dependence and subordination.

It is in precisely this context — of gender power relations — that homosocial spaces like Masonic lodges had a profound impact on women. By further restricting women's already limited access to the extra-domestic world, homosociality helped keep women subordinated. Explaining how all-male associations buttressed "the edifice of male exclusionary power," Tosh argues that they "are integral to any notion of patriarchy beyond the household. They embody men's privileged access to the public sphere, while simultaneously reinforcing women's confinement to household and neighborhood." In this way, the associational world of men is one aspect of what Eve Kosofsky Sedgwick has identified as a broader homosocial dynamic (the other manifestations of which include "male friendship, mentorship, entitlement, rivalry, and hetero-and homosexuality") that helps sustain masculine authority.[37] Freemasonry excluded women from its lodges and, in so doing, from the identities and roles it encouraged its members to adopt. As we will see, transforming oneself, through Masonry, into a cosmopolite or an imperial citizen was an opportunity available only to men.

Although women were significant for their exclusion from Masonry's inner sanctum — the lodge — they did play key roles in the wider world of Masonry's fraternal culture. In fact, their presence was crucial for the "public demonstration of masculinity." First, women served as spectators and observers of impressive public Masonic ceremonies throughout the empire.[38] (Ironically, Masons needed women to help constitute their audiences, but they cited women's unrestrained curiosity as one of the main reasons they should never be admitted into the brotherhood.) Second, Masons envisioned women as worthy objects of their charity. Lodges recorded countless instances of allocating their funds for the upkeep of widows and orphans of deceased members. Membership in the brotherhood thus enabled Masons to fulfill their masculine duties to their dependents even from beyond the grave. Masonic charity underlined the central fact of women's dependence — first on their fathers, then on their husbands, and, if ultimately widowed, on the brotherhood. Finally, Freemasonry encouraged men to act appropriately at home and preserve their reputations as upstanding heads of households. In its sixth charge, which specifically concerned the Mason's "Behaviour at Home and in your Neighbourhood," the constitutions governing the brotherhood urged: "Masons ought to be Moral Men, as above charged; consequently good Husbands, good Parents, good Sons, and good Neighbours, not staying too long from Home and avoiding all Excess; yet wise Men too, for certain Reasons known to them." In these ways, Freemasonry served to uphold the "hegemonic masculinities" at play in a given period, reinforcing widely held notions about how imperial men should act, what qualities they should possess, and what their responsibilities were.[39]

The fifth and final theme — *fraternalism* — is closely related, conceptually and in practice, to masculinity. In fact, Mary Ann Clawson, a historian of American fraternalism, identifies masculinity, along with a "corporate" idiom, ritual, and proprietorship, as a defining characteristic of fraternalism.[40] Fraternalism is the process by which biologically unrelated men undergo a shared ritual experience designed to create the bonds and obligations that supposedly characterize the relationship between actual brothers. Bound by ritual and often ideology, members of fraternal associations were pledged to privilege one another's interests over those who did not belong to the brotherhood. What did fraternalism have to do with imperialism? According to imperial historian Ronald Hyam, we know very little about the role of Freemasonry's "doctrines of brotherhood in sustaining the worldwide activities of traders and empire-builders."[41] My argument that the modern world's first and most successful fraternal organization was, from its very beginnings, intimately bound up in imperialism suggests that to a very great extent the British Empire was a fraternal enterprise.

The idiom that lent the most power to contemporary explanations of Masonic fraternalism was that of the family. As we will see, lodges used familial labels, even "mother," "sister," and "daughter," to describe their relations with one another, and Masonic writers and orators drew on idealized understandings of the family to convey expectations concerning members' behavior. Describing eighteenth-century Freemasonry as a "fictive family," historian Steven C. Bullock explains, "Masonic fraternity gave emotional weight to enlightened social relations by asserting their similarity to the widespread, seemingly natural experience of the family. Members were knit together by the same permanent bonds of affection and responsibility as actual kin."[42] Freemasonry was understood as a kind of family, but it differed significantly from traditional families. As a sex-specific family, it excluded two groups usually seen as critical, if subordinate, members of the family: women and children.[43] For the entire period covered here, British Freemasons consistently and unequivocally maintained that their fraternal family had no need of women. The brotherhood also excluded men under the age of twenty-one. Members of this fraternal family were thus connected to one another on the basis of their shared values, interests, and ideology, rather than on the basis of shared blood.

In the absence of blood ties, Masons and other fraternal groups used rituals to create a sense of community and mutual obligation. Masonic ritual derived primarily from two sources: the craft practices of medieval operative masons' guilds and Judeo-Christian accounts of the building of Solomon's Temple. Brethren learned a new ritual, along with its accompanying password and symbols, as they passed each level, or degree, in Freemasonry. Though some branches of Freemasonry would develop dozens of degrees, British Freemasonry was limited to three degrees, known as the Craft or "Blue" degrees.[44] In the first, the Entered Apprentice degree, the master and brethren introduced the initiate into the world of Freemasonry. Partially naked, blindfolded, and constricted by a rope that was tied around his neck, the initiate experienced the mystery of Freemasonry as he learned about its meaning. The ritual conveyed the central "landmarks" of Masonry: the charity brethren demonstrated toward one another and the external world, "the perfect spirit of Equality among the brethren," and the universality of brotherhood. The next degree, the Fellow Craft, was even more esoteric in nature, as the initiate learned the secret meanings of geometry and the Great Architect of the Universe. The Craft degrees culminated in the ritual of the Master Mason, which reenacted the murder scene of Hiram Abiff, the master builder of Solomon's Temple, said to have sacrificed his life to protect the secret knowledge of his craft brotherhood.[45]

These allegorical rituals had several functions. They performed a pedagogical role by conveying Masonic principles to initiates and members. Over time, they also combined with an elaborate system of handgrips, passwords, and symbols to develop into a lingua franca for Freemasons throughout the world to identify and communicate with one another. Most important for the purposes of family building, they created fraternal bonds among the brethren.[46] Masonic cere-

monies functioned like a marriage ceremony, another form of ritual that sought
to create permanent bonds where blood ties did not exist. As in the exchange of
marriage vows, the initial ceremony impressed upon the Entered Apprentice
the idea that he was entering into a new set of relationships that demanded a
lifelong commitment. By undergoing the subsequent rituals of Fellow Craft and
Master Mason, the new member completed the necessary steps in becoming a
full-fledged, equal member of a sworn brotherhood. He was now bound to a
group of men—his brethren—who pledged to respect, help, and love each
other through all circumstances. Speaking before an audience of Freemasons in
1799, the Reverend Joseph Inwood exhorted: "To you my brethren, who have
attached yourselves to each other, in the grand and royal order of Masonry,
besides these various bonds of union with which all men are united as brethren,
I address myself to reminding you of the solemn obligations and engagements
with which we have entered into the union of brotherhood, before God and our
brethren."[47]

But just how far were British Freemasons willing to take their fraternalism?
Brotherhood in Masonry was envisioned as a subset of a wider fraternalism that
Masons like to refer to as "the common fatherhood of God and the brotherhood of man." As we have seen, as long as he professed belief in a supreme being
and was over the age of twenty, any man was eligible for admission. It was this
latitudinarianism that enabled Freemasonry to serve, according to its Constitutions, as "a centre of union and the means of conciliating true friendship among
persons that must have remain'd at a perpetual distance." Masonic fraternalism
was thus not just about British men taking care of one another in strange
colonial environments, but also about believing in a basic affinity with "others"
encountered in those same strange colonial environments. Not surprisingly, the
exigencies of imperial rule consistently put to the test Freemasons' commitment to the idea of universal brotherhood. As several scholars of Masonry have
pointed out, Masons were engaged in a constant balancing act, weighing the
inclusive claims of their ideology with the need they felt, given their particular
circumstances, to be exclusive in their admissions practices.[48] But though the
circumstances might change, Masonry's claims to inclusiveness remained constant over time, and excluded groups—women, free blacks, emancipated slaves,
Parsis, and Hindus—were always challenging the institution to live up to these
claims. In responding to such challenges, British Freemasons were engaged in a
process of defining not only the boundaries of their institution but also their
identities as Britons, Freemasons, and men.

Supranational identities like fraternalism and cosmopolitanism warrant our close attention. But because historians have been so focused on how Britons defined their national, racial, and gender identities *through difference*, the "connection-building" dimensions of identity formation have been almost completely overlooked. The historiography of imperialism has become overly preoccupied with questions of otherness.[49] As the case of Freemasonry makes clear, colonial identities and ideologies were more complex than just "us versus them." Moving to the other extreme — by overemphasizing "affinity-building" — is not the kind of corrective we need.[50] Rather, the time has come to explore what Jane Samson, a historian of British missionaries in the Pacific, has aptly described as "the constant tension between alterity and universalism . . . , or, to put it another way, between 'othering' and 'brothering.'"[51] While Freemasons were clearly imperialists interested in upholding the rule of colonial difference, they were at the same time propounding an ideology that claimed the other as their brother, even through the period of high imperialism. It was an ideology of rule that was powerful and insidious, to be sure, but one that was also susceptible to revolutionary interpretations.

ONE

A Vast Chain Extending Round the Whole Globe

In 1785, the Reverend Joshua Weeks explained to Masons gathered to hear his St. John's Day address in Halifax, Nova Scotia, that they possessed a "key" that would give them "admittance to the brotherhood" anywhere in the world. "Were the providence of God to cast you on an unknown shore; were you to travel through any distant country, though ignorant of its language, ignorant of its inhabitants, ignorant of its customs," he assured his listeners, the key would "open the treasures of their charity." The following year, on the other side of the Atlantic, the Grand Lodge of England issued a proclamation that revealed the profound accuracy of Weeks's remark. Freemasonry's reputation for taking care of its members had become so well known and its network so extensive that strange impostors were after its "treasures." Grand Lodge officials warned the English brethren that "many idle persons travel about the country, (some particularly in the dress of Turks or Moors) and, under the sanction of certificates, and pretending to be distressed Masons, impose upon the benevolence of many lodges and brethren." The Grand Lodge described this practice as "disgraceful to the society and burthensome to the fraternity" and instructed lodges to bar such dissemblers from admission.[1]

How did British Freemasonry became so important and so extensive over the course of the eighteenth century that cunning Englishmen resorted to the complex deceit of posing as Turks and Moors to infiltrate its network? What were the salient characteristics and primary functions of the institution they hoped to cheat? To answer these questions, we need to examine both its macrocosmic and microcosmic dimensions. A bird's eye view of the Masonic network reveals that the brotherhood was, from its beginnings, British (as opposed to English) in its origins and global in its scope. It was built as a result of the activities of four grand lodges, each responding with varying degrees of enthusiasm to the opportunities for global expansion presented by the growing British Empire. The Irish and one branch of English Masonry, the Ancients, were the network's primary builders; they were particularly effective in adapting Masonry's administration to facilitate global expansion and in opening the brotherhood's "treasures" to a wide range of men. And they were primarily responsible for connecting Masonry to that crucial institution of empire building, the British army. Examining the resulting network reveals this cultural institution's important role in the accelerating processes of globalization underway during the second half of the eighteenth century.

The microcosmic perspective, revealed in the operations of individual lodges, indicates that Freemasonry was fundamentally imperial in its functions and fraternal in nature. It buttressed British imperial power, in very public ways, by making its buildings available for official purposes, playing a prominent role in the ceremonial aspects of imperialism, and offering recreational outlets for British expatriates. It had an even more profound impact, however, as a result of the homosocial activities that took place within the private inner sanctum of the lodge. Here men underwent experiences designed to encourage convivial, intellectual, and spiritual fellowship and to nurture the growth of fraternal bonds. Freemasonry proved especially attractive and useful to men in inherently imperial occupations — merchants, colonial administrators, and British army personnel — who could call on their brethren for all manner of assistance as they moved around the empire. In both cases — public Masonic events and hidden fraternal rituals — women were as significant in their presence as in their absence. British Freemasons never allowed women to participate in their lodge rituals and conviviality, but they did embrace them as spectators of their public ceremonies, guests at the balls they hosted, and dependent objects of charity. In these ways even a primarily homosocial environment such as that created by Masonry reveals how masculinities are constructed and reinforced with women in mind.

The Network's Hub

As Freemasonry spread throughout the empire, it became an expansive network that connected men across vast distances. In fact, the model of the network is very useful for understanding Freemasonry during this expansionary phase of its history. A network is an interconnected system; more specifically, it is an interrelated group of people who share interests and concerns and interact for mutual assistance. While some networks operate only on a local scale, others, like the Masonic network examined here, function concurrently on a variety of levels: local, national, regional, and even global. Freemasonry's multilayered, supranational network comprised several interrelated elements. Individual brethren and the local lodges to which they belonged constituted the most basic units of the network. Provincial grand lodges were its regional nodes and metropolitan grand lodges its central hubs. A shared Masonic ideology, a Masonic lingua franca, and complex administrative structures and policies linked these elements together.

Close attention to the institutional development of this network over time and across space reveals that historians of Freemasonry, whether amateur or professional, have not paid sufficient attention to the British dimensions of the brotherhood's history, particularly in the eighteenth century. Masonic historians have written separate histories of Freemasonry in England, Ireland, and Scotland. Academic historians have focused on Scotland in the search for Freemasonry's origins and, for the eighteenth century, studied aspects of English and Welsh Freemasonry. As yet, no work examines how the three jurisdictions interacted and influenced one another, not only in the British Isles, but also in the empire. Though it is certainly possible and reasonable to discuss "Irish Freemasonry" or "English Freemasonry," to ignore "British Freemasonry" is to miss a critical dimension of the brotherhood's history. This British dimension is evident in the nature and functions of its nascent administration and in a schism that divided the Masonic world — with great consequences for its spread through and role in the British Empire — between the 1750s and the early nineteenth century.

The building of a Masonic administration that facilitated the growth of the global network would not have been possible without the establishment of metropolitan grand lodges. In 1717 four Masonic lodges assembled at London's Goose and Gridiron alehouse to form a grand lodge, to which each English lodge would belong and send representatives.[2] Originally motivated to congregate for social reasons, members of the young Grand Lodge soon became anxious to control the proliferation of lodges. To this end, it distinguished between "regular" and "irregular" Freemasonry. Only by gaining permission from the Grand Lodge for its formation could a new lodge secure inclusion in the approved *List of Lodges*, a compilation published initially in 1723. Lodges that did not submit to the authority of the Grand Lodge were considered irregular and their members called "clandestine" and banned from visiting regular lodges. The Grand Lodge also started to extend its authority into the English counties and beyond Britain's shores and in the process became the central node in a nascent Masonic network. As such, it performed a variety of governing functions including standardizing Masonic practices, setting up guidelines for the establishment of new lodges, enacting legislation to guide members and lodges, overseeing the membership, and administering a charity fund.[3] Freemasons in Ireland and Scotland followed the English example with the establishment of the Grand Lodge of Ireland in Dublin (1725) and the Grand Lodge of Scotland in Edinburgh (1736). The three grand lodges were separate entities and, early on at least, they did not coordinate their administrative efforts. But British Freemasonry in this period was standardized enough to make the practices of any of the three systems recognizable to members of the other two jurisdictions.[4]

The grand lodges performed other centralizing administrative functions that facilitated the network's expansion. They collected fees and dues and served as the highest authority in matters of Masonic jurisprudence. They guarded Freemasonry's gates by keeping track of lodges and members. And they devised, printed, and circulated basic statements of the guiding principles and regulations of Masonry. In 1723, the prominent London Freemason James Anderson, a Presbyterian minister (who had been educated at Marischal College in Aberdeen), composed the first published edition of English Freemasonry's constitutions. Anderson offered a history of the brotherhood and explained recently codified policies that were to govern members and lodges. Discussing the Freemason's relationship to the state, religion, general society, and the institution, the *Constitutions* included a detailed code of behavior, known as "The Charges of a Free-Mason." "The Charges" provided instructions and general regulations for lodge procedures, such as the admission of members, election of officers, chain of command, and Masonic ceremonies. John Pennell, an Irish Freemason, devised a set of constitutions in 1730 based on Anderson's, but even more tolerant in its handling of religion. With little variation in wording and procedures, future editions published in the British Isles and abroad reflected the grand lodges' success in standardizing the basic principles and policies of British Freemasonry.[5]

Certificate of William Forman, Lodge No. 195 (Irish Registry), Royal Highlanders Regiment, 1761 (Grand Lodge of Ireland).

As Freemasonry grew in popularity, the institution became vulnerable to outsiders who sought to take advantage of the benefits reserved for members. After all, the successful operation of the network depended on the ability of complete strangers to identify and trust one another. The *Constitutions* instructed: "You are cautiously to examine [a strange brother] in such a method, as prudence shall direct you, that you may not be imposed upon by an ignorant false pretender, whom you are to reject with contempt and derision, and beware of giving him any hints of knowledge."[6] The problem of impostors led the grand lodges to issue repeated warnings, like the one quoted at the beginning of this chapter, to guard their lodges, secrets, and funds. But placing such a burden on individual brethren was risky and, especially once lodges began proliferating worldwide, impractical.

Irish Masonic authorities were the first to address the problem of how to recognize brothers who were strangers by issuing certificates to individual brethren. Demonstrating that in its origins the brotherhood was a fundamentally British institution, the English and Scottish Grand Lodges readily adopted this and other Irish strategies for governing Freemasonry as it spread within and outside the British Isles.[7] A certificate identified a man as a regular Mason to whom a lodge could legitimately offer the benefits of membership. In essence they operated as passports in the Masonic world and were especially important for brethren who traveled from one outpost of the empire to another. Lodge No. 241 in Lower Canada granted six certificates "to Brethren who were on the point of leaving for England" in November 1790. In 1792 Lieutenant John Ross, recently arrived in Plymouth from Gibraltar, revealed the importance of these documents by urging the English Grand Secretary to send certificates that he had requested "some time ago." His regiment would be embarking for Ireland as soon as the transports arrived, and he did not want to depart without the certificates in hand.[8] Though responding innovatively to the problem at hand, the Irish authorities had devised only a partial solution: certificates were not always necessary for admission to a lodge, and they could be forged.

Since lodges could not rely entirely on the authenticity of certificates or the trustworthiness of those presenting themselves as Freemasons, the true test of a brother's Masonic credentials was his knowledge of passwords, symbols, and rituals. A member gained more and more knowledge of the society's rituals and teachings as he progressed through the various stages of Freemasonry. Upon successful completion of each degree, he received secret recognition words and committed new rituals to memory. Practices developed in the metropole were exported to the colonies, so men throughout the empire who had proceeded through the three degrees of Craft Masonry shared the same basic knowledge. Taken together, the rituals, teachings, passwords, and handgrips constituted a Masonic lingua franca spoken in both the metropole and the colonies. Masonic knowledge itself became the key to both admission to lodge meetings and access to benefits. As the Reverend Weeks quoted above observed, Freemasons were "Masters of a secret language, by which they can make themselves known to each other at a distance."[9]

The grand lodges developed sophisticated strategies for ensuring the integrity of their network, but in the 1750s the emergence of a rival English grand lodge, known as the Ancients, and the schism that followed rendered Freemasons' ability to identify legitimate brethren increasingly difficult. The schism created disorder and instability, but it also resulted in Freemasonry's transformation into a more broadly based and more thoroughly British institution and actually contributed to the proliferation of the global Masonic network. During the schism Freemasonry became a dynamic organization that could adapt to various circumstances and draw members from a wide range of men. As a result, the nodes of its network multiplied rapidly.

The emergence of a rival grand lodge in England was due primarily to the activities of Irish Masons in London, where Irish Freemasonry once again exercised a transformative influence. During the 1740s, agricultural crisis combined with a population explosion in Ireland to create conditions of dearth, disease, and famine that provided the fuel for the satiric commentaries of Jonathan Swift (who is believed to have belonged to a London lodge) and the compassionate inquiries of George Berkeley. Thousands of Irishmen crossed the Irish Sea to find work in London. Freemasons among them naturally desired to continue their membership in the fraternity, and their decision to establish their own lodges, rather than joining existing lodges in the metropolis, had great consequences for the nature of Freemasonry and its spread throughout the empire. Suffering from inefficiency, overextension, and ineffective leadership in the 1740s, the original English Grand Lodge had become lax. It did not bother to challenge the existence of these new lodges. By the 1750s Irish migrants had established six of their own lodges. In 1751 a group of eighty to a hundred Masons representing these Irish lodges gathered at the Turks Head Tavern in Soho. Their object was the establishment of the Grand Committee of the Most Ancient and Honourable Society of Free and Accepted Masons — in short, the setting up of a supreme Masonic authority to rival the "Premier" Grand Lodge of England. Within three years the number of lodges affiliating with the Ancient Grand Lodge (as it came to be known) had grown from the original six to thirty-six. Englishmen (and some Scots) from the middling ranks — artisans, semi-professionals, and tradesmen — began to join Ancient lodges.[10]

Realizing they were up against a firmly established, if disorganized, institution in the Premier Grand Lodge, the Ancients were by necessity well organized. Their attention to administrative detail contributed to their quick success not only in the British Isles but also abroad. They immediately compiled a set of rules and orders laying out the conditions for membership in and operation of their new Grand Lodge. The regulations called for regular monthly meetings of the Grand Lodge, even going so far as to assess fines on those who failed to attend. Determined to keep their records straight, the Ancients required every lodge to make regular returns and entered the information regarding membership and payments in registers. They set up a central charity fund and a system for determining worthy applicants. Instrumental in the administration of the Ancients at this stage was Laurence Dermott. An Irish Catholic who was relatively well educated and possessed strong organizational skills, he had joined a lodge in Dublin in 1741 and crossed the Irish Sea in 1748. In London, he worked as a journeyman painter and eventually became a successful wine merchant. In 1752 the Ancients elected Dermott Grand Secretary, a position he held for nearly twenty years; he later became Deputy Grand Master (1771–77 and 1783–87). In his capacity as Grand Secretary, Dermott served as a director of ceremonies and instructor of rituals, duties that enabled him to enforce uniformity in the practices of the Ancient lodges. He also emphasized record keeping and firm grand lodge control over subordinate lodges, and he was responsible for compiling the regulations of the Ancients. Dermott's conscientious approach combined with the broad-based appeal of the new body ensured the success of the Ancient Grand Lodge.[11]

With the Ancients firmly established, a nasty — though in some ways constructive — rivalry soon developed. The Premier Grand Lodge fired the opening salvo in 1755 when it declared the Ancients irregular Freemasons and dismissed them as lower-class, Irish impostors who practiced illegitimate Masonic rituals. The Ancients responded with a catechism included with the 1764 edition of the *Constitutions*, in which Dermott ridiculed the practices of the Premier Grand Lodge and claimed that its very formation was irregular. The Premier Grand Lodge not only envied the success of the Ancients and disapproved of the social composition of their lodges; it also resented the fact that the Ancients had described them as "Moderns," an appellation that stuck. In a period when well-rooted origins conferred legitimacy, charges of innovation were considered a serious assault. Seeking to preserve the integrity of their lodges, each Grand Lodge issued repeated warnings to its members throughout the next decades. The Premier Grand Lodge admonished: "Persons who assemble in London and elsewhere in the character of Masons, calling themselves Ancient Masons . . . are not to be countenanced or acknowledged as Masons by any regular lodge or Mason under the Constitution of England."[12]

The Moderns had to do more than just warn their members about the upstart Ancients; they had to make certain their own ship was in order, a task undertaken by the grand masters of the 1760s. Installed in 1764, Lord Blayney improved grand lodge administration by paying official visits to London lodges and enforcing strict uniformity. He encouraged Henry, Duke of Gloucester, to join the order in 1766 and arranged for the Grand Lodge to elect the duke as well as the Dukes of York and Cumberland to high Masonic office. Their attendance rekindled the interest of other nobility and gentry. The Duke of Beaufort took over in 1767. He attempted to incorporate the Grand Lodge, initiated plans for the construction of a permanent building (completed in 1776), and further improved grand lodge administration. The Moderns also benefited from the tireless efforts of Thomas Dunckerley, who was an illegitimate but acknowledged son of George II. Dunckerley served in the navy until 1767, at which point he returned to England and dedicated his energies to reviving Freemasonry. As Provincial Grand Master for nine English counties, he encouraged firm administration and established new lodges at the provincial level.[13] With the Ancients growing and the Moderns rejuvenated, there was little hope that the breach in British Freemasonry would be healed any time soon.

The schism between the Ancients and the Moderns had far-reaching implications for the composition and character of the fraternity both in the British Isles and in the empire. First, the rise of the Ancients changed the social composition of the fraternity's membership, broadening it into a more popular institution and thus making it more likely to succeed across space and time. Starting in 1721, when the first nobleman assumed the helm of the Premier Grand Lodge, English Freemasonry had become increasingly fashionable in the world of polite aristocrats and well-educated gentlemen. Its ranks included those at the highest levels of society as well as men from just below the nobility and gentry, like the gentlemen of the Royal Academy whose attraction to Masonry stemmed from their interest in Newtonian science and the ancient world.[14] Primarily artisans and tradesmen, the Ancients drew their members from a level below this world of genteel, aristocratic (or nearly aristocratic) men. The first edition of the Ancients' constitutions described its members as "men of some Education and an honest Character; but in low Circumstances." It urged the Mason to "treat his Inferiors as he would have his Superiors deal with him, wisely considering that the Original of Mankind is the same." Margaret Jacob aptly characterizes the rise of the Ancients as "a revolt of lesser men against their betters." Yet while their literature celebrated artisans and small merchants, the Ancients maintained due deference toward the monarchy and the court. As Jacob puts it, Ancient egalitarianism was "very finely honed." Probably unaware of such nuances, the Moderns challenged the social credentials of their rivals. The Moderns' Grand Secretary, in a report to his superiors in 1775, described the Ancients as being composed of "the very lowest people we have in London, such as Chairmen, Brewers, Draymen . . . so very contemptible [that] I have heard a Gentleman of their body say he was ashamed to be seen among them." He also related that a "stranger" who visited one of their lodges would fear for his purse and his life "from the appearance of its members." The subsequent Grand Secretary stated that the Ancients consisted of "the lowest order of the people" and their officers were "in very mean occupations." Its reputation among Modern Freemasons aside, the Ancients' more broad-based character was also reflected in their fairly democratic approach to administration. Unlike his counterpart in the Premier Grand Lodge, the Grand Master of the Ancients could not act independently; in all matters, including the establishment of new lodges, he had to seek the approval of other members of the Grand Lodge.

Finally, whereas the Grand Master appointed the officers of the Premier Grand Lodge, the Ancient Grand Lodge elected its officers.[15]

The rise of the Ancients not only broadened the socioeconomic basis of the fraternity; it also effected the intersection of Irish and English, and eventually Scottish, Freemasonry and in the process created an institution that had an essentially British character. Like the wider empire of which it was rapidly and thoroughly becoming a part, Ancient Freemasonry brought together men of the four "nations" of the British Isles, enabling them to create new, composite institutions and identities. The Ancients drew from both Irish and English Freemasonry in setting up and operating their organization. Dermott used Anderson's *Constitutions* in compiling the Ancients' first *Book of Constitutions*, the *Ahiman Rezon*, but his primary inspiration came from Irish texts like Spratt's *Irish Constitutions*. The Irish Grand Lodge's adoption of the *Ahiman Rezon* as its official *Book of Constitutions* further demonstrates the close links between Irish and Ancient Freemasonry.[16] Meanwhile, the Ancients, being based in London and including English members, were also subject to English influences. By combining Irish and English Masonic traditions, Dermott and his fellow Ancients made their version of Freemasonry into an institution that was at once new and reminiscent, that lay in the fuzzy realm of Britishness.

Another factor that reveals the British character of the Ancients was its approach to leadership, specifically in filling the grand mastership. Despite (or perhaps because of) their appeal to the middling classes, the Ancients sought a grand master from the ranks of the nobility. When they had trouble finding an English nobleman to serve as their leader, they turned to the Irish and Scottish peers. From 1756 on, every grand master of the Ancients was either Scottish or Irish. These grand masters included two Irish earls who had served as the Grand Master of Ireland and three Scottish peers who held concurrent appointments as the Grand Master of the Ancients and Grand Master of Scotland. All would have been familiar with Irish and Scottish Masonic practices and thus have offered a British perspective.

Finally, the establishment of regular relations among the Ancient, Irish, and Scottish grand lodges demonstrated Freemasonry's development into a British institution. Dermott arranged in 1758 for the Grand Lodge of Ireland to bypass the Moderns and communicate only with the Ancients. For the first time, Irish and English (and then Scottish) authorities corresponded regularly with one another and kept track of each other's activities and decisions. A mutual compact among the three grand lodges formalized this relationship in 1772. The Ancients assured the Scottish Grand Lodge that "a brotherly connexion and correspondence" would "be found productive of honour and advantage to the Fraternity in general." From this point on, the grand lodges frequently consulted with each other about difficult matters affecting Freemasonry. Writing to the Ancients in 1783, the Grand Lodge of Ireland assured its counterpart that they would "always concur with them in everything for the mutual advantage of the Ancient Craft."[17] Though they retained their regional administrative structures and a single British grand lodge was never contemplated, their combined efforts, especially abroad, resulted in an indisputably British institution.

Only recently have historians begun to realize the significance of the Ancients in transforming Freemasonry in the British Isles; generations of Masonic historians completely ignored them (perhaps because of their Irish, lower-status origins).[18] By passing over the Ancients, they have overlooked the Ancients' role in spreading Freemasonry abroad and thus underemphasized a key dimension of British Masonic history. As we will see, the Ancients were especially effective outside the British Isles; they were more instrumental in this regard than their rivals the Moderns. Their success in both contexts was due to their conscientious administration and their openness — to men from various rungs on the social ladder and to influence from the Irish and Scottish. Together the Ancients and the Irish would take the lead in globalizing the Masonic brotherhood.

The Globalization of the Masonic Network

Shortly after the establishment of the first grand lodge in 1717, British Freemasonry began spreading to the European continent, the Mediterranean basin, the Atlantic world, and parts of Asia. Freemasonry's transfer to Europe and its subsequent role in European societies has occupied several historians' attention, but its concurrent spread outside Europe has garnered little analysis. Yet it is clear that Freemasonry's intra-European and extra-European chronologies were interacting. The English warranted a lodge for Bengal the same year they warranted one for Gibraltar (1728). By the time the English and Scottish had succeeded in establishing lodges in the Netherlands in the 1740s, lodges were already at work in the North American and West Indian colonies, as well as in Turkey. Here was a European institution, but it was a European institution with a global reach. To bypass this basic fact is to neglect a critical and defining characteristic of eighteenth-century Freemasonry.

Metropolitan officials did not have a preconceived plan for global expansion, but they did embrace any opportunity to extend their brotherhood beyond the

British Isles. The development of the institution's bureaucracy coincided with Freemasonry's worldwide diffusion, and key elements of its administration clearly reflected this fact. During the mid-eighteenth century, therefore, the grand lodges became not only centralized authorities within the British Isles but also metropolitan governors of an ever-expanding Masonic empire abroad.

If the metropolitan grand lodges willingly accepted their position at the center of a growing Masonic empire, the impetus for the global spread of the fraternity originated at the peripheries. It is doubtful that Freemasonry would have become an imperial institution had the soldiers, administrators, and colonists who built the empire not felt so strongly about maintaining their Masonic affiliations while abroad. Those who wanted to practice Masonry in places where no lodge had been established were able to take advantage of several mechanisms by which Masonry spread abroad, including ambulatory lodges attached to British army regiments. Just as it was in the development of the brotherhood's metropolitan bureaucracy, the Grand Lodge of Ireland was especially responsive to the opportunities presented by imperial expansion, willing to adapt Masonic administration, and thus instrumental in exporting Freemasonry abroad.

AMBULATORY LODGES

Freemasonry's close association with the British army contributed more than any other factor to the brotherhood's global spread. Eighteenth-century regimental lodges not only served the needs of soldiers and officers; they also opened their doors to civilians and often helped them establish permanent lodges in distant parts of the empire. Although Freemasonry certainly benefited from its associations with the army, it was also sensitive to local conditions, geopolitical shifts, and the exigencies of war.

Once again, administrative innovations on the part of the Irish Grand Lodge were crucial to Freemasonry's success. To facilitate the spread of Freemasonry abroad, Irish authorities adapted their system of issuing warrants. The term "warrant," as used in Masonic documents dating from the 1720s, referred only to the *permission* of the grand master or grand lodge to constitute a new lodge. Starting around 1731, Irish Freemasons went a step further by issuing an actual document that indicated a lodge had received grand lodge permission to operate. Warrants were "designed to be the visible authority for the existence of the Lodge"; eventually lodges were required to display their warrant in order to constitute themselves and hold meetings.[19] As Freemasonry spread throughout the British Isles, Europe, and the empire, warrants served two primary functions: first, they enabled lodges to prove their status as regularly and officially constituted. Local Masonic authorities had the right to refuse recognition to a lodge that did not have a warrant. For example, in 1772 authorities in Quebec rejected Freemasons in the 21st Regiment, who claimed membership in an Irish lodge but could not produce their warrant. Second, since warrants were sequentially numbered, they helped the British grand lodges to keep reasonably accurate registries and accounts. By the mid-eighteenth century, both the Scottish and the English authorities had adopted the practice of their Irish counterparts.[20]

The Grand Lodge of Ireland adapted this system to respond to opportunities for global expansion by developing the "traveling warrant." In so doing, they became the leading exporters of British Freemasonry. Typically lodges in the British Isles were identified with a particular locality — a town, a city district, or even a specific tavern. During the 1730s, the Irish Grand Lodge began issuing warrants to Freemasons in the British army and, to a lesser extent, the Navy. As their name suggests, ambulatory lodges accompanied peripatetic regiments or ships, giving military Masons the authority to hold lodge meetings anywhere. The Irish Grand Lodge granted the first traveling warrant to the First Battalion in the Royal Scots (the oldest Regiment of the Line) in 1732; it traveled the globe with its regiment for over a century. In 1737 the Grand Lodge established a traveling lodge in the Second Battalion of the regiment. By 1762, with a second lodge constituted in the First Battalion, three Irish lodges were at work in the Royal Scots alone.

Having gained a head start on their rivals, the Irish introduced military Freemasonry to several parts of the empire and warranted the most military lodges over time. The Irish Grand Lodge warranted the first military lodge in the American colonies, which operated in Colonel Harward's Regiment of Foot (1st Bn. East Lancashire) while it was garrisoned in Louisbourg in 1746. The first lodge to serve with a British army regiment (as opposed to an East India Company Regiment) in India was also Irish and was warranted in 1742. It arrived in Madras with the 39th Regiment in 1754. Particularly successful purveyors of military Masonry, the Irish warranted 190 regimental lodges between 1732 and 1813. The close connection between Ireland, Irishmen, and the British army surely played a role here. Many of the first regiments to have lodges had either been raised in Ireland or served there at some point in their history. Ireland was an important recruiting ground for the army, and Irishmen held positions of command in several regiments that had lodges attached to them.[21]

In time, the other British grand lodges followed the Irish example. Scottish military personnel were acquainted with the idea of traveling warrants in the early 1730s when the Irish Grand Lodge constituted lodges in two Scottish regiments (No. 11 in the 1st Foot and No. 33 in the 21st Foot). In 1747 the Scottish Grand Lodge adopted the practice, issuing a traveling warrant to Freemasons in the Duke of Norfolk's Regiment (the 12th Regiment of Foot). During the mid-eighteenth century, this regiment served in Germany, Flanders, Holland, and Minorca. In 1762 the regiment was back in Scotland, where it participated in the Masonic foundation stone laying ceremony of the North Bridge in Edinburgh. Such occasions, which revealed to the general public the growing connection between Freemasonry and the military, were becoming increasingly frequent during the second half of the eighteenth century. By 1813, the Scottish had given warrants to twenty-one regimental lodges.[22]

The Ancients enthusiastically embraced the idea of traveling warrants, but the Premier Grand Lodge was more reluctant. This divergence would contribute directly to the relative success of Ancient Masonry vis-à-vis the Moderns, especially in the empire. Both English grand lodges issued their first traveling warrants, to the 8th and 57th Regiments, respectively, in 1755 (by this point the Irish had warranted twenty-nine military lodges and the Scots at least five). But in its sixty-year history the Ancient Grand Lodge issued 108 traveling warrants, over twice as many as the 48 issued by its rival.[23] What accounts for the Moderns' reluctance to adopt a technique that was proving so conducive to the spread of Masonry? Perhaps it was because traveling warrants were already by this point associated with both the Ancients and the Irish, two groups from whom the Moderns were trying to distance themselves. The result was that the Ancients and the Irish were the most productive builders of Masonry's imperial network.

The history of a typical Irish military lodge, Lodge No. 227, demonstrates how regimental lodges served as the primary mechanism for spreading Freemasonry throughout the empire. The Grand Lodge of Ireland founded Lodge No. 227 (later named The Lodge of Social and Military Virtues) in 1752 when it issued a warrant to Masons in the 46th Regiment of Foot. During the Seven Years' War, the lodge was active in Halifax, Nova Scotia (1757–58), and then in the West Indies (1762). During the War of American Independence, the regiment participated in General Grey's expedition against colonists in Massachusetts in 1778. The chest of the lodge fell into the enemies' hands, though Brother General Washington soon ordered its return, under a guard of honor, to the 46th Foot. At the conclusion of hostilities, the regiment went back to the Caribbean for ten years. It returned to Ireland in 1788; interactions with local Masons led to a revival of the lodge. The lodge traveled to Gibraltar and subsequently to the Caribbean during the wars against France. It lost its chest again and, once again, it was returned. In the early nineteenth century, No. 227 was active in New South Wales, southern India (though it lost most of its members to a cholera outbreak), and ultimately Montreal, where it became a stationary lodge associated with the garrison in that city. In New South Wales and Lower Canada, the Lodge of Social and Military Virtues was active in setting up permanent civilian lodges.[24]

The activities of a military lodge resulted in the permanent establishment of Freemasonry in a locality. Interested civilians — usually merchants and civil servants — often participated in meetings of military lodges. When they initiated civilian candidates, military lodges contributed directly to the spread of Freemasonry by exposing the societies with which they came into contact to the ideology, practices, and architecture of Freemasonry. For example, military lodges attached to regiments active in the conflicts of the 1750s through the 1780s were especially instrumental in planting Freemasonry in North America. Halifax was a hub of military Masonry from the late 1740s. All thirteen regiments that used Halifax as a base during the siege of Louisbourg (in 1758) had lodges associated with them either during or immediately following the Seven Years' War. The presence of so many military lodges contributed to the Masonic activity in the town, which was significant enough to require a provincial grand lodge; it operated between 1757 and 1776. The American War and the Anglo-French wars brought more regiments, and consequently more lodges, to the city.[25] Meanwhile, in Quebec City, at least nine regiments (including the 15th, 28th, and 48th) in General Wolfe's army that took the city from the French in 1759 had lodges attached to them. After their victory on the Plains of Abraham, the British occupied Quebec City and within two months representatives from the regimental lodges met to form a permanent local grand lodge. Lodges present in regiments involved in capturing Montreal from the French in 1760 opened their doors to civilians, who then formed their own lodges after the regiments moved on to new destinations.[26]

Sometimes regimental lodges would help civilian members arrange for the establishment of a lodge, even if it involved bending the rules a bit. Active in Albany, New York, during the 1750s, the Irish lodge (No. 74) in the Second Battalion Royal initiated several townsmen into Masonry. Upon the regiment's transfer in 1759, the lodge informed Irish authorities that it had decided to copy its warrant in order to set up a new lodge: "Our body is very numerous by the addition of many new members, merchants and inhabitants of the City of Albany, they having earnestly requested and besought us to enable them to hold

a Lodge during our absence from them." Because the practice of copying warrants was highly irregular, the Grand Lodge authorized the Provincial Grand
Master of New York to grant the lodge its own warrant within a few years.[27]
Several decades later, during the first British occupation of the Cape (between
1795 and 1802), a group of sergeants and privates in the 91st Regiment took the
unusual step of petitioning the primary Dutch lodge in the colony (Lodge de
Goede Hoop) for a dispensation to meet as an English lodge. The Dutch Lodge
granted permission for the establishment of Africa Lodge No. 1 but forbade it
to initiate new members. The British Masons ignored this restriction, and several members even established an offshoot lodge (Lodge de Goede Truow) in
1800. The Ancients eventually caught up with the situation and issued a warrant
for Africa Lodge; by 1812, at least 125 Masons had either undergone initiation
in or joined the lodge.[28]

Freemasonry benefited from its connection to the British army, but it also
suffered from the vicissitudes to which eighteenth-century regiments were
prone. Transfers of personnel could of course be very disruptive, but the outbreak of war was especially detrimental. Although military lodges furthered the
spread of Masonry in Canada during the Seven Years' War, lodges like the
Minden Lodge in the 20th Foot went into dormancy during the War of American Independence and the Anglo-French Wars. On the other side of the empire,
the Second Mysore War (1780–84) sent lodges in Bengal into abeyance, and
the Provincial Grand Lodge of Bengal ceased meeting for three years. In 1784 a
Mason stationed at Fort William, the garrison of Calcutta, reported that the
brotherhood had "greatly suffered under the public calamity of war" but was
starting to revive thanks to "Peace being now happily restored."[29] The Third
Mysore War (1790–92), against Tipu Sultan, had a similar effect, reducing the
Carnatic Military Lodge to only a few members. In 1791 a brother who was
soon to be transferred from Madras to Gibraltar told the Moderns that they
should not expect "our Noble Art" to flourish in the midst of war, given that
"many of our Brethren are with the Army in the field." Summing up the situation for eighteenth-century lodges in the empire, the officers of the Provincial
Grand Lodge of Madras regretted that "from the Nature of our situation in this
Quarter of the Globe, great fluctuations in Masonick affairs must constantly
occur, as the Event of War and the Departure of Persons for Europe frequently
suspend the operations of Masonry in different lodges."[30] Clearly lodges operating in places like India, where civilians were not likely to participate, were more
vulnerable to dissolution during wartime than those in settlement colonies.

Freemasonry also claimed a presence in the Royal Navy, although it was much less evident than in the army. The cramped and constantly shifting conditions of naval service proved less conducive to Masonic activity than army life, especially when regiments remained for years on end in colonial garrisons. Nevertheless, at least three naval lodges, operating on board the HMS *Vanguard*, *Prince*, and *Canceaux*, were at work in the second half of the eighteenth century, and they too proved instrumental in spreading Freemasonry abroad. The driving force behind all three lodges was Thomas Dunckerley, mentioned above in connection with the revival of the Moderns in late 1760s. He had a long naval career, primarily as a gunner and warrant officer, and was initiated into Freemasonry in 1754 during one of his stays in Plymouth (he joined three lodges there). Around 1760 the Moderns presented him with a patent to "Inspect the Craft wheresoever he might go" as well as a warrant to set up a lodge on board HMS *Vanguard*. Two years later he received a warrant for a lodge on board HMS *Prince*. He later used both warrants to set up permanent lodges on land. Stationary lodges also attracted naval personnel. During the eighteenth century, three "Royal Naval Lodges" were founded, one each in London (1739), Deal (1762), and Gosport (1787). The Maid's Head Lodge at Norwich (1724) and the Phoenix Lodge at Portsmouth (1786) included naval personnel in their ranks.[31]

In sum, though at times military life worked against the spread of Freemasonry, the military lodge developed into the most important mechanism for the globalization of the Masonic network during the eighteenth century. Nearly every regiment had at least one lodge in its ranks; many had several. Gould estimates that "there were no less than seven in the 52nd and six in the 28th Foot, while among the other regiments of cavalry and infantry there were four with five, six with four, twenty-one with three, and forty-six with two Lodges each." The 1st, 17th, 23rd, and 51st Foot each had lodges warranted by all three British jurisdictions at various points in their histories. The Royal Artillery boasted the most Masonic lodges, with twenty-eight Ancient lodges. From Gibraltar in 1773 a member of Ancient Lodge No. 148 in the Royal Artillery reported that, in addition to several Modern lodges, Irish lodges were operating in the 1st, 2nd, 38th, 76th, 56th, and 58th regiments of foot and a Scottish lodge in the 12th Regiment. Most historians estimate the total number of lodges formed by all four jurisdictions as close to 500. As Irish Masonic historian Chetwode Crawley succinctly put it at the end of the nineteenth century: "These lodges permeated everywhere; everywhere they left behind the germs of Freemasonry."[32] Thus, through the traveling warrant, the Grand Lodge of Ireland had introduced a new dimension — geographical flexibility — to British Freemasonry.

THE MEN ON THE SPOT

As military lodges crisscrossed the globe with their regiments and planted Freemasonry in distant parts of the empire, the metropolitan grand lodges adapted their administrative structures to facilitate the fraternity's global diffusion. The military lodge itself represented a direct administrative response to the opportunities presented by British imperial expansion. But administrators (particularly the Irish and the Ancients) did more. Specifically, they added nodes to Freemasonry's growing bureaucratic network by expanding the number of provincial grand lodges.

The provincial grand lodge system initially emerged in England in the 1720s when the Grand Lodge established the Provincial Grand Lodge for Cheshire in 1725. It adopted the same approach to its nascent overseas empire shortly after it constituted its first lodge in Bengal. In 1729 it named Captain Ralph Farr Winter of the East India Company as Provincial Grand Master for the East Indies to monitor the fraternity's progress there. Metropolitan authorities appointed a Provincial Grand Master for New York, New Jersey, and Pennsylvania in 1730, the year of the first known lodge meeting in the American colonies. From that point on the grand lodges deputized provincial grand masters wherever a strong Masonic presence had emerged or wherever they anticipated Freemasonry would find fertile ground. By the 1740s, the Grand Lodge of England had also appointed provincial grand masters for New England, Georgia, South Carolina, New York, Antigua, and Nova Scotia.[33]

As with certificates and warrants, the practice of appointing provincial grand masters was adopted by the other British grand lodges. Alexander Drummond, who oversaw lodges in western Scotland, received a commission to serve as a provincial grand master when he went to Turkey to serve as British Consul in 1747. The Grand Lodge of Scotland gave "full power . . . to him, and to any other whom he might nominate, to constitute Lodges in any part of Europe or Asia bordering on the Mediterranean Sea, and to superintend the same, or any others already erected in those parts of the world." Two decades later, in 1767, Scottish authorities named Governor James Grant of East Florida "Provincial Grand Master over the Lodges in the southern district of North America."[34] The first provincial grand lodge set up by the Grand Lodge of Ireland was active in Munster in the 1750s; its first overseas provincial grand lodge started operating in Barbados in 1801.

For all the British jurisdictions, the provincial grand master served as the grand master's representative in a locality (much as colonial governors represented the crown abroad). In accepting an appointment as a provincial grand master, the nominee was required to pay additional fees. These "men on the spot" had extensive Masonic powers as they managed Masonry in their jurisdictions. Samuel Middleton, Provincial Grand Master of Bengal, monitored the activities of twelve lodges, including several that the Provincial Grand Lodge had constituted among the brigades stationed at Fort William, in the early 1770s. Like his counterparts in other areas of the empire, his duties included collecting fees and dues, keeping registers, corresponding with and reporting to the metropolitan grand lodge, settling disputes, and disciplining lodges or brethren who violated regulations. He was also responsible for the operation of the provincial grand lodge itself.

Provincial grand masters contributed to the extension of the Masonic network by establishing new lodges in their jurisdictions. Governor William Mathew, appointed Provincial Grand Master for the Leeward Islands in 1738, set up two lodges in Antigua and two in St. Kitts by 1743. The Provincial Grand Lodge of Massachusetts established fifty lodges, including six in what would become Canada, before the American War of Independence. In the colony of Upper Canada, the provincial grand master warranted twenty lodges between 1792 and 1799. Sometimes provincial grand masters defined their jurisdictions quite broadly. Robert Tomlinson, Provincial Grand Master for North America, constituted a lodge of "old Boston Masons" on Barbados when his ship stopped there on the way to England in 1738; the lodge then initiated the governor and "several gentlemen of distinction." Members of the provincial grand lodge in Quebec reported to the Grand Lodge of England that they had issued warrants to constitute two lodges in New Brunswick. The first, New Brunswick Lodge, was comprised of "a number of Gentlemen resident in that Province," while the second one was to be formed in the "New Settlements above Montreal."[35]

Another man on the spot who contributed to the extension of the network by broadly interpreting his brief was Terence Gahagan, the chief Masonic authority for the Coast of Coromandel (southern India). En route to England in 1797, Gahagan stopped off at St. Helena where the lieutenant governor, Francis Robson, asked him to set up a lodge. Local Masons had been acting under a Scottish warrant dated 1761 but now sought to "abide by the rules of English Freemasonry." The new lodge consisted of "several of the principal Inhabitants, and gentlemen in the Service of the Honble . . . East Indian Company," including Robson (a lieutenant colonel in the East India Company Army), the chief surgeon, four other officers, and a factor on the island. Shortly thereafter, local Masons requested the English Grand Lodge make Robson a provincial grand master in his own right, so he could constitute a second lodge for "several respectable people on the Island, tradesmen and others, who are already *Masons*, but not members of the St. Helena Lodge." Robson established his Masonic credentials by informing metropolitan authorities that he was well acquainted with the principal members of lodges at Madras as well as several members of the Modern Grand Lodge in England. "I confess myself to be," he wrote, "an ardent enthusiast for promoting the good, and the honor of *Masonry*; and esteem myself bound to keep my work of honor sacred to the Craft; as well as to the Character and Rank I hold in life, as a gentleman, not to swerve therefrom."[36] Metropolitan authorities readily granted Robson the appointment.

Although men like Robson adopted a conscientious approach to the office of provincial grand master, the provincial grand lodge system was at times problematic. Acting as deputies, provincial grand masters were supposed to notify the grand lodge when they warranted new lodges and keep in regular, if infrequent, communication. But the travel and communication challenges of the mid-eighteenth century, combined with the grand lodges' reliance on individuals who had other preoccupations or acted independently, made such contact difficult. Moreover, when provincial grand masters did write to metropolitan authorities, they often complained that the British grand lodges, especially the Grand Lodge of England, were unresponsive to their petitions and concerns. These deficiencies aside, the provincial grand lodge system did allow for metropolitan authorities both to extend Masonry's increasingly global network and to oversee it. As we have seen, provincial grand masters had the authority, granted to them by the metropolitan "mother" lodges, to establish new lodges abroad. They also monitored the conduct of their lodges and implemented the policies and procedures of the metropolitan government. Colonial brethren were generally unwilling to defy the appointed representatives of the British grand lodges. In fact, requests for the establishment of provincial grand lodges continued to be made, and there were no major reforms to the system, until the second half of the nineteenth century.

The final mechanism that worked along with military lodges and provincial grand masters to spread Freemasonry abroad from the 1750s was the process of emigration. Settlers ventured out to the Caribbean, the North American colonies, and ultimately Australia during the eighteenth century. One colonist residing in Nova Scotia in the early nineteenth century observed: "From Europe, the Royal Art [Freemasonry] crossed the Atlantic with the first Emigrants, and settled in various parts of America." If they arrived at their destination and found no local Masonic lodge or determined that existing lodges were too crowded, colonists who were Masons sent petitions to metropolitan authorities to set up new lodges. In response, the grand lodges issued "deputations to constitute lodges." To cite just one example, in 1787 the Grand Lodge of Ireland received, and ultimately granted, a request from three brethren "praying for [a] Wart [warrant] to hold a lodge in the town of Kingston in Jamaica."[37] Local lodges might also grant "dispensations" to new lodges until their warrants arrived. In these ways, countless unofficial "men on the spot" played a role in extending the Masonic network overseas, particularly in the settlement colonies. While military lodges had been critical in setting up the Masonic network during the eighteenth century, the processes of migration and the activities of provincial grand masters were more important in strengthening the network once it had been established.

As a result of these proliferating mechanisms — ambulatory lodges, provincial grand masters, and requests from colonists — Freemasonry achieved a global presence during the eighteenth century. The fact of Freemasonry's global diffusion allows us to take up Anthony Hopkins's invitation to consider detailed historical evidence to arrive at "an improved and more refined understanding of globalization in world history." While several commentators have identified globalization as a distinctly modern phenomenon (qualitatively different from anything that has preceded it), the evidence discussed here demonstrates that key globalizing processes were at work well before the advent of modernity.[38] A fully operational supranational institution was functioning during the eighteenth century, which historians typically include under the rubric of the "early modern" or at least describe as the hinge between the early modern and the modern worlds. In fact, social scientists seem to be preoccupied with proving a fundamental and reciprocal relationship between globalization and modernity, which, given the lack of historical specificity in this literature, leads most theorists to ignore the world before the nineteenth century.[39]

But historians can obviously do more than just point out that globalization is not a new phenomenon; we can also bring more precision to the attempt to periodize globalization and to identify and explore its historical manifestations. The few globalization theorists who have attempted to contextualize globalization over the *longue durée* have a tendency to identify huge chronological swaths as distinct phases in the history of globalization. Hopkins and his coauthors provide a much more nuanced approach, one that distinguishes four types of globalization (archaic, proto, modern, and postcolonial) but allows for complexity and unevenness: "the four types are best viewed as overlapping and interacting sequences rather than as forming a succession of neat stages. Typically, one form coexisted with another or others which it may have nurtured,

Diffusion of British Freemasonry, 1727–1751 and 1752–1816

▼ Lodges established 1727–1751
▲ Lodges established 1752–1816

absorbed, or simply complemented. The relationship, whether symbiotic or competitive, does not therefore foreclose on the future. There are interactions and tendencies but there is no inexorable logic."[40]

Evidence from the world of Masonry allows us to refine our understanding of the protoglobalization phase (1600–1800) by identifying the "long eighteenth century," and more specifically the period between 1750 and 1815, as a key turning point in the history of globalization. Though Freemasonry's network began reaching outside Britain in the early decades of the eighteenth century, its period of most significant proliferation came after 1750 (see map). The Masonic network experienced, to borrow the terms of a prominent globalization theorist, David Held, greater intensity (more nodes) and extensity (nodes in new places), especially once the Ancients emerged.

It is not surprising that the period between 1750 and 1815 was a watershed in the history of Freemasonry and globalization, because it was a watershed in the history of imperialism.[41] It witnessed both the intensification of processes that were already at work and new developments. Existing trading networks grew, capital and commodity flows intensified, and the by now well-established European empires became even more entrenched abroad. What was new was the pecking order of these empires — Britain emerged on top. Britain's predominance on the world stage was the outcome of another new development: warfare on a global scale. This period saw both the first world war (the Seven Years' War) and the second (the Napoleonic Wars). Global warfare and imperial rivalry were accompanied by substantial troop movements and adjustments to imperial administration. These, in turn, brought new levels of intensity and extensity to the Masonic network, which grew in large part because of the brotherhood's associations with the most powerful and farflung empire on earth.

The history of Freemasonry thus allows us to peer into a moment when various globalizing agents, some old and some new, interacted to effect the transition from protoglobalization to modern globalization. Although it is not hard to think of precedents, such as the Jesuit Order, Freemasonry was one of the first, if not the first, modern sociocultural institutions to develop an international network that lubricated other agents of globalization (such as trade networks, migration flows, and imperialism). Its emergence anticipated the multiple and varied sociocultural institutions (including business societies like Rotary International and other fraternal organizations) that would increase global connexity in the nineteenth and twentieth centuries.

The Triumph of the Ancients

Masonic administration displayed a significant degree of centralization in the eighteenth century, but it was also characterized by fluidity and confusion. Bureaucratization proceeded fitfully. The grand lodges never had a premeditated plan to extend Freemasonry abroad, though, as we have seen, they did respond once this process was underway. Some, like the Irish and the Ancients, reacted more quickly and effectively than others. The very existence of rival grand lodges created an uncertain and difficult situation, especially in the colonies. While the Irish, Scottish, and English grand lodges generally respected one another's jurisdictions in the British Isles, the colonies and extra-imperial world were viewed as free and open territory. Provincial grand masters appointed from Britain and Ireland had overlapping authority; they saw little reason to communicate with one another and coordinate their efforts. Meanwhile, each governing body received applications for warrants to establish lodges overseas and authorized military lodges to take their brand of Freemasonry abroad. Confusing as these circumstances were, they actually favored the extension and adaptation of the Masonic network. It was, in many ways, a productive rivalry, one that benefited the Ancients in particular. The Ancients were most eager to extend the Masonic network to global proportions and most willing to give the network's key to a broad range of men.

While the schism contributed to Masonry's overall growth, on the ground it became a source of regret and frustration for colonial Masons. In 1767, Edward Ward, a lodge secretary in Calcutta, described "the present animosities that disturb the concord of Lodges in this remote part of the world" but was able to report that "Masonry daily gains ground" in Calcutta and its environs. The same year, the master of a Modern lodge in Quebec who was visiting London described the schism in a letter to his brethren across the Atlantic: "I am sorry to inform you that in London there is a great Division amongst the Craft, those under your Grand Master are the most universal and tho' they Call themselves ancient masons works the Modern way, and those under Esq Mathews works [*sic*] the ancient way, and are called York Masons." To secure a warrant for a provincial grand lodge to operate in Quebec, he was required to learn "a new lesson" (presumably the ritual variations that had come to distinguish the Moderns from their rivals) and pay additional fees for the privilege.[42] As we have seen, the metropolitan grand lodges also asserted their authority by issuing circulars that warned against fraternizing with rival Masons. These circulars made their way through the empire. In 1785 a letter from the Carnatic Military lodge in Calcutta mentioned the Moderns' 1777 circular (quoted earlier). A decade later, Modern Masons in Gibraltar requested an update, stating that they "shall be glad to know if these differences Continue in England. . . . We expected when that Incendious Dermot died that all those contentions would have ceased when you write. . . . Let us know the Grand Lodge sentiments about it."[43]

Life in the colonies was not always conducive to strictly following metropolitan directives on these matters. Sometimes prominent men were affiliated with the Ancients; should an aspiring new lodge refuse to acknowledge their fraternal connection with high-ranking brothers in their midst on the basis of a metropolitan quarrel? What effect might this have on one's relations in the world outside Masonry? This was the dilemma some Modern brethren faced in Arcot (in southern India) in 1784. Well aware of the Moderns' rule against associating with Ancients, members of the recently formed Carnatic Military Lodge nonetheless admitted some Ancient Masons. They justified their actions by claiming they had been "actuated by laudable and generous views to promote Harmony amongst the Craft in general" and lamenting the existence of distinctions "in an order that should be universal."[44]

The Carnatic Military Lodge of the Moderns was in a difficult position because military bases like the station at Arcot (as well as Halifax and Gibraltar) offered especially fertile ground for the Ancients. Its main rival was Lodge No. 152, established in 1768 by the Ancients for army officers, ship captains, and merchants. In 1778 the lodge had forty members (including captains, lieutenants, a surgeon and a major, masters of vessels, attorneys, and inhabitants who were listed as residing throughout the wider Indian Ocean — in China, Manila, and "at sea").[45] By 1779, the Ancients set up a provincial grand lodge under John Sykes, a Madras barrister and past master of No. 152; it built a Masonic hall and operated a charity fund. Though the Ancients experienced a slight downturn due to the war and the death of their provincial grand master, by 1785, when the Carnatic Military Lodge of the Moderns appeared on the scene, the lodge had a membership of fifty-three (comprised primarily of military officers but also of merchants and factors).

Subsequent relations among these lodges in Madras reveal that the metropolitan dispute between Ancients and Moderns could lead to an untenable situation for Masons in the empire. In 1785, the Ancients reported to London that "in the Provinces remote from the Mother Country" the various "evils" that attended the schism "are experienced in a degree of which the Brethren in England can have no conception." To rectify matters, members of No. 152 proposed a solution that foreshadowed developments in the metropole a quarter century later. "We wish a Union of the Craft could be effected," they urged. The timing for such a step was right. Not only were Madras Ancients frustrated with their own grand lodge for neglecting its correspondence, but the Moderns had also recently appointed the commander-in-chief, Brigadier General Matthew Horne, as their Provincial Grand Master for Madras. Though preoccupied by his military duties (which had led to his capture and detention on Mauritius by the French), Horne eagerly accepted in the hope that he could stem the spread of Ancient Masonry. Terence Gahagan, a military surgeon and long-time Modern Freemason then stationed in Madras, served as Horne's deputy. After negotiations with Lodge No. 152, whose members Gahagan described as "some of the first characters of the Settlement," the Ancients surrendered their warrant and jewels to Horne. The union was sealed with a ceremony consecrating Horne's new provincial grand lodge in 1786.[46]

Meanwhile, frustrated Masons in Gibraltar informed metropolitan authorities in the mid-1780s that Masonry "is now in a very unsettled and confused state in this place from the Old Dispute between Ancients and Moderns." Several Ancient lodges had been vying with the Moderns there since the 1770s. An artillery regiment that arrived in 1772 brought an Ancient lodge, and within five years the Ancients had warranted a civilian lodge—Inhabitants Lodge No. 202—on the island. In the wake of the Franco-Spanish siege that finally failed in 1783, the Ancients seem to have gained the upper hand, as evidenced by requests from Modern lodges to come under the Ancients' banner. Observing that the Ancients were "advancing in their cause," William Leake (master of one of the Modern lodges and garrison chaplain) urged the Moderns to renew their provincial grand lodge in order to "eradicate . . . the pretended Authority of the Spurious Grand Lodge of England." With the Moderns' authority reasserted, "many very old and good Masons" would rethink their decision to switch to the Ancients. Gibraltar Moderns had their provincial grand lodge by 1788 and did experience a bit of a revival, but too much ground had already been lost to the Ancients. They would warrant at least nine lodges in the subsequent two decades. So prevalent were the Ancients that they claimed to take "not the least notice of [the Moderns] or their proceedings" and "scrupulously attended" to their grand lodge's warning not to admit any Moderns into their lodges.[47]

Bolstered by the success of its lodges in places like Madras and Gibraltar, the Ancient Grand Lodge confidently reported in 1792 on "the increasing prosperity and extension of the Ancient Craft, not only under our government, but also under that of the Grand Lodges of Scotland and Ireland . . . in different Quarters of the Globe." These "different Quarters" included the Caribbean and

British North America. In Jamaica the Moderns managed to hold on until the late 1790s, but thereafter the Ancients were in the ascendancy. Ancient Masonry had become so popular, a local lodge secretary reported to London, that it was very vulnerable to impostors. As a result of his letter, the Grand Lodge issued a circular cautioning its lodges as far north as Nova Scotia against three dissemblers: Moses Levy, "a Jew, near six feet, well proportioned, and a good looking man," a saddler named Cuthbert Potts, "a squat, well proportioned man," and an excise officer named Alexander McCallum, "a thin man and much pock-pitted in the Face." Ancient brethren in Bermuda and Barbados had also triumphed over the rivals by the century's end.[48]

Masons in Halifax, which had long been a stronghold of the Ancients due to its role as a military base, also celebrated the "extension of our Ancient Craft throughout the Globe." A brother in rural Nova Scotia informed authorities in Halifax that "there is not a lodge throughout this province, but are strangers to what is understood of Modern Masonry, we hold fast to the old Land marks." Though Modern Masons in Lower Canada were in a stronger position than their counterparts in Nova Scotia, by 1792 they too were on the decline. When Prince Edward arrived in Quebec from Gibraltar that year, he affiliated with both Moderns and Ancients and, like Mathew Horne in Madras, ushered in a union of the competing factions. An address to the prince upon his departure anticipated future events by expressing "a confidential hope that under the conciliatory influence of your Royal Highness, the Fraternity in General of Freemasons in His Majesty's Dominions will soon be united." Finally, the Moderns posed absolutely no threat to the Ancients in the relatively young colony of Upper Canada. In 1798 the Ancients' Provincial Grand Master, William Jarvis (Provincial Secretary and Registrar of the colony), reported: "It is with singular satisfaction that I am enabled to inform you of the flourishing state of the Ancient Royal York Craft in this Province under my immediate care, and also that the influence of Masonry under the Modern Sanction is now totally done away and extinguished."[49]

The Ancients were more successful in the colonies than the Moderns because they were more willing to accept members from across the middling ranks of society and thus more attentive to the needs and lives of a wider range of men. As Steven C. Bullock notes, the Ancients "proved the more popular and adaptable body." While the Ancients both in Britain and the colonies welcomed tradesmen and professionals, the Moderns hoped to preserve a more genteel membership.[50] In 1785, the Modern Provincial Grand Master of Bengal refused to grant an application to establish another lodge in Calcutta because he "was dubious of the Characters of the men," but he did not hesitate to authorize the "gentlemen" at a military station "to form themselves into a lodge." The strong position of the Ancients Lodge No. 152 in Madras had contributed to a broadening of the membership of Freemasonry there. Returns from the lodges in the region indicated men from the lower orders were joining lodges shortly after the union of Ancients and Moderns under Horne. In addition to its military members, a lodge at Fort St. George included a tavern keeper, a coach maker, a schoolmaster, a carpenter, and a jeweler. Another thriving lodge in the region was composed of over thirty men identified as "labourers," as well as hairdressers, carpenters, and various other tradesmen. Two labourers even held offices in the lodge.[51]

In the Caribbean men of comparable rank had become interested in Masonry, and the spread of the Ancients gave them confidence that they could win admission into the brotherhood. If refused admission to a Modern lodge, they could always try their luck with an Ancient (or Irish or Scottish) lodge. As in Madras, the threat posed by the Ancients led some Modern lodges to broaden their own memberships. The membership of St. John's Lodge, Antigua, fluctuated greatly between 1738, when the lodge was founded and initially flourished, and the 1780s. The lodge was so dormant in the 1770s that it was forced to rent the lodge room to the army. Revived in 1787, the lodge enjoyed a membership of thirty-five within three years. Most were in their twenties when they joined the lodge and they represented a wide range of occupations, including eight planters, seven merchants, three accountants, several doctors and architects, a lieutenant and an ensign, a ship captain, a barrister, a customs officer, a coachmaker, a wheelwright, a shipbuilder, and a mariner. (The majority had become Freemasons in Antigua, though, notably, several had been "made" in London, Scotland, and Ireland.) The other Modern lodge on the island experienced a comparable broadening of its membership. Though in the early 1780s its officers surmised that the lodge's "select" membership—composed "of all the Grand Officers and Past Masters of different lodges of the Island"—would ensure Freemasonry's respectability, within a few years the lodge was admitting artisans (a tailor, an engraver, a blacksmith, a mason, a cooper, a ship wright, a limner, and a vintner) and several clerks.[52]

In addition to their more liberal admission policies, the Ancients put pressure on Modern lodges by having an administration that was better suited to overseas expansion. As they had in compiling their regulations and running their lodges, the Ancients followed the lead of the Grand Lodge of Ireland in their strategies for spreading Freemasonry overseas, including providing warrants to brethren who sent in requests from overseas (they had issued over 200 warrants by 1777) and establishing provincial grand lodges. One administrative discrepancy in particular put the Moderns at a disadvantage: the Moderns insisted on appointing provincial grand masters while the Ancients, deferring to the expertise and wisdom of local Masons, often allowed their subordinate lodges in the colonies to nominate or even elect their leaders. The Moderns hoped to exercise some control over local Masonic administration, but their insistence on appointing leaders often led to difficulties for colonial Masons, especially if an appointed provincial grand master moved or died in office. In 1769 George Errington, an ardent Mason in Barbados, informed the Moderns that the provincial grand master appointed for the island (John Stone, Solicitor General of Barbados) was quite incapable of fulfilling his duties from London, where he had been residing for the last three years. Although the Grand Lodge took his advice and appointed another provincial grand master (the Hon. Samuel Rouse), subsequently they did not keep up with their correspondence. Errington must have been frustrated when he observed Ancient, Irish, and Scottish Masons electing their own leaders, as was the case in Jamaica in 1770. The story was the same in North America. The warrant of the Ancient Provincial Grand Lodge of Nova Scotia, established in 1784, allowed members of the lodge to elect their own provincial grand master. Meanwhile, Modern Masons in Quebec admitted that their grand lodge's policy worked to their disadvantage as they awaited the warrant appointing Sir John Johnson, provincial grand master: "We are at this moment without it, and consequently without such a head, as would tend to establish and encourage Masonry in the Province: which we are sorry to inform you, is on the decline. We feel more sensibly the want of such a Provincial Grand Master, and regular correspondence, from seeing the York Masons (calling themselves Ancient York) gaining every day upon us, and in general, attended by any Strangers who come to the country, which must arise from the attention paid to them, by the Grand Lodge *they acknowledge* in Britain."[53]

Two final factors contributed to the success of the Ancients over the Moderns outside the British Isles. First was their friendly relationship with the Irish and Scottish grand lodges. Not only did grand lodge representatives in the British Isles correspond regularly with one another; the grand lodges also cooperated abroad in their resistance to the Moderns. Officers of an Ancient lodge in St. John's, Newfoundland, acknowledged this state of affairs when they described themselves as being united with the Grand Lodges of Scotland and Ireland in "the strict prohibition of all Modern Innovations."[54] Second, and most significantly, the Ancients' administrative flexibility, openness, and liberality made Ancient Masonry especially popular within the British army. As we have seen, next to the Irish, the Ancients warranted the most regimental lodges. A Modern Mason in Gibraltar took note of this relationship in 1785 when he observed that with the arrival of each new British regiment, the number of Ancient, Irish, and Scottish lodges increased. He complained that their members "will not associate with us calling us Modern Masons, they call themselves Ancient."[55] Thus, the regimental lodges were the primary exporter of Ancient Masonry, enabling it to gain ground over the Moderns in colonial societies.

To summarize the argument to this point: in its origins and administration, eighteenth-century Freemasonry was, at base, a British institution. English, Irish, and Scottish Freemasonry developed concurrently, and though their proponents did not officially coordinate their activities until the early nineteenth century, the actions of each jurisdiction had an impact on the others. It is therefore impossible to understand the history of this institution unless one studies it from a self-consciously British history perspective. But examining the history of the brotherhood from the perspective of British history takes us only so far. We need an even wider lens to capture fully Freemasonry's dimensions. If the Masonic network was fundamentally British in its origins and administration, it was global in its scope, thanks in large part to the efforts of the Irish and Ancient grand lodges. As we have seen, Freemasonry spread — with remarkable success — throughout and beyond Britain's formal empire. The primary reason for its success was the fact that the Masonic network effectively serviced the needs of the growing empire and its builders. To see how this was so, we now turn from the macrocosm of the network to the microcosm of the lodge.

Imperial Brotherhood

Peering into the world of Masons — their lodge meetings and buildings, their processions and events, their ceremonies and charity — reveals that the brotherhood served a broad range of both public and private functions in the eighteenth-century empire. The global Masonic network became deeply embedded in the community structures of British expatriates in the Caribbean, North America, Gibraltar, and India. Even "the profane" — women as well as men — were involved in Masonry, as spectators of impressive Masonic ceremonies, guests at Masonic balls, and recipients of Masonic charity. But it was in the private, exclusively masculine world of the lodge that Freemasonry had the most profound impact. By assisting the empire's builders, Freemasonry emerged as an important sociocultural institution that helped extend British power overseas and made imperialism into a fraternal enterprise.

All lodges throughout the eighteenth-century British Empire shared some basic characteristics. They had been founded either as offshoots of a military lodge or via warrants from a provincial or metropolitan grand lodge. Regardless of its location — on the empire's frontier or on a ship, in a well-established colony or an army garrison — a lodge was supposed to meet, circumstances permitting, at least once a month. Regular meetings were fairly standardized: the brethren performed the rituals of the first three degrees, conducted lodge business, and usually shared a meal. "Special communications" of the lodge supplemented the regular monthly or bi-monthly meetings; these included meeting for the annual festivities of St. John's Day or gathering in public for processions, banquets and balls, and ceremonies.[56] In addition to meeting in their local lodges, brethren would also gather for regular meetings of their provincial grand lodge, presuming a provincial grand master was active in their area.

The size of lodges varied greatly across time and space, but every lodge had to have enough members to fill the officers' positions: a master, senior and junior wardens, a treasurer, senior and junior deacons, a secretary, and a tyler. A lodge thus had to have at least eight members to function effectively, but colonial lodges often had many more than this. One lodge working in Calcutta in 1770 listed sixty-five members in its ranks; its officers noted that though "several of our Brethren have dyed [sic] abroad . . . Masonry flourishes in this part of the world." Indeed, its return for the next year identified ninety-five members. Another lodge in Calcutta had two hundred members in 1785. Large memberships were not a disadvantage for colonial lodges because all members were not always present, and lodges could not count on members to pay dues if they were away for extended periods of time. The Lodge of Perfect Unanimity in Madras counted seventy-eight members on its rolls in 1796. Many lived outside Madras, not only in Bengal and Bombay, but also England, Denmark, America, and China. Yet sometimes lodges grew too large to work effectively and had to split into two, as happened to St. John Lodge in Gibraltar in 1789. Along with the regular members, lodges often welcomed visiting brethren who swelled their ranks. For example, a brother listed as "Captain Savage," visiting from the Lodge of Amity in China, attended meetings of the Royal Lodge in London in 1778 and 1779.[57]

Before turning to the private functions of the fraternalism nurtured within Masonic lodges, it must be stressed that the brotherhood played an important public role in the eighteenth-century empire. Ordinary colonists and prominent colonial administrators alike relied on the brotherhood for a range of practical, ceremonial, and recreational purposes. During many of these occasions, Masonry even provided a heterosocial environment that included women, sometimes as active participants and other times as observers. The presence of women, as well as men who did not belong to the brotherhood, proved crucial as Masonry built its reputation as a respectable brotherhood tied to those in positions of power.

Freemasonry was a critical institution for imperial pioneers who devoted themselves to transforming remote localities into enclaves of British society. Often a Masonic lodge was among the first community buildings constructed in frontier settlements. Settlers and imperial administrators used Masonic halls as gathering places for recreational activities, business transactions, and civic meetings. Indeed, Masonic halls functioned like taverns in pioneer societies, except that they could be used for official meetings and religious services as well as convivial purposes. Freemasons' Hall in Niagara, Upper Canada, offers an example of a multipurpose edifice that residents prioritized when designing and constructing the town. The British established the colony of Upper Canada to absorb the northward migration of loyalists during and after the War of American Independence. The colony's principal town, Niagara, was founded in 1780, when Lieutenant Colonel John Butler and the disbanded members of his famous Butler's Rangers settled in the environs of Fort Niagara as a government-sanctioned farming community to service the needs of the garrison. In 1791 the Niagara Land Board met to determine a site for a town; construction began late that year. Although the government had recommended that the board prioritize the building of a marketplace, a church, and a school, its members, most of whom were Freemasons, decided instead to erect a public house and a Masonic hall (and then a jail). Freemasons' Hall quickly became the center of community life in Niagara. The edifice was two stories, the first open to the general public and the second accessible only to members of Niagara's two Masonic lodges. Town members gathered at the Masonic hall for community dances called "Niagara Assemblies." The first agricultural society of Upper Canada held its monthly meetings at Freemasons' Hall. Perhaps most significantly, the building also served the needs of the town's nascent religious congregations. Anglican minister Robert Addison had little success soliciting funds from Niagara's niggardly merchants for the construction of a church, so he was forced to hold services in Freemasons' Hall for seventeen years (as noted in the diary of Lady Simcoe, the first governor's wife).[58]

Lieutenant Governor John Simcoe found Freemasonry to be a very useful institution when he established the seat of the colonial government in Niagara in 1792. A long-standing Freemason, Simcoe had been initiated in England in 1773 while an ensign in the 35th Regiment of Foot. Simcoe's overriding goal as governor was to ensure that Upper Canada developed a distinctly British, as opposed to American, tenor. Though the Constitutional Act of 1791 institutionalized a political and legal system based on the British model, the settlement of so many people from the United States troubled the governor. "The utmost Attention," Simcoe explained, "should be paid that British Customs, Manners, and Principles . . . be promoted and inculcated."[59] To this end, he conferred British place names throughout the territory, vigorously promoted the established church, and sought to develop a loyal colonial aristocracy. And he also encouraged a British institution that was becoming closely associated with the British state, Freemasonry.

Simcoe readily made use of Masonic buildings for official government functions and in so doing endorsed the brotherhood's role in colonial society. In fact, he opened the first parliament of Upper Canada in Freemasons' Hall, Niagara. Hoping to impress the elected and appointed representatives, settlers, officers and soldiers, and Native Americans attending the opening of the legislature on 17 September 1792, he arranged for all the pomp and circumstance he could muster in such a distant outpost of the empire. Freemasons' Hall, which colonists associated with the practice of elaborate ceremonies, was an ideal venue. The Horse Guards and Queen's Rangers were at attention in full dress; the guns of Fort Niagara and the ships in the harbor bellowed in the background. At high noon, Simcoe, accompanied by a guard of honor, arrived at Freemasons' Hall and called the assembly to order. From the master's chair he spoke of the incomparable benefits of the British constitution for ensuring the speedy colonization of Upper Canada and for establishing "the foundation of union, of industry and wealth, of commerce and power, which may last through all succeeding generations." Notably, the first legislative action of the new parliament was to validate the marriages of the British settlers. In addition to using Freemasons' Hall for the assembly, the colonial government used it as a courthouse and an Indian Council House until it built structures dedicated to these purposes.[60]

Upper Canada's most prominent citizens joined Simcoe in his patronage of the Masonic brotherhood. They regularly met in Freemasons' Hall for lodge meetings as well as official business. Among them was Sir John Johnson, son of Britain's primary point man with the Iroquois, Sir William Johnson. Johnson had undoubtedly been exposed to Freemasonry by his father's extensive involvement in the brotherhood prior to the American War of Independence. The younger Johnson, who had been initiated in London at the age of twenty-five and appointed Provincial Grand Master for Quebec in 1788, was an advisor to Lord Dorchester and a member of the Executive Council of Quebec. Other prominent Freemasons included Robert Hamilton (the dominant merchant and main wielder of patronage in Niagara), Robert Kerr (the colony's preeminent surgeon), and Ralfe Clench (clerk of the township, legislative assemblymen, and a judge).[61] Thus, from offering a multipurpose edifice to lubricating patronage networks, Freemasonry functioned as a key institution in the early years of Upper Canada's history.

Britons in more established parts of the empire also took advantage of the recreational activities Freemasonry offered. Masonic balls were especially popular affairs. During the 1780s, the Provincial Grand Lodge of Bengal regularly organized grand balls and suppers for Calcutta Masons and their guests. Masons in the neighboring Dutch, French, and Danish settlements were invited to attend the festivities. Likewise, Madras Masons hosted a grand ball that more than three hundred people (including Lord Clive, who was visiting Madras at the time) attended. With a military guard and the town band overseeing the festivities, the Masons and their guests supped in large tents and danced in the Pantheon. In these ways the primarily homosocial world of the brotherhood provided heterosocial forms of recreation that helped women as well as men overcome the boredom that often characterized life in the empire. Yet Masonic balls could also complicate the colonial social scene. Lady Anne Barnard, a resident of Cape Town during the first British occupation, reported in a letter home that "there is much taste for Masonry here" and that local Masons had planned "a great Ball in town" in January 1801. She noted that while all the "English Ladys of fashion" had received invitations, their husbands had not unless they happened to be Masons. She and her friend were still contemplating attending until they found out that the organizer, Colonel Cockburn (the aide-de-camp), had invited the governor, lieutenant governor, admiral, and general, even though they were not Masons. So she sent a "civil excuse . . . expressing my sorrow that it was not in my power to make *one* at their ball & supper."[62]

Another source of distraction and amusement were the Masonic processions and foundation stone laying ceremonies that caught the attention of curious onlookers and were reported in local newspapers. These elaborately staged public affairs functioned not only as a recreational outlet but also as performances of British imperial power, displaying to assembled crowds the grandeur of Britannia and her subjects. Eighteenth- (and nineteenth-) century Masons were very fond of marching in processions — between their lodge and a church when they celebrated the annual Festival of St. John, when they approached a building for the ceremonial laying of its foundation stone, and when they accompanied the body of a deceased brother to his grave. The lodges of Quebec gathered in June 1787 to mourn the death of Brother Charles Carleton, Provincial Grand Master and lieutenant colonel in His Majesty's Service. The Masons had received permission from Lord Dorchester to attend his funeral with Masonic honors, and, according to one witness, the resulting ceremony "far surpassed anything of the kind ever seen in this country." Masonic foundation stone laying ceremonies attracted crowds throughout the eighteenth-century empire; as will be seen, they occurred with increasing frequency during the subsequent century. In the case of both processions and ceremonies, participants wore colorful Masonic regalia, carried symbolic props, and marched in an order prescribed by the *Constitutions*.[63]

Some Masonic ceremonies, especially St. John's Day observances that took place every December, included both public and secret dimensions, which served further to pique onlookers' curiosity. In September 1786, Modern Masons, preceded by a band, marched around "a very large elegant House" in Madras. A substantial crowd looked on. Then, one by one, the Masons disappeared into the house to conduct, for the first time "in this part of the world," a solemn ceremony of consecration. One of the brethren reported that "the largest assembly of Masonic *Gentlemen*, sixty and upwards, attended upon the occasion, and were *agreeably* surprised, and *extremely* pleased at the ceremony." Upon hearing of this event, the Moderns' Grand Secretary observed that "so much splendour and éclat" helped "raise the respectability of the Craft in the estimation of the Public." St. John's Day celebrations were often extended affairs with both public and private dimensions. In 1792, Quebec Masons were instructed to attend church "clothed Masonically" and then disperse to their lodges' "respective places of meeting" to celebrate the day. They were to gather again at 7:00 at Lane Spring's Gardens to install provincial officers. The day concluded with a program of Masonic songs and toasts (presumably accompanied by a meal). The all-day comings and goings of prominent Masons clad in their regalia, including a royal prince stationed in Quebec at the time, must have been an intriguing sight. Meanwhile, in Upper Canada, lodges also regularly observed St. John's Day by marching in procession to a local church and then adjourning to their lodges or a tavern for a meal. In 1799, however, lodges in York marched not to a church but to the chamber of the Legislative Council to hear the sermon by Reverend Addison. That the private meeting took place in an official space indicated the extent to which Masonry was ensconced among the powerful.[64]

Freemasonry was thus a prominent feature of the public landscape of the British Empire during the second half of the eighteenth century. It performed a range of functions that buttressed the imperial state: providing buildings for public and official meetings, offering recreational outlets, and contributing to the ceremonial dimensions of British imperialism. As important as the public activities of Masons were, however, it was really in the seclusion of the lodge that Freemasonry had the most significant impact. In their private lodge meetings, men entered the ultimate homosocial refuge. There, they enacted rituals designed to create bonds of fellowship, obligation, and love — in short, they learned how to be brothers.

Before they could work on building their fraternal bonds, colonial Masons had to ensure the privacy of their meetings. Finding a convenient but appropriate place to meet was a challenge. Often the best local Masons could do during the eighteenth century was to meet in a public house. Lodge Industry and Perseverance was preoccupied with this issue as it moved around Calcutta looking for a permanent home in the 1780s. The lodge first met at the Town Hall (formerly a school and a court house) and then at Le Gallais's tavern, the private residence of one brother, and another tavern (which the master described as "too public for the Initiation of Brethren"). Finally, in 1787, the members of this wealthy lodge were able to purchase a one-story house in Lall Bazar and build a lodge room on top of it.[65] A two-story edifice seems to have been the ideal situation, as we saw with the lodge in Niagara, Upper Canada, that used its lower level for public meetings and its upper level exclusively for the brethren. Once they found an appropriate venue, Masons enacted further measures to exclude "the profane." They covered any windows that exposed their operations to the outside world and posted an officer — the tyler — to guard the door of the lodge.

The very fact of Masonry's secret workings must have attracted colonial men in need of recreational, intellectual, and spiritual outlets. Boredom was particularly acute for British soldiers. When the 43rd Regiment was stationed in Nova Scotia in 1758, Captain John Knox complained that "the time passes very heavily." Freemasonry offered him and his fellows a welcome diversion, a form of recreation that proved more respectable and fulfilling than the typical options of drinking, whoring, and gambling. "When the calendar does not furnish us with a loyal excuse for assembling in the evening," he noted, "we have recourse to a Free-Mason Lodge, where we work so hard that it is inconceivable to think what a quantity of business, of great importance, is transacted, in a very short space of time." A member of the Minden Lodge in the 20th Regiment later reflected that "the freshness and beauty of Freemasonry" offered crucial relief for soldiers. "Those who have sojourned in the isolated scenes amid which it is the soldier's lot to be stationed in that distant land, where there is nought to redeem the monotony of an every day existence, nought to satisfy the yearnings of the mind after the knowledge which befits man as an intellectual being," were profoundly grateful for the distractions Freemasonry afforded.[66] Of course, soldiers and other empire builders beset by boredom were undoubtedly attracted to the conviviality of post-lodge meals and banquets. At the same time, Masonry, with its elaborate rituals and symbolic system, appealed to those with more spiritual needs. Soldiers in an army that recognized only the Church of England benefited from the opportunity to acknowledge their faiths within an institutional setting. In the Masonic lodge, the soldier could privately worship the god of his choice while still being a part of a community of believers. He enjoyed fellowship with men who professed faith in the Great Architect of the Universe, who could be at one and the same time the god of Anglicans, Presbyterians, Roman Catholics, Jews, and others.

Outside the lodge, the fraternal bonds formed through rituals and refreshment translated into forms of direct assistance that eased the inherently risky lives of the empire's soldiers, administrators, merchants, and colonists. In the days before disability and life insurance, before governments helped their most needy citizens, voluntary associations (like friendly societies) were crucial for helping people deal with the tenuousness of life. Freemasonry was among the first voluntary associations to perform these functions; it was certainly the first such institution to operate on a global scale. A member's access to services was limited only by the extent of the network. As we have seen, this network stretched across much of the globe by the 1780s. Thus, a Mason could rely on Masons in his particular locality and in other parts of the world. In addition to operating on a global scale, Freemasonry's safety net worked because the brethren had a sense of familial obligation toward one another. In 1771, the Grand Lodge of Scotland ordered that any member applying to the general charity fund would, as long as he produced a certificate, "receive all the honour due to a faithful Brother of the same household with us."[67]

Eighteenth-century Freemasons responded to crises affecting individuals as well as whole communities, to man-made and natural disasters, to misfortune and even mistakes on the part of their brethren. Money and brotherly compassion flowed not only out from the metropole but also from one colony to another and from the empire to the British Isles. Early evidence of the transatlantic scale of Masonic charity came in 1733 when the English Grand Lodge urged members to make generous contributions to help "send distressed Brethren to Georgia where they might be comfortably provided for." Some decades later, in the midst of the Seven Years' War, residents in Quebec faced war-time conditions compounded by difficult winters. Lodges in Quebec reported that they were "extending our Charitable Collections not only to Distress'd Brethren and poor Widows of Brethren who have fallen in the fields of Battle but even to relieve the distresses and miserys [*sic*] of some hundreds of poor miserable Canadians [d]uring the Course of a long and Severe Winter." During the War of American Independence, the Premier Grand Lodge of England sent £100 to alleviate "the distressed brethren at Halifax, Nova Scotia." When a hurricane ripped through Barbados in October 1789, members of the prominent St. Michael's Lodge helped one another build "temporary habitations," assisted one member who had been completely "reduced to want," and then directed the rest of their charity toward other "poor Masons" on the island. Having used lodge funds to relieve the suffering of the brethren, the lodge had to request money from the English Grand Lodge to rebuild their hall, which lay "in a heap of ruins."[68]

With or without natural disasters, migration to the empire was often a risky proposition. It usually took some time for an immigrant to achieve financial stability. The settlement colonies thus had a substantial temporarily indigent population. In British North America, Masonry provided material assistance to brethren in this category. During the early 1780s, three lodges in Montreal established a permanent charity fund and purchased a house for £1,000 "for the relief of necessitous Brethren" and use as a hall. In 1790 a Masonic official in Nova Scotia noted in a letter to metropolitan authorities that in six years the Provincial Grand Lodge had given away £365 to many "traveling brethren, from England, Scotland and Ireland, driven to distress by divers misfortunes, in this distant part of His Majesty's Dominions, far from their native homes."[69]

Of course, lodge charity funds were only available as long as members paid their initiation fees and regular dues, an expensive obligation that was often difficult to meet. But lodges across the empire demonstrated flexibility when it came to payment. In 1799 a lodge in Kingston excused "indigent" brethren from paying their dues until their financial situations improved, while the Barton Lodge (in Hamilton) allowed members who did not have enough currency to pay their dues in the form of "good merchantable wheat." On the other side of the empire, in India, members of Lodge Industry and Perseverance sent assistance to brethren who were in Debtors' Prison in Calcutta as a result of the wars with France in the 1790s. One of these brethren asked for the lodge's forbearance in paying his dues, "till I have some kind of employment, or till my return from another voyage, as my losses by the French, and my being so long without employment makes cash just now rather scarce." His brethren were in fact bound to help him. Masonry's *Constitutions* required that if a brother was "in want" he must "be relieved"; the brethren "must employ him some days or else recommend him to be employed."[70]

Recommendation letters from Masonic brethren were especially useful to colonial Masons who were moving back to Britain or from one part of the empire to another. They eased the passage of countless colonial servants and ordinary colonists. In 1793 when Charles Stuart was returning "to his Native Country [England], to enjoy that repose which he has so justly merited by his Services in the Eminent Station he has lately held in this Government," the officers of the Provincial Grand Lodge of Bengal sent a letter recommending him to the English Grand Master as "a very Worthy and Benevolent Man, and as a faithful and zealous Mason." Stuart had gone out to India as a member of the Supreme Council of Bengal and subsequently served as interim governor during Lord Cornwallis's tenure as governor general from 1786 to 1793. The practice of recommending brethren to other brethren worked for less prominent men as well. A Masonic official in India wrote to the English Grand Secretary on behalf of his son, Captain Thomas Williamson, who was proceeding to England "on account of an injustice which has been done to him here [Calcutta]." He assured the secretary that he was a worthy Mason, asked him to introduce his son to the Grand Lodge and the fraternity, and expressed the hope that he would "find that support which his good works entitle him to, and of which being a stranger in England he will stand in need." Meanwhile, a former master of Windsor Lodge in Nova Scotia took a letter of recommendation from his Nova Scotian brethren when he relocated to Bermuda in 1796. A Mason's certificate could also serve the same function; the certificate of James Badger, of Dorchester, Lower Canada, read: "His upright Masonic conduct during his residence among us induces us to recommend him in the strongest terms to all the Fraternity wheresoever convened or congregated round the Globe."[71] These examples reveal how a Mason could receive assistance not only from his own lodge but also from brethren in other parts of the empire to whom he was connected through a shared knowledge of Masonic ideals, rituals, and practices.

While Masonic fraternalism was built on men's homosocial experiences in the lodge, the presence of women was nonetheless significant to its operation.

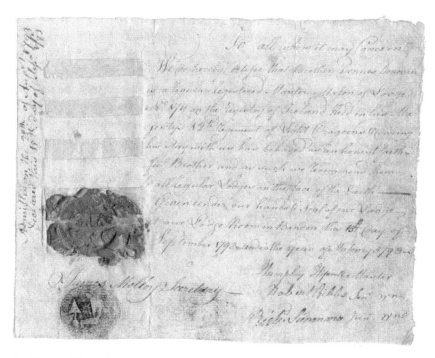

Certificate of Denis Donovan, Lodge No. 79 (Irish Registry), 12th Regiment Light Dragoons, 1793 (Grand Lodge of Ireland).

Women played a crucial role as spectators of Masonic ceremonies and dependent recipients of Masonic charity. When William Leake, the garrison chaplain, assembled all the brethren stationed on Gibraltar to hear the proclamation appointing him Provincial Grand Master, he invited not only the army officers, naval officers, and local merchants but also the "ladies of the garrison" to attend.[72] Many other women, in various parts of the empire, became part of the Masonic world when their husbands needed to rely on their brethren for support. Being able to count on one's brethren allowed men to meet their obligations as heads of households and thereby reinforced assumptions about men's roles as reliable breadwinners. It also gave them peace of mind. It is not a coincidence that when William Johnson composed his will, he identified five Masons as the guardians of his eight children with Mary Brant, his third wife, "in full confidence that . . . they will strictly and as *Brothers* inviolably observe and Execute this my last charge to them." Allocating £300 to purchase rings for them, he went on to explain that his "strong dependence on, and expectation of" these brethren "unburthens my mind, allays my cares, and makes a change less alarming." Masons in Calcutta also acknowledged Masonry's ability to bring comfort to men by enabling them to fulfill their role as providers. In 1788 they raised money to help one of their brethren who had fallen onto hard times. "We hope, by the united efforts of the several lodges in Calcutta, this our worthy Brother may be restored to that former peace of mind he enjoyed, and thereby be enabled to support himself and family with the comforts of life."[73]

Membership in Freemasonry helped men who were apart from their dependents meet their obligations to them. Terence Gahagan, a Masonic leader in Madras, noted in one of his many letters to the Moderns' Grand Secretary, William White, that he was sending his sons back to England for their education. He asked White to look out for them. In response, White assured the worried father that "I shall be happy in having the pleasure of seeing your Sons on their coming to England and to render them every Service in my power."[74] A man's Masonic credentials were even good from beyond the grave. Lodges regularly supported the widows and orphans of deceased brethren. Lodge Industry and Perseverance in Calcutta granted money to the widow of Brother William Barrington. Barrington had been a passenger on board the Danish ship *Nathalia* that left Bengal on New Year's Day 1770. When Arab pirates attacked the ship, Barrington escaped, but he died of exhaustion crossing the desert as he tried to reach Cairo. His widow, who remained in Calcutta, became reliant on his Masonic brethren for her upkeep. In the same period, but on the other side of the world, the Lodge of Philanthropy in Upper Canada established a benevolent fund "for the benefit of Free Masons' widows, the education of orphans, and indigent brethren's children."[75] Such examples illustrate how the fraternal bonds forged through homosocial lodge activities could have a profound and lasting impact outside the lodge, not only on the members but on their dependents as well. By enabling men to maintain their families, even in death, Masonry reinforced prevailing attitudes about men's responsibilities as men and their position vis-à-vis women and children.

The same dynamic was at work in the world of military Masonry in this period. We might think that Freemasonry flourished in the army because officers and soldiers, immersed in an all-male world, had few opportunities for heterosocial interaction. For many this was undoubtedly the case, especially since the demographics and the policies of the army encouraged the development of various forms of male companionship and required men to look to each other for stable, long-term relationships. But research is beginning to reveal the prevalence and multifaceted roles of women (both indigenous and British) in eighteenth-century regiments. Officers' wives often accompanied their husbands abroad. And although regulations limited the number of privates' wives "on the strength" to six per one hundred, illegitimate hangers-on swelled regimental populations to an extent that distressed commanders. Within this relatively significant population of married army personnel, we still find Masons such as Brother Alexander Galloway of the Royal Artillery. When Galloway died in 1793, he left behind a widow and two children who came under the care of the regimental lodge (Galloway was interred in a Masonic ceremony led by the garrison commander and the regimental band). So many brethren in the 20th Regiment met a similar fate that its regimental lodge set up a fund specifically for the upkeep of their widows and orphans.[76] It thus seems that men chose to participate in Masonry not because they were denied the company of women but because even in a primarily male world at times they desired a place to escape women's presence. And though there is evidence of Freemasonry's fraternal subculture cutting across the ranks of the eighteenth-century army (privates as well as officers were eligible for admission), it never trespassed the gender boundaries that preserved the lodge as a homosocial space.

In conclusion, this institution that was fundamentally British in its origins achieved a global reach through the activities of competing grand lodges, particularly the Irish and the Ancients. It performed a wide range of functions — both private and public — that helped the British maintain and extend their power overseas. At the same time, Freemasonry served to reinforce assumptions about men's roles as providers and women's status as dependents. Masonry thus defined its expectations of British men quite clearly. But were other, non-British, men who joined this supposedly cosmopolitan brotherhood expected to live by the same standards? What were the feelings of the brethren of Ancient Lodge No. 152 in Madras when their most prominent member, Umdat-ul-Umrah Bahadur, son of the Nawab of Arcot, failed to live up to his duties as "an English Mason"?[77] To answer these questions, we must now define the precise nature and extent of Masonic cosmopolitanism.

TWO

In Every Climate a Home

"The persons admitted [as] members of a Lodge must be good and true men, free-born, and of mature and discreet age, no bondmen, no women, no immoral or scandalous men, but of good report," proclaimed "The Charges of a Free-mason," which appeared for the first time in print in James Anderson's 1723 *Constitutions*. A subsequent edition (1738) elaborated: candidates had to be "of good Report, hail and sound, not deform'd or dismember'd at the Time of their making. But no Woman, no Eunuch." Though clearly excluding many classes of people, this new society of Freemasons was relatively inclusive in its admissions policy. The only other stated requirement for membership was belief in the existence of a supreme being. Thus, the institution claimed to admit able-bodied, free men of any religious, political, national, or racial background: "We are . . . of all Nations, Tongues, Kindreds, and Languages."[1] Their ideology was, I submit, a supranational ideology, one that is best described as *cosmopolitan* and one that existed in constant tension with the exclusivity members sought to uphold, particularly in colonial contexts.

British Freemasons promoted a particular form of cosmopolitanism, first formulated in the eighteenth century and then constantly reiterated through the nineteenth and twentieth centuries. It was a supranational identity, a mode of seeing oneself as being connected to communities that extended beyond the British nation. Five salient characteristics defined the cosmopolitanism Masonry advocated: tolerance and inclusiveness, a belief in the fundamental unity of mankind, a rudimentary sense of global citizenship, affection and sociability, and benevolence. Together they formed a coherent cosmopolitan outlook that was central to the institution's identity and consistently evoked in its prescriptive rhetoric, as distilled from Masonic constitutions and handbooks, speeches and sermons, and toasts and songs.

Like all discourses, this manifestation of cosmopolitanism was marked by tensions and inconsistencies, which become especially clear when examining how empire-building Freemasons put their cosmopolitanism into practice. As Chapter 1 demonstrated, Freemasonry spread from Britain and Europe to other parts of the world during a particularly expansive phase of imperialism. British gains from the wars of the first part of the century (the wars of the League of Augsburg, Spanish Succession, and Austrian Succession) allowed them to establish further their presence in the Mediterranean, the Caribbean, and far north America. But it was really during the first world war — the Seven Years' War (1756–63) — that the British found themselves engaged in empire building in a great number of different places: all up and down the eastern seaboard of North America, the Caribbean, the Mediterranean, West Africa, and now South Asia. By the 1780s, they were colonizing New South Wales and Van Dieman's Land and exploring the Pacific Ocean. This expansive, multicultural imperial context provides a laboratory for seeing how Freemasons practiced their professed ideology of cosmopolitanism. How, given the supranational ideology Freemasonry promoted, did British Freemasons navigate "otherness" when they came into contact with the diverse cultures of the empire? What happened when a Muslim Nawab or a Mohawk chief or an "Atlantic African" presented himself as a candidate for admission in the brotherhood?

As it turns out, during the last third of the eighteenth century, Freemasonry was a relatively open and pluralist institution that partially succeeded in its declared mission to transcend the differences imposed by religion, politics, and even race. The brotherhood's credentials as a cosmopolitan institution also rested on its ability to facilitate men's movements from one nation to another and to bring together men of different nations, even in a climate of intensive international rivalry. But looking closely at Masonic practice — especially in light of Margaret Jacob's question of "what gender exclusion tells us about the nature of this new and enlightened fraternity" — reveals another defining feature and set of underlying assumptions of British Masonic cosmopolitanism.[2] While British Masonic rhetoric and practice, to a limited extent, transcended religious, racial, and national difference, British Masonic cosmopolitanism was always defined in exclusively masculine terms. Being a cosmopolite was an identity available only to men. Reflecting and reinforcing the "hegemonic masculinities" of the late eighteenth century, Masonic cosmopolitanism is thus best described as a fundamentally *fraternal* cosmopolitanism.[3]

Citizens of the World

Since the end of the eighteenth century, the term "cosmopolitan" has had many meanings, from the relatively neutral "traveler" and "Francophile" to the pejorative "person without a country" and "traitor." A less frequently used but nonetheless significant synonym of "cosmopolitan" is "freemason." This equation indicates the close relationship between the ideology of cosmopolitanism and the Masonic brotherhood. Scholars of both cosmopolitanism and Freemasonry have made note of this connection. For example, Thomas Schlereth argues that it was in Masonic lodges (as well as salons and scientific societies) that "this abstract claim [of cosmopolitanism] took on a certain degree of reality for a small minority of eighteenth-century intellectuals." Margaret Jacob also describes cosmopolitanism as an ideal articulated by Masonic orators as well as famous philosophes; it was an ideal, she remarks, that "encouraged fraternal bonding."[4] But no one has fully probed the cosmopolitan dimensions of Masonic ideology and practices. Similarly, scholars have failed to take advantage of the opportunities that Freemasonry's history as an imperial brotherhood presents for improving our understanding of specific manifestations of cosmopolitanism.

Before we can examine how Masons put their cosmopolitan ideal into practice in the context of imperialism and contemporary gender relations, we must first get a sense of the vision of cosmopolitanism—including its limitations and inherent tensions—that Masons projected in their writings and orations. Looking at a range of eighteenth-century Masonic texts reveals that Freemasons promoted a version of what Pauline Kleingeld defines as a "moral cosmopolitanism": "the view that all human beings are members of a single moral community and that they have moral obligations to all other human beings regardless of their nationality, language, religion, customs, etc. Its defenders regard all humans as worthy of equal moral concern and advocate impartiality and tolerance."[5] Masonic writers and orators consistently returned to the constellation of themes that I have identified above as the defining features of Masonic cosmopolitanism.

The first aspect of Masonic cosmopolitanism was its emphasis on the related ideals of tolerance and inclusiveness. A concern evident in much Enlightenment thinking, advocating tolerance was the philosophes' strategy for coming to grips with the horrors of the seventeenth-century religious wars and trying to avoid them in their own century. They frowned upon narrow-mindedness and overly sentimental local attachments, encouraging instead an awareness and appreciation of the world's diversity.[6] Schlereth explains that toleration was a "pragmatic acknowledgment of the necessity to insure political and religious peace amidst worldwide pluralism" (though he does not make explicit that what enabled Europeans to realize the extent of worldwide pluralism was the violence of imperialism). Kleingeld describes this attitude as "cultural cosmopolitanism"; it is a variant of moral cosmopolitanism. Cultural cosmopolitans of the eighteenth century, according to Kleingeld, acknowledged that "humanity expresses itself in a rich variety of cultural forms" and sought "to preserve open-minded engagement with other cultures in a way that t[ook] their particularity seriously."[7]

Freemasonry's ideology promoted moral cosmopolitanism by tolerating, even celebrating, difference. Envisioned as a fundamentally pluralistic body, Freemasonry was meant to serve as a "centre of union" that welcomed men of vastly different backgrounds. Its stance on religion demonstrates this latitudinarianism. The *Constitutions* explained that Masonry "oblige[d] [the brethren] to that Religion in which all men agree, leaving their particular opinions to themselves; that is, to be good Men and true, or men of honour and honesty, by whatever denominations or persuasions they may be distinguish'd." The idea was to find a least common spiritual denominator, what Jacob describes as "a single creed, one that could be embraced by a variety of Christians, as well as by Mohammedans and Jews." One Masonic orator, speaking in Liverpool in 1788, explained that Masons pursued "the universal Religion, the Religion of Nature."[8] For Masons, the Craft was neither a religion in and of itself nor a threat to religion (despite detractors' claims to the contrary). Rather, Masonry was described as the "handmaid of religion," encouraging a member faithfully to follow the precepts of whatever religion had summoned his soul. The essence of a Mason's religiosity was, therefore, "unity amid multiplicity."[9]

In fact, from the beginning, the brotherhood had enforced strict rules against the discussion of both religion and politics in lodge meetings. It was a policy designed to preserve a tolerant space in which men of diverse backgrounds and persuasions could practice the rituals and learn the lessons of Masonic fraternalism. The *Constitutions* insisted: "Therefore no private Piques or Quarrels must be brought within the Door of the Lodge, far less any Quarrels about Religion or Nations, or State Policy, we being only, as Masons, of the Catholick Religion above-mention'd." Lodge masters instructed new initiates that "Religious Disputes are never suffered in the Lodge." Masons even used their institution's reputation for discouraging inflammatory discussions as a selling point. In the turbulent days of 1793, when they were concerned about being shut down as an unlawful society, English Freemasons assured King George that their rules instructed them against entering "into religious or political discussions, because composed (as our fraternity is) of men of various nations, professing different rites of faith, and attached to opposite systems of government, such discussions sharpening the mind of man against his brother, might offend and disunite." Meanwhile, the Grand Lodge of Ireland issued a circular reminding Irish lodges that "interference in religious or Political matters is contrary to the Constitutions of Masonry."[10]

The emphasis on tolerance points to a key difference between cosmopolitanism and the related idea of universalism. Universal characteristics are those that can be observed in all humans; universal truths are claimed to be true for all mankind; universal human rights are to be defended for all people, regardless of their particular circumstances. Thus, by "positing commonalities of needs, interests, or ideals between members of different cultures," universalism seeks to erase particularities, to make all mankind subscribe to commonly held ideas and values. Historically, the universalizing ideologies of the West (Christianity, Liberalism, and Marxism) have posed the greatest threat to local cultures. Such ideologies typically went hand-in-hand with, and often disguised, European imperialism. Though it too had Western roots, cosmopolitanism was not just another ideological wolf masked in sheep's clothing. The moral/cultural cosmopolitanism described here was based on some universalist assumptions but its purpose was not to universalize. Rather, it encouraged engagement with and appreciation of difference. Juxtaposing universalism and cosmopolitanism, Pratap Mehta explains that the latter "attempts to create a space in which genuine dialogue and opening of horizons are possible. Unlike some forms of universalism that seem to deny the claims of our embeddedness, our locations, and subject positions, cosmopolitanism is aware of the inevitable pull of our locations, our embeddedness in particular cultures and contexts."[11]

Freemasonry displayed both cosmopolitan and universalizing tendencies. Indeed, the history of British Freemasonry, closely allied as it was with an imperial power, reveals a constant interplay between the cosmopolitan and the universal — and the tensions generated by this interplay — in Masonic ideology and practice. The universal aspects of Freemasonry are evident in members' subscription to the idea of a universal human family.[12] Professing belief, as they put it, in "the common fatherhood of God and the brotherhood of man," Masons maintained that all men had proceeded from the same common stock and belonged to the same universal family. Masonic tracts made this claim over and over again, not just in the eighteenth century, but, as we will see, throughout the nineteenth century as well. Preaching a sermon in 1764, the Reverend Thomas Davenport rhetorically asked the Masons gathered before him: "What am I to understand by the term 'brother'?" He responded, "I am not to confine it to him that is born of the same Parents, not to a Fellow-Member of any particular Society in which I may happen to be engaged; nor am I to bound it within the Limits of my Fellow-Citizens, or those of my own Country or nation, much less to any Sect or Party. No, the Relation is far more extensive, stretching itself, like the Benevolence of our one God and common Father, even to the Ends of the Earth." The brethren could read about this idea in their handbooks as well. One from the 1790s reminded its readers: "By the Exercise of Brotherly Love, we are taught to regard the whole human Species as one Family, the High, Low, Rich and Poor; all created by one Almighty Being, and sent into the World for the Aid, Support, and Protection of each other. On this grand Principle, Masonry unites Men of every Country, Sect and Opinion."[13]

Being tolerant, practicing inclusiveness, and believing in a universal human family dictated how the cosmopolitan Freemason should feel and behave. With an open mind and an awareness that he was always among his brothers, the Mason was expected to feel at home in any part of the world. This ideal corresponded closely to the definition of the cosmopolite as a citizen of the world.[14] In *Working the Rough Stone*, Douglas Smith identifies this attitude in eighteenth-century Russian Freemasonry: "Free from the narrow constraints that segregated humanity, the Mason, as a true cosmopolitan, was at home everywhere in the world: 'The universe is the Freemason's homeland, and nothing characteristic of man can be foreign to him.'" Russian Freemasons took their lead from their British brethren. William Preston, whose *Illustrations of Freemasonry* became a bestseller in England during the eighteenth century and continues, to this day, to come out in new editions, explained that Masonry "unites men of the most opposite religions, of the most distant countries, and of the most contradictory opinions, in one indissoluble bond of unfeigned affection. . . . Thus, in every nation a mason may find a friend, and in every climate he may find a home."[15] (Note that Alexander McLeod's certificate recommends him "to all men enlightened wherever spread on the face of the Earth.")

The obligations of moral cosmopolitanism, and, by extension, Freemasonry,

Certificate of Alexander McLeod, Lodge Humility with Fortitude No. 317 (English Registry), Fort William, Bengal, 1813 (copyright, and reproduced by permission of, the United Grand Lodge of England).

went beyond expecting a man to be comfortable in any part of the world. The cosmopolitan was supposed to feel and express love for mankind (even if he could not muster it for all individuals he encountered). Freemasons adopted the attitude of most Enlightenment thinkers that man was naturally inclined toward love and affability. "By building bonds of affection that moved outward from the inner-most circles of benevolence," Steven C. Bullock explains, "Masonic brotherhood attempted to expand the 'particular love' of families and neighbors into a 'universal love' that would eventually include the entire world." Brotherly love was a favorite topic for Masonic sermons, usually delivered before Masons gathered in churches for annual Festivals of St. John. In 1785 the Reverend Joshua Weeks delivered a sermon to fellow Masons gathered to celebrate the festival of St. John the Evangelist in Halifax, Nova Scotia. He argued that though social gradations rightly existed in human society, before God all men were equal. Institutions like the Christian religion and Masonry obligated men to love one another. According to Weeks the benevolent spirit of Freemasonry "doth not restrain its enlivening influences to one sect or religion, to one nation or climate: It reaches, like the power of attraction, to the smallest and the largest bodies in the universe, uniting men of all degrees and of all nations in the bonds of friendship." A Mason was to feel and express love for all mankind, but particularly for his brethren in Masonry. The mutual affection and concern of Freemasons even surpassed those of kin. *A Dissertation on Free-Masonry* explained: "United by the endearing name of *brother*, *Free-Masons* live in an affection and friendship rarely to be met with even among those whom the ties of consanguinity ought to bind in the firmest manner."[16] Here brotherhood became an ideal that even surpassed the familial model on which it was based.

For Weeks and other eighteenth-century Masonic commentators, the idea of a universal human family toward which one expressed love and friendship led logically to another aspect of moral cosmopolitanism, the practice of benevolence. Cosmopolites were dedicated to the "promotion of a philanthropic humanitarianism toward the brotherhood of mankind." For Masons, the practice of charity was a defining experience of belonging to the brotherhood; benevolence was thus a regular theme of Masonic orations. According to Preston, "Mankind, in whatever situation they are placed, are still, in a great measure, the same; they are exposed to similar dangers and misfortunes." The goals of Masonry, therefore, were "to soothe the unhappy, by sympathising with their misfortunes; and to restore peace and tranquility to agitated spirits." William Dodd, the Grand Chaplain of English Freemasonry in 1776, encouraged his listeners to provide the "readiest relief we can give to the woes and distresses of our fellow creatures — of *all mankind*; — of every *being*." Masons owed a particular duty to one another, but they should not limit their charity to members of the brotherhood. Charitable acts toward the poor were especially important for the cultivation of Masonry's public image. John Turnough, Masonic orator and author of *The Institutes of Freemasonry*, pointed out: "We are connected with Men of the most indigent Circumstances. . . . Out of a Lodge, the most abject Wretch we behold, belongs to the great Fraternity of Mankind; and therefore, when it is in our Power, it is our Duty, to support the Distressed, and patronize the Neglected." Thus, the Freemason was "a man of universal benevolence and charity."[17]

By encouraging the brethren to feel love for one another as well as mankind and to demonstrate a spirit of benevolence, Freemasons subscribed to the culture of sensibility at work in eighteenth-century imperial Britain. Summarizing this development, Kathleen Wilson describes sensibility as "the bedrock of an ethical system in which the moral qualities of compassion, sympathy, and benevolence guided men and women in their negotiations with modern commercial society." Sensibility contributed to shifts in notions of masculinity. Men were encouraged to develop a highly refined sensitivity in their emotions, manners, and tastes while being careful to avoid charges of effeminacy. Sensibility also had an impact on perceptions of Britons as empire builders. "The 'man of feeling' with a capacity for sensibility and sentiment generated new requirements for imperial leaders," explains Wilson; she goes on to list General Amherst, Lord Clive, and General Wolfe as "examples of military men who were also noble men of Empire, revealed in their sympathies for vanquished foes and indigenous people alike." Captain Cook was another "exemplar of this new imperial masculinity, combining expertise, humanitarianism, and compassion in equal measure." Lord Cornwallis, who served as governor general of Bengal in the aftermath of Warren Hastings's impeachment trial, and Arthur Philip, first governor of New South Wales, also embodied this new version of imperial masculinity.[18] All of these men were Freemasons. While each was undoubtedly preoccupied by the business of empire building, their affiliation with Masonry, even if limited, would have reinforced assumptions about how a sympathetic, cosmopolitan man of empire should act.

It is here that we see that, even as an ideal, British Masonic cosmopolitanism was marked by limitations and tensions. As Douglas Smith points out in his discussion of eighteenth-century Russian Freemasonry, "While Freemasons may have seen the entire universe as their homeland and acknowledged a common divine spark animating all of humankind, this did not mean that everyone was welcome into the order, or that all men were essentially the same — indistinguishable and equal." Similarly, the toleration and openness to difference advocated in British Masonic texts were not unrestrained. Masons did not consider all religions worthy of respect, only monotheistic faiths that allowed a member to profess belief in the Great Architect of the Universe. And they never tolerated atheists. Moreover, Masonic pronouncements regarding the equality of men as brothers operated only within the limits that stadial theories of human progress, and the imperial endeavors that had been instrumental in their formulation, would allow. Preston described Freemasonry as "a science confined to no particular country, but diffused over the whole terrestrial globe." Claiming that Masonry offered its members a universal language, he continued: "By this means many advantages are gained: men of all religions and of all nations are united. The distant Chinese, the wild Arab, or the American savage, will embrace a brother Briton; and he will know, that, besides the common ties of humanity, there is still a stronger obligation to engage him to kind and friendly actions." Though all men shared a common humanity, some men were clearly more advanced than others. The Masonic ideal of equality was similarly bounded. The *Constitutions* instructed that "all preferment among Masons is grounded upon real worth and personal merit only." One of the most central Masonic symbols was the level, a tool used to remind the brethren that they were equals. But Masonry was not interested in sweeping away social gradations. As Preston explained, "though as masons we rank as brethren on a level, yet masonry deprives no man of the honour due his rank or character, but rather adds to his honour."[19]

Finally, though they might embrace the idea of a universal human family toward which they felt love, Masons were always keen to distance themselves from "the profane"—those who did not belong to their brotherhood. A Mason's general love for mankind did not always materialize into a particular love for the people in his midst. After all, one point of participating in Masonry was for a man to distinguish himself from everyone else—common, uneducated, and amoral men and all women who did not meet basic admissions requirements. Admission into a lodge, undergoing initiation, participating in secret rituals, acquiring esoteric Masonic knowledge—all served this function of distinguishing Masons from those they excluded. Even the practice of charity had this effect. "To relieve the Distressed," urged one Masonic handbook, "is a Duty incumbent upon every Man, but more particularly upon Masons, who are linked together, by one indivisible Chain of sincere Affection." Masons were thus constantly engaged in a process of deciding who was eligible to become a brother. Jacob explains that the notion of the profane "defined the borders of the Masonic polity, and, predictably, those boundaries shifted, depending on time, place, and circumstance."[20] To get a sense of Masonry's boundaries, to gauge the extent to which British Masons made good on their cosmopolitan claims during the second half of the eighteenth century, we will now examine British Masons' response to the diversity contained in the British Empire during a particularly expansive phase of its history.

Practicing Cosmopolitanism

During the second half of the eighteenth century, the fraternity was a relatively fluid and open institution that did, at times, live up to its ideology of cosmopolitan brotherhood. As we have already seen, the extension of Ancient Freemasonry had resulted in the social broadening of the membership so that lodges included elites and artisans and representatives of every social gradation in between. Chapter 3 will examine the brotherhood's appeal to men of diverse, even antithetical, political opinions. The focus of the present discussion is on how men of various religious, racial, and ethnic backgrounds found their way into Freemasonry. It must be acknowledged at the outset that eighteenth-century lodges that spread into the empire were lodges created by and for empire builders, be they merchants, colonial administrators, sailors, soldiers, ministers, or ordinary colonists. But though lodges were unquestionably dominated by white men, British Freemasonry did occasionally realize its promise of inclusion. Meanwhile, belonging to Freemasonry encouraged British men to transcend national distinctions by welcoming French, Danish, and Dutch men as their brethren in Masonry, even in a climate of intensive international rivalry. In these ways, Freemasons enacted their view of the world as "one republic of which each nation forms a family, and each individual a member."[21]

Addressing the Sea Captains' Lodge in Liverpool 1788, an orator made the very typical Masonic claim that "All Masons, therefore, whether Christians, Jews, or Mahometans . . . we are to acknowledge as Brethren." And, in fact, the brotherhood did admit men of various sects and religions during the eighteenth century. Catholics regularly sought, and won, admission into the brotherhood. The Vatican issued the first in a long series of bulls and encyclicals condemning Freemasonry in 1738; it reiterated its position in another bull denouncing the institution in 1751. Nevertheless, the Catholic presence in British Freemasonry was significant through the end of the century. Catholics even occupied the highest position in Freemasonry: the Duke of Norfolk was elected Grand Master in 1730. Later in the century, during the years of the schism, Thomas Matthew, a substantial County Tipperary landowner and Provincial Grand Master for Munster in 1757, headed the Ancients (between 1766 and 1770) and Catholic Lord Petre was at the helm of the Moderns (in 1772 and 1776).[22] Obviously if the English grand lodges accepted Catholics as leaders, private lodges would be more likely to welcome Catholics as brethren.

Freemasonry's willingness to include Catholics was most evident in Ireland, where the Church's anti-Masonic pronouncements did little to dissuade Catholics from joining. The same year that the Vatican issued its first anti-Masonic bull, Roman Catholics participated in the establishment of Boyne Lodge in Ireland. Three decades later Catholics still belonged to the lodge. Some lodges in Ulster had Catholic majorities or were even exclusively Catholic in membership; other lodges in the region repeatedly referred in their minutes to these lodges as "Roman Bodies." Remarkably, toward the end of the century the majority of Freemasons in Ireland were Catholics. Since the penal laws did not restrict Catholics from engaging in trade and practicing medicine, a significant Catholic middle class had emerged.[23] These were just the sort of men who joined the brotherhood, which in many ways offered a refuge from the penal laws. It helped, of course, that the Irish Catholic clergy did not enforce the papacy's position against the brotherhood until well into the nineteenth century.

At the same time, the Grand Lodge of Ireland encouraged the participation of both Catholics and Protestants. In 1787 it warned Freemasons in County Londonderry "not to give any obligation contrary to the Constitutions of Masonry in general, touching religious principles under the penalty of Expulsion." Six years later it reaffirmed its position by sending a letter to all lodges in Ireland "informing them that their interference in religious or Political matters is contrary to the Constitutions of Masonry." At this point Irish Freemasonry was under the leadership of Lord Donoughmore, who actively championed the cause of Catholics in Ireland. Serving as grand master between 1789 and 1813, Donoughmore was a conscientious Masonic and political leader. In 1792 he attended the meeting to organize the Catholic Convention and thereafter devoted his parliamentary career to emancipation, which he hoped to secure by voting for the Union in 1800.[24]

Finally, the fact that Roman Catholic churches publicly associated with the fraternity demonstrates the entente between Freemasonry and Catholicism in late-eighteenth-century Ireland. In 1799 the Grand Lodge of Ireland needed to raise funds for its Orphan School, so it organized a charity sermon at an Anglican church. At the same time it decided to ask "a Clergyman of the Romish Church . . . to present a sermon in one of their Chapples in aid of the said School." The next year Lodge No. 60, working in Ennis, County Clare, observed its annual St. John's Day celebration in a Catholic church and heard a sermon by the Reverend Patrick McDonogh, a high-ranking official of the diocese.[25]

Across the North Atlantic Ocean, in Quebec, members of the Catholic Francophone community actively participated in Freemasonry until the mid-nineteenth century. The British had won Quebec as a result of Wolfe's 1759 victory over Montcalm (an event that nineteenth-century Masons would play an instrumental role in commemorating), thereby inheriting a French Canadian population of over 60,000. Freemasonry, in its French guise, had already taken root in New France, thanks in large part to the operation of dozens of regimental lodges in the French Army. In the midst of the Seven Years' War, as the British conquest of New France was proceeding, two British lodges emerged: the Provincial Grand Lodge of Quebec set up by military brethren, and Merchants' Lodge established by civilians in 1759.[26] In this early period Masonry in New France was not segregated along national lines. An English Masonic official in Montreal observed in 1768 that Pierre Gamlin had a French warrant appointing him provincial grand master for "Canada" but noted that he "thought it better to assemble together promiscuously than set up any such distinction as English and French workmen." About this time, one of the French lodges in Quebec changed its name to "Frères du Canada" and affiliated with the Ancients. In 1788, the lodge moved to Montreal; it included members of both the Francophone and Anglophone communities. French Canadians were serving as officers of the lodge in 1792 when the lodge came under the jurisdiction of the Provincial Grand Lodge of Lower Canada.[27]

The significant participation of Catholics in British lodges of the eighteenth century calls into question Linda Colley's argument about the role of anti-Catholicism in the forging of British national identity in the period between 1707 and 1837. Identifying themselves vis-à-vis the French Catholic enemy and the subject populations of the British Empire, Britons, Colley argues, built their sense of nationalism on a foundation of "intolerant Protestantism." She identifies anti-Catholicism as a hallmark of British national identity through the early nineteenth century.[28] But Freemasons' willingness to include Catholics in their brotherhood, and even accept them as their leaders, points to a more tolerant attitude at work, at least by the last third of the eighteenth century. That Britons were not as stridently anti-Catholic as Colley claims is also demonstrated by the broader political context. The imperial Parliament passed legislation giving official sanction to the Catholic institutions and traditions of French Canada in 1774 and preserved them for Lower Canada (Quebec) again in 1791. And prominent British politicians, including Pitt, Fox, and the Grenvilles, publicly supported the rights of Catholics (and ushered Catholic relief acts through Parliament), even at a time when Britain was at war with France.

Jews in Britain could not claim, like Catholics, that the disabilities under which they lived were beginning to ease, but they could become Masons. Jews had joined lodges in London as early as the 1730s. One lodge welcomed a Jewish candidate named Edward Rose in 1732. Though the event occasioned debates over the admissibility of Jews into Freemasonry, the participation of Jews "in significant numbers" during the ensuing years reveals that British lodges had decided in favor of admitting them. Jews, some of whom attained high Masonic offices, were also active in grand lodge affairs. Jewish participation in local and grand lodges was officially recognized at a time when anti-

Jewish sentiment was tangible. Parliament passed a Jewish naturalization act in 1753 for a Jewish population of fewer than 8,000. But shrill public outcry led to the act's immediate reversal. When Laurence Dermott published the Ancients' constitutions, *Ahiman Rezon*, three years later, he included a prayer that could be uttered "at the Opening of the Lodge, & c. used by Jewish Free-Masons" and referred to the operation of "Jewish lodges." Half of the signatories of a petition to establish a new lodge in 1759 were Jewish. Thus, by the 1750s, Jews composed a significant proportion and sometimes even the majority of some lodges' membership. Many decades later, in the 1840s, the Grand Lodge of England highlighted its long tradition of admitting Jews when it cut off all official communication with the Grand Lodge of Prussia when certain German lodges adopted anti-Semitic admissions policies.[29]

If British lodges were developing a reputation for tolerating Jews, Continental Freemasonry was more ambivalent about their admission. Lodges in Holland copied English policies and practices, and thus Dutch lodges were open to Jews. Arguing that both English and Dutch Masons were "accustomed to allowing Jews to mix in their company," Joseph Katz claims that "the admission of Jews into the lodges of England and Holland is a sign that tensions between Jews and their surrounding environment, at least for some segments of both populations, were abating." French lodges of the 1730s abided by the principles of English Masonry, but published statements of 1742 and 1755 effectively excluded Jews from participation. When the French decided to make baptism an admission requirement, French Freemasonry became much more closely identified with Christianity than its British and Dutch counterparts. Such policies were due, in part, to the hostile position of the Catholic Church. Nevertheless, Katz suggests that lodges in France did occasionally admit Jews. A Masonic encyclopedia published in 1766 noted, "Only as an exception, as an expression of deference to the Old Testament, is a Jew able, on rare occasions, to take part in [Freemasonry]."[30]

Freemasonry attracted Jews for the same reasons it attracted men of other religions. Many must have embraced its cosmopolitan ideology as they sought acceptance into broader society in Britain and on the Continent. Through Masonic lodges, Jews entered circles from which they had previously been excluded. Participation conferred prestige and practical benefits. Noting that most Jews who joined Freemasonry were Sephardic, Katz explains that "membership was especially desirable for those whose business affairs took them to other cities and even abroad." The returns of British lodges in the Caribbean to the Grand Lodge of England indicate a strong Jewish presence among the merchant communities of the Atlantic world. A lodge active in Newport, Rhode Island, included Jews, presumably merchants, from the Caribbean and Portugal.[31]

And what of the "Mahometan" brethren mentioned to the members of the Sea Captains' Lodge? The admission of Muslims, of course, allows us to test Masonry's claims to cosmopolitanism with regard not only to religion, but also to other perceived categories of difference. Eighteenth-century Britons encountered Muslims primarily in South Asia. Much of the region was under the control of regional Muslim rulers (nawabs) as British interests and power in the subcontinent expanded during and after the Seven Years' War. In 1776, Umdat-ul-Umrah Bahadur, son of the Nawab of Arcot (also know as the Carnatic), was initiated into Freemasonry. The Grand Lodge of England attached great importance to the event, as demonstrated by its willingness to spend close to £40 on an embroidered Masonic apron and a specially bound *Constitutions* to mark the occasion (carried out to India by Sir John Day, Advocate-General of Bengal). In their address to the prince, Grand Lodge officers affirmed that "the good moral Man of every country or denomination is qualified to participate . . . without regard to the mode in which he pays his adoration to the Supreme Architect of the Universe." They also reiterated the principle that "universal charity and benevolence are the foundation of Masonry." The prince responded, in turn, with an illuminated letter informing his new British brothers, in Persian, that he "had long wished to be admitted of your Fraternity." Drawing on the ideas of cosmopolitanism, he claimed that he considered "the Title of an English Mason as one of the most honorable I possess, for it is at once a cement to the Friendship between your Nation and me and conferred on me the friend of Mankind" (though his English brethren would later complain that he was not living up to his duty to provide for needy brethren). Within a few years, the second son of the Nawab of Arcot also sought admission into the brotherhood. The initiations of these two Muslim princes set a precedent that would be cited for the inclusion of other South Asians several decades later.[32]

During the 1770s at least one prominent Native American and several Africans were members of the brotherhood. The same year of the Umdat-ul-Umrah's initiation, the brethren who met at the Falcon Tavern in London initiated the great Mohawk leader, Joseph Brant, into the fraternity. Membership in the brotherhood proved useful to Brant in his interaction with English colonists in New York and later Upper Canada. Closely tied to the Johnson family (Sir William Johnson married his sister Mary in 1753), Brant was a staunch Loyalist and crucial ally of the British during the American War of Independence. He received a commission as an officer in the British army after the war; this provided him with a pension and a land grant along the Grand River in Upper Canada, where he joined two lodges, the prominent Barton Lodge No. 10 at Hamilton and Lodge No. 11 in Mohawk Village where he lived. Throughout his life, Brant belonged to two worlds, Native American and British. Traveling to England several times, he accepted many aspects of British culture, including a Western education, the English language, and the Anglican faith. On his visits to England he conversed with Boswell, sat for a portrait by Romney, and had dinner with the Prince of Wales. He also translated the Bible into the Mohawk language. Meanwhile, Brant was a respected Native American leader who attended meetings of the Iroquois Grand Council prior to and during the war and played an instrumental role in the military operations of the Iroquois Confederacy. He fought fiercely alongside the British (he was called "Monster Brant" by the patriots) because he believed the British would reward their allies by returning Mohawk lands after the war.[33]

Membership in Freemasonry was strategically useful to Brant as he nimbly negotiated the middle ground — "the place in between: in between cultures, peoples, and in between empires and the nonstate world of villages." According to Richard White, Brant had multiple loyalties, "to the league of the Iroquois, to the Indians as a race, and to the British Empire."[34] He also identified himself as a Mason. Belonging to the brotherhood gave Brant an entrée into British society and eased his interactions with British Masons both in America and the British Isles, where he had been initiated. He spoke a common language, not just English, but also Masonry and Anglicanism. Brant's membership in Freemasonry conferred legitimacy on him in the eyes of the British and thus helped him cultivate alliances with British commanders in his struggle to fend off predatory patriots. In this case Masonry's cosmopolitan ideology worked to the practical advantage of a brother whose cultural background was strikingly different from that of his British brothers.

To an extent, David Cannadine's argument in *Ornamentalism* — that the British governed their empire as an "authoritarian and collaborationist" entity that "always took for granted the reinforcement and preservation of tradition and hierarchy" — helps explain why British Freemasonry welcomed men like Umdat-ul-Umrah Bahadur and Joseph Brant into its lodges. Both were precisely the higher-status indigenes on whom ornamentalism depended. Umdat-ul-Umrah Bahadur's father, the Nawab of the Carnatic, had sided with the British in their struggle with the French to gain control over southern India. During his own reign, the British would take over the civil administration, revenue collection, and defense of the Carnatic (under the subsidiary alliance system). In 1776 Grand Lodge officers observed that his son's initiation had had the effect of "strengthening the cement of friendship and alliance" between Great Britain and "your Illustrious House." Meanwhile, on the other side of the empire, Brant was clearly an important ally of the British, whose American policies were causing tremendous dissension at the very moment of Brant's initiation. Freemasonry, in the eighteenth as well as the nineteenth century, could thus work to the advantage of British colonial governors in their search for collaborators. But social status was not always on the forefront of Free- masons' minds (as Cannadine would have us believe). Even lower status "oth- ers" enjoyed the full benefits of Masonic brotherhood. In 1784, for example, the Irish Grand Lodge granted £10 to Brother Abraham Raish and his son Ali of Constantinople who were "praying relief to carry them home." So cosmopolitan was the brotherhood by this point, in fact, that two years later the Moderns issued its warning to lodges (cited at the beginning of Chapter 1), urging them to beware of the "many idle persons" who, dressed as Turks or Moors and bearing counterfeit certificates, were "pretending to be distressed Masons."[35] Apparently crafty English impostors had realized that, given Freemasonry's diverse membership, the best way to infiltrate lodges was to disguise themselves as needy Turkish or Moorish Freemasons.

In this period, British Freemasonry was open enough to include not only prominent indigenous collaborators like Umdat-ul-Umrah Bahadur and Joseph Brant, but also some African Americans. One was Prince Hall, founder of what would later become known as Prince Hall Freemasonry. Hall was a freed slave working in Boston as a leather dresser in the 1770s; he achieved prominence as a community leader (he was particularly concerned about education) and an outspoken challenger of slavery.[36] The circumstances of Hall's admission into Freemasonry are a matter of considerable debate. He and fourteen other promi- nent blacks from Boston gained admission into an Irish regimental lodge (in the 38th Foot), No. 441, in 1775, paying the impressive sum of £45.5 for the privilege. What is unclear is if they were initiated in a legitimate ceremony. One author contends that the initiation was a very unmasonic scam to take their money. Hall's successors naturally claimed that it was above board. Whether regularly or irregularly made Masons, Hall and the others did gain access to Masonic knowledge and started attending meetings of Lodge No. 441.[37]

Shortly thereafter, when the regimental lodge moved on, Hall established "African Lodge." Setting up a lodge without a warrant was not atypical, espe- cially if a group of local Masons affiliated with a regimental lodge wanted to continue meeting after the regiment's departure from their town. It is unknown if Hall and his brethren initially attempted to join an existing Boston lodge. By 1784, he was anxious for the legitimacy only an official warrant could provide. That year he wrote to William Moody, a member of the Lodge of Brotherly Love, meeting in London, requesting he act as an advocate for African Lodge in procuring a warrant from the Moderns. Hall informed Moody that the lodge — composed of "poor yet sincere brethren of the Craft" — had been meeting for eight years (with permission from the Provincial Grand Master of Massachusetts to "walk on St John's Day and Bury our dead in form which we now enjoy") and they now hoped the Grand Lodge would grant them a warrant "as long as we behave up to the Spirit of the Constitution." In September 1784 the Grand Lodge of England complied and issued a warrant to African Lodge No. 459, the last warrant granted by the Moderns to a lodge in the United States. For a number of years African Lodge functioned as a regular lodge, making returns to London and contributing to the Charity Fund. In 1788 Hall reported that the lodge had four new brethren, a "melato" and three others, "all Black men and of good charecters and we hope will make good men," but that it also had to expel two members for failing to pay their dues. He also noted that "one of our brothers was kednapted" by "Ruffens" but was now home. The following year, he observed that the lodge "in general behaves very well in there station so that ther no just complantes made agenst them" and noted it had just initiated "a Blacke man," Samuel Beean, and a black minister who had recently arrived from Burchtown, Nova Scotia. The lodge was growing so quickly that Hall inquired about the possibility of setting up a second lodge.[38]

The minister to whom Hall referred in his 1788 return was John Marrant, another African American community leader who was publicly involved in Freemasonry. A free black born in New York in 1755, he moved to the South at a young age and received an education as a musician. Marrant encountered George Whitefield and converted to Methodism while in South Carolina as a young man. After living among the Cherokee for a while (because his family had rejected him for becoming a Methodist), he was pressed into the Royal Navy to serve as a musician on board the *Scorpion* during the American war. Marrant ended up, after many years' service, in a hospital in Plymouth, England, where he was discharged from the Navy. He resolved to track down Whitefield, was introduced to Lady Huntingdon, and became part of the Countess of Huntingdon's Connection. The Countess convinced him to publish an account of his life in 1785 during the time he was in seminary in Bath. After his ordination as a minister, he journeyed to Nova Scotia (where he experienced tension with local Wesleyan Methodists and became a leader of black loyalists relocated from the rebel colonies). In 1789, Marrant went to Boston and was initiated into Free-masonry. He delivered the St. John's Day sermon that year (Prince Hall sent a copy of this to the English Grand Lodge) and thereafter returned to England.[39]

As African American community leaders, Hall and Marrant derived many benefits from their membership in the fraternity. First, it gave them an oppor-tunity to build on the transatlantic networks that connected them to the world outside Boston. Marrant's service in the Royal Navy and subsequent sojourn in Britain had expanded his horizons. When he returned to North America, he remained in contact with Lady Huntingdon, with whom Hall also corre-sponded. Both were more likely to view themselves as citizens of the Anglo-American Atlantic world than as Americans. Freemasonry's ideology encour-aged them to think in supranational terms, as evidenced by the fact that Hall included in his letters to the English Grand Lodge salutations of his "Love, Peace, & Happiness to the Noble Fraternity all round the Globe." Second, according to Bullock, Hall's connections with Freemasonry gave him a "public identity" by providing Hall with opportunities to speak in public, a privilege generally reserved for black religious leaders. His tombstone inscription attests to his achievement of a public identity via Freemasonry: "Here lies the body of Prince Hall, First Grand Master of the Colored Grand Lodge of Masons in Mass." Moreover, Masonry's ideology of fraternal cosmopolitanism gave Hall and Marrant ammunition to challenge slavery, the abuses blacks suffered in Boston (especially personal violence and kidnapping, which Hall had men-tioned in one of his letters to the English Grand Lodge), and blacks' general subordination to whites. By referring to Masonic concepts of brotherly love and equality Hall argued that Africans deserved to be treated with respect and not subjected to the "daily insults [they met] with in the streets of Boston." Accord-ing to Joanna Brooks, Freemasonry was highly instrumental in the creation of an effective black "counterpublic sphere" in the 1780s and 1790s. She argues that through their processions and publications, black Masons like Hall and Marrant pursued "the black counterpublic strategy of reclaiming individual black subjects from public use and abuse and reconstructing black identity oppositionally within the refuge of black-only incorporations and collectives."[40]

It is difficult to determine, however, whether theirs was a strategy of choice or of necessity. That Prince Hall wrote consistently to the English Grand Lodge (up until 1806) indicated his desire to remain within the fold of British Ma-sonry, a world composed primarily of whites. Rather than setting up his own lodge, Hall probably would have preferred to see Masonry live up to its ideol-ogy of universal brotherhood. But this was, of course, beyond the realm of possibility. White Masons in Boston and other U.S. cities did not want black men joining Masonry, either in white lodges or black lodges. Their attitude prompted Peter Mantone of Philadelphia to write to Hall in 1797; he requested a warrant for eleven brethren to meet as a lodge since white Masons had refused to allow the establishment of a black lodge in the city. Hall agreed to sanction their lodge's formation, though he had not received authority from the Grand Lodge of England to act as a Provincial Grand Master (it was not unusual for an existing lodge to give a new lodge a dispensation to meet until an official warrant could be secured). He issued another warrant to a lodge in Providence, Rhode Island, at the same time. Despite the fact that, at least until 1806, Hall remained under the impression that African Lodge was subordinate to the English Grand Lodge, 1797 marked the beginning of "Prince Hall" Masonry's spread throughout the northern United States.[41] As discussed in Chapter 6, Prince Hall Masons then began a nearly two-hundred-year struggle to gain recognition as legitimate Freemasons.

The evidence presented thus far reveals the relative openness of eighteenth-century British lodges. Eighteenth-century lodges included in their ranks Protestants, Catholics, Jews, and Muslims. Some men of color also joined the brotherhood. Even though the numbers of non-European candidates admitted was small, the institution itself was prominent and influential within the imperial establishment and just having a reputation admitting different sorts of men was significant. Moreover, thanks to the success of the Ancients, an artisan might very well rub shoulders with a gentleman in eighteenth-century lodges, which drew members from across the ranks of the humble as well as the prominent. Yet these men of diverse religions, political positions, social classes, and, to a limited extent, races, were all part of what was essentially a pan-British world. Freemasonry's credentials as a cosmopolitan institution also rested on its ability to facilitate men's movements from one nation to another and to bring together men of different nations, even ones that were at war with each other. As seen in the Masonic career of Benjamin Franklin, in Masons' treatment of one another during wartime, and in the complex trading networks of the Indian Ocean, the brotherhood does seem at times to have enabled members to transcend the climate of imperial rivalry, mercantilism, and warfare that characterized the last third of the eighteenth century.

Benjamin Franklin, artisan turned inventor and statesman, considered himself a cosmopolite, a citizen of the world. Much, of course, has been written about Franklin, so we focus here on how his involvement in Masonry facilitated the cosmopolitan inclinations of a man operating at the intersection of the national, imperial, and international spheres. Franklin was initiated in St. John's Lodge, Philadelphia, in 1731. He quickly climbed the ranks of Modern Masonry in Pennsylvania, serving several times as Provincial Grand Master of the Pennsylvania region (via appointments from the Modern Provincial Grand Master of Boston). In 1734, he printed the first American edition of Anderson's *Constitutions*; he later played an instrumental role in the building and dedication of the first Masonic building in America (1755). In his analysis of colonial American Freemasonry, Bullock stresses how Franklin utilized Freemasonry in his ascent into the genteel culture of Philadelphia's elites (though he also demonstrates the misapprehensions surrounding early colonial Masonry). But Freemasonry was also important to Franklin for other reasons. According to William Stemper, he embraced Masonry's latitudinarianism and toleration in his effort to promote "a public religion as a progressive colonial public ethic." He championed universal brotherhood as well, especially in his embrace of the idea of a transnational "republic of letters": the widespread belief in the eighteenth century that the pursuit of science and cosmology and the practice of benevolence should transcend the political realities, such as war, that divided men. During the Cook expedition of 1779, at the height of the American war, Franklin composed a paper that he circulated to captains of American warships, warning them not to molest the English scientists onboard as they were the "common Friends of Mankind." Yet, as Schlereth points out, a moral elitism underlay Franklin's cosmopolitanism, as evidenced in his plan to bring together the world's elite thinkers into a "United Party for Virtue" modeled along Masonic lines.[42]

At the time of the Cook voyage, Franklin was serving as American minister to France, in which capacity his Masonic membership proved very useful. In Paris between 1776 and 1785, Franklin helped Americans escaping from Britain, negotiated loans from the French government, purchased and shipped arms, and coordinated the activities of American privateers (like his Masonic brother John Paul Jones). He also composed and disseminated American propaganda and generally nurtured the French-American relationship. All the while, he accepted countless social invitations from enthralled Parisians who were eager for the company of this fascinating American. Franklin's Masonry, according to Claude-Anne Lopez, was a primary reason for his tremendous popularity in France. "His association with Freemasonry plunged him into French affairs and placed him at the center of the social and intellectual circles of Madame Helvetius, Voltaire, and others." In 1778, the same year he secured a French loan of six million livres a year, signed mutually defensive and commercial treaties, and was received by Louis XVI, Franklin also joined the prestigious Lodge des Neuf Soeurs in Paris. Conceived by the philosopher Claude-Adrien Helvetius and founded by Joseph-Jerôme le Français de Lalande in 1776, the lodge was named for the nine muses and soon became a primary gathering place for artists, free thinkers, and men of letters. Voltaire became a member in 1778, shortly before his death. Franklin not only joined the lodge but, in his capacity as master of the lodge in 1779 and 1780, was instrumental in rescuing it from expulsion after a scandal involving its memorial service for Voltaire. Finally, some authors have also speculated that Masonic connections facilitated his operations as post-master general and a spy.[43]

The Atlantic world of Franklin's era was rent by international rivalry and warfare, circumstances that put Freemasonry's fraternal cosmopolitanism to the test. It was not unusual in the confusion of war for a regimental lodge to lose its chest (containing its warrant, records, and regalia) to the enemy. If recovered by Freemasons among the enemy, the property was typically returned. In 1779 after an engagement at Stoney Point, some documents of Unity Lodge No. 18 in His Majesty's 17th Regiment of Foot came into the hands General Samuel Parsons. Parsons, a member of American Union Lodge, immediately returned the documents to his brethren in the opposing army. In the letter accompanying the Masonic items, he explained how Masons acted in war: "However our political sentiments may impel us in the public dispute, we are still Brethren, and (our professional duty apart) ought to promote the happiness and advance the weal of each other."[44] As we saw in Chapter 1, Washington, who ordered his army to return the property of English Masons, seems to have shared Parsons's attitude.

The crossroads of several trading empires, the Indian Ocean region was another testing ground for Masonic cosmopolitanism. Freemasonry could be put to very practical uses in this context. Masons representing different European nations appear to have had a fairly regular intercourse with one another. English and Dutch Freemasons visited each other's lodges in Bengal in the 1770s and in the Cape during the 1790s. In Bengal they took part in the same processions. At the Cape, British Masons, including General J. H. Craig (first governor of the Cape Colony) and John Malcolm (aide-de-camp to General Clarke), were welcomed at the preeminent Dutch Lodge, the Lodge de Goede Hoop, in the early years of the first British occupation.[45] During the 1780s, the French Lodge Triple Hope at Mauritius opened a correspondence with the English Lodge of Perfect Unanimity at Madras. "Desirous of fastening more and more the ties which unite us to you, by the firm Bonds of Brotherly

Affection," the French Freemasons sent their British "brothers" a list of their members and the degrees they had attained. They asked the British Masons to "accept from us Dear Brethren the solemn assurance of a Brotherly reception to those amongst you who may visit our Lodge. Grant the same to those of ours we beseech thee." In the same year, the Lodge of Perfect Unanimity began corresponding with the recently established — and appropriately named — French lodge at Pondicherry, La Fraternité Cosmopolite. One of the British brethren delivered a packet to the French lodge and reported on the warm reception he had received. Frequent allusions to this lodge in the minutes of Perfect Unanimity indicate "the utmost goodwill and friendly feeling obtained" between French and British Masons in this period. Meanwhile, across the Bay of Bengal, the primary English lodge on Sumatra reported that they had "established a fraternal Correspondence with the Lodges in the Isle of France and that the politest intercourse subsists between us."[46] (Note that the certificate of Charles Wallington is in both English and French.)

Foreign Masons also seem to have participated in meetings of provincial grand lodges and social events hosted by British lodges in India. The 1789 membership list of the Provincial Grand Lodge on the Coast of Coromandel included Le Chevalier de Fresne, Colonel of the Regiment of Bourbon, described as a "Member by particular favor." To their ball in 1789, British Freemasons invited other European residents of Calcutta, as well as Masons from the neighboring Dutch (Chinsurah), French (Chandernagore), and Danish (Serampore) settlements. Even the governor of Chinsurah, identified as "Brother Titsingh," attended the festivities. Danish merchants were active and regular members of Lodge Industry and Perseverance at Calcutta. Its rolls at the end of the century included several Danish merchants, like Niels Peter Mossin and Harmand Schroeder, and, later, the governor of Serampore, Jacob Krefting. The outbreak of war with France had led to closer associations with these Danish merchants of Serampore, which remained a neutral port during the conflict. In the 1790s, a lodge for Englishmen engaged in the service of the Danish King and Company's Service was operating at Serampore, and the Provincial Grand Lodge of Bengal waived the fees for Danish brethren seeking to constitute a lodge.[47]

One reason why European Masons were so eager to welcome one another in their lodges and maintain a fraternal correspondence was the belief that belonging to this increasingly international brotherhood could benefit prisoners of war. In 1783 Brother Baker of Bengal's Lodge of Industry and Perseverance reported "on the great civility and kindness he experienced from the members of such Lodge [Lodge of Perfect Harmony] during his residence on the Island of

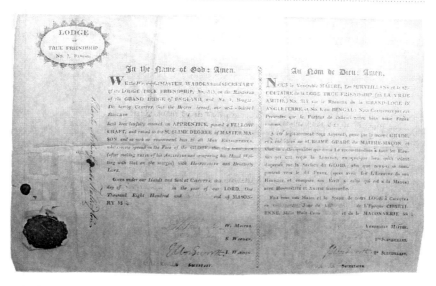

Certificate of Charles Wallington, Lodge of True Friendship No. 315, Calcutta, Bengal, 1813 (copyright, and reproduced by permission of, the United Grand Lodge of England).

Bourbon where he was a prisoner of war." The lodge officers drafted a letter expressing their appreciation to the French lodge "for such attention and house [hospitality?] to the English in general, but particularly to Brother Baker." Two years later General Matthew Horne informed the English Grand Lodge that many British Freemasons whom the French were holding as prisoners of war on the Island of Bourbon (Reunion) "received from them very handsome relief and assistance." Those who did not need material assistance "met with great attention to every endeavor by the Principal member to render our situation on the Island pleasant and agreeable." He even participated in a meeting of a French lodge composed of French officers; he noted some variation in rules but was able to identify the "true principle of Masonry" at work. At this same time, Ancient Freemasons in Madras observed that French Freemasons' reputation for taking care of "unfortunate Bros" captured in war had "reached the remotest parts of India" and was responsible for "increasing the number of our Brethren throughout the British settlement."[48]

In sum, Britons participated in Freemasonry not only because of the fellowship, conviviality, and assistance it promised, but also because membership might serve them well were they to fall into enemy hands. Becoming a prisoner of war was a distinct possibility for soldiers and officers of the British army given the almost continuous warfare between the 1750s and the 1810s. The same colonial wars that put Britons at risk resulted in an expansion of British influence overseas and the inclusion of a greater diversity of peoples within the empire. Though in their lodge meetings Britons interacted primarily with one another, they might also encounter men of other nations and races, and certainly of various religions and social positions. Within the limits that imperialism would allow, Freemasonry did practice the inclusiveness and toleration its cosmopolitan ideology prescribed. But what happens when we take what Margaret Jacob describes as the "inexorable logic" of Masonry's ideology to its logical conclusion?[49] Was Masonic cosmopolitanism expansive and tolerant enough to include women?

Fraternal Cosmopolitanism

Expansion of the empire, particularly toward the end of the eighteenth century, coincided with shifting attitudes toward men, women, their respective roles, and their relations with one another. British ideas about masculinity, which were increasingly informed by encounters with "others" (most notably the French and colonial subjects), had always been defined vis-à-vis women. But the decades bracketing the turn of the century witnessed the crystallization of a domestic ideology that was heavily influenced by evangelicalism, associated primarily with the middle class, and focused on appropriate roles for men and women. Forms of sociability that had included men as well as women were called into question for their effeminizing influence on men. Men thus found themselves having to balance the need to spend time with other men with expectations concerning their roles as breadwinners and patriarchs. British Freemasonry, especially when considered in light of the decision of continental Freemasons to include women, not only reflected the solidification of this ideology but also played a significant role in helping men address shifting expectations. While on the continent lodges demonstrated a "cosmopolitan universalism, here defined to include women" that was "the hallmark of Masonic idealism," the cosmopolitanism of British Freemasonry was gendered decidedly as masculine.[50]

The first lodge of adoption, as lodges that included women as well as men came to be called, was established under the sanction of the Grand Lodge of the Netherlands and met in The Hague in the 1750s. Jacob argues that La Loge de Juste "permitted a degree of sexual egalitarianism" that was unprecedented and unimaginable in other, more public circumstances. This basic equality between the sexes is evident in two ways. First, the lodge officers' ranks were open to women as well as men. Second, the men and women in the lodge participated in complex rituals, specifically designed for this lodge, that expressed not only their "mutual search for virtue and wisdom" but also their fundamental equality. Jacob therefore identifies in the activities of this lodge a kind of "egalitarian socializing," though she is careful to point out this always took place behind closed doors.[51]

La Loge de Juste is notable in its own right, but it is also important because it became the model for similar lodges of adoption appearing elsewhere on the Continent. The pressure to include women was greatest in France, where the authorities had arrested some women Freemasons and their brethren during the 1740s. Lodges of adoption were clearly evident (despite official prohibition) by the 1760s. During the 1770s, the French grand lodge, The Grand Orient, granted official recognition to the lodges of adoption, and women's Freemasonry began displaying a public presence. French Freemasonry drew its female membership from the aristocracy and haute bourgeoisie, though some women of lesser rank (like actresses) also participated. All were literate. Countering Dena Goodman's argument that women occupied only a subordinate, dependent place in such lodges (where, essentially, they were duped by men), Burke and Jacob contend that "as women came together regularly behind the doors of their lodges, they grew in confidence, power, and awareness." They characterize these women as autonomous agents engaging in a purposeful activity: to experience the Enlightenment. Masonic lodges served as "entry points to the organizing concepts of the Enlightenment." Thus they credit the lodges with being responsible for nothing less than the origins of modern feminism. Lodges of adoption proliferated to almost every city in pre-Revolutionary France, and they even started popping up outside France. John Robison, a Scottish professor of natural philosophy, visited lodges in Belgium, France, Germany, and Russia at the end of the eighteenth century. In St. Petersburg, he described attending "a very elegant entertainment in the female Loge de la Fidelité, where every ceremonial was composed in the highest degree of elegance, and every thing conducted with the most delicate respect for our fair sisters, and the old song of brotherly love was chanted in the most refined strain of sentiment."[52] Robison mentions nothing about women participating in Freemasonry in the British Isles. While they migrated east, the lodges of adoption, it appears, did not cross the Channel.

In eighteenth-century Britain and its ever-growing empire the Masonic lodge remained a male preserve. British Freemasons' intransigence on this issue had attracted attention as early as the 1720s when critics denounced members of the early lodges as women haters. People assumed lodge meetings were social gatherings and wondered why women, who did have a role in most social functions, were not included. Of course there were also accusations of Masons' engaging in immoral behavior during their secret meetings. But such accusations met with rebuttals, some even from women who defended the new brotherhood. In 1732, a Mrs. Younger delivered the epilogue to a play that London Freemasons had sponsored at the Theatre in Lincoln's-Inn-Fields. Describing herself as an "advocate" for the "Art of Masonry," she chimed:

> What monstrous, horrid Lies do some Folks tell us?
> Why Masons, Ladies! — are quite clever Fellows;
> They're Lovers of our Sex, as I can witness;
> Nor e'er act contrary to Moral Fitness.
> If any of ye doubt it, try the Masons;
> They'll not deceive your largest Expectations.[53]

British Masonry's official prohibition against the initiation of women was highlighted in scattered reports that women occasionally found their way into the brotherhood. The most famous incident involved Elizabeth Aldworth (née St. Leger). She was the daughter of Viscount Doneraile, who held one of the first lodges in Ireland at his house near Cork. The accounts of Elizabeth's admission into the mysteries of Freemasonry vary. Some state she walked in on her father and his Masonic brethren when they were performing their Masonic rites. Others attribute more guile to the seventeen-year-old: according to one account, she eavesdropped through a crevice in the wall; another has her concealed in a clock. Regardless of how it happened, she witnessed secret rituals and members of the lodge felt compelled to initiate her. She remained an active member of the lodge throughout her life and has come down in posterity as a patroness of the order. There are other scattered references to British women sneaking into or stumbling upon lodge meetings, but they are always related to indicate the extreme novelty of the situation.[54]

So irregular, in fact, was the admission of women into English lodges that discussing it became a way to discredit rival factions. Despite their many differences on matters of Masonic practice, the Ancients and Moderns agreed on the place of women in Masonry, as seen in their attacks on each other. One of the leaders of the Ancients accused the Moderns of subverting Masonic custom and law by admitting a eunuch and, "upon a late tryal at Westminster," a woman called "Madam D'E——" (presumably a French woman). A commentator from the nineteenth century discredited the Ancients by claiming it was their practice to admit women. "The result was that ceremonies once solemn and intended to convey lessons of truth and virtue, became debasing orgies of the vilest description, and cloaks for systems of grossest immoralities."[55]

Welcoming women into Masonic lodges was simply beyond the realm of possibility in Britain. It was unfathomable because of Britons' shifting attitudes toward sociability, politeness, and domesticity, attitudes which Masons shared and to which they contributed. As many scholars have demonstrated, the eighteenth century witnessed the proliferation of new forums that encouraged sociability (the idea that man was by nature inclined toward association with others). While some of these venues were exclusively male, many, like theaters, gardens, and even coffee houses, were heterosocial spaces where men and women socialized together. For much of the century, historian Michele Cohen argues, the presence of women in these contexts was deemed crucial for helping men achieve politeness. Conversation with women, as well as knowledge of French ways and the French language, enabled men to refine their manners and present themselves as cultured and polished. (The idea of politeness was closely related to cosmopolitanism: "Through careful attention to manners and speech, gentlemen could move easily within a polite social world that reached across local and even national boundaries.") But, according to Cohen, a shift was underway by the 1780s when heterosocial spaces became perceived as fraught with danger for British masculinity. Widespread concerns that the influence of women and the French would render men effeminate emerged. Quoting William Alexander's *History of Women* (1779), Cohen describes the challenge faced by British men: "Men must spend some time with women . . . but, to 'retain the firmness and constancy of the male,' they must also spend time 'in the company of our own sex.'" As Cohen puts it, "Homosociality alone could secure manliness."[56]

Freemasons had, of course, long emphasized sociability. William Dodd opened his remarks at the dedication of Freemasons' Hall in 1776 by affirming the sociability of man: "Every feeling of the human heart, every trait in the human character, every line in the history of civilized nature . . . serves to convince us 'That man is a being formed for Society, and deriving from thence his highest felicity and glory.'" British lodges had never (knowingly) admitted women, but in the 1780s and 1790s, at precisely the moment of heightened British anxieties over effeminacy and when lodges of adoption were proliferating in France, Freemasons made explicit their assumptions that Masonic sociability was available to men only. In addition to the example of French lodges of adoption, some faint calls for women's inclusion in British Masonry prompted this rededication to fraternal sociability. Captain George Smith, a military academy inspector and high-ranking English Mason who published *The Use and Abuse of Freemasonry* in 1783, argued that since there was "no law ancient or modern that forbids the admission of the fair sex amongst the society of Free and Accepted Masons, and custom only has hitherto prevented their initiation," all "*ladies* of merit and reputation" should be admitted or at least be allowed to form their own lodges, as in Germany and France. Women could spend a few hours a week studying Freemasonry, he maintained, and still have time "for domestic concerns, and the acquisition of the usual accomplishments." Viewing female minds "as capable of improvement as those of the other sex," Smith suggested that participation in Masonry would allow women to cultivate virtue and thereby counteract "the profligacy of female manners." But Smith's argument went unheeded. In fact, viewed as a troublemaker, he was expelled from the brotherhood two years later. Though the stated reason for his expulsion was his role in "uttering an instrument purporting to be a certificate of the G.L. recommending two distressed brethren," one cannot help but wonder if his radical views on women also played a part.[57]

In response to developments in France and the few arguments in favor of women's exclusion, a chorus of voices swelled up to affirm that British Masonry was, and should always remain, a male preserve. They provided many justifications for this policy. There were the usual claims that women were constitutionally incapable of keeping secrets, but this reason was not as prevalent as one might think. Addressing the Sea Captains' Lodge in Liverpool in 1788, John Turnough acknowledged that women were capable of keeping secrets and that Masons regarded them highly. But he felt their exclusion was justified because their admission would provoke jealousy: "then we should no longer be kind Brethren, but detested Rivals, and . . . our harmonious Institution would by that means be annihilated." Others felt that the presence of women would seriously compromise the sanctity of lodge meetings. "Our lodge is sacred to *silence*," explained William Hutchinson (1796); "it is situate[d] in the secret places, where the cock holdeth not his watch, where the voice of railing reacheth not, where brawling as the intemperate wrath of women, cannot be heard." Another common reason eighteenth-century British Masons gave for excluding women was, simply stated, that everybody else did it. "The not admitting them into our Institution is not *singular*, but that they are likewise excluded from the *Priesthood*, from *Universities*, and many other *Particular Societies*." An anonymous commentator writing in 1790 complained that criticizing the Freemasons for excluding women was unjustified, "as in this they but imitate the conduct of all clubs, universities, and corporate bodies, who have most assuredly never been censured on that account." Noting the existence of French lodges of adoption, he defended British practice: "Though our fair sisters are not initiated into the more profound mysteries of the art, they are sufficiently acquainted with its general tenets, and tendency, to derive the most important advantages from their knowledge."[58]

Its homosocial sanctity thus reinforced, the Masonic lodge was preserved as an ideal space for men to counteract the feminine influences in their lives. Conviviality was of the utmost importance; lodge meals and banquets became increasingly significant and elaborate features of British Masonry over time. Formal toasts and songs punctuated Masonic evenings. Both the act of singing and the lyrics of songs encouraged convivial celebration; popular Masonic song titles included "Let masons be merry each night when they meet," "With cordial hearts let's drink a health," and "With harmony and wine flowing."[59]

But Masonic homosociality went far beyond providing opportunities for conviviality. The lodge was also billed as an alternative to heterosocial spaces that had hitherto facilitated men's refinement. Preston nicely captured the brotherhood's vision of men being refined by each other when he described Masonry as "a moral science calculated to bind men in the ties of true friendship, to extend benevolence, and to promote virtue." A more abridged version of this "mission statement" was the endlessly repeated mantra that Masons' were bound to pursue "brotherly love, relief, and truth." A Masonic handbook from the 1790s explained the Mason's pursuit of "truth" (virtue): "To be good Men and true, is a Lesson we are taught at our Initiation; . . . by its [Masonry's] Dictates, we endeavour to rule and govern our Lives and Actions." Through Masonry, a man could examine and improve upon his character, gain "a proper knowledge of arts and sciences," and cultivate "every virtue, for the correct government of every passion, and for the refinement and proper use of every feeling." Masonry taught discipline: "Our tongues should be perfectly in our possession. A Mason, above all men, should be modest, moderate, and no vain talker." "Hypocrisy and Deceit are supposed to be unknown to us, Sincerity and plain Dealing our distinguishing Characteristics." The Mason, in short, was supposed to "promote morality and beneficence."[60] By being a Mason, a man could therefore achieve politeness without the help of women.

Participation in Freemasonry could also help British men answer what John

Tosh has described as the challenging "double call" of home and associational life at the turn of the nineteenth century. These decades marked the beginning of an "era of domesticity" for middle-class Britons. Prosperous, growing, and heavily influenced by the currents of Evangelicalism, the "middling sort" of the late eighteenth century was emerging as a self-conscious class that keenly looked out for its own interests. As Leonore Davidoff and Catherine Hall so convincingly demonstrated in the path-breaking *Family Fortunes*, this "consciousness of class" took on highly "gendered form," demonstrated by the solidification of an early Victorian domestic ideology based on the idea of separate spheres. Many historians have since pointed out that separate spheres was not an idea new in the 1780–1850 period. Historians, including Davidoff and Hall, have also taken pains to demonstrate that the circumstances of men's and women's lives often did not conform to the conditions set out by the ideology. Nevertheless, the turn of the nineteenth century did witness an intensification and clarification of middle-class ideas about the sexual division of life and labor. A woman's charge was to cultivate the home as a place to nurture children and to serve as a refuge from the harsh external world. Men were the ones to venture into this external world — to engage in work that would allow them to fulfill their obligations as providers and independent men. As home and work separated, domestic space, rather than public spaces, emerged as the preferred site for heterosocial (and of course heterosexual) interactions.[61]

While early Victorian domestic ideology placed a straightforward ban on women's participation in public life, men's relationship to domestic life was more complex. Davidoff and Hall went to great lengths to show how middle-class men were "in fact, embedded in networks of familial and female support which underpinned their rise to public prominence." More recently, Tosh has gone even further to argue that domesticity was as central to masculinity as men's engagement in the world of work, politics, and association. Men's status *as men* had long been tied to their position as heads of households and their involvement in the domestic realm. By the early nineteenth century, their roles as protectors and providers were supplemented by the expectation that they would also be devoted to "hearth and family." New calls for masculine domesticity, however, conflicted with another longstanding dimension of British masculinity — homosocial association. Describing homosociality as the "conceptual other" of domesticity, Tosh argues that late-eighteenth-century men spent time with other men because they viewed too much domesticity as dangerous and that all-male settings retained their pull on men through the Victorian period. Thus, men found themselves engaged in a careful balancing act negotiating the new calls for domesticity with the well-established culture of homosociality.[62] Tosh therefore concludes that masculinity was concurrently defined in three arenas: work, home, and all-male associations.

Though Tosh only mentions Freemasonry, being a Mason helped a man strike a balance between homosociality and domesticity in two ways. First, as we have already begun to see, the functioning of Masonry's homosocial world depended on the absence of women in some circumstances and the presence of women in others. British Masons always had women on their minds, if not in their lodges. They had a place as spectators at public events (such as the dedication of Freemasons' Hall in London in 1776, festivals, and annual balls) and as dependents on Masonic benevolence. The English Grand Lodge opened a Masonic Female Orphans' School in 1788; lodges could nominate the daughters of indigent or deceased brethren for admission into the institution. As Chapter 1 illustrates, this mutual assistance network extended throughout the British Empire and often supported Masons' wives and children. Though not physically present, women also had a place in meetings of the lodge as the subjects of toasts and songs. One well-known eighteenth-century Masonic song was entitled "A Mason's Daughter Fair and Young." Gathered in an exclusively male space, Masons drank to "Each charming fair and faithful she, Who loves the craft of masonry" and "To masons and to masons bairns [children], And women with both wit and charm, That love to lie in Masons' arms."[63]

Second, Freemasons' unique activities allowed them to justify homosocial bonding by arguing that it actually made men better husbands and fathers. Masonic writers and orators constantly assured their audiences that Masons were not a carousing sort. Turnough sought to answer detractors who accused Masonry of corrupting "Men who, before they were Free-Masons, were Lovers of Sobriety, and a domestic Life" and now spend all their time in taverns. He assured his audience that the Order "forbids in the strongest Manner, Irregularity and Intemperance." He also explicitly noted that though some might see a conflict between the homosocial world of Freemasonry and the heterosocial domestic sphere, Masonry itself, in emphasizing the duties of men as brothers, husbands, and fathers, posed no threat to the home. Even women were "well convinced that none esteem and love them more than Free-Masons" and willing to acknowledge "that it has made *those* with whom *they* have been connected (what it ought to make all), more faithful Lovers, and more affectionate Husbands." Smith agreed that belonging to Freemasonry inspired members with "a far greater desire and reverence for" marriage. A Mason's schooling in the art of self-improvement included lessons on how Masons should behave in the home.

As we have seen, the *Constitutions* instructed the Mason "to act as become a moral and wise Man" and admonished him not to neglect his family by succumbing to gluttony or drunkenness. How a Mason treated his wife and children served as one gauge of his progress in Freemasonry. By being "worthy *men* and worthy *Masons*," Freemasons could, according to one orator, "distinguish and exalt the profession which we boast."[64] In short, being a good Mason meant being a good man.

Situating Cosmopolitanism

In presenting a specific example of an institution with a cosmopolitan outlook, eighteenth-century Freemasonry offers an opportunity to contextualize the phenomenon of cosmopolitanism. Cosmopolitanism has yet to receive the close historical and analytical scrutiny with which scholars have approached nationalism and imperialism. Historians have not used the term with much precision. Historians of British imperialism, for example, are fond of describing the eighteenth-century empire as an increasingly "cosmopolitan" entity but actually seem to be saying that the British became governors of a bigger and more culturally *diverse* empire in this period.[65] Other historians have presented cosmopolitanism as having a transcendent status. Consistent over time and space and lending itself to straightforward definition, it can be tracked — in attitudes, policies, institutions, and individuals — through the ages. In his study of the rise of English nationalism, Gerald Newman describes this transcendental quality: "The cosmopolitan ideal, like others deeply rooted in constant human aspiration, thus possessed a sort of historical life and momentum of its own, an internal power capable of carrying it without external help into the mental life of the eighteenth century."[66]

More recent scholarship (primarily in disciplines other than history) has started to get away from making such bold pronouncements about cosmopolitanism. In much the same way that scholars are investigating the idea of alternative modernities, scholars of cosmopolitanism are identifying its multiple origins, moments, and manifestations. Bruce Robbins, introducing a collection of essays by scholars of literature, philosophy, international politics, and anthropology entitled *Cosmopolitics*, writes: "Like nations, cosmopolitanisms are now plural and particular. Like nations, they are both European and non-European, and they are weak and underdeveloped as well as strong and privileged. . . . Like nations, worlds too are 'imagined.'"[67] Thanks to work of this nature, we are beginning to detect historical shifts in the meaning and practice of cosmopolitanism: to appreciate the fact that different kinds of cosmopolitanism were put to different uses, by various groups of people in various times and places. But much work remains to be done on the nature of cosmopolitanism in specific moments and places.

As we have seen, the history of the Masonic brotherhood offers one avenue into cosmopolitanism's complex and shifting past. Eighteenth-century Masons viewed themselves as cosmopolites, as citizens of the world who practiced toleration and inclusiveness, believed in the fundamental unity of mankind, and prized affection, sociability, and benevolence. At times, by admitting various sorts of men into their brotherhood, eighteenth-century British Masons lived up to the ideals of their particular form of cosmopolitanism. Yet, as we have seen, both the rhetoric and practice of Masonic cosmopolitanism were marked by tensions and limitations from the start. Attention to the broader context reveals that the world of British Masonry usually upheld racial and religious hierarchies and always upheld gender hierarchies. Freemasonry suggests, therefore, that scholars keep two issues at the forefront of their analyses of cosmopolitanism. The first is the relationship between cosmopolitanism and imperialism. The "age of Enlightenment" that gave birth to new forms of cosmopolitanism coincided with a particularly expansive "age of empire."[68] Indeed, it seems impossible to imagine the emergence of cosmopolitanism without the experiences provided by imperial encounters. In this way, imperialism and cosmopolitanism might be considered as opposite sides of the same coin. Imperial expansion led to Europeans' encounters with unfamiliar places and peoples, which in turn led to the development of sophisticated cosmopolitan ideas, which factored into further imperial ventures. Cosmopolitanism, for the eighteenth-century philosophe, scientist, and even ordinary Freemason became a way to negotiate (both intellectually and practically) the diversity of the world that imperialism had revealed. We can extend Jacob's observation that "the Masonic vision wanted a European cosmopolitanism that would not interfere with national identity or monarchical glory" to include empire building.[69] In this way, a cosmopolitan outlook did not necessarily undermine imperialism, though it had the potential to be interpreted in ways that could call imperialism into question.

If the history of Masonry makes clear the centrality of empire to the formulation of supranational identities like cosmopolitanism, it also reveals the great extent to which particular varieties of cosmopolitanism are fundamentally gendered constructs. As we have seen, British Freemasonry departed dramatically from what Jacob describes as the gender-inclusive "cosmopolitan universalism" of certain Dutch and French lodges.[70] British Masons could not take cosmopolitanism to its logical conclusion and admit women because to do so would have violated the sanctity of the lodge as a place for men to spend time in the company of other men. Only the friendship and love of men produced the right environment and the harmony necessary for them to internalize the lessons of Masonry and, in the process, transform themselves into cosmopolites. The centrality of fraternalism to British Masons' notions and practice of cosmopolitanism rendered the institution impervious to calls for including women.

The relationship between Freemasonry and women did not change as the new century dawned. The doors of British lodges remained closed to women. And, despite repeated claims from Masonic orators that theirs was a cosmopolitan brotherhood, they were beginning to close to certain kinds of men as well. The moment of relative inclusiveness that I have described here did not outlive the 1700s. In the first half of the nineteenth century, neither women nor colonial subjects would be permitted to enter the lodge and use its language, symbols, and rituals to lay claim to the Enlightenment ideals of liberty and equality. By this point, as we will see in Chapter 5, Freemasonry was ensconced in the new order that had taken shape, one that defined the citizen as a white, Protestant (until 1829) man of sufficient property. But before we can see how the brotherhood played a part in defining this new order, we must place Freemasonry in the context of eighteenth-century British Atlantic politics to get a sense of whether, along with men of various religions and nations, the brotherhood attracted men of diverse political opinions.

THREE

Resolv'd against All Politics?

British Freemasonry's first constitutions, compiled by James Anderson for the Grand Lodge of England in 1723, urged a Mason to "be a peaceable subject to the Civil Powers" and avoid plots and conspiracies against the state. It claimed that kings and princes encouraged the fraternity because of its members' reputation for "peaceableness and loyalty." If a brother did rebel against the state, he was to be discountenanced, but the regulations made clear that he could not be expelled from his lodge on the basis of his being a rebel. His relationship to his lodge "remain[ed] indefeasible." The *Constitutions* even went so far as to ban the discussion of politics — the brethren were enjoined to leave their "Quarrels about Religion, or Nations, or State Policy" outside their lodges.[1] For much of the eighteenth century, these words constituted the extent of the British grand lodges' directives to individual Masons concerning politics.

When the English Grand Lodge published a revised version of the *Constitutions* almost a century later in 1815, the clause protecting political rebels from expulsion was conspicuously absent. It took a Mason's loyalty for granted: "A Mason is a peaceable subject to the civil powers wherever he resides or works, and is never to be concerned in plots and conspiracies against the peace and welfare of the nation."[2] As Chapter 4 demonstrates, during the early nineteenth century British Freemasonry did everything in its power to cultivate its reputation as a loyalist institution. It made a conscious effort to identify itself with the defining features of the British state: constitutional monarchy, Protestantism, and empire. This effort marked a dramatic departure from the brotherhood's relationship to politics during the eighteenth century — the focus of this chapter — when Freemasons could be found along the complex political spectrum of the period between the 1720s and the 1790s. The changes in the language of Freemasonry's *Constitutions* are thus emblematic of a broader shift in the nature of the brotherhood's role in the political culture of the British Atlantic world.

Although historians have written more about Freemasonry between 1720 and 1800 than any other period and added significantly to our understanding of the relationship between Masonry and politics, they have seemed too eager to see Freemasonry as either fundamentally conservative or fundamentally radical. Examining English Freemasonry in the second half of the eighteenth century, John Money, for example, argues that the brotherhood was a "major agent" in the process by which "the varied potential elements of loyalism at the grass roots [were] drawn together in a single chorus of national devotion to the Crown."[3] H. T. Dickinson, on the other hand, includes Freemasonry as part of the "many-headed hydra of heterodoxy." Eric Hobsbawm, John Brewer, and Kevin Whelan emphasize the brotherhood's associations with radicalism. Margaret Jacob presents an interesting twist: an institution that was "aggressively royalist" and never really posed a threat to established institutions in Britain became, in the European context, radical and subversive.[4]

Yet, as I argue here, during the eighteenth century British Freemasonry was never associated with a particular political position, movement, or even leaning. Rather, it demonstrated tremendous elasticity and adaptability. As Irish Masonic historians John Lepper and Phillip Crossle put it, eighteenth-century Freemasonry "include[d] men of the most diverse theories in regard to civil government." To be fair, several historians have made this point. In *Living the Enlightenment*, Jacob admits: "Predictably in a British context lodges were, on the whole, remarkably supportive of established institutions, of church and state. Yet they could also house divisive, or oppositional, political perspectives. They could be loyalist to the Hanoverian and Whig order, yet they could also at moments show affiliation with radical interests, whether republican or Jacobite, and, possibly at the end of the century, Jacobin."[5] Building on this idea, James Melton describes Freemasonry as "a protean form of association that could be appropriated for very different political ends. Its social and ideological elasticity enabled Masonry to accommodate a broad spectrum of political attitudes, ranging from royalist celebrations of absolute monarchy to Jacobin assaults on it."[6] While these observations squarely hit the mark, no historian has explored the *extent* of British Freemasonry's elasticity and explained why men of such wide-ranging political views found membership useful.

One reason historians have not been able to take full account of Freemasonry's elasticity vis-à-vis eighteenth-century political culture has been their propensity to limit their area of analysis to a particular place (e.g., Wales), political movement (e.g., Wilkite radicalism), or event (e.g., the American War of Independence).[7] Because of this circumscribed approach, Philip Jenkins's observation, made in 1979, that "the [British Masonic] movement urgently needs to be placed in its contemporary political context" remains valid today.[8] For Masonry's "contemporary political context" in the eighteenth century included not only Britain but also Ireland, the continent, and the American colonies. To demonstrate the extent of Freemasonry's appeal to men of wide-ranging political positions and the various uses to which they put the brotherhood, this chapter therefore examines the brotherhood's concurrent connection to the Whig establishment and the various political challengers it faced across the eighteenth-century British Atlantic world: the Tory opposition, the Jacobite movement (to 1745), the Wilkite agitation (1760s), American Patriots (1776–83), and the Society of United Irishmen (1798).

Using the wide angle afforded by "British history" and "Atlantic history" reveals that, even in an era known for its vibrant club life, Freemasonry was a singularly successful and useful form of association.[9] It was unique in many ways. Masonry served as an incredibly powerful connective force, linking men throughout the British Isles and the colonies with its ideology, practices, and far-reaching network of lodges. There were other connective forces, to be sure. Whether in the colonies or in the British Isles, British men were bound together by common language, culture, trading networks, and consumption patterns; they shared many assumptions about what it meant to be a Briton.[10] And other institutions—like coffee houses, reading clubs, and political societies—facilitated men's association with one another. But no other eighteenth-century institution matched Masonry's combination of widespread reach, coordinated administration, and cosmopolitan orientation. Coffee houses and associations brought men together, but usually only at a local level. Missionary churches sent members far and wide and had centralized administrations, but they were certainly not cosmopolitan organizations. Some institutions met men's convivial needs, others their spiritual needs, and still others their social and material needs, but none provided the kind of "one-stop-shop" offered by Masonry. As seen in Chapter 1, by joining a Masonic lodge an eighteenth-century man could re-create with his fellows, challenge his intellect, nurture his spirit, improve his character, facilitate his social ascent, and, if necessary, gain access to various forms of material assistance. And he could do this anywhere in the British imperial world.

A man who underwent Masonic initiation was also joining an institution that, despite its claims to being above politics, had a unique and intimate relationship to the political realm. Few, if any, other institutions could claim its members represented a range of political positions. The *Constitutions*, written in the aftermath of the political-religious turmoil of the early modern period, placed no restrictions on the political orientation of prospective members.[11] It bears repeating that the rules of Masonry, at least during the eighteenth century, protected the membership rights of brethren a state might construe as rebels. The unusual premium Masonry placed on toleration therefore enabled men of oppositional political identities to belong to the same brotherhood (if not the same lodge within it). Second, Jacob has convincingly argued that Masonry was one of the first widespread institutions that instructed men in the practices of citizenship: operating according to constitutions, voting, and serving as elected officers. Thus, she writes, "lodges were deeply concerned with the political without ever wishing to engage in day-to-day politics."[12] Third, as we see in this chapter, sometimes members and lodges did wish to engage in day-to-day politics, and when they did, they found that their brotherhood offered a highly portable and adaptable organizational form — a network of lodges — that could be co-opted for political purposes. While such activities clearly violated the spirit and the letter of Masonic law, Jacobites, patriots, and United Irishmen, as well as those loyal to the Hanoverian establishment, did use Freemasonry to facilitate individual political careers and forward particular political agendas. Finally, Freemasonry provided a model for other societies that were explicitly political. Especially in Ireland, societies like the Defenders, the Orange Order, and United Irishmen mimicked the lodge structure, practices, and fraternalism pioneered by Freemasons.

Freemasons' implication in movements that challenged the British government, especially the United Irish Rebellion, had profound consequences, felt far beyond Britain's shores. As it experienced the heated crucible of metropolitan politics at the turn of the century, the brotherhood would undergo a dramatic transformation, one that witnessed the contraction of its openness. By the 1790s, the brotherhood that had, for seven decades, neither prescribed nor proscribed political behavior of any kind would begin telling its members exactly how they should act vis-à-vis the British state.

Britain: Oligarchy and Opposition

The Grand Lodge of England emerged in 1717 amid an atmosphere of political instability. The country was adjusting to its new German-speaking king, George I, who had occupied the throne for only three years. The House of Stuart, in exile on the Continent, was constantly on the lookout for opportunities to reclaim the throne. Meanwhile, a true party system was just beginning to take shape, with momentum shifting in favor of the Whigs who supported the Hanoverian succession. The Tories had held the upper hand during the reign of Anne, but they found their influence waning under George I. Though the Whigs suffered many internal divisions and weathered the profound financial crisis caused by the bursting of the South Sea Bubble in 1720, Robert Walpole, as of 1721 the leader of the Whigs and chief minister to George I, was firmly in command of his party when George II ascended the throne in 1727. Under Walpole and his successors, the Whigs became the dominant political force of the eighteenth century, though it is important not to underestimate the significant subculture of oppositional politics represented, in turn, by Jacobites, Tories, and radicals (and even within the Whig Party itself). Freemasons could be found not only among the oligarchy's supporters but also in the ranks of those who challenged Whig ascendancy.

Early in the history of speculative Freemasonry, the brotherhood — at the national level — became closely identified with the Whig oligarchy and was associated with powerful men (for this reason, it also attracted those seeking social and political advancement). The men active in founding the first grand lodge in 1717, the first nobleman to serve as grand master in 1721, and most of its subsequent leaders were all "resolutely Whig." They lost control of the grand lodge for a year (to the Duke of Wharton), but in 1723 prominent Whigs who were loyal to the Hanoverians resumed control over its operations. According to Jacob, grand lodge leaders actively supported Walpole, and "the mythological history and official constitutions of British freemasonry self-consciously argued for ministerial and court-centered government based on the constitutional settlement of 1689." Walpole himself was a Freemason. At a lodge meeting held in Walpole's Norfolk home, several prominent supporters, including the Duke of Newcastle, were initiated into Freemasonry.[13] In London, supporters campaigned for Walpole in taverns, hosted party dinners, and issued pamphlets. Masons like Sir Robert Rich (army commander), the Hon. Charles Stanhope (Treasury Secretary), the Duke of Chandos (Paymaster General), and Martin Bladen (Comptroller and later commissioner of the Board of Trade and Plantations) benefited from the extensive Whig patronage networks and used their positions to their own financial advantage.[14]

Freemasonry's identification with the Whig regime is also evident in the basic ideas and practices of the brotherhood. Its official publications championed strong constitutional monarchy and loyalty to the royal ministry. The lessons conveyed through Masonic rituals elaborated upon natural liberties like justice and toleration that Whigs championed. Moreover, the governing practices of lodges were largely Whiggish in inspiration. One of Jacob's central arguments in *Living the Enlightenment* is that Masonry was a constitutionally governed society; from the national through the provincial and to the local level, lodges were expected to abide by the published *Constitutions*. "The goal of government by consent within the context of subordination to 'legitimate' authority was vigorously pursued by the Grand Lodge of London and was demanded of all lodges affiliated with it." In terms of governing practices, this meant majority rule, elections by ballot, the investing of the master with executive power, and deliberation through committees. It also required members to pay dues and demanded civil behavior and allegiance to the national government.[15]

Loyalist Whigs who took over the Grand Lodge in 1723 sought to position the brotherhood in line with the ruling establishment in large part because of concerns that Freemasonry would be associated with Jacobitism. Jacobitism—defined here as support for the Catholic Stuart line that was exiled from the British Isles as a result of the Revolution of 1688—in its pan-British context was a movement that stretched between two key historical moments, James II's defeat at the Battle of the Boyne in 1690 and the Jacobite invasion of James's grandson Bonnie Prince Charlie (the Young Pretender) in 1745. Though for a time professional historians dismissed Jacobitism as an insignificant movement, recent studies have proved otherwise. In the process, they have demonstrated an undeniable link between Jacobitism and Freemasonry.[16] Freemasonry took root in opposition networks for the same reasons it appealed to the Hanoverians' supporters—it could be used to further individual political agendas and the broader movement, in this case by facilitating men's movements within the transnational Jacobite network and rallying sympathetic members to the cause.

The brotherhood appears to have helped grease the wheels of the Jacobite network in Europe and parts of Britain. As Paul Monod has argued, Jacobitism was a varied political and social phenomenon characterized by "contrasting forms of individual adherence to the banished Stuarts: the peaceable, sociable Jacobitism of the gentry, and the militant loyalty of the rebels of 1715 and 1745." We find Freemasons among both the "social Jacobites" and those willing to risk their lives for the exiled king, including the Duke of Wharton. It was Wharton whom Whig Freemasons had usurped to regain control of the Grand Lodge of England in 1723. The duke was the most infamous English magnate of the period. Blessed with significant literary and political talent, he spent most of his life squandering his gifts as well as his fortune. He amassed huge debts and developed a reputation as a rake, but remained important in fashionable society (there were only twelve dukedoms at this point in George I's reign). Wharton seems to have become a Freemason primarily for what the brotherhood could offer him socially rather than for its principles (though he was a deist). Like many in this age of clubs and associations, he was a consummate joiner. In addition to joining various existing societies, he also founded new ones. In 1718 he established the infamous Hell-Fire Club, a rowdy association — for promi-nent ladies as well as gentlemen — whose central purpose was to blaspheme traditional religious tenets and practices. He was initiated into Freemasonry in 1722 at the age of twenty-three. Wharton coveted the highest position in this new society and positioned himself to take over as grand master from the popular Duke of Montagu (who had much more sober interests in Free-masonry). He achieved this goal within a year of his initiation.[17]

Though Wharton was not yet firmly in the Jacobite camp in 1723, his politics were suspicious enough to raise alarms among Whigs who belonged to the English Grand Lodge. His inherited political home was among the opposition Tories, but in late 1721 he had abandoned them to ally himself with Walpole's challenger within the Whig Party, the Earl of Sunderland. His reasons for shifting allegiances were primarily financial, and so in addition to his reputation as a rake, he was seen as an opportunist. In 1722, when he took over the grand mastership, people correctly suspected his Jacobite proclivities, even though he was formally identified with the Whigs. The band at his installation banquet reportedly played the Jacobite tune, "The King shall enjoy his own again." Moreover, the King's Army Lodge to which Wharton belonged included many members of Tory, and probably Jacobite, sympathies. So problematic were Wharton's politics that some of his supporters in the Grand Lodge issued a statement professing Freemasonry's support for the Hanoverian succession. The response of the secretary of state revealed the government's lack of concern: "they need not be apprehensive about any molestation from the Government," he replied, "as . . . the secrets of the Society . . . must be of a very harmless na-ture, because, as much as mankind love mischief, nobody ever bothered to betray them."[18]

As was typical of his behavior, Wharton did not stay a Freemason for very long. Bored, he left the brotherhood in 1724 once his tenure as grand master had expired. Shortly thereafter, he formed the Gormogans, a club whose *raison d'être* was to mimic and mock Freemasonry. Within a year, saddled with debts totaling over £70,000 and with no political allies in England, Wharton openly "converted" to Jacobitism and suddenly left for the Continent. Wharton fared about as well among the émigré Jacobite community as he had in England. But he did renew his interest in Freemasonry and found the first lodge in Spain in 1728. His resumption of Masonic activity on the Continent indicates his hope that membership in Freemasonry would prove socially and politically useful.

The links between Jacobitism and Freemasonry extended to the institutional level, as evident in Wales during the 1720s. Though Welsh Jacobites had not participated in the 1715 uprising, the decade after the '15 witnessed significant Jacobite activity in Wales. Disaffected landed magnates, including Lewis Pryse and William Powell (south-west Wales) and Lord Bulkeley and Watkin Williams Wynn (north Wales), led the cause. In addition to localized riots and the harassment of local Whig authorities, Welsh Jacobitism involved invasion plots. Pryse, the Tory who controlled Cardiganshire, was in communication with the Stuart Court in 1717 to make a "last push . . . towards a happy restoration to old England." A few years later rumors of a French invasion involving another key Jacobite leader, the Duke of Beaufort, were circulating. According to Philip Jenkins, Jacobites among the Welsh gentry were so optimistic about the possibility of overthrowing the Hanoverians that by the 1720s they organized Jacobite clubs, including the Society of the Sea Serjeants in southern Wales, that had overtly political functions.[19]

Jenkins traces continuities in the origins and the membership registers of the Sea Serjeants and the Masonic lodges founded in southwestern Wales at this time. The first Welsh lodge was established in Carmarthen, the heart of Serjeant activity, in 1726, about the time the Sea Serjeants emerged. Its first master, Sir Edward Mansell, belonged to the Sea Serjeants; Mansell later served as an officer in the English Grand Lodge and as Provincial Grand Master for Wales. His successor to the office of Provincial Grand Master was also a Sea Serjeant. Similar connections and continuities existed with the second Welsh lodge (in Haverfordwest). Members of both Freemasonry and the Sea Serjeants referred to one another as "brothers." All this crossfertilization leads Jenkins to conclude that "under George II it was virtually impossible to distinguish between Jacobite secret societies and Masonic lodges."[20]

The connection between Jacobitism and Freemasonry was even stronger on the Continent, where a significant Jacobite diaspora had been developing since the end of the seventeenth century. The Masonic network helped English, Scottish, and Irish Jacobites move through European society; they were instrumental in extending this network across Europe and clearly influenced early continental Freemasonry. Charles Radcliffe, who became Earl of Derwentwater when his brother James was executed for his part in the 1715 uprising, played an instrumental role in Freemasonry's spread through Europe in the 1720s. It is likely that he founded the first lodge in Paris in 1725; it was composed of both English and Irish Jacobite exiles. Derwentwater later became Grand Master of the lodges in France. As has been mentioned, the Duke of Wharton set up a Jacobite lodge in Spain in 1728. Other Jacobite exiles set up lodges in Russia, Switzerland, and Avignon. One of the exiles of the 1715 Jacobite Uprising, Lord Wintoun, ran a lodge in Rome between 1735 and 1737 that included several English Roman Catholics and Nonjurors.[21]

By the mid-1730s a connection between Scottish Jacobitism and Freemasonry had also become clear. In 1736 Scottish gentry with Jacobite proclivities, like the earls of Eglinton, played a role in the founding of the Grand Lodge of Scotland. Chevalier Andrew Michael Ramsay, the Scottish mystic, political theorist, and former tutor to Charles Edward, had gained admission into London's Horn Lodge in 1730. He was very active in spreading Freemasonry in Europe and published an influential tract, *Discours*, in 1738. According to Monod, the "main effect of the *Discours* was to establish Masonry as a pursuit worthy of the noble classes of Europe." One result of his efforts was the establishment of complex higher degree systems, the "Scottish rite" in France and "Strict Observance" Masonry in Germany, Sweden, and other parts of Europe. The latter claimed that Jacobite exiles had initiated Charles Edward Stuart as the secret Grand Master of the Knights Templar Order in Paris.[22]

Finally, Freemasonry's network of lodges also proved useful as Jacobites, in both Britain and on the Continent, hatched their plans to usurp the Hanoverians. We have already seen that leaders of the first Jacobite Uprising in 1715, like the Earls of Wintoun and Derwentwater, set up continental lodges. In 1737 the London papers reported that "Jacobites, Non-jurors and Papists" were entering Masonic lodges that were preparing for another invasion. By this point, both the French and British governments were watching French Freemasons in the service of the Stuarts. Dominic O'Heguerty, one of the founding members of the Paris lodge set up by Derwentwater, was a member of a prominent French-Irish ship-owning family and a Jacobite. He and fellow ship builder, Jacobite, and Freemason Antony Walsh furnished Prince Charles with the ship that took him to Scotland in 1745. Meanwhile, Jacobite agents from the Continent were welcomed in sympathetic lodges in Scotland. It must have helped that William, 4th Earl of Kilmarnock, was Grand Master of Scotland in 1743; the earl and one of his sons joined the rebels two years later. Further south, the Jacobite tenor of lodges in parts of England (such as Newcastle and the Tyne Valley) convinced later observers that Freemasonry was "a gigantic Jacobite conspiracy."[23]

Despite this strong connection between the brotherhood and Jacobitism, continental Freemasonry was in no way an exclusively Jacobite domain in the mid-eighteenth century. As in England, loyalist Whigs on the Continent worked hard to counter their brotherhood's associations with Jacobitism and were instrumental in founding some of the earliest European lodges. Hanoverian Whigs had established the first official continental lodge (sponsored by the English Grand Lodge) in The Hague. The English ambassador, Lord Chesterfield, and Jean Desaguliers, the Newtonian churchman who was a founder of the English Grand Lodge, were brethren in this lodge. Lord Waldegrave, the British ambassador to France in the 1730s, also sponsored a lodge, probably as a challenge to the lodge set up by Derwentwater and his fellow Jacobite émigrés. Suspicious of Freemasonry in any guise, the French authorities searched his residence in the aftermath of a lodge meeting in 1738. Meanwhile, the Vatican officially condemned Freemasonry for the first time and suppressed the Jacobite lodge in Rome.[24]

While historians have pointed out the Masonic associations of some Jacobites, they have underestimated its significance to the movement. Daniel Szechi argues that Masonic lodges (like Sea Serjeant Clubs) were "part of a wider network of patrician conviviality with an overtly Jacobite tinge." Likewise, Paul Monod sees Freemasonry more as an element of Jacobite sociability than of the movement's political culture. Like sporting events, clubs, and mock corporations, lodges encouraged elite comradeship. "Safely detached from Whiggish knavery, ensconced in a hidden withdrawing room, surrounded by trustworthy friends and protected by the rules and regulations of their secret societies, Jacobite gentlemen could indulge themselves in the dream of a Stuart restoration."[25] Certainly, Freemasonry was an important social forum, but Jacobites were also interested in its political uses. In fact, drawing a distinction between "the political" and "the social" in this period is in some ways to impose a false division (to socialize *as Jacobites* was in itself a political act). If Freemasonry had merely offered a social venue, government authorities and the Catholic Church probably would not have been so suspicious. And English Whigs would not have gone to such lengths to be certain the Grand Lodge was in their camp. Although the Jacobites never fully realized it, Freemasonry's subversive potential would become clear in oppositional movements later in the century.

Freemasonry's appeal to a variety of political groups is suggested not only by the participation of Whigs and Jacobites but also opposition Tories and the Prince of Wales, who too used the brotherhood to forward political agendas. Sir Walter Blackett, the Lord Mayor of Newcastle and a Tory MP, dominated Northumberland Freemasonry during the 1720s and 1730s. Freemasons among the Tory supporters of Bolingbroke took part in the political activities of the Brothers Club and the Beef-Steak Society and dined in taverns affiliated with the Tory Party. Masons John Byram and Edwin Ward were among the Tory pamphleteers who critiqued Walpole's government. Frederick, Prince of Wales, joined the brotherhood in 1737. Jean Desaguliers, one of the royal chaplains, and other members of the English Grand Lodge initiated the prince in a ceremony at Kew. Historians have noted that the prince's initiation marked a turning point for English Freemasonry: no longer would it be consistently subject to the public insults and parodies it had experienced in the 1720s and early 1730s. But, like Wharton earlier, Frederick seems to have had political motives for joining. His initiation coincided with his entering into active opposition against the royal ministry. Several politicians attended his initiation. According to Masonic historian Aubrey Newman, "At a time when he was already canvassing as many factions as he could find in Parliament, when it was important for him to build up as much support as possible in the House of Commons, Frederick chose to join an organization which contained a number of Members of Parliament in its ranks." After his initiation, Frederick did not demonstrate much interest in Masonic affairs, and so the brotherhood failed to secure in the prince the kind of royal patron its leaders sought.[26]

Whatever the prince's motives for joining the brotherhood, his participation, at the very least, provides further evidence of Freemasonry's ability to accommodate a range of political positions during the mid-eighteenth century. Its protean nature and role in furthering individual political agendas became apparent again during the radical Wilkite agitation of the 1760s. John Wilkes, an Aylesbury squire who was elected to Parliament for the first time in 1757, took over the ownership of a middle-class London paper, the *North Briton*, in 1762. The paper became an outlet for Wilkes's radical political views; in it he not only denounced the Peace of Paris, but also accused the king of being a liar. Arrested for seditious libel, he mounted a successful defense based on the argument that his detention represented an assault on English liberty itself. He was released but shortly thereafter fled to France (and as a result was expelled from Parliament). After being convicted of libel and sentenced to four years of exile, he returned to England in 1768, stood for election, and was returned by the shopkeepers of Middlesex. The government immediately put him in prison, where street mobs rioted on his behalf and in opposition to oligarchic government. Two times, Wilkes was again elected and expelled by the house.

Wilkes joined the Freemasons during the height of his troubles, in 1769, while serving his sentence for libel and blasphemy. On 3 March 1769, the *Gentleman's Magazine* reported that "the officers and members of the Freemasons' Lodge, held at the Jerusalem Tavern in Clerkenwell, by virtue of a deputation, signed by the Deputy Grand Master, attended at the King's Bench Prison, and made Mr. Wilkes a Mason. It was said in the papers that the dispensation was obtained from the Grand Master, but this was contradicted." Newman points out that Wilkes's initiation was a serious breach of Masonic regulations, which required an initiate to be a "free man." He argues that Wilkes's participation in Freemasonry was another instance of his joining as many societies and associations as possible in order to gain more publicity.[27] While Wilkes was certainly a joiner, the connection between Masonry and the radical agitation of the early 1770s was not based on Wilkes's political opportunism alone. John Brewer contends that "the political implications of Wilkes's admission were obvious." English and Welsh Masons were among those who supported the Wilkite cause. Some Masonic lodges had taken part in the agitation drummed up by the Society of Supporters of the Bill of Rights, founded to champion Wilkes's agenda. Even Newman admits, "It is clear that those Masons associated with Wilkes were undoubtedly acting politically, and that many of the individual lodges involved in these waves of agitation had political overtones." In Wales, Jenkins argues, Freemasonry was instrumental in carrying on the tradition of Country opposition during and after the 1760s. He demonstrates this by tracing the continuities between the political organization and social contacts of Jacobitism, Wilkite radicalism, and Freemasonry. Several close friends of Wilkes, such as John Pugh Pryse (of Gogerddan) and Robert Jones (of Fonmon in Glamorgan), were descendants of ardent Jacobite families and Freemasons.[28]

Further testifying to the elasticity of Freemasonry during the eighteenth century, the Wilkite agitation coincided with the strengthening of the relationship between the brotherhood and the royal family. Though Frederick was not an active Freemason, he set an example for his sons, three of whom joined the Craft in the 1760s. Edward, Duke of York, became interested in Freemasonry while on the Continent and was initiated in 1765 in Berlin. His brothers, William Henry (Duke of Gloucester) and Henry Frederick (Duke of Cumberland), joined in 1766 and 1767, respectively. In a letter to the master of a lodge in Calcutta in 1768, one grand lodge official noted: "Masonry flourishes with amazing success in the present era, Their Royal Highnesses the Dukes of Gloucester and Cumberland have joined the fraternity and the first noblemen in Britain vouchsafe to protect us. . . . In short, every thing tends to cultivate and promote our Royal Art here, and we earnestly hope that the zeal and ardour of our worthy brethren abroad will not fail in this respect, but emulate them to vie with each other in establishing the virtues of our ancient and honourable society." The Modern Grand Lodge, under the leadership of the Duke of Beaufort between 1767 and 1771, actively encouraged the participation of all three royal princes by conferring the high Masonic rank of "Past Grand Master" on each.[29]

The evidence presented here enables us to rethink the role of Freemasonry in Hanoverian political culture. John Money argues that under Beaufort's administration during the late 1760s the brotherhood emerged as an agent of conservatism, loyalism, and nationalism. He identifies a formal association between Freemasonry and the established church in this period and also points out that local lodges made contributions in support of crown forces. Other efforts — the grand lodges' eagerness to avoid any implication in popular radicalism and the increased associations with the royal family — contributed to "consolidating the craft's place in the panoply of Royalty and Nationality." As we have seen, the evidence of Freemasonry's serving as a buttress of the establishment during the mid-eighteenth century is certainly extensive. But Money dates the consolidation of Freemasonry as a loyalist institution too early (as we will see, it narrowly escaped being identified as an "unlawful society" in 1799). Likewise, Jacob's argument that in Britain the Masonic lodge "offered no opposition to established institutions" oversimplifies a rather more complex situation.[30] The English political world of the period between the 1720s and the 1770s provides much evidence for the argument that Freemasonry was compatible with a range of political positions. Widening the lens to include the British Atlantic world of the last third of the eighteenth century further solidifies this interpretation. For while the members of one lodge in Kelso, Scotland, were so loyal that they marched at the head of a regimental recruiting party and offered a bounty of three guineas to every man who enlisted to serve in the American war, thousands of their Masonic brethren across the ocean had decided to throw in their lot with the patriots.[31]

Colonial British America: Patriots and Loyalists

At the Battle of Bunker Hill, Joseph Warren, American volunteer and Provincial Grand Master for America, sacrificed his life for the rebel cause. Across the battle lines, Lord Rawdon (future English Grand Master and governor general of India) distinguished himself to such an extent that General Burgoyne reported in a dispatch that "Lord Rawdon has this day stamped his fame for life."[32] As the war unfolded, patriot Masons paid tribute to heroic brethren by raising their glasses to "Warren, Montgomery and Wooster." Meanwhile, loyalist Masons expressed their attachment to their brother who was next in line for the British throne. Masonry, it seems, was more invested in than "resolv'd against" the bloody political struggle unfolding in North America during the late 1770s.

Historians of the American War of Independence have paid more attention to Freemasonry than historians of other events and processes examined here. Granted, the historiography is uneven, ranging from hagiographic accounts detailing, for example, the *Masonic Membership of the Founding Fathers* to the precisely argued work of Steven C. Bullock. Yet all, from the celebratory to the scholarly, focus on the patriots, and neglect the extent to which Masonry was evident on both sides of the conflict. It is clear, however, that Freemasonry during the 1770s was not yet sufficiently identified with a particular political position to preclude men of both sides from seeking membership in the same brotherhood. Patriots and loyalists alike deemed Freemasonry an organization worthy of their energies and attention — even during the chaos and upheaval of war — because it helped them negotiate social position, adjust to dislocation, and even further their political causes. Thus, we see Freemasons in *both* the patriot and loyalist camps: Freemasons participated in the Boston Tea Party, presided over the Continental Congresses, signed the Declaration of Independence, and commanded the Continental Army. At the same time members of the fraternity enforced the Townshend duties, served in His Majesty's regiments, commanded the king's armies, and fled to the West Indies and British North America when the patriots triumphed.

In determining whether he identified himself as a patriot or a loyalist during the American War, a Freemason faced a difficult decision, a choice made more complicated by his membership in the brotherhood. First, the institution charged its members to be loyal to the established authorities and to refrain from engaging in rebellions and conspiracies against the state. "The Charges" thus conveyed the expectation that a Mason's loyalty should be reflexive. Yet, as we have seen, "The Charges" still contained an "escape clause" that proved critical in helping Masons who supported the American cause to resolve this dilemma. As long as he convinced himself that the government had become oppressive enough to warrant revolution, a Freemason in this period could justify opposing the state in open rebellion.[33]

The harder issue was the fact that the lodges in the American colonies had derived their authority from the British grand lodges and their members identified themselves as British, not American, Freemasons. During the middle decades of the eighteenth century, Freemasonry was a sociocultural institution that connected the British Atlantic world, functioning, like the consumer economy and an inherited set of ideological assumptions, to foster the Britishness of American colonists.[34] Even through the conflict, Freemasonry remained a single, transatlantic institution. British American Masons did not seek independent Masonic government until after the conflict had resolved in the colonies' favor. Throwing off the political connection with Britain thus put one's Masonic legitimacy in jeopardy. Yet, since many colonial Freemasons were willing to take this risk, we find both rebels and loyalists drawing on the brotherhood in a range of social and political situations.

Patriot Masons called upon the fraternity in numerous ways, at times even using it to pursue their political agenda. Of course, such activities went against both the letter and spirit of the brotherhood and lodges did not formally endorse the colonists' cause. Nevertheless, certain lodges and prominent brethren were clearly implicated from the beginning in the effort to drive the British out of the thirteen colonies. Over half of the 134 members of St. George's Lodge in Schenectady, New York, for example, fought for the patriots.[35] The connection between Freemasonry and the Revolution was particularly evident in New England. On the night of 16 December 1773, the members of St. Andrew's Lodge (Ancients) in Boston held a regularly scheduled meeting but only five brothers — the officers — showed up. While they transacted their limited business at the Green Dragon Tavern, the nearby waters of Boston Harbor were swallowing the tea cargoes of three large "Indiamen." Bullock suggests that they had scheduled the meeting as an alibi for the members who participated in the Boston Tea Party. The tavern, which was the Masonic hall of the Boston Ancients, was also the meeting place of several proto-revolutionary groups including the North End Caucus. St. Andrew's membership overlapped with these political societies. Its master, Joseph Warren, belonged to the North End Caucus; the lodge's Senior Grand Warden, Paul Revere, joined three other St. Andrew's brothers as members of the more militant Sons of Liberty. The connections between

St. Andrew's meeting place and membership and the patriot cause were not coincidental. St. Andrew's would later assert that the Boston Tea Party had been plotted in their lodge room. Though a few loyalist members of St. Andrews left with the British, the membership of the lodge even grew during the war, adding almost a hundred new members between 1777 and 1780.[36]

Patriots also found Freemasonry useful as they negotiated personal advancement in the stormy political climate of the 1770s and 1780s, as we can see in the case of social climbers like John Paul Jones. Jones used Freemasonry in his rise from humble Scottish origins to a position of prominence in the American Navy. He joined the brotherhood in Scotland in 1770, at which point he had already served as a mate on at least four Atlantic merchant ships. His biographer notes: "John Paul would find Masonic lodges wherever he went on his journeys. He used them both as refuges and stepladders." Jones's Masonic credentials proved helpful as he sought entrance into Fredericksburg, Virginia, society in 1774. Though initially shunned by the local gentry because of his Scottish background and lack of connections, Jones was admitted into the Fredericksburg Lodge and befriended by its master (and fellow Scotsman), Dr. John Read. Jones joined the rebels, along with over thirty other members of the Fredericksburg Lodge, in 1775. Thomas suggests that because of Jones's Masonic connections, the Naval Committee in charge of building a rebel navy commissioned him as a first lieutenant and gave him command of a converted merchant vessel. For the next four years, he hounded British ships on both sides of the Atlantic, capturing prizes and prisoners, steadily building his reputation as a fearless naval raider. Whenever Jones found himself on land for extended periods of time (whether negotiating with American leaders about his commissions or waiting for ships to be built or repaired), he sought out the company of fellow Masons. He did so in Boston in 1777. Three years later, in Paris, he was initiated in the famous Lodge of Nine Sisters, which Franklin had joined in 1778. A well-known naval hero, he was admired by ladies and "feted by the local Masons" wherever he went.[37]

Membership in Freemasonry facilitated social climbing, promotion, and class cohesion of officers in the Continental Army. Freemasonry flourished among the officers: 42 percent of the army's generals joined the brotherhood before or during the war. Bullock argues that membership had such widespread appeal because it offered lower-status officers an entrée to polite society and social endorsement and contributed to the development of an esprit de corps among officers who came from very diverse geographical, social, and religious backgrounds. Bullock also demonstrates that the brotherhood "provided a counterweight to the fragmentation that threatened the officer corps, helping create the sense of common purpose necessary for the survival of the army — and thus the success of the Revolution itself." Freemasonry was so popular that at least ten traveling lodges were warranted during the war. Like their counterparts in the British army, American regimental lodges had ambulatory warrants that allowed their members to meet wherever they happened to be stationed. The most active was American Union Lodge, which had been chartered by the Modern Provincial Grand Lodge in Boston in 1776 and over the course of the war met in Connecticut, New Jersey, New York, and Massachusetts. In 1799, several brothers applied to the Grand Lodge of Massachusetts for a warrant to establish another military lodge, which they named Washington Lodge. By the end of the war the lodge membership rolls boasted 250 brethren. Officers of the Continental Army continued to find Freemasonry useful after the war. Membership helped ease veterans' transition into civilian society and enabled them to maintain group solidarity, as well as friendships and contacts, forged in wartime.[38]

The supreme commander of the American forces, General George Washington, embodied the connection between Freemasonry and the rebel army. He found both practical and ideological uses for the brotherhood. Initiated by a Virginia lodge in 1752, Washington was so serious about Freemasonry that he took time out from coordinating the war to attend meetings and participate in processions. On 27 December 1778, he led a procession of three hundred brethren dressed in full Masonic attire through the streets of Philadelphia to Christ Church, where they attended a Masonic service to commemorate the colonists' capture of Philadelphia from the British. The following June at West Point Washington participated in another Masonic celebration. Over one hundred Masons — each one an officer in the Continental Army — marched in a procession and then, edified by a sermon and addresses, enjoyed a convivial reception. As Bullock demonstrates, Washington "stressed 'Discipline and Subordination' as the key to a successful fighting force." He therefore encouraged Freemasonry as a way to maintain distinctions between officers and men and used its ceremonial aspects to foster the cohesion of the officer class. More broadly, Washington drew on the lessons of Masonic fraternalism in his successful attempt to subordinate the egalitarian impulses of the revolutionary era to the interests of the elite class he represented. In all its various eighteenth-century guises, British Masonry never threatened social hierarchy. It encouraged its diverse members to see one another as brethren, but it did not suggest they should treat one another as equals.[39]

Nineteenth-century portrait of George Washington hanging in Freemasons Hall, London (copyright, and reproduced by permission of, the United Grand Lodge of England).

At the same time the fraternity was evident in patriot circles and flourished in the Continental Army, it had a significant presence among loyalists, a point that eighteenth-century historians have insufficiently addressed. As it did for the patriots, Freemasonry helped loyalists handle war-time dislocation and provided a venue not only for conviviality but also (contrary to Masonic rules) for the expression and forwarding of the loyalist political agenda. Loyalist Masons from North Carolina relied on Masonry's Atlantic network as they fled to other parts of the British Empire when expelled by the patriots. Mason Alexander Telfair and his biological brother organized passage for fellow loyalist families on board their ship *The Brothers*. Initially given sixty days to leave in May 1777, Telfair was able to secure an extension for their departure from Governor Caswell, who was also a Freemason. It is likely that Telfair's decision to name the ship *The Brothers* contained a double meaning since several other loyalist Masons, including Chief Justice Martin Howard (master of New Bern Lodge), were on board. Though harassed by privateers, the loyalists made their way safely to New York and then London.[40]

Masons in London were indeed responsive to the needs of brethren caught up in the commotion across the Atlantic. In 1778 the Premier Grand Lodge sent £100 to "alleviate the distresses of many worthy members of the Fraternity" in Halifax. Members of a Halifax lodge reported back to the Grand Lodge that they applied the money to those "who in consequence of their loyalty to the best of Princes, in this Time of general Confusion, have subjected themselves to various kinds of insults and abuses, and also to a deprivation of the greatest part of their Property." Grateful for the attention from their "Mother Grand Lodge," the members of this lodge expressed their allegiance to the British Government. "We are determined to persevere in cultivating the Principles which we have imbibed, to all around us," they reported, "and heartily wish that those concerned in supporting the present Rebellious Commotion may be speedily sensible of their Error . . . and that intestine Broils may cease in every part of the British Empire." They further demonstrated their loyalty by enclosing donations of £5 for the General Fund of Charity and almost £24 for the building of the Grand Hall in London.[41]

Back in the rebellious colonies, high-ranking Masons also remained loyal to the crown. Four of the five Modern provincial grand masters serving at the time of the conflict were loyalists: William Allen of Pennsylvania, Egerton Leigh of South Carolina, John Rowe of Boston, and Sir John Johnson of New York. Their decisions to side with the British had a definite effect on the lodges in their jurisdictions. Allen, a merchant who built a fortune large enough to rank him as Philadelphia's richest man, served as provincial chief justice and, at the outbreak of the war, joined the British army at Trenton, New Jersey. The patriots confiscated all his property. The Moderns, whom Allen had represented since 1750, had already lost most lodges to the Ancients by the outbreak of the war, and his departure marked the end of Modern Masonry in Pennsylvania.[42] Leigh, the attorney general for South Carolina, had been appointed Grand Master of the Provincial Grand Lodge by the Moderns in 1770, though he had already been serving in the position for a few years. He left Charleston in 1774 because of his loyalist sympathies, and many lodges became dormant. Though the disruptions of the war in the early years made it difficult for Charleston lodges to meet, the provincial grand lodge was revived when the British occupied the city in 1780. Its membership was loyalist in composition.[43]

In Boston, the obviously patriotic sympathies of certain lodges, like St. Andrew's, made the city an inhospitable place for loyalists, and many left during the early years of the conflict. John Rowe, a prominent merchant whom the Moderns had appointed Provincial Grand Master for North America in 1768, was shunned by patriot Masons for remaining neutral; he also socialized with British officers. A crowd of rebels led by Paul Revere harassed another Modern brother, the customs commissioner Benjamin Hallowell. He and his brother (also a Mason) were among the many loyalist Masons who left with the British. These included St. John's Lodge (the provincial grand lodge) and twenty brethren of another lodge. There were also loyalists among Boston's Ancients, as evidenced by the departure of Lodge No. 169, whose warrant eventually found its way, via Canada, to New York. Its members were instrumental in establishing an Ancient Provincial Grand Lodge in New York in 1781.[44]

New York City, occupied by the British and serving as the headquarters of the British army for the course of the war, was a center of Masonic loyalism. Gathering to celebrate their annual Masonic holiday, St. John's Day, in 1776, the Masons of New York drank to "loyal and Masonic" toasts. Masons who were patriots either left the city or kept a low profile. Because of his sympathies with the rebels, the master of St. John's Lodge chose to depart and took the lodge warrant with him. While some lodges shut down during the war, others, including St. John's, continued to meet with the help of the many regimental lodges then stationed in the city.[45]

The Provincial Grand Lodge of New York, under the leadership of Sir John Johnson, was overtly loyal to the British. We have already met Johnson as Provincial Grand Master for Quebec in the late 1780s. Prior to the war, he was very active in New York, being appointed Provincial Grand Master in 1767. Like his father, William Johnson, he was a dedicated Mason, and he established strong relations with Native Americans in the Mohawk Valley, many of whom he brought to the side of the Loyalists. Johnson and his Deputy Grand Master, Dr. Peter Middleton, worked hard to keep the Moderns afloat during the war (their biggest challenge was from the loyalist Ancients in exile from Boston). When the British capitulated in New York the staunchly loyalist Johnson settled in Montreal, where he became Superintendent General of Indian Affairs for Quebec in 1782 and Provincial Grand Master in 1788. He was joined in British North America by other loyalist Masons from New York such as the master of Union Lodge in Albany, several officers of St. Patrick's Lodge in Johnston, and the Mohawk chief Joseph Brant.[46]

British North America was not the only refuge for loyalist Masons; others went to the Caribbean, where they found Freemasonry firmly in line with the establishment. In Bermuda, the lodge attached to the 47th Regiment took part in all the festivals, church services, and other Masonic activities on the island during the war. Even though normal shipping lanes were disrupted, Barbadian lodges flourished — with merchants, professionals, and crown officials swelling their ranks — until a hurricane hit in 1781. The Caribbean theater of the war was hazardous in other ways, especially once Spain entered on the side of the Americans and the French in 1779. Walter Davidson, member of Amity Lodge, reported that "by the capture of St. Georges Quays in the Bay of Honduras many of the Brethren who composed the Amity in that place No. 309 were made Prisoners and carried away by the Spaniards with whom they still Remain. The few who have escaped have formed a lodge at Masons' Hall, Kingston."[47]

In sum, when we look at Freemasonry in the British Atlantic world of the 1770s and 1780s, we see what had been evident in Britain and Europe since the 1720s — that the brotherhood was elastic enough to include men of opposing political loyalties. Despite American Masons' fondness for claiming that their fraternity occupied a crucial and privileged place in the conflict that gave birth to the United States, it seems clear that for every patriot Mason there was a brother who maintained allegiance to the king. The brotherhood helped patriot and loyalist alike negotiate social advancement, pursue political objectives, and adjust to new circumstances in an extremely turbulent context. As the momentum of revolutionary activity swung back across the Atlantic in the 1780s and 1790s, we see, once again, Freemasonry's being put in the service of both radical and conservative agendas.

Ireland: Freemasonry and "the Ninety Eight"

Traditional scholarship on the revolutions of the late eighteenth century has typically concentrated on revolutionary moments in particular places such as North America and France. Some scholars have adopted a more consciously "Atlantic" approach, but much of this work remains focused primarily on developments in the thirteen British American colonies. Only in recent years have historians given the Haitian Revolution the kind of historical attention it warrants and included the Latin American independence struggles of the early nineteenth century in broader assessments of the period. But Ireland's place in this milieu has received extremely limited notice (except of course from Irish historians). This is due, in large part, to the fact that unlike in the cases of colonial British America, France, and Latin America, the efforts of revolutionaries to overturn the status quo failed miserably. However, including the United Irish Rebellion of 1798 in our examinations of the "age of Atlantic revolutions" is highly instructive, because it demonstrates not only the power of the forces of British conservatism during this revolutionary era but also a profound shift taking place in Freemasonry. To an even greater extent than in other parts of the eighteenth-century British Atlantic world, Freemasonry, particularly at the local level, was implicated in Irish radicalism. While United Irishmen adapted the Masonic network to revolutionary ends, other Masons, especially those in positions of leadership, used Masonic channels to express their loyalty to Britain. Thus, the United Irish Rebellion of 1798 is best characterized as a "hinge event" that reveals, on the one hand, aspects of Freemasonry's eighteenth-century past (relative inclusiveness and involvement in revolutionary movements) and, on the other hand, the loyalist and Protestant character it would purposefully assume in the early part of the nineteenth century.

The United Irish Rebellion took place in the early months of 1798, sixteen years after the Volunteer (citizen militia) movement had managed to secure a degree of legislative independence for Ireland's Anglican ruling class, the Ascendancy, under the leadership of Henry Grattan. The limited independence of "Grattan's Parliament," characterized by narrow Whig oligarchy, oversight by the English government, and continued restrictions on the rights of Catholics and Dissenters, did not satisfy large sections of Irish society, notably Ulster Presbyterians and middle-class Catholics. Both groups, as well as reform-minded Anglicans, found a forum for their grievances in the Society of United Irishmen. Emerging in Belfast and then in Dublin on the heels of the French Revolution in 1791, the Society championed the unrealized objectives of the Volunteers: the reform of Parliament and the enfranchisement of Catholics. As its name implied, the Society aimed to be nonsectarian and sought to provide a space that could accommodate the many varieties of Irishness vying for political legitimacy in the 1790s.

Inflammatory rhetoric that appeared mainly in the Society's newspaper, the *Northern Star*, and negotiations with France by United Irish leaders led the British government to suppress the hitherto constitutional organization in 1794. The Society went underground the following year, and members committed themselves to the creation of an Irish republic separate from Britain. Now a secret, oath-bound organization, the Society increased its contacts with potential allies in the struggle against England: the French government, Societies of United Englishmen and Scots, and the Defenders.[48] These alliances led to the creation of a revolutionary coalition that transformed the United Irishmen into a primarily Catholic popular organization with Protestant leadership and pledges of assistance from France. The government, having infiltrated the society with informers, tried to suppress treasonable activities in Ulster and arrested United Irish leaders there in 1796. Despite government repression, meted out rigorously by General Gerard Lake, revolt broke out in May 1798 in Leinster and Ulster. The French arrived too late — by the time United Irish leader Theobold Wolfe Tone landed in County Mayo with a French invasion force of over 1,000 men, the rebellion had lost most of its steam. As the government squelched the rebellion over the course of four months, more than 30,000 people, mostly Irish peasants and republicans, were killed.

Freemasonry was a part of Ireland's long tradition of political societies that both preceded and followed the United Irishmen. It influenced the Volunteer movement of the 1780s. Existing lodges helped constitute Volunteer corps; in 1782 members of Lodge No. 547 in County Tyrone formed themselves into the First Free Masons Corps of the kingdom of Ireland. Moreover, lodges grew out of Volunteer corps, such as the First Volunteer Lodge, No. 620, which was warranted in Dublin in 1783. The most prominent Volunteer leaders, including Lord Charlemont and Henry Grattan, were Freemasons, and the chair of the 1782 Dungannon Convention, William Irvine, was Provincial Grand Master of Ulster. As a result of Freemasonry's associations with the popular Volunteer movement and the brotherhood's general appeal, Masonic lodges and influence began to spread. Ireland witnessed a dramatic proliferation of Masonic lodges in the 1780s and 1790s, as men from both the Protestant and Catholic communities sought admission into the Craft. Other clubs and societies patterned their terminology, practices, and organizational structures after the Freemasons. On opposite sides of Ireland's politico-religious spectrum, both the Defenders and the Orangemen adapted Freemasonry's preexisting organization, its symbols, its ideology, and at times its networks to their own needs.[49]

The relationship between Irish Freemasonry and the Society of United Irishmen was complex and multifaceted. Like their brethren in Britain and the American colonies, Irish Freemasons did not display a single, uniform response to radicalism. Rather, their involvement in and reaction to the United Irish movement varied from place to place, according to the level within the organization (viz., individual member, lodge, or grand lodge), and depending on the phase of the rebellion under consideration.[50] Both this high degree of variation and the changes the brotherhood underwent as a result of its connections to the rebellion indicate that this was indeed a pivotal event, one that simultaneously recalled the past and heralded the future.

First, several aspects of the relationship between Freemasonry and the United Irish movement echoed precedents set earlier in the century. Take, for example, the United Irishmen's reliance on the ideals of Masonic cosmopolitanism: toleration and brotherhood. United Irish ideology and political strategy hinged on the notion that only the cooperation of the Protestant and Catholic communities would effect change in Ireland. The United Irishmen disparaged Ireland's sectarian past and blamed the government for exacerbating communal tensions. As one early United Irish pamphlet put it: "The intestine divisions among Irishmen have too often given encouragement and impunity to audacious and corrupt administrations." The United Irish goal of bringing together members of both communities to achieve political reform demanded toleration and sympathy on the part of all. In an address to radicals in Scotland, United Irish leaders described their vision of a society in which Catholics and Protestants were committed to "holding out their hands and opening their hearts to each other; agreeing in principles, concurring in practice."[51]

Freemasonry offered both an ideological and a practical precedent for the United Irish program. As Kevin Whelan points out, it was one of the United Irishmen's "most effective recruiting, organisational and ideological vectors." There are striking parallels between the discourses of Masonry and the Society of United Irishmen, both of which emphasized the ideals of toleration, equality, and brotherhood and used words like "benevolence," "convivial," and "universal." These discursive relationships indicate that they were both part of the Enlightenment milieu that prized, if it did not always demonstrate, openmindedness and the acceptance of difference. Moreover, Freemasonry served as a model for actually bringing Catholics and Protestants together in a nonsectarian setting. The brotherhood was, according to A. T. Q. Stewart, one of the few arenas in which Catholics and Protestants could embrace each other as equals.[52] In these ways the fraternity laid the groundwork for the Society of United Irishmen, which aimed to be a meeting ground for men of various communities.

The writings of William Drennan most clearly display the connection between Freemasonry and United Irish ideology. Though he eventually distanced himself from the United Irishmen, Drennan played a key role in the early development of the Society. The son of a Presbyterian minister, Drennan was trained as a physician in Edinburgh but turned his attention to politics early in life. In 1784 he wrote a series of letters that were published in the *Belfast Newsletter* and subsequently as a widely distributed pamphlet. His intervention came at a point when the Volunteers had failed to realize their lofty goals and become a spent force. Frustrated by the lethargy that had infected radical politics, Drennan attacked the Parliament, urged reform, and called for the Volunteers to renew their agitation. Significantly, he also beseeched Ireland's alienated communities to unite under the banner of Irish patriotism. While his published letters reveal Drennan's political philosophy, his private letters from this period indicate his increasing interest in using Freemasonry as a model for a new society that would push for the achievement of these radical objectives. The role of Freemasonry in promoting the objectives of certain American patriots and French revolutionaries must not have been far from his mind. For Ireland, he wanted to mimic certain aspects of Freemasonry, particularly its secrecy, in creating an exclusive group of dedicated radical Volunteers. "I should like to see," he wrote, "the institution of a society as secret as the Free-masons, whose object might be by every practicable means to put into execution plans for the complete liberation of the country." He felt that a certain level of secrecy would excite people's curiosity, just as it had done for the Freemasons. In 1791 Drennan anonymously published the most sophisticated formulation of his plan for the creation of a new political society. He proposed the new society be called the "Irish Brotherhood" and highlighted Freemasonry in his opening sentence: "It is proposed, that at this conjecture a Society shall be instituted in this city, having much of the secrecy, and somewhat of the ceremonial attached to Free-masonry." While secrecy would make people curious, he argued, ceremony would "strike the soul through the senses" and help secure members' emotional investment in the cause.[53]

Though the founders of the Society of United Irishmen did not use Drennan's "Irish Brotherhood" as the precise organizational model for the society they established in Belfast in October 1791, they did draw upon the discourse of fraternity evident in Drennan's writings. The United Irish constitution proclaimed that the society had been formed "for the purpose of forwarding a brotherhood of affection, a communion of rights, and an union of power among Irishmen of all religious persuasions, and thereby to obtain a complete reform in the legislature, founded on the principles of civil, political, and religious liberty." Similarly, each new member declared in the United Irish oath that he would help form and uphold this "brotherhood of affection" among all Irishmen regardless of their religion.[54] In conceiving of their organization as a brotherhood and in emphasizing religious toleration, the United Irishmen directly associated themselves with Freemasonry.

By the time the United Irish movement entered its revolutionary phase in 1795, Freemasonry had become more than an ideological influence. Early indications of Freemasons' direct involvement with the Society began to emerge in 1792, when Masonic lodges first ignored the cardinal rule of Masonry to avoid politics and issued statements in support of the United Irishmen. The first lodge to enter the debate publicly was Lodge No. 650 in Bellaghy, which published its proceedings in the *Belfast Newsletter* on 11 December 1792. Its fifty-two members resolved to affirm their "invariable attachment" to the king but at the same time expressed support for reform, as long as it was achieved through constitutional means. Other lodges in central and eastern Ulster followed suit in early 1793. In mid-January delegates representing 1,432 Freemasons gathered at Dungannon, County Tyrone. After conducting regular lodge proceedings, during which no political matters were discussed, the lodge adjourned. The delegates immediately reconstituted themselves as an "Assembly of Masonic Citizens." As such, they passed resolutions calling for the reform of Parliament and advocating Catholic emancipation. Their published statement indicated their reluctance to "speak on political subjects" and offered the assurance that "the virtuous Brother however he may differ from us in religious or political opinions, shall ever be received with the cordial embrace of fraternal fellowship." Yet the circumstances of the time demanded that Masons take action: "We are from our souls sincerely loyal, but ours is not the loyalty of slaves, it is that of Masons — Masons who know their Rights, and are determined to die or be free." Consciously drawing on their brotherhood's associations with radical movements in other parts of the Atlantic world, they expressed their approval of events in France and described their "illustrious brother Washington and the Masons of America" as the "Saviours of their Country, and the first founders of the Temple of Liberty." Finally, they thanked the Volunteers for their efforts and closed the assembly by urging: "Let every Lodge in the Land become a company of Citizen Soldiers. Let every Volunteer Company become a Lodge of Masons."[55]

When the movement went underground in 1795, the United Irishmen realized that they could co-opt Freemasonry's existing structure as a powerful organizational tool in fomenting revolutionary activity. In the spring United Irish leaders, based in Belfast and Dublin, sent "emissaries" throughout Ireland to spread the United Irish message and recruit new members. Many of these emissaries joined the brotherhood. As Masons, they were entitled to make use of the lodge network that crisscrossed the Irish countryside and receive assistance and hospitality from their brethren.[56] Contemporary British intelligence reports also reveal that the United Irishmen used lodge meetings, which had earned a reputation as harmless gatherings, as covers for their seditious activities. The government learned in late 1797 that United Irish delegates in

Derry were meeting "under the mask of masonry" on St. John's Day, the most important event in the Masonic calendar. It received reports of similar meetings in County Meath in March 1798; the chief constable there told Thomas Pelham, Ireland's Chief Secretary, "I am informed there is a new society swearing under the name of Freemeasons [*sic*] but the[y] are not Fremeasons [*sic*] only give that name." A contemporary Masonic periodical published in England told readers not to be surprised that "amidst the violence of politics, or rather that mental fever which has spread with such rapidity of late throughout Europe, and especially in the sister kingdom, some of the Masonic fraternity should be led away by popular, and to weak minds, pleasing theories."[57]

In addition to using lodges as covers for United Irish meetings, the Society utilized the Masonic network to circulate information and gather recruits. Protected by members' oaths to keep lodge proceedings secret, Masonic channels were ideal for spreading information about the planned rebellion. For instance, one Richard Gally of Ballinderry received word from Masonic brethren about the location of gunpowder stolen from Belfast in 1797. In terms of recruiting, United Irishmen used the Masonic network to gain new members through questionable means. In April 1797 a man from Dublin reported to the government that a Mason had "carried him into an ale house." Once inside, the man claimed, he was confronted by several other Masons and forced to take the oath of the United Irishmen and "aid the French."[58]

Such activities, as well as alleged connections between Freemasonry and other secret societies like the "Dublin Library" and the Illuminati, raised the suspicions of the government. Pelham, though not a Mason himself, understood the threat posed by members of the fraternity who had joined the United Irishmen. The intelligence he received prompted him in late 1797 to write to the Irish grand master, Lord Donoughmore, and ask him to "check the designs of those who wish to make Freemasonry a political engine." Freemasons with connections to the United Irishmen in Ulster and Dublin did not heed any warnings that the Grand Lodge might have issued. Their continued abetting of the United Irishmen soon brought General Knox, the man in charge of subduing Ulster, to the conclusion that all Masonic lodges should be shut down. Though the government never took this step, it did use its broad powers to arrest suspected Masons. In May 1798 the authorities arrested an entire lodge (of twenty-three men) in Newry for assembling after the curfew. The authorities rejected the explanation that they were merely attending a lodge meeting.[59]

As was the case during the Jacobite, Wilkite, and American patriot movements, many Irish Masons fervently proclaimed their loyalty to the government while other brethren sought its demise. In 1792, prior to the Masonic convention at Dungannon, twenty-five Armagh lodges gathered in support of the government and published resolutions indicating their loyalty and contentment with the status quo. Freemasons in other parts of Ireland — Dublin and County Derry — followed the example. Three years later one government informer reported that "Freemason Lodges in Different counties have recently come forward, and publicly avowed their sentiments of Loyalty, and their marked disapprobation of United Irishmen." Several lodges in Irish regiments printed and distributed handbills condemning the United Irishmen and expressing loyalty to the government in 1797.[60] Notably, like the Masons who had become involved with the United Irishmen, those lodges that sided with the government and made public declarations to that effect were also violating the strictures against political involvement. The willingness of Irish Freemasons to ignore or reinterpret this central rule in order to make expressions of loyalty anticipated future policy of the British grand lodges.

Throughout the crisis the Grand Lodge of Ireland sided completely with the forces of order. From the early 1790s the Irish Grand Lodge remained stalwart in its loyalty to the government and consistent in its attempts to discourage members who were attracted to the United Irish cause. In January 1793 it issued a circular to all subordinate lodges, reminding them that any political or religious discussions and publications were "utterly inconsistent with the Fundamental Principles" of Freemasonry. Political activities, they warned, fostered animosity and ill will among brethren. In a succinct statement of Masonic ideology, they emphasized toleration and loyalty: "True Masonry prefers no Sect, and acknowledges no Party. A Mason's religion is the faithful worship of God, his politics a strict obedience to the Laws of the Country in which he resides, and, a most cordial and unremitting attachment to his Sovereign."[61] To demonstrate Irish Freemasons' loyalty when war broke out with France in 1794, Donoughmore called for the formation of a Masonic Volunteer regiment.

As circumstances began heating up in 1797, Armagh Freemasons who remained loyal to the government felt compelled to reassert their law-abiding intentions. In June of that year, thirty-four Masonic lodges assembled in the city of Armagh to pass resolutions and draft a declaration of loyalty. After announcing their firm attachment to George III and their respect for the Constitution, the Armagh Masons disclaimed "all connection with any traitorous society or rebellious association." They explained that their Masonic oaths bound them to be good, peaceful subjects and that the institution discountenanced the discussion of political matters, though they regretfully acknowledged some of their members had strayed into the United Irishmen. Assuring the government that their institution promoted "Peace and Harmony, Love and Loyalty," they hoped to "wipe away from Masonry a stigma which should never rest upon it."[62]

By this point Donoughmore was in regular communication with the government, which expressed concern about Freemasonry's increasing implication in United Irish movements. In response to Pelham's request to curb recalcitrant lodges, the Grand Master assured him that the Grand Lodge had ceased warranting new lodges in the North because of the political situation there. The rapid spread of Freemasonry that had characterized the early 1790s came to a grinding halt. Donoughmore's and Pelham's cooperation on a plan to monitor the activities of northern lodges provides further evidence of the Grand Lodge's loyalty during the crisis.[63] The outbreak of rebellion in May 1798 forced the Grand Lodge to suspend its meetings immediately. When meetings of the Grand Lodge resumed in November, it summoned individuals it suspected of participating in the rebellion and ordered lodges in Dublin to investigate the conduct of their members during the upheaval. Suspected lodges and members had to answer to the Grand Lodge for their participation in the rebellion. But what should the Grand Lodge do with men whose right to rebel was protected by the constitutions themselves? As the next chapter shows, members of the Irish Grand Lodge, torn between Freemasonry's commitment to inclusiveness and the loyalist response demanded by wider affairs, were divided in their opinions on this point.

The Threat of Radical Freemasonry

In the British Atlantic world of the eighteenth century, Freemasonry proved to be a highly elastic and adaptable institution. As we have seen, its members included men who held a striking diversity of political opinions, both in support of and opposition to the Whig oligarchy that dominated Britain. To be sure, the Grand Lodges of England, Ireland, and Scotland made every effort to remain loyal to the establishment, but during this early phase of Freemasonry's history they had limited control over local lodges and individual brethren. The lack of centralized oversight enabled some brethren, especially in times of political upheaval, to ignore their brotherhood's strictures against the discussion of politics and co-opt Masonic lodges for various oppositional political agendas. Especially in Ireland, radicals realized Freemasonry presented a ready-made network of lodges that could be put to seditious political uses (had Jacobitism posed a more serious threat earlier in the century, Masonic lodges would have likely played a comparable role in facilitating a Jacobite coup). In sum, as a result of the activities of Masons *as* Jacobites, Wilkites, American patriots, and Irish radicals, British Masonry developed a tradition of being associated with the politics of opposition and radical causes. It was not as strong as Freemasonry's reputation for radicalism in France, but it was significant nonetheless.

Radical Freemasonry was perceived as a threat not only in 1790s Ireland, but even in the nascent United States and the new British colony of New South Wales. The brotherhood's associations with troublemaking were exported along with exiled United Irishmen. John Caldwell was one United Irishman who made his way to the United States and took his politics and Masonry with him. A wealthy merchant and shipping agent in Belfast (where he joined both the Freemasons and the Society of United Irishmen), Caldwell was close to United Irish leader Wolfe Tone and became a key member of the Ulster Directory. He was arrested by the government in 1798, but unlike his brother who was executed, he was allowed to sail to America. As he settled down in New York, one of his first moves was to join a Masonic lodge. The arrival of men like Caldwell prompted Uriah Tracy, Federalist congressman of Pennsylvania, to observe after a tour of his state in 1800: "In my very lengthy journey through this state, I have seen many, very many Irishmen, and with a very few exceptions, they are United Irish, Free Masons, and the most God-provoking Democrats on this side of Hell." Shortly thereafter, on the other side of the world, United Irishmen were provoking suspicions about Masonry in New South Wales. Governor Philip King officially banned Freemasonry in 1803 in the wake of the arrival of 780 Irish political prisoners, some of whom would conspire in rebellion at Castle Hill, New South Wales, the following year.[64] King's reaction to Freemasonry indicates the growing concerns of colonial officials that the migration of "Orange" and "Green" would create new Irelands overseas.

British Freemasonry's associations with radicalism had become so significant that its leaders in England, Ireland, and Scotland had no choice but to try to take control of the brotherhood during the turbulent decades of the 1790s and 1800s. Nineteenth-century British Freemasonry could not absorb the diversity of political opinions evident in the brotherhood during the eighteenth century. Metropolitan authorities made a conscious move to ensure that British Freemasonry at all levels was in the hands of loyalists. Their concerns resonated with members throughout the empire. In mid-1799 Major General Collins and other officers of the Provincial Grand Lodge of Madras wrote to the English Grand Lodge. They reported that they had received word of events in France and expressed their "extreme regret" that on the Continent their order was being used "as a Veil to conceal and propagate principles at which every true mason must revolt." They continued: "We hope these infamous associations against religion Government and Social Order have long before this been dissolved and fully exposed; and that the faithful member of the Fraternity (and such is to be found in every well regulated British Lodge) whose professions and action uniformly tend to the peace and happiness of his fellow Creatures, will be restored to his proper rank in the esteem of his *Fellow Subjects*."[65] The next chapter looks at what the grand lodges had to do to ensure that the Freemason was "restored to his proper rank in the esteem of his Fellow Subjects," in short, to prove the brotherhood posed no threat but rather could be counted on to buttress the state. In the process, they would have to deny the radical heritage bequeathed by some of their eighteenth-century brethren.

FOUR

Our First Duty as Britons

As Britain prepared to enter the war against revolutionary France in early 1793, the Modern Grand Lodge of England addressed His Majesty King George III. The rules of their order forbade Freemasons from engaging in politics, they pointed out, but the Grand Lodge had decided to sweep this stricture aside: "Our first duty as Britons superseding all other considerations," they declared, "we add, without farther pause, our voice to that of our fellow-subjects, in declaring one common and fervent attachment to a government by king, lords, and commons, as established by the Glorious Revolution of 1688."[1] Thereafter, British Freemasons readily set aside the rule against political discussions to repeat the refrain that they were the most loyal and patriotic of all His Majesty's subjects. Circumstances demanded it.

Convincing the government of the fraternity's salubrious intent was nothing less than a matter of institutional survival. By the 1790s, Freemasonry could no longer afford to operate as a politically ambivalent institution. The tense atmosphere generated by the wars with France, popular radicalism within Britain, and the increasingly sectarian nature of Irish society in this period made the government view societies like Freemasonry with intense suspicion. Between the 1790s and the 1820s Parliament passed legislation curbing its citizens' political freedoms and outlawing associations it deemed subversive. On more than one occasion Freemasonry narrowly escaped the government's attempts to identify it as a seditious society. In such a turbulent context, Freemasons chose the politically prudent course, to bring their institution firmly in line with the Hanoverian establishment.

British Freemasons' adoption of the discourse of loyalty and attachment to the principles of 1688 — including, most importantly, Protestant succession — reflected a dramatic change in the institution's identity, policies, and priorities. For much of the eighteenth century, as we have seen, men of various religious and ethnic backgrounds had composed the fraternity. And, prior to the 1790s, it would have been impossible to associate Freemasonry with a single political position or identity. Fluid and open, Freemasonry included men who were "attached to opposite systems of government," including Jacobites, Tories, Whigs, patriots, loyalists, United Irishmen, and unionists.[2] But during the wars and rebellions of the nineteenth century, Freemasons would invariably position themselves on the side of the British state. By this point the fraternity was so clearly identified with a particular political position — ardent loyalism — that a radical would have felt very uncomfortable, and out of place, in a Masonic lodge.

While mid-nineteenth-century observers could take Freemasonry's loyalty for granted, Freemasons of the previous generation had to prove the brotherhood's allegiance to the state. To do so, the fraternity consciously exchanged the cosmopolitan ideology and identity that had characterized the institution during the eighteenth century for a reputation as an institution that unfailingly upheld, and even promoted, the monarchy, state, and empire. This process involved several steps and took place over three decades. It included concerted efforts on the part of Freemasons to nurture the fraternity's association with the royal family, to avoid government repression, and to cultivate a reputation — and invent a tradition — of unfailing Masonic loyalism. As will be seen, they sidestepped the ban on politics by convincing themselves that their actions — as loyalists — were not, by definition, political. Meanwhile, the Grand Lodges of England, Ireland, and Scotland consolidated their own authority as the only legitimate governors of Masonry. The final aspect of this process, Freemasonry's increasing identification with Protestantism, resulted not so much from the conscious efforts of the grand lodges but rather from the actions of the Vatican and local Masons by whose efforts Freemasonry's ecumenical vision began to recede, particularly in Ireland. While Irish historian Kevin Whelan has argued "radical Freemasonry shuddered to a sectarian-induced halt" in the late 1790s, the developments examined here suggest that the "deradicalizing" of Freemasonry played out not in a single moment (the squelching of the Rebellion) but over the course of several decades, between the 1790s and the 1820s.[3]

Royalty and Loyalty

As the Revolution unfolded in France during the early 1790s, most Britons, especially those who ran the government, watched on in horror. Any broad-based support the Revolution might have enjoyed in its early years quickly dissipated when it entered its more radical phases. By 1793, Britain was once again engaged in a war against its long-time continental nemesis. In Britain, the war produced a climate of menacing repression (the government harassed those who expressed sympathy for revolutionary ideals and advocated even a modicum of reform) but also patriotic zeal. Caught up in this heated atmosphere, Freemasonry became a focus of the government's suspicion. In response, Freemasons made a concerted effort to prove their loyalist intentions. The brotherhood's multifaceted strategy included cultivating its relationship with the royal family, securing exemption from repressive legislation, reinterpreting its central rules to allow it to engage in political activity, and inventing for itself a loyalist tradition suitable to the exigencies of the times.

Freemasons had long identified their brotherhood as "The Royal Art," yet it was not until the end of the eighteenth century that they solidified their relationship with the royal family. Their successful attempts to do so were part of the broader program to associate British Freemasonry firmly with the establishment and thereby raise it above suspicion. Prior to the 1780s, four royal princes had joined the brotherhood and participated with varying degrees of enthusiasm. In the 1780s the Modern Grand Lodge intensified its courting of the royals. In 1782 it elected the Duke of Cumberland (initiated 1767) as its grand master. He was the first in a long line of royal princes to hold the highest office in English Freemasonry (see the appendix). Though Cumberland was not involved in the day-to-day running of the fraternity, his titular leadership had an incalculable effect on Freemasonry's reputation as a loyal, respectable institution especially when he publicly supported the development of the Royal Masonic Institution for Girls (founded in 1788).

Most importantly, Cumberland actively encouraged his nephews to become members of the fraternity and in so doing helped to extend the relationship between Freemasonry and royalty long into the future. Between 1786 and 1789, the first four sons of George III, including the future kings George IV and William IV, were initiated into the mysteries of Freemasonry; sons five and six joined in the 1790s (the seventh, the Duke of Cambridge, never underwent initiation). When the Duke of Cumberland died in 1790, the Prince of Wales took over as Grand Master of the Moderns. Grand Lodge officials were pleased "to obtain such a distinguished honour." As Grand Master, he founded his own lodge, served as an intermediary between the king and the Grand Lodge, and participated in Masonic ceremonies, such as the laying of the cornerstone of the Covent Garden Theatre. He indicated his commitment to Freemasonry in a response to expressions of condolence upon the death of his daughter, Princess Charlotte. Telling the Grand Lodge that membership in the brotherhood had offered him both solace and pleasure, he assured: "This mutual intercourse must ever more firmly cement the ties of affection between me and the Craft, which it will be my unceasing duty and inclination, under the protection of the Great Architect of the Universe, ever most studiously to cultivate and improve."[4] The prince held the position until 1813, when his second youngest brother, the Duke of Sussex, became grand master.

By the time the Prince of Wales took over the leadership of the Moderns in 1790, his brother Prince Edward (George III's fourth son [1767–1820]) was putting the brotherhood's association with the royal family on display far beyond Britain's shores.[5] Prince Edward (who became Duke of Kent in 1799 and, in 1819, the father of the future Queen Victoria) embodied the link between Freemasonry, loyalism, and empire building that was then developing and that would become a hallmark of the Craft in the nineteenth century. Edward was initiated in the late 1780s in Switzerland and was immediately given a high Masonic rank by the English Grand Lodge. In 1790 Edward embarked on an imperial military career. Before his departure with the 7th (Royal) Regiment of Fusiliers to Gibraltar, the Moderns appointed him Provincial Grand Master for Gibraltar and Andalusia, a position he held until 1800. Little evidence remains of Edward's Masonic activities in Gibraltar, but his attitude toward the men in his charge did make a lasting impression. He soon developed a reputation as a tyrannical martinet (his penchant for severe discipline would eventually cost him his military career). Under Prince Edward parade duty was almost as exacting as combat. Officers stumbled into the hairdresser at four in the morning to tame their mops according to his precise instructions. They then had the unpleasant duty of smelling their NCOs' breath (and the NCOs that of the men) to ascertain whether anyone was inebriated. The men found themselves "endlessly polishing and pipe-claying, drilled to exhaustion and mercilessly punished."[6] In less than a year, he was removed to Canada as a result of the stress his command had put on the garrison at Gibraltar. Notably, his personal discipline did not extend to his management of his income and he found himself perpetually in debt.

What was especially interesting, and consequential, about Edward's Masonic career was his concurrent affiliation with both the Moderns and the Ancients. Though formally affiliated with the Moderns, Edward started associating with the Ancients, who were in the ascendancy in Lower Canada when he arrived in 1791. Once Edward made himself known as a brother, local Ancient Masons quickly invited the illustrious colonel to serve as their provincial grand master. They secured the approval of the Ancient Grand Lodge, which sent a warrant appointing Edward provincial grand master with power to grant warrants, make Freemasons, "Rectify Irregularities, and to hear, adjudge, and determine all and singular Matters of Complaint, Controversies, or Disputes." Given his obsession with discipline and order, it is not surprising Edward turned out to be an effective Masonic leader in Lower Canada. Although he remained there for only two years, his tenure as provincial grand master clearly helped to solidify Ancient Freemasonry's presence in the colony. Edward and his deputies closely regulated the brotherhood by visiting lodges, enforcing regulations, and requiring lodges to instruct their members through lectures. They demanded strict lodge accounting, encouraged donations to charities, and instituted the regular celebration of Masonic festivals. On Edward's watch applications for membership increased significantly: he warranted ten new lodges prior to his departure in 1794. Though he treated the men of his regiment severely, he nonetheless looked out for those who belonged to the brotherhood (it was Edward who saw to it that Brother Galloway received a Masonic funeral and helped raise a subscription for his dependents in 1793).[7]

The responses of Freemasons in other parts of British North America to Edward's presence demonstrated his positive impact. An officer of the Provincial Grand Lodge of Nova Scotia reported to the Ancients in 1793 that Freemasonry was flourishing in Canada and it was "highly honored" in having the prince at the helm. Freemasons in Lower Canada who had interests in the new province of Upper Canada were similarly impressed with Edward's effect on the fraternity and requested the extension of Edward's authority to include Upper Canada. They believed his appointment would assist them as they fulfilled their "most earnest desire of diffusing the principles of the Royal Craft in that inhospitable part of the world, which will ever be essential to the civilization and moral improvement of mankind." So beneficial was Edward's patronage that members of the Provincial Grand Lodge of Lower Canada continued to install him as their grand master until 1810, even though he left the colony in 1794.[8]

After a brief West Indian tour of duty in which he distinguished himself for bravery, Edward arrived in Halifax, where he continued to participate actively in Freemasonry while serving the empire as commander-in-chief of Nova Scotia and New Brunswick. The Ancient brethren of Nova Scotia greeted Edward with an unambiguous expression of loyalty: "Permit us . . . to participate in the general joy and respectfully to assure your Royal Highness of our firm adherence to that excellent form of Government which is the peculiar blessing of a British subject, and to express our unshaken loyalty to His Majesty, and zealous attachment to every branch of his Royal family." In response, Edward assured members of the Grand Lodge that he viewed it as his duty "to give every attention to the Royal Craft as far as my abilities go" and promised to offer public prayers "for the protection of the Craft in general, and more particularly for that of the Grand Lodge of Nova Scotia." He not only offered prayers but also appeared with his brethren in important public celebrations. As a holder of high Masonic office in 1800, Edward laid the cornerstone of Halifax's first Masonic hall in a ceremony that was a "gala day for the town." Two lodges in the Royal Fusiliers, the prince's regiment, participated, as well as Sir John Wentworth, the lieutenant governor and master of the Royal Nova Scotia Regiment Lodge. Edward's role in the ceremony was yet another indication of his dedication to the brotherhood and his willingness to encourage it wherever he was assigned. This commitment continued, with great consequences for the future of Masonry, even after his military career had come to an end shortly thereafter.[9]

British Freemasonry's association with the royal family was fostered not only by the princes' willingness to participate in the brotherhood, but also by words of encouragement from the grand lodges and ordinary Masons throughout the empire. Masons enthusiastically lent support to the royals, as their national leaders and their brother Masons, through the medium of official addresses. Whether commemorating a royal birth or celebrating a family member's escape from assassination, the address was a time-honored, regulated custom that people in late Georgian and Victorian Britain took very seriously. The addresses were generally printed in the newspapers; without fail their authors claimed to be the most loyal subjects in the kingdom. Although from the vantage point of the twenty-first century it is tempting to dismiss such addresses as effusive, inconsequential pandering, they were, like parliamentary petitions, an important medium for the expression of political identity.[10] They gave Freemasons, who at this time were actively promoting themselves as a loyalist institution, ample opportunities to participate in the political life of the nation.

Freemasons in Bengal sent one such address home in the winter of 1793. Earlier in the year the Provincial Grand Lodge there had publicly expressed regret about the execution of Louis XVI (and in the process noted that Louis had been an active Freemason and even founded the Lodge Militaire des Trois

Frères Unis). Gathered for their annual Festival of St. John in late December, members of the English lodges in Bengal were even more concerned about the political situation in Europe. They resolved to join in "the cry of loyalty which appals the fanaticism of Democracy in our native country" by sending an address to the Prince of Wales. Appealing to his membership in Freemasonry, they asked him to permit them "to gratify our feelings as subjects, as Members of a Fraternity to which you are personally endeared." The address then confirmed their attachment to the fundamental principles of British citizenship: freedom ("equal *protection* from just and impartial laws and an exemption from the control of *individuals*"), loyalty ("unalterable veneration for the House of Brunswick as our *Sovereign*"), and constitutional monarchy ("as settled by the Revolution of 1688"). In so doing, Calcutta Masons struck an early note in a steadily building chorus sung by Freemasons at the turn of the nineteenth century.[11]

If Masons as far away as India felt events in France warranted an unqualified expression of loyalty to the throne, Masons in Britain were even more anxious to stress their connection to the royal family. The leader of the Moderns at the time was Lord Moira (1754–1826). Francis Rawdon-Hastings (who became Earl of Moira in 1793 and would later, while serving as governor general in India, become Marquess of Hastings) had distinguished himself in the army during the American War of Independence and returned to a political career in the Lords. Though the circumstances of his initiation into Freemasonry are unknown, he was closely connected to the household of the Duke of Cumberland (the Moderns' Grand Master since 1782) and was, in 1790, appointed to the position of Acting Grand Master to oversee grand lodge affairs on Cumberland's behalf. Moira led the political circle around the Prince of Wales, so it is not surprising that he asked Moira to continue in the post when he took over as Grand Master later that year. And so it was under Moira's direction that the Moderns composed the loyal address quoted at the opening of this chapter. It concluded with a mission statement, frequently reiterated by Masons in Britain and the empire: "The Heir Apparent of the Empire is our Chief. We fraternize for the purpose of social intercourse, of mutual assistance, of charity to the distressed, and good-will to all; and fidelity to a trust, reverence to the magistrate, and obedience to the laws are sculptured in capitals upon the pediment of our Institution." The Grand Lodge sent copies of the address to its lodges in India and the colonies. It was read, for example, "in open lodge" when Lodge Perfect Unanimity (Madras) met in July 1794.[12] In making such a proclamation, the officers of Perfect Unanimity, along with British Masons everywhere, set aside the constitutions' injunction against the discussion of politics within lodge walls. Such contradictions between Masonic ideology and the practices of lodges would soon require careful resolution.

By associating their brotherhood with the crown, Freemasons contributed to what Linda Colley has described as the "face-lift" of the British monarchy in the aftermath of the American War. No longer seen as a collection of dull and aloof foreigners, the royal family became a beloved and celebrated national symbol. A combination of factors, including George's own efforts to improve the monarchy's image, the sobering effects of the French Revolution, a more advanced infrastructure of communications (including an enthusiastic press), and the security guaranteed by the proliferation of volunteer and militia regiments, contributed to George's increased popularity and elaborate public celebration of his reign. Freemasons' public addresses reflected their approval of the monarch and in so doing contributed to this shift in the image of the monarchy. In 1800 the Ancients praised George for his "private Virtue" and "uniform Concern for the Welfare of [his] people," while the Grand Lodge of Scotland noted George's magnanimity and hoped for the "permanent, unimpaired, and undisturbed felicity of [His] Majesty, and of every branch of [his] Illustrious House."[13] Of course while George III might have received the freely given assent and praise of his subjects, his sons, scandalized and unpopular, were often the brunt of public ridicule if not contempt. Yet even though individual members of the royal family departed from respectable mores in their own lives, they nonetheless represented an institution and an ideal that was deemed inherently respectable. Thus Freemasonry's association with the royal house, despite the princes' tarnished reputations, did bring prestige to the Craft.[14]

Freemasons' efforts to cultivate relationships with members of the royal family paid off during the second half of the 1790s, when Britain was at war with France and the government cracked down on suspicious individuals and associations. It took the threat of internal rebellion as well as external invasion very seriously. Since entering the war in 1793 it had enacted a series of repressive measures to keep control over the country, including the suspension of Habeas Corpus (1794), the Treasonable and Seditious Practices Act (1795), and the Seditious Assemblies Act (1795). Even after it had thoroughly infiltrated and soundly routed the United Irishmen, the government kept up its guard, and in the aftermath of the rebellion it passed the Unlawful Societies Act (1799). This piece of legislation banned all societies that had "taken unlawful Oaths and Engagements of Fidelity and Secrecy, and used Secret Signs, and appointed Committees, Secretaries, and other Officers, in a secret Manner" for the purpose of challenging the laws and government of Great Britain and Ireland.[15]

Freemasonry presented a likely target. Given the fraternity's connections with the Society of United Irishmen and, prior to that, British Jacobites, radicals, and American patriots, as well as its insistence on keeping its proceedings secret, it easily met the criteria for being shut down. Moreover, 1797 had witnessed the publication of two sensationalist exposés: John Robison's *Proofs of a Conspiracy against all the Religions and Governments of Europe carried on in the Secret Meetings of Free Masons, Illuminati, and Reading Societies* and Abbé Augustin Barruel's *Mémoires pour servir à l'histoire du jacobinisme*. The first Masonic conspiracy theorists to receive widespread attention, both authors argued that Freemasonry was, to quote Professor Robison's words, an association formed "for the express purpose of ROOTING OUT ALL THE RELIGIOUS ESTABLISHMENTS, AND OVERTURNING ALL THE EXISTING GOVERNMENTS OF EUROPE." Both laid the blame for the Revolution, and especially the Terror, at the doors of France's Masonic lodges.[16] Yet in this climate of suspicion and uncertainty, the British government decided not to apply the act to Freemasonry. Private meetings between the grand masters (Lord Moira and the Duke of Atholl) and Prime Minister Pitt, as well as expressions of support from several members of Parliament, convinced the government to introduce a revised version of the bill that specifically exempted the brotherhood. The government made it clear that it wanted to keep a close eye on the fraternity—in exchange for the exemption, it required each lodge to report annually to the local clerk of the peace and furnish a list of members and meeting times.[17]

In order to ensure their institution's survival, Freemasons readily complied with these provisions by enacting administrative reforms and offering assurances to the government; meanwhile, they boasted of the special treatment they had received. The Moderns issued a circular in July 1799 commanding all lodges to send their returns to the clerk of the peace by 11 September. The Grand Lodge of Scotland met the conditions of the act by requiring its subordinate lodges to apply for new warrants. It viewed the "flattering" law "as bearing honourable testimony to the purity of the Order, and thus silencing the daring breath of calumny." In an address to the king in 1800 the Ancients commented that their institution was "honorably exempt" from government suspicion and expressed their appreciation "that amidst the Restraints which the Vigilance of your Government has found necessary to impose, we are permitted to hold our regular Assemblies." By this point, they had already adopted a resolution preventing all public Masonic processions and irregular meetings and revised their official return forms to include a statement outlining the provisions for compliance.[18]

But the campaign to prove their loyalty to the state, of which abiding by the Unlawful Societies Act was but a first step, presented Freemasons with a serious dilemma: how to live up to the terms of the deal while also preserving Masonic ideology. The institution had always boasted of its rule forbidding the discussion of politics at Masonic gatherings. This injunction lay at the heart of Masonic ideology. Indeed, the grand lodges' insistence that their members observe this rule had played a part in the institution's exemption from government repression. Exemption in the future depended on Freemasons' ability to continue claiming that theirs was an apolitical society. Yet the momentous events of the times had compelled Masons (at both the grand lodge and the local level) to enter the realm of politics. Expressions of loyalty, no matter how necessary, were unquestionably political statements. As such, they marked a departure from the sacred traditions of the order, a departure that gave contemporary Freemasons pause.

In their efforts to resolve this dilemma, the grand lodges adopted different approaches, but they all ended up in the same place: overt politicization of the brotherhood. Masonry's position was most precarious in Ireland, where the extensive involvement of some Irish Freemasons in the United Irish Rebellion had led to profound, and well-placed, suspicions on the part of the government. Irish Grand Lodge officials thus took the most drastic steps, though not before having to confront head on the dilemma over Masons' engagement in politics. Members of the Grand Lodge were split in their opinions about whether to punish those Masons who had taken part in the rebellion. Most believed that the escape clause in the constitutions protected the Masonic rights of any brethren who had been engaged, in one way or another, with the United Irishmen. That no lodges or members were expelled for their conduct during the rebellion revealed that this group won out in the short term. But immediately after the Grand Lodge decided not to punish United Irishmen, it instituted sweeping reforms, including a profound alteration in the rules governing the institution, to prevent its hands from being tied in the future. Its overall strategy was to keep Freemasonry above politics and, in so doing, align the institution — by default — with the establishment. It issued official announcements to subordinate lodges that the discussion of political and religious subjects within lodge walls was "utterly subversive of and abhorrent from the fundamental principles of Masonry." It also passed a resolution stating "that the true principles of Masonry inculcate an affectionate loyalty to the King and a dutiful subordination to the State." But the Grand Lodge felt that even these policies were insufficient. In a highly significant move, the Grand Lodge also revised the second charge, eliminating the escape clause that had preserved the membership of a brother who rebelled against the state.[19]

The Moderns' path to outright political engagement was both more gradual and more subtle than that of the Irish. Violating Masonry's cardinal rule to eschew politics had clearly made Masonic leaders uncomfortable since the 1790s. In 1793, the "overthrow of all peace and order" in France had required them to "depart from a rule which had been till then religiously observed in our association." They even openly acknowledged their discomfort to the king: "It is written, Sire, in the institute of our order, that we shall not, at our meetings, go into religious or political discussion; because, composed (as our fraternity is) of men of various nations, professing different rules of faith, and attached to opposite systems of government, such discussions, sharpening the mind of man against his brother, might offend and disunite." But the circumstances of the times, as well as their sense of duty as Britons, had demanded a temporary policy shift: "A crisis, however, so unlooked for as the present, justifies to our judgement a relaxation of that rule." "Relax" was the operative word. They did not seek to overturn the rule, just to sidestep it. Assuming it was a one-time event ("a singular juncture"), they eased their consciences by resolving that "no precedent should be drawn from that step."[20]

But, in 1800, a "motive of equal consequence" required a subsequent relaxation of the rule to allow them to make another "public declaration of their political principles." In May a "daring Assassin" fired shots on George III while he was attending the Theatre Royal on Drury Lane. Though still somewhat concerned that political declarations were against the rules of Freemasonry (as evidenced by a delay in the submission of their address), the Moderns were less troubled than they had been in the early 1790s. "We should think ourselves wanting in the first duty towards your Majesty and towards that constitution," they explained to the king, "did we not approach your Majesty with a testimony of our feelings on this awful occasion." They assured him that Freemasons had the most loyal intentions and professed their "unalterable attachment to the present happy form of government in this country." Likewise the Grand Lodge of Scotland confessed to George the "purity and simplicity of our ancient Order, and of our sincere attachment to the glorious constitution of our country." Not to be outdone, the Ancients issued a circular, sent to all Ancient lodges throughout the empire, containing the text of their address to George III. "We assure your Majesty," they wrote, "that no Class of your Subjects entertain a more sincere Attachment to your Person, and to the Constitution, or will shew a greater Zeal in their support."[21]

Zealous support did in fact come from the West Indies, though Ancient Masons there were still wrestling with the conflict between Masonic ideology and taking a political stand, even one that was loyalist. Masons in Barbados reported that they had maturely considered the "Charges" and decided that sending an address "so far from being in the smallest degree contrary to the principles of Masonry, would be perfectly consonant to them." In congratulating George on escaping assassination, the Barbadian Masons, like their counterparts in the British Isles and Bengal, referred to the particular blessings they enjoyed as subjects of the British crown. They also reminded the king that Parliament had seen fit to preserve the right of "real Free Masons" to meet and alluded to the Unlawful Societies Act as a proper "guard against the Abuses which might possibly be committed, by false pretenders to that Name assembling." They concluded with an assurance that "genuine Free Masons" could never engage in conspiracy since their brotherhood strictly charged them "never to suffer any Political Disquisition in a Lodge" and "always to be peaceable Subjects of the Government."[22] In claiming for Freemasonry an exclusively loyal pedigree, these Masons conveniently overlooked the fact that lodges had, in recent years, engaged in disquisitions of a political nature.

By 1800, British Masons of all stripes were well on their way to a more permanent and effective resolution of their dilemma. Rather than relaxing or, even worse, abandoning their cardinal rules, they subtly altered the definition of "politics." They continued to assert their aloofness from politics yet, at the same time, identify themselves as loyalists. In so doing, they made the implied claim that loyalism was outside the definition of "political." The label "political," it seems, applied only to those who sought to challenge the state. In an address to the monarch some years later, the Grand Lodge of Ireland succinctly characterized nineteenth-century Freemasons' understanding of loyalism: "We feel it to be peculiarly the duty of the Masonic Body to offer your Majesty a loyalty free from the asperity of political and religious controversy."[23] Freemasons' manipulation of the semantics of the political was a creative solution that allowed them to become effusive loyalists, and delegitimate those who sought to challenge the imperial government, without compromising their Masonic ideals.

Thus freed from their dilemma, Freemasons took their loyalist program to the next level by inventing the tradition that their brotherhood had *always* been loyal. To be sure, the *Constitutions* had, since their first publication in 1723, included wording that encouraged a Mason to be loyal to the state: "A Mason is a peaceable subject to the Civil Powers, wherever he resides or works, and is never to be concern'd in plots and conspiracies against the peace and welfare of the nation." It was this statement that allowed the Grand Lodge of Ireland to describe loyalty to the king and subordination to the State as "true principles of Masonry" and the Barbadian Masons to claim that Freemasons were always "peaceable Subjects of the Government under which they live." And, as we have seen, eighteenth-century Freemasonry did have a strong tradition of supporting the Hanoverian establishment. Moreover, Freemasons could justifiably claim that the rule forbidding political discussions in lodge meetings had existed "from time immemorial" (or at least since the publication of Anderson's first *Constitutions*). But the *Constitutions* had never *required* a brother to be loyal; and until 1800 they had included the clause that protected the Masonic rights of rebellious brethren.

Turn-of-the-century Freemasons not only erased the escape clause and reached the conclusion that the "no politics" rule did not apply to loyalist expressions; they also purged Freemasonry of its past associations with those oppositional forces — Jacobitism, radicalism, and American patriotism — that had challenged the state. By highlighting the loyalist tradition in Freemasonry, they glossed over the radical counter-tradition of the not-too-distant past (which had put Freemasonry in the very position in which it now found itself). "Deradicalizing" the brotherhood's past squelched its potential for radical associations in the future. We see this deradicalizing happening in Quebec, where the Provincial Grand Master of Lower Canada described loyalty to the crown as "the first of Masonic virtues." Claude Dénéchau urged members of the fraternity to attend to their public and private duties: "As Citizens, as Husbands, as Fathers, and as Brothers, let your conduct be straight and exemplary, each fulfilling with honesty and cheerfulness the station to which it has pleased God to call him." But loyalty to the crown and empire was the most important obligation of the Mason. Dénéchau encouraged his audience to emulate their "brethren of exalted rank and eminent character, whose names are foremost in Patriotism." He concluded, "Masonry has at all times prospered under the powerful and protecting arm of the British Government, and accordingly our Lodges are *proverbially Loyal*."[24]

Dénéchau's description of the Craft as "proverbially Loyal" was a clear example of a tradition in the process of being invented, of an "attempt to establish continuity with a suitable historic past."[25] In short, Freemasonry's claim to an exclusively loyalist past assured its future as a loyalist institution, one protected by the British state. Freemasonry secured exemption from the Unlawful Societies Act in 1799 only because the brotherhood's leaders agreed to an implicit quid pro quo — the government's toleration in exchange for the fraternity's public loyalty. What was at first a calculated response to the exigencies of a crisis thereafter became, through continued excursions into the politics of patriotism, an identity, a pattern of identifying Freemasonry with loyalism.

Consolidating Grand Lodge Authority

Proclaiming their institution's loyalty from the dais of a grand lodge room or in an official communication from the grand master meant little if local Masonic lodges were left to their own devices. Freemasonry's position in the 1790s was precarious, not only because of its historical associations with radicalism but also because the three grand lodges had yet to establish complete control over their respective jurisdictions. Lord Moira, the leader of English Freemasonry, acknowledged this when he told the Depute Sheriff of Edinburgh that Freemasons had been exempted from the Unlawful Societies Act "in consequence of my assurances to Mr. Pitt that nothing could be deemed a lodge which did not sit by precise authorization from the Grand Lodge, and under its superintendence."[26] Freemasonry could simply not afford to tolerate the presence of unauthorized lodges or activity. If a disgruntled Grand Lodge officer ran off with the membership registers or a recalcitrant lodge declared itself the only interpreter of true Masonry, a schism could easily erupt. Internal dissension could seriously compromise Freemasons' attempts to prove to the government that theirs was a loyal and trustworthy institution. During the first two decades of the nineteenth century, it was thus essential for the British grand lodges to consolidate and assert their own authority as the only legitimate governing bodies of British Freemasonry. The Grand Lodges of Scotland and Ireland confronted and defeated internal rivals. In England, the time had come to resolve the quarrel that had plagued Masonry since the 1750s. The schism in English Freemasonry had become a serious blot, an impediment in the institution's efforts to bill itself as a loyal and respectable institution. Accomplishing all these goals required Grand Lodge officials throughout the British Isles to act as effective leaders and put their administrative houses in order.

Given the turbulent events of the 1790s, establishing the loyalty of Irish Freemasons and consolidating the authority of their grand lodge was even more a matter of survival than it was for their English and Scottish counterparts. The leadership of Lord Donoughmore (Grand Master, 1789–1813) proved crucial. In attempting to keep politics outside of Freemasonry, he revealed his faith in the power of Masonry to bring Irishmen together. The son of John Hely, Provost of Trinity College and Irish Secretary of State, and a lawyer by training,

The Masonic Hall and Club Buildings, Molesworth Street, Dublin, Ireland, from *The Builder*, 28 September 1867 (copyright, and reproduced by permission of, the United Grand Lodge of England).

Donoughmore served as Commissioner of the Customs in Ireland between 1785 and 1802 and also as a member of Parliament until 1788. He was an ardent supporter of Catholic emancipation, involving himself in the planning of the Catholic Convention of 1793 and speaking on behalf of Irish Catholics in the House of Lords. He viewed Freemasonry as playing an important part in his efforts "to unite my countrymen and fellow subjects of every religion, description, and degree." Donoughmore also firmly believed in the brotherhood's encouragement of "loyalty to the Sovereign to whom [citizens] owe their allegiance and attachment to their common country which all may feel bound alike and interested to defend."[27]

In addition to trying to keep Freemasonry above the Irish political fray, the Grand Lodge under Donoughmore's rule became more efficient and stronger. A popular and dedicated grand master, Donoughmore traveled extensively, visiting lodges and making the presence of the Grand Lodge felt throughout the counties. More than once Donoughmore found himself in the position of peacemaker, reconciling the Grand Lodge and provincial leaders. Under his administration, the Grand Lodge also reined in recalcitrant lodges that acted independently and failed to pay dues. Shortly thereafter it appointed a salaried officer to collect the past dues of negligent lodges. Once the deputy grand treasurer had contacted all of the 907 lodges on the grand lodge rolls to request their compliance, the Grand Lodge—in a move that departed from its laissez-faire approach during the eighteenth century—boldly canceled 169 lodges that had not responded. From then on, failure to maintain contact with the Grand Lodge was considered sufficient cause to cancel a lodge's warrant.[28]

Unpopular for requiring lodges to pay back dues and stay in regular contact, the Grand Lodge soon faced a very serious challenge to its authority. In 1806 a schism erupted when a number of brethren belonging to lodges in Ulster and Dublin took over the physical premises of the Grand Lodge and established a rival grand lodge. The lodges were led in their rebellion by a disgruntled and corrupt official, Alexander Seton, who had served as deputy grand secretary since 1801. Seton had a vested interest in keeping the financial records of the Grand Lodge from coming to light—he had been embezzling dues since his first year in office. But by whipping up opposition to the centralization then underway, he managed to distract his supporters from his criminal motives. The Grand Lodge put up a formidable fight: it filed a series of lawsuits against Seton and others; it tried to convince rebellious lodges it was the only legitimate Masonic authority in Ireland; and it gained the support of the other British grand lodges. When members of the rival grand lodge began suspecting

Francis Rawdon-Hastings (1754–1826), first Marquess of Hastings (Earl of Moira), Acting Grand Master of English Freemasonry, 1790–1813 (copyright, and reproduced by permission of, the United Grand Lodge of England).

Seton of stealing their own funds in 1811, most of the lodges decided to return their allegiance to the original Grand Lodge and the revolt petered out. Even during the height of the rebellion, the Grand Lodge continued to implement policies designed to consolidate its authority and streamline its administration.[29] Though the turbulence of the 1790s had put Irish Freemasonry in a particularly precarious position, the brotherhood emerged from the decade stronger, more administratively efficient, and less threatening to the government. Yet its future was not entirely assured. As we will see, the unrest of the 1820s would sweep up Freemasonry in sectarian politics and, as a result, government bans designed to keep order during troubled times.

Like the Irish Grand Lodge, the Grand Lodge of Scotland proved it was firmly in charge of Scottish Freemasonry in this period. Between 1805 and 1820 the Prince of Wales served as the Grand Master and Patron of Scottish Freemasonry. As in England, however, the day-to-day running of the Craft was left to an acting grand master. The most effective person in this role was the Earl of Moira, who led the Grand Lodge between 1806 and 1808 while concurrently serving as Acting Grand Master of England. Moira once again demonstrated his effective negotiating skills as Scottish Grand Master by bringing about a reconciliation between the Grand Lodge of Scotland and Mother Kilwinning Lodge, one of the original Scottish lodges that had resisted the authority of the Grand Lodge and established its independence in 1743. Another serious threat to grand lodge authority emerged during Moira's tenure in 1807, when Dr. John Mitchell, master of Lodge Caledonian, caused commotion in grand lodge ranks. After proposing a highly controversial resolution that failed to pass by only one vote, Mitchell suggested his own lodge should secede from the Grand Lodge. Incensed, the Grand Lodge suspended him but Lodge Caledonian seceded anyway. A long and bitter fight ensued, with the Grand Lodge eventually expelling Mitchell and suspending several of his supporters. The issue would not be finally settled until 1813; by that point the Grand Lodge had exerted control over the vast majority of lodges in Scotland.

The first step in consolidating grand lodge authority in England, and thereby to help solidify the brotherhood's reputation as a loyalist institution, was to resolve the quarrel between Ancients and Moderns. The existence of rival grand lodges not only failed to inspire the confidence of the government; it also caused administrative headaches and pointed to embarrassing contradictions in an institution theoretically dedicated to brotherly love. By the early nineteenth century both parties recognized the benefits of uniting. The Moderns wanted the schism to come to an end because they realized their rivals were more popular and growing faster. As we have seen, the Ancients enjoyed tremendous success in the British army and the empire. That the Moderns were willing to negotiate with their upstart rivals reveals the great extent to which colonial developments could affect Masonry in the metropole (the union of Ancients and Moderns in Madras and Lower Canada also set an important precedent for metropolitan Masons). For their part, although they enjoyed the support of the Grand Lodges of Scotland and Ireland, the Ancients envied the prestige the Moderns drew from their connections with the royal family.[30]

Effecting the union between the Ancients and the Moderns was critical for solidifying Freemasonry's future. Lord Moira acknowledged that until English Masons resolved the conflict, others would look upon their order with suspicion: "The Unity of Masonic Constitution . . . is the only security for

regularity and uniformity of observance, without which the character of a Masonic Lodge might be assumed by any act of individuals for conducting in
secrecy the most nefarious designs." But effecting such a union was a long and
delicate process. In 1809 the Moderns changed their rituals to conform more
closely to those of the Ancients and appointed a committee, which met between
1809 and 1811 and was called the Lodge of Promulgation, to study the remaining ritualistic differences. The Moderns had also established relations with the
Grand Lodges of Scotland and Ireland. The following year the Ancients passed
a resolution in support of a union on the condition that the so-called "ancient
landmarks" of the Craft were preserved. After the two grand masters, the Earl of
Moira and the Duke of Atholl, held a series of meetings, special grand lodge
committees were constituted to work out the administrative details and coordinate the two sets of rituals. Negotiations dragged on for two years and hit an
impasse in 1813.[31]

Fortunately for both sides, the stalled negotiations coincided with the increased involvement of the royal princes, whose willingness to hold positions
of leadership and to help reconcile the two sides of the Craft indicated the
seriousness with which they approached the fraternity. In 1813 Edward, Duke
of Kent (who had been recalled from Gibraltar in 1802/3 because he inflicted a
disciplinary regime too severe even for that mutinous garrison), became Grand
Master of the Ancients. It was an appropriate appointment since, as Cecil
Woodham-Smith describes, "he united a pedantic love of detail with a love of
interfering and setting right."[32] Meanwhile his brother, the Duke of Sussex, had
replaced the Prince of Wales as Grand Master of the Moderns, and their intervention proved critical to the resolution of the sixty-year-old schism. Removed
enough from the details to maintain perspective and still sufficiently engaged
to command the respect of both parties, the royal brothers quickly ushered in
the union. The grand lodges signed twenty-one Articles of Union and on 27 December 1813 combined to establish the United Grand Lodge of England. The
Duke of Kent graciously stepped down, and the Duke of Sussex took charge of
this new grand lodge.

The firm administration of the Duke of Sussex (1813–43) allowed the new
grand lodge to assert its authority over the former Ancient and Modern lodges
throughout England and the empire. In addition to introducing significant
changes in Masonic ritual, he oversaw the renumbering of all the lodges, a
complicated process that usually provoked discontent, and a major restructur-
ing of grand lodge administration. The Grand Lodge carefully outlined the
duties of existing grand officers, including most importantly the provincial

grand masters, and created new positions. To monitor the expansion of the Craft, the Grand Lodge required new lodges applying for warrants to secure the sponsorship of an existing lodge in its locality. It also insisted that new initiates receive an official grand lodge certificate.[33] Finally the Grand Lodge envisioned building suitable premises: "such an Edifice in the Metropolis of the British Empire, as should make it the Centre for the resort, intercourse, scientific culture, and fraternal conviviality of the Masonic World." Its ambitions were indeed global, as evidenced by an 1814 circular urging members to abide by the new regulations and thus ensure the perfect unity "by which the English Masons will be recognised as uniform with the Antient Brothers throughout the world."[34]

In addition to solidifying their internal authority vis-à-vis their subordinate lodges, the British grand lodges also sought to consolidate their power by improving their relations with one another. A regular, friendly correspondence between the Ancients and the Grand Lodges of Scotland and Ireland had taken place since the 1780s. Records from the 1780s to the 1810s reflect a commitment to keeping one another informed about the election of officers and grand lodge proceedings. The Irish Grand Lodge assured the Ancients in 1783 that it would "always concur with them in every thing for the mutual advantage of the Ancient Craft." Their grand secretary wrote regularly to the Ancients to inform them about the Irish Craft and ask for information and advice. He expressed his hope "that the proceedings in both kingdoms should correspond as nearly as possible."[35] Periods of stress and uncertainty, such as those occasioned by schisms, often led the grand lodges to turn to one another for support and confirmation of their own legitimacy. In the midst of its troubles with Dr. Mitchell, for example, the Scottish Grand Lodge sought support from the Grand Lodge of Ireland and the Ancients. Articulating an opinion already shared by its Irish and English counterparts, the Grand Lodge argued that the welfare of Masonry depended on the authority of a "Super-intending power, competent to control the proceedings of every acknowledg'd Lodge, and of every member of the Craft." The Irish Grand Lodge, having itself just defeated a rebellion, concurred. It assured the Grand Lodge of Scotland it would correspond regularly and cooperate with it "in every measure which may tend to the general good of the Craft and particularly in giving its most zealous support to the maintenance of good order, subordination and respect for authority."[36]

The effort to improve Grand lodge relations culminated in 1814 with the signing of the International Masonic Compact. In July of that year the Irish and Scottish grand masters journeyed to London for a series of meetings with the

Duke of Sussex and other officials of the recently consolidated United Grand Lodge. Negotiating "to settle the points of communion, intercourse, and fraternization among the three GRAND LODGES of the United Kingdom," the representatives agreed to a number of regulations "for the maintenance, security, and promotion of the Craft." They decided upon the essential elements of Masonic ritual and pledged to maintain "a constant fraternal intercourse" with one another through correspondence and exchange of proceedings. Ensuring their independent jurisdictions, the grand masters pledged that they would not encroach upon one another's territories or members. They set a minimum initiation fee to guard the benevolence funds from "irregular and improper applications." Along these lines, they agreed that a grand lodge certificate was necessary for admission into a lodge in the jurisdiction of another grand lodge; and they promised to look carefully into the character of candidates before admitting them. Finally, they pledged to discountenance "in all their Meetings every question that could have the remotest tendency to excite controversy in matters of Religion or any political discussion whatever."[37]

By 1814 Freemasonry in the British Isles was governed by three separate yet cooperating bodies. Each had recently consolidated its authority over subordinate lodges in its jurisdiction, and although provincial lodges occasionally acted out, the grand lodges experienced no further serious challenges to their power. The compact signed in 1814 ensured that within the British Isles at least, the three grand lodges had clearly defined territories and friendly relations. But the international arena posed a number of challenges and problems that made grand lodge relations far from cordial. Before examining the state of imperial Freemasonry in the early nineteenth century, it is instructive to revisit Ireland, whose status as both a kingdom and a colony sheds light onto processes evident throughout the overseas empire. In particular, the Irish case reveals the early development of a new aspect of British Freemasonry that came to characterize the nineteenth-century brotherhood from Nova Scotia to the Cape Colony: its fundamentally Protestant nature.

Sectarian Shoals

Though British Masonic authorities reinterpreted strictures against political discussions in order to identify their fraternity with loyalism, they were not willing to overlook the rule forbidding the discussion of religion. As they had since the early eighteenth century, British lodges continued to claim to admit men of any faith and to describe the lodge as a meeting ground of the world's religions. But Ireland in the aftermath of the Union presented special challenges to the Masonic ethos of toleration and brotherhood. Nowhere else in the British Isles did politics and religion combine to produce such a divisive atmosphere. In the face of this situation the Irish Grand Lodge made significant efforts to encourage toleration and maintain the lodge's function as a neutral space for Anglicans, Presbyterians, and Catholics. Masonic authorities in Dublin opened negotiations with the head of the Irish Church, punished lodges that persecuted Catholics, and eventually suspended troublesome Masonic processions. But the highly sectarian atmosphere of early-nineteenth-century Ireland proved too much even for Masonic idealism. Circumstances outside grand lodge control dictated that Irish Freemasonry began to lose its Catholic constituency and take on an increasingly Orange complexion. In Ireland, and then throughout the British Isles and the empire, the fraternity soon became identified not only with loyalism, but with its constant bedfellow, Protestantism.

The decades between the Union and the Great Famine might be fairly described as one of Irish history's several "pressure cooker" periods. A massive population explosion increased pressure on the unstable agrarian economy. Ireland did not undergo the processes of industrialization transforming England, Wales, and the Scottish lowlands in this period, and it did not have the urban outlets necessary to absorb an expanding population. Parts of Ireland, especially Ulster, became fertile ground for agrarian secret societies and rural protest movements that sought to regulate the moral economy and redress perceived injustices. Ireland's Catholic majority had the most significant grievances. In 1823 Daniel O'Connell founded the Catholic Association to agitate for Catholic emancipation and the repeal of the Union. Both political and agrarian violence escalated. Throughout this period, an insecure government addressed the situation by implementing coercive measures, including restrictive legislation and the introduction of the world's first modern police force, the Irish Constabulary. On top of all this, potent memories of ageless enmities between Ireland's competing religious communities fueled sectarian discord.

Changes in Irish Freemasonry both reflected and contributed to this volatile situation. Lord Donoughmore transferred the grand mastership to his hand-picked successor, the Duke of Leinster, in 1813. A member of the prominent Ascendancy family, the Fitzgeralds, the third duke was the son of a former Irish grand master and nephew of Edward Fitzgerald, the United Irishman. Educated in England, Lord Leinster had an active political career, supporting Catholic emancipation, advocating parliamentary reform, and serving as president of the Board of Commissioners of Ireland's first nondenominational system of national education. During the first part of Leinster's long watch (1813–74), Irish Freemasonry reached its maximum extent but then steadily contracted as the number of active lodges decreased.[38] The decline is easily explained: after the 1820s Catholics distanced themselves from the fraternity and Freemasonry soon became closely and permanently identified with Protestantism.

The hostile attitude of the Catholic Church — which was obviously outside the control of Masonic authorities — contributed to Masonry's increasingly Protestant character. Although the Vatican had issued encyclicals against Freemasonry in the eighteenth century, they were neither widely publicized nor strictly enforced in Ireland until the early 1800s. By the time Irish prelates made their congregations aware of the Church's position on Freemasonry, the Vatican had stepped up its efforts to curtail Catholics' participation in Masonry. In the 1820s alone, the Vatican issued three official statements condemning the order. Throughout the rest of the century the Church consistently reiterated its position that it viewed Freemasonry as a dangerous enemy. Hostility between the Church and Masonry bubbled up at the lodge level during the 1810s. The Grand Lodge received numerous reports from Catholic members complaining of persecution at the hands of priests. "The Pulpits and communion tables," the Grand Lodge reported, "teem with anathema's [sic] against them [Freemasons]." Taking a hard line against parishioners who belonged to the fraternity, priests withheld the most important rites of Catholicism: baptism for the children of Masons, post-childbirth purification for their wives, and last rites for the dying. The Grand Lodge also claimed that priests were attempting to squeeze information about Freemasonry out of vulnerable members. Only when a man renounced Freemasonry and provided information about Masonic practices did priests perform the soul-saving ceremonies.[39]

In 1814, with the hopes of redressing its members' grievances, Grand Lodge officials decided to bring the situation to the attention of the highest-ranking Irish bishops. Writing to the Reverend Dr. O'Reilly, head of the Irish Church, they described "a most unexplained . . . and unjustifiable persecution with which numbers of our Brethren of the Roman Catholic persuasion have been visited by the Pastors for no other cause whatsoever but the *avowed* one of their being Free Masons." The Grand Lodge informed the bishop that priests, especially in the North, were refusing to minister to members of the parishes who belonged to the fraternity. Not surprisingly, the Grand Lodge pointed out to the bishop that the British legislature had sanctioned their order and that the Prince Regent himself was a member. In language reflecting their increased emphasis on loyalism, they assured O'Reilly that Masonic obligations helped strengthen the social compact and "bind [the citizen] more firmly and zealously to his King, his Country, and his God." Finally, Irish officials threatened to urge the other British grand lodges to make "the many and grievous vexations to which the Roman Catholic Brethren are exposed" a matter of parliamentary investigation.[40]

The communications with Roman Catholic officials and the appeals to the English Grand Lodge failed to produce the desired results, and the Grand Lodge continued to receive reports of persecution in subsequent decades. The situation for most of its Catholic members became unbearable. Church officials in Ireland were bound by Rome's decisions and had to enforce the edicts against Freemasonry, which culminated in threats of excommunication against those who refused to renounce the brotherhood. As a consequence, Catholics left the fraternity in droves. Whole lodges were depleted. In 1819 the Grand Lodge discussed reports "from several lodges relative to the persecution of Brethren of the Roman Catholick persuasion by their Priests." The master of Lodge No. 445 in County Westmeath wrote to the Grand Lodge in 1830 and inquired whether he should return the lodge warrant since "the members have all withdrawn thro' the influence of Priests."[41]

The priests' actions against Freemasons were not the sole reason for Catholics' departure from the fraternity. Sometimes lodges with predominantly Protestant memberships either forced Catholic members out or prevented Catholics from joining in the first place. For example, during the 1820s Lodge No. 424, in County Antrim, instituted a rule requiring members and candidates to swear they had never "professed the Roman Catholic Religion." When the Grand Lodge became aware of the situation, it suspended several members of the lodge, ordered the questionable bylaw expunged, and required No. 424 to admit Catholics.[42] But although the Grand Lodge had the power to monitor the regulations of lodges, it could not become involved in their mundane affairs nor oversee their unstated admissions policies. Moreover, what right-minded Catholic would venture into a lodge that had a reputation for anti-Catholic policies? Thus, over time more and more lodges forsook their ecumenical mission and became exclusively Protestant arenas, a process that reflected the religious stratification increasingly evident in Ireland during the 1820s.

In the highly sectarian atmosphere of the 1820s, the fate of Irish Freemasonry became intertwined with that most ardent champion of Protestant rights, the Orange Order. O'Connell's campaign to win civil rights for his fellow Irish Catholics reinvigorated Orangeism, which had experienced a period of decline in the first part of the nineteenth century. Orange activities, particularly the 12

July parades commemorating the Battle of the Boyne, fed the siege mentality of Irish Protestants, who feared their privileges and liberties would evaporate if Irish Catholics achieved emancipation. They were also a source of constant concern for the authorities because processions inevitably inflamed community tensions and resulted in deadly clashes with Catholics. Another source of sectarianism and violence were the Ribbonmen, members of agrarian secret societies that fought for the rights of tenant farmers, protested against the payment of tithes, and challenged the Orangemen. In the summer of 1815, over a thousand Ribbonmen attacked a public house in Derry where Orangemen and Freemasons held lodge meetings. During the 1820s they stepped up their tactics of intimidation to push forward their anti-Protestant agenda.

Apprehensive about these dangerous forces threatening the peace, the government attempted to defuse the Irish powder keg through coercive legislation. Between 1822 and 1824 it suspended habeas corpus and passed a series of insurrection acts, including the 1823 Act for Preventing the Administering of Oaths, to try to restore stability. Such measures were designed to curb the activities of the Orange Order and the Ribbonmen, and, as it had in 1799 with the Unlawful Societies Act, Freemasonry was swept up in the commotion. Both Freemasonry and the Orange Order suspended their activities in August 1823. The circular letter informing Irish Masons of this action, which was published in several newspapers, indicated that the action was necessary even though Freemasons "invariably profess[e]d unbounded allegiance to their Sovereign, fidelity to the Government, [and] obedience to the Laws." That the government did not automatically extend the exemption secured in 1799 indicated that Freemasonry, at least in Ireland, had yet to prove its loyalist credentials.[43]

That fall, Grand Lodge officials worked to devise a strategy for getting Freemasonry back into the government's favor and putting it on a sound legal footing. They decided to submit a petition to Parliament. It reached the House of Commons in early 1824. In the petition the Freemasons described theirs as a charitable, benevolent, and peaceful institution whose lodges forbade the discussion of political and religious matters. Naturally, they pointed out that the king and his male relations, as well as numerous members of the nobility and magistracy, belonged to their fraternity. Reminding the MPs that the government had exempted Freemasons from the Unlawful Societies Act, the petitioners assured them that they were "not yielding to any class of His Majesty's subjects in loyalty to the Throne or in obedience to the Laws of the Realm." Notably, Freemasonry's supporters in Parliament emphasized the brotherhood's potential for reconciling the differences between Ireland's warring communities. As a result of its efforts in Parliament, Irish Freemasonry became a legal institution again in June 1824.[44] Yet the hiatus had exacted a cost on Irish Freemasonry: the Catholic Church was more adamantly opposed than ever, and many lodges never resumed meeting after the interruption.

Freemasonry's growing identification with Orangeism — as evident in the issue of party processions — did not endear it to Catholics. Contrary to the principles and rules of the order, Masonic lodges had begun associating publicly with the Orange Order by marching in Orange processions, wearing Orange ribbons on their Masonic aprons, and playing Orange songs during their marches. The Grand Lodge took a firm stand against this behavior. As early as 1822 it suspended a lodge "for walking in procession as Masons, and causing party tunes to be played to them, and also for walking with the Orangemen on the 12th of July." By the time it passed the 1824 ruling requiring a magistrate's approval for a procession to take place, the Grand Lodge had suspended additional lodges over the issue. The matter put the Grand Lodge in a delicate situation. While it was receiving reports from the police concerning unauthorized processions and dealing with government prosecution of offenders to the peace, it also had to confront complaints from lodges around Ireland about the strictures against marching. Some lodges even threatened to stop sending dues until they were allowed to hold processions whenever they chose. The Grand Lodge responded by banning processions altogether and thus found itself regularly punishing the many lodges and individuals that ignored the ban.[45] When the Grand Lodge felt sufficiently in control of the situation in 1831, it decided to restore to lodges their marching privileges, but once again its affairs became intertwined with those of the Orange Order. This was hardly surprising considering the degree of association between the two institutions. In 1835 Parliament opened an investigation into the Orange Order. The Whigs who led the inquiry were suspicious of the order's connection to certain members of the royal family, its political activities, and its presence in the army. The government decided, on the advice of the select committee, to ban the Orange Order and in early 1836 it dissolved.

Although Irish Freemasons were anxious that they too would be subject to the ban, their loyal behavior had raised them above suspicion. Noting that "there is no country where the principles of our Order are more applicable than in Ireland," Leinster informed English authorities that he was proud to have preserved the rights of Irish Freemasons. He and his fellow Grand Lodge officers thanked Freemasonry's advocates in Parliament and pledged to exert control over insubordinate lodges. The Grand Lodge took a series of steps to curb processions. In anticipation of the annual commemoration of St. John's Day it sent notices to all lodges, dispatched deputations to various parts of the country, and posted placards in towns, all warning that marching would not be tolerated. Despite the Grand Lodge's efforts the government informed them that Freemasons continued to violate the ban against processions. The Grand Lodge finally got the situation in hand by launching a major investigation, cooperating with the police to get information on offending lodges, sending representatives to enforce its rulings, and suspending numerous lodges. In August 1838, for example, it canceled one lodge and suspended eighteen.[46]

But the Grand Lodge was fighting against an inexorable Orange tide. By the time it regained control, Irish Freemasonry had already lost much of its potential to serve as a meeting ground for Protestants and Catholics. Its goal to serve as a neutral space further evaporated when Daniel O'Connell decided in 1837 to renounce his connections with the fraternity. In April of that year he wrote a letter to the editor of *The Pilot*. O'Connell explained that he had belonged to Lodge No. 189 in Dublin and had even served as its master, but he assured his readers that at the time he did not realize the Church forbade membership in the brotherhood. Once he became aware of the Church's censure, he unequivocally renounced Freemasonry. Although he felt that Freemasonry had no evil tendencies, he explained that he strongly objected to the taking of oaths required for membership. Such oath taking, he remarked, "is alone abundantly sufficient to prevent any serious Christian from belonging to that body."[47]

The position of the Catholic Church, the government's suspicions of Freemasonry, the obvious association between Freemasonry and Orangeism in many lodges, and the disavowal of Catholic Ireland's cherished demagogue combined to compromise any appeal Freemasonry had to the Irish majority. An institution that had served in the late eighteenth century as a meeting ground for Protestants and Catholics had become, over four decades, an almost exclusively Protestant domain. As Roy Foster explains, both Freemasonry and Orangeism became "part of the social cement of Protestantism in the new era."[48] Despite its ecumenical ideology and intentions, Freemasonry had contributed to the spread of sectarianism in Ireland.

Freemason = Loyal Briton = Patriot

The process by which a brotherhood with a history of radical associations aligned itself with the church-and-king establishment has much to add to our understanding of patriotism, loyalism, and nationalism at the turn of the nineteenth century. The current historiography consists of a sophisticated literature on patriotism and a few key works that focus on either loyalism or nationalism. This extensive historiography barely mentions Freemasonry, which is surprising given that Freemasonry was the most popular association of the "respectable classes" in eighteenth-century Britain, and, as demonstrated here, its members were engaged in patriotic activities and made regular expressions as loyalist Britons. Indeed, as we have seen, turn-of-the-century Freemasons would likely have considered themselves among the most patriotic subjects of the Hanoverian realm. The brotherhood's transformation into a "stabilizing factor" between the 1790s and the 1820s thus offers a window onto all three phenomena, allowing us to examine their interrelationship and suggesting the need to distinguish much more explicitly and carefully their respective characteristics.[49]

First, Freemasons' response to the events of the 1780s and 1790s can shed light on the differences between patriotism and loyalism as well as their relationship to one another. The differences are subtle but nonetheless important.[50] Patriots, who identified with and fought for an abstraction (like a constitution or a nation), were found all along the political spectrum. In fact, many historians have taken pains to demonstrate that the label "patriot" was contested vigorously between the mid-eighteenth and the mid-nineteenth century, when people of various political affiliations, including radicals, could and did claim to be "patriots."[51] Whereas patriotism was up for grabs, loyalism had a much more specific meaning, though it too could shift over time. Loyalists, who identified with a particular ruler, government, or party, were generally conservative supporters of the establishment and upholders of the existing political system. Patriotism was thus a more flexible concept: while we might discuss various kinds of patriotism (radical, oppositional, loyalist), we would be hard-pressed to find, for example, "radical loyalism" pressing forward its agenda.[52]

In this case, Freemasons came to define their brand of patriotism in specifically loyalist terms. To be a Freemason was to be a patriot; to be a patriot was to be a loyal Briton. Between the late 1780s and the 1820s, they pursued a deliberate strategy to impress upon the government and the public this association (Freemason = loyal Briton = patriot). Their tactics included encouraging the involvement of the royal princes in the brotherhood, joining the chorus of loyal expressions to the king, and consolidating the authority of the grand lodges. Yet this was by no means just a top-down effort: evidence of loyalist addresses coming in from North America, the Caribbean, and India demonstrates the active participation of the Masonic rank-and-file in this program. Through these methods, metropolitan and colonial Freemasons positioned themselves firmly as loyalists willing to support the narrow political elite governing the country.

The history of Freemasonry in this period also allows us to gauge the extent to which the loyalist patriotism of Britons was genuinely felt or merely induced by government repression during the crucial decade of the 1790s. Historians concur that although the label "patriot" was contested vigorously earlier in the century, the government, the king, and conservatives enjoyed a monopoly on patriotism during the 1790s. Driven by fear of invasion, loyalty to the monarchy and the constitution, and pride in Britain's fabulous naval victories, people rallied to the king and his government to an unprecedented degree. But historians disagree about what led to this groundswell of conservative patriotism. One prominent school argues that conservative ideology, by force of its better, more practical, and more appealing arguments, triumphed over its radical counterpart. Because their arguments were less convincing and their political organization less effective, radicals could not come close to gaining the kind of widespread support that greeted conservative loyalism.[53] Other historians have challenged this argument, which they call the "Dickinsonian consensus," by emphasizing the role of broader circumstances, and specifically government repression, in leading to the conservatives' victory over radicals.[54]

The case of Freemasonry suggests that though government repression clearly affected how Freemasons behaved and responded to broader events, their conservative loyalism was genuinely felt. Granted, the Unlawful Societies Act put Masons in a very uncomfortable position, and they had to act fast to avoid being swallowed up by the legislation. But by 1799 (when the act was passed), the grand lodges had already laid much of the groundwork to associate their brotherhood with loyalism. They had joined the loyalist address movement of 1792–93, even though their deliberations over whether Masonic rules allowed them to do so caused them to be a bit tardy in getting their address to the king. By 1793 the Moderns could boast that the Prince of Wales was their grand master, while the Ancients could point to Prince Edward's close associations with the brotherhood in the empire. Finally, the grand lodges themselves observed that they were living in "a time when nearly the whole mass of the people anxiously press[ed] forward and offer[ed] with one heart, and one voice, the most animated testimonies of their attachment to [his] Majesty's person and government." Likewise, a Masonic orator proclaimed to assembled brethren that they were living in unprecedented times by exhorting:

Perhaps the history of man no where affords us any information, of any period, like the present, of national unity in our national politics; . . . It is almost an undiscoverable mystery, that a nation, so averse to its present engagements of war and tumult, both from interest and humanity of sentiment, should almost universally unite to encourage, support, and continue, the utmost exertions of that, which naturally exhausts our wealth, draws rivers of tears from many of our fellow creatures eyes, and gives every disagreeable sensation to all the feelings of our national and Christian humanity.

This Masonic address concluded with a prayer that reflected the brotherhood's new priorities: "May this kingdom, gracious God, never want a Protestant prince to wear its crown, or to sway its sceptre; nor may our Order, by any species of disloyalty, forfeit its present high respectability, of being a valuable and honourable Society, for Royal Union."[55]

In responding to the dilemma into which the circumstances of revolution and war had put them, Freemasons arguably went further than the situation demanded. They not only complied with the government's requirements for exemption from the Unlawful Societies Act (annually registering their members and reporting to the clerk of the peace), but also voluntarily underwent a profound ideological and institutional shift. Freemasons *as Freemasons* became public loyalists, and in so doing they abandoned a cardinal tenet of their order. They comforted themselves by assuming that acts and expressions of loyalty were not actually political. This allowed them to take other steps toward loyalism, like inventing the tradition that their institution had always been loyal and contributing, as a body, to the Patriotic Fund ("for the relief of the widows and families of those brave men who have fallen or may suffer in their country's cause during the war"). But even these measures were deemed insufficient: British Freemasons added yet another dimension to their loyal program. They took upon themselves an evangelical mission to cultivate loyalty in their fellow citizens. As the Modern Grand Lodge put it, Freemasons were "to labour, as far as their feeble powers may apply, in *inculcating* loyalty to the King and reverence to the inestimable fabric of the British Constitution." According to Claude Dénéchau, the French Canadian/Briton/Provincial Grand Master quoted earlier, membership in the brotherhood bound the brethren, "collectively and individually as far as our influence may extend among our fellow subjects, to inculcate principles of Loyalty to the King and obedience to His Laws." A verse printed in a guide for Freemasons living in India during the early nineteenth century urged that Freemasonry offered a path to the fruits of Britishness:

YE free-born sons of Britain's Isle,
Attend while I the truth impart,
And shew that you are in exile,
Till science guides you by our art;
Uncultivated paths you tread,
Unlevelled, barren, and blindfold be,
Till by a myst'ry you are led
Into the Light of Masonry.[56]

Without Masonry, they would remain exiled from Britain's liberty and civilization.

The verse's linking of Freemasonry with Britishness was quite typical of Masonic discourse in this period, a practice that allows us to look at one final historiographical issue: the nature of British national identity and, specifically, the place of the monarch (and thus loyalism) therein. In *Britons*, Linda Colley argues that during the two decades on either side of 1800 more people began to perceive of themselves as Britons, an identity that could be effectively grafted on to other local or regional identities. The wars against Catholic France, the influence of Protestantism, the consolidation of the ruling class, the facelift of the monarchy, and the participation of ordinary men and women in the political life of the nation all contributed to a heightened sense of Britishness in this period. The rehabilitated monarchy was a crucial element of this process. George and his ministers worked hard to make the monarchy a successful "focus for patriotic celebration": "Officially sponsored patriotic celebrations were thus made, as far as possible, identical with celebration of the king."[57]

Both the actions and the words of Freemasons lend support to Colley's emphasis on the royalist (and thus loyalist) dimensions of turn-of-the-century patriotism.[58] Their language reflected the intensification of British national consciousness and demonstrated that loyalty to the monarch (and his family) was a fundamental component of the Britishness then under invention. Their campaign to court the royal family as actively engaged patrons of their brotherhood was a clear sign that they wanted to be associated with the House of Hanover. Moreover, the fact that they invariably mentioned the king or the Prince of Wales when they expressed their sentiments as Britons provides evidence of this feeling. Masonic sources are rife with examples. In 1793 the Premier Grand Lodge stated that it felt compelled to drop the rule against political statements and express their loyalty to the crown because their duty "as Britons" demanded it. The next year, Freemasons in Nova Scotia announced to Prince Edward that they were firmly attached to "that excellent form of Government which is the peculiar blessing of a British subject" while at the same time they expressed their "unshaken loyalty to His Majesty, and zealous attachment to every branch of his Royal family." Commemorating George III's Jubilee in 1809, the Earl of Moira described how as "men and Britons" Freemasons enjoyed the fruits of George's reign, including the extension of arts and sciences, a degree of national wealth "unexampled in history," and the "manly defiance of every foe." Finally, at a Masonic festival in Madras in July 1811, it was reported that when the Deputy Provincial Grand Master gave a toast to George III ("the Most Gracious and Beloved Sovereign"), "the finest sensations of British patriotism glowed in the breast of every individual of the assembly" and that the whole event "was conducted in a manner highly patriotic and truly worthy of the Fraternity."[59] Thus, for Britons who belonged to Freemasonry, loyalism had become a reflex. The stamp of loyalty and Protestantism that came to characterize Freemasonry in the British Isles was thus also on display in the colonies, to which we now return.

FIVE

Men of the Best Standing

On the first day of March in 1824, the *Calcutta Gazette* reported on the ceremony to lay the foundation stone for the New Hindoo College, then being erected for "the moral and intellectual improvement" of Britain's Hindu "native subjects." The event had been staged on the previous afternoon at four o'clock, when the Masonic lodges of the city gathered at the old Hindoo College in Bowbazar to march in procession to the new building site in Potuldunga Square. Constables and soldiers were in attendance to monitor the crowd of natives and Europeans that the *Gazette* described as "dense in the extreme." High-ranking Masonic officials performed the ritual of consecrating the building site: they prayed, deposited coins of the reign into the stone, covered the cavity with an inscribed silver plate, lowered the stone into place, tested it with their symbolic tools, and anointed it with corn, oil, and wine. According to the report: "In the Square area stood the Brethren of the mystic Institution in their badges and jewels of ceremony listening bear-headed to the impressive invocation going on. As far as the eye could reach, it met Tiers above Tiers of human faces, the house tops in every direction being crowded to cramming by the natives anxious to have a view of the imposing scene. Behind the Brethren standing in square might be seen many Ladies and gentlemen of the first respectability." Brief speeches, greeted with applause, followed, and then the officers and lodges filed off to the tune of "God Save the King." Four months later, the Provincial Grand Lodge of Bengal performed a comparable ceremony for the New Mahommedan College, which was similarly dedicated to interrelated objectives of spreading civilization and securing collaborators.[1] None of the thousands of Europeans and Asians in attendance could doubt the Masonic order's reputation for loyalty and respectability. The events were but two of countless early-nineteenth-century Masonic ceremonies that evinced the brotherhood's role in building the empire — by simultaneously helping construct its architecture and constitute its ruling establishment.

The British Empire of the early nineteenth century was a sprawling multicultural entity the likes of which the world had never before seen. Though thirteen colonies had been lost to the Americans, the empire had expanded to even greater proportions with the development of the new colonies of Upper Canada, New South Wales, and Van Dieman's Land and, in the aftermath of the Napoleonic Wars, the acquisition of Trinidad, St. Lucia, British Guiana, Malta, Mauritius, Ceylon, and the Cape. The forms of colonial governance were as diverse as the colonies themselves. The white settlement colonies of British North America were governed by oligarchies aptly described as "merchantocracies." The islands of the Caribbean remained in the hands of defensive, slave-oppressing plantocracies. The Indian Empire, once governed exclusively by the East India Company, was under the control of an evolving "company-state" that received increasing directions from the British government. Garrisons like Gibraltar and Malta experience direct military rule. Finally, autocratic governors representing the British crown enjoyed a monopoly of authority in the penal colonies of Australia, the Cape Colony, and various other crown colonies scattered around the globe. Despite vastly different governing arrangements, one common feature was the concentration of political power in the hands of an elite few, usually a governor and his appointed advisors.[2]

With its well-established colonies and new territories, the British Empire was also comprised of populations of greater diversity than any previous empire. British administrators faced the challenges of governing British settlers, slave populations, and indigenous peoples as varied as the Iroquois of North America, the Marathas of central India, Australian Aborigines, and the Khoikhoi of the Cape. While historians generally acknowledge the complexities of the indigenous societies that were under British sway, it seems easy to forget that the "British" who ran, defended, and populated the empire were also an increasingly diverse group in this period. The massive migration wave that took 22.6 million Britons out of the British Isles by 1914 had its origins in the migration streams of the 1810s. British people were not only making their way along well-traveled routes to established colonial capitals like Halifax, Calcutta, and Cape Town but also into the colonial interiors.[3] The period also witnessed a shift in the class dynamics of the British Empire. The growing demands of colonial administration, trade, and military service combined with private initiatives to expand the imperial middle class. These demographic movements took place in close interplay with the shift in the economic basis of imperialism from mercantilism to free trade, a shift that clearly reflected middle-class interests.

Back in Britain, the move toward free trade was but part of a series of moral, political, and economic victories that revealed the growing consciousness and influence of the middle class. The work of Leonore Davidoff and Catherine Hall has demonstrated how the "middling sorts" of the eighteenth century were transformed into an assertive middle class that developed a distinctive culture and defended its interests during the first half of the nineteenth century. Their analysis focuses on the crucial role of early Victorian domestic ideology in bringing unity to the middle class and separating it from their social betters and inferiors.[4] Armed with deeply held attitudes concerning the proper places of men and women, religious enthusiasm, and profits gained from industry and empire, the middle class spearheaded the campaigns for abolition, the improvement of society, and parliamentary reform. The latter, achieved in the Reform Act of 1832, brought middle-class men into a power-sharing arrangement with traditional elites while leaving working-class men and all women out in the cold. Thanks to the work of Hall and others, our understanding of middle-class construction and experience is beginning to approach that of the aristocracy and the working class, groups that have long captured the attention of British social historians.

Even though some social historians of Britain have begun factoring the empire into the equation and historians of particular colonies have certainly examined questions of class, the literature on what we might call "the new imperial social history" is very much in its infancy. As David Cannadine asserts in *Ornamentalism*, "There has never been an authoritative social history of the empire."[5] Rather than claiming to offer such a history, this chapter uses Freemasonry to suggest ways to think about the issues of class formation, social mobility, and class relations across the nineteenth-century empire. Evidence from a range of distinct colonial contexts — Nova Scotia, Bermuda, New South Wales and Van Dieman's Land, India, Lower Canada, Upper Canada, and the Cape Colony — reveals that the brotherhood performed similar functions and Freemasons shared similar goals and preoccupations across the empire. First, Masons carefully cultivated their reputation as members of a loyal and respectable institution that was closely connected with imperial elites. This identity was constantly displayed in public ceremonies for all to see. But because of

Charles Aburrow, Deputy District Grand Master of the Transvaal, laying the foundation stone of the new temple for Royal George Lodge at Krugersdorp, Transvaal, 29 October 1898 (copyright, and reproduced by permission of, the United Grand Lodge of England).

Freemasonry's associations with established elites, it also attracted rising men, especially in the settlement colonies. To accompany their new fortunes, social climbers sought more elusive commodities that required skillful negotiation to attain: status, respectability, and political power. Freemasonry helped them acquire these and, in so doing, played an instrumental role in constituting the colonial ruling establishment at a crucial moment in its expansion, during the period from the 1800s through the 1840s. Finally, at the same time it facilitated the broadening of colonial elites, Freemasonry also played an important regulating function. The remarkably fluid social environments of the early-nineteenth-century settlement colonies produced anxieties on the part of established power brokers, the newly prominent, and rising men, and led to contests over men's claims to status and power. Colonial Freemasons deployed various strategies, particularly the subtle use of the discourse of respectability, to balance their institution's claims to inclusiveness with their desire for it to remain exclusive. In this way, as historian James Melton acutely observes, Freemasonry "established new criteria of social distinction that accentuated the gap between the propertied and the unpropertied even while it reduced the distance between the nobility and the middle classes."[6]

Men of Prominence

In 1819 a Mason residing in Nova Scotia noted that "Masonry in this Province has ever been conducted by persons of the most respectable characters; and . . . those who have had the direction and management of public affairs have generally been zealous and active in promoting its growth."[7] His assessment applied to other parts of the world that had been part of the empire since the 1760s or earlier, namely Bermuda, several West Indian colonies, Lower Canada, and Bengal. Whether operating in a plantocracy, a merchantocracy, or a company-state, Freemasonry had developed a reputation as an institution patronized by those in power and useful to those who aspired to prominence. Its very public presence had long received the sanction of colonial governors, who appreciated the usefulness of Masonic venues and beneficial effect of Masonic ceremonies on the societies in their charge.

In the Caribbean and North America, the brotherhood had succeeded in achieving a solid reputation due to its associations with the army, the oversight provided by provincial grand lodges, the active participation of leading citizens, and government patronage. These factors were typically interdependent: if there were no provincial grand lodge to oversee local Masons, leading citizens might shy away from participating; if leading citizens took part in Masonry, metropolitan authorities were more likely to set up a provincial grand lodge. Regardless of local circumstances, Masonry's historic connection with the army did ensure the brotherhood's association with the upper ranks, especially in important military bases like Bermuda and Halifax and in cities conquered from other imperial powers, like Quebec. Regimental lodges had regularly cycled through all three places, and the participation of officers contributed to the esteem in which the brotherhood was held.

The relationship between military officers, colonial governors, and local elites was evident in turn-of-the-century Bermuda. An Irish military lodge attached to the 47th Regiment held private meetings and participated in Masonic church services and festivals on the island between 1783 and 1801. It also helped set up the first civilian lodge. Bermuda Lodge No. 507, established on the western coast of the island in 1793, was identified as the lodge of "a number of the first and most respectable characters in the Government," including Henry Tucker, the lodge's first master, who served as "President" of Bermuda four times between 1796 and 1806. Men of prominence on the other side of the island, in St. George, sought to establish a second civilian lodge in 1797. The prime mover behind this lodge was John Van Norden, a Loyalist who had lived in New Jersey and Nova Scotia (where he had been a master of Windsor Lodge No. 13) before arriving in Bermuda in 1796 to take up a naval post. Van Norden and seven other prominent Bermudians successfully applied to the Grand Lodge of Scotland for a warrant, and St. George's Lodge No. 266 came into being in May 1798. Flourishing in the early nineteenth century, the lodge worked under the sanction of the government. In 1812 Governor James Cockburn granted it a plot of land for a Masonic hall. Van Norden, who was by then both mayor of St. George and Provincial Grand Master, conducted the building's foundation stone laying ceremony. But the lodge outgrew its premises, and, just three years later, the governor deeded the former Sessions House to the lodge for the yearly rental of one peppercorn.[8]

Likewise, in Nova Scotia, Masonry's close connection with the military and governing elites — frequently put on public display — ensured that it was viewed as a respectable and officially sanctioned body. Since the earliest days of British settlement, Freemasonry had enjoyed the patronage of Nova Soctia's "principal inhabitants." Governors Edward Cornwallis and Charles Lawrence headed the First Lodge of Nova Scotia in the 1750s. In 1751, the two lodges in Halifax decided to observe St. John's Day "with the usual pomp" (though mourning the recent death of the Prince of Wales) by walking in procession first to the Governor's House and then to St. Paul's Church. During the next decade and a half, Jonathan Belcher, Chief Justice, legislative councilor, and later lieutenant governor, led the brotherhood as Provincial Grand Master for the Ancients. Belcher's death and the outbreak of the American War interrupted the progress of the Craft, but in 1784, as Loyalists began flocking to Nova Scotia, the Provincial Grand Lodge was revived.[9]

Leading citizens and imperial officials were at the helm of Nova Scotian Masonry for the next four decades. John George Pyke, Provincial Grand Master from 1784 to 1785 (and again from 1811 to 1820), was one of the original settlers of Halifax. He was a prosperous merchant, legislative assemblyman, and police magistrate who saw the renewal of the Provincial Grand Lodge as the "means of cementing us in the bonds of peace and brotherly love" and making "our universal charity and benevolence . . . conspicuous." Within two years, Pyke and his fellow officers set up ten lodges in Loyalist settlements throughout Nova Scotia. Though effective and diligent, Pyke lacked the high social standing of other Freemasons in Halifax at the time, namely the governor, John Parr, who had served as an officer in the 20th Foot between 1745 and 1776. Called up from retirement due to the influx of Loyalists, he became governor in 1782 and was installed as the Provincial Grand Master in 1785. A contemporary history reported Parr as showing "a friendly disposition to promote the honour and welfare of the Craft." Speaking at Parr's installation, the prominent Loyalist Reverend Joshua Weeks observed that local Masons had "unanimously chosen the first personage in the Province to be their Grand Master, that he who governs them as subjects, may govern them as brethren." Parr's willingness to serve, according to Weeks, united Masons in the colony and rendered his authority "more respected."[10] Parr continued in both offices until his death in 1791, when local lodges marched at his funeral.

A fellow Irishman and close advisor to Parr, Richard Bulkeley took over as Provincial Grand Master (and interim administrator of the colony) in 1792. Like Parr, he embodied the link between Freemasonry, the army, and the colonial service: he was an officer in the 45th Foot, an original settler of Halifax, a founding member of the first lodge, and a lifelong colonial administrator who served thirteen governors as provincial secretary and in various other positions. It was during Bulkeley's administration that Prince Edward was in residence in Halifax. As we have seen, he associated publicly with the brotherhood when he laid the foundation stone of Halifax's first Masonic hall in 1800. Governor John Wentworth, who had arrived with the Loyalists in 1783, attended the ceremony in his capacity as master of Royal Nova Scotia Regiment Lodge. Maintaining the brotherhood's longstanding tradition of being associated with Government House, Wentworth became Provincial Grand Master in 1802. He did much to build Nova Scotia into a loyal British enclave. His departure for England in 1810 necessitated the identification of a successor. Former Grand Master Pyke agreed to serve. Under his watch, the brotherhood performed a foundation stone laying ceremony for the Province House (1811), publicly celebrated Nelson's victories over the French, and distributed assistance to the veterans of the War of 1812 — all of which helped Freemasonry maintain its reputation for loyalty and respectability. But Pyke encountered difficulties in dealing with the recently formed United Grand Lodge of England, and on three occasions during his second term local brethren tried to secure a more prominent brother as their leader, first Attorney General Richard Uniacke, then Governor James Kempt (who turned out not to be a Mason), and finally Governor George Ramsay (Lord Dalhousie). Uniacke and Dalhousie refused for fear of ruffling Pyke's feathers, though the latter did associate publicly with the brethren when, for example, he laid the foundation stone of Dalhousie College in 1820. By the end of Pyke's tenure, Freemasonry had enjoyed a seventy-year association with Nova Scotia's most powerful men. It was this illustrious history that, as we will see, made the appointment of a former tanner to the office of provincial grand master in 1820 controversial.

Long-running connections with the military and local elites were thus very important for putting Freemasonry above reproach and suspicion, but the attitude of a colony's governor had an especially profound effect on its fortunes. A comparative examination of Freemasonry's position in the fledgling colony of New South Wales and the solidified Indian empire at the turn of the nineteenth century clearly demonstrates the impact of official sponsorship on the brotherhood's position in local contexts. The British settlement at New South Wales had been in existence for less than a decade when local Masons attempted to set up a lodge. In 1797 the Irish Grand Lodge received a petition from George Kerr, Peter Farrell, and Ger. Black "praying for a War[ran]t to be held in the South Wales Corps serving at Port Jackson in NSW." Though no lodge was working in New South Wales, the colonial authorities had just licensed James Larra, a Jewish emancipist (a convict whose terms had expired but faced an uncertain social status), to build a tavern, The Freemason's Arms, in Parramatta. Despite apparent interest, the Grand Lodge deferred the matter indefinitely.[11] Irish officials likely hesitated to grant the petition because, given the government's increasing suspicion about the associations between Masonic lodges and the United Irishmen, Freemasonry's position in Ireland was tenuous. Grand Lodge authorities certainly did not want to risk alarming the government by spreading Irish Freemasonry in its radical guises to an insecure new colony on the edge of the known world. Moreover, they probably knew very little about the settlement's status, let alone the prospects for Freemasonry there.

Given the unique social geography of the colony, the brotherhood's prospects were not nearly as good as in other parts of the empire. Male convicts had been arriving since 1788, females since 1789; they constituted the majority of the Europeans present. The governor, who oversaw a growing population of convicts, Aborigines, military personnel, and maritime sojourners, enjoyed complete executive power. But he faced challenges from many quarters. The three men who petitioned the Irish Grand Lodge in 1797 were members of the New South Wales Corps, which had been raised and dispatched by the British government in 1789 to oversee convicts and maintain order in the colony. Emerging from the earliest days when the colony was engaged in a basic struggle for survival, the Corps had become, by 1795, the primary military, economic, and political force in the colony. Officers of the Corps amassed substantial landholdings, dominated the judicial system, and made huge profits by monopolizing the rum trade and all imported spirits. Rum became a form of currency, paid to laborers in exchange for their services. Their rum monopoly thus allowed the Corps to control the nascent colonial economy during the administrations of the colony's second and third governors. The third, Philip King, arrived in 1800 to find the economy starting to diversify but the Corps still firmly entrenched. The society he encountered was also starkly stratified: colonial officials and Corps officers at the top, convicts at the bottom, and a small number of free settlers and emancipists wedged in the middle.

Both metropolitan developments and the local state of affairs led Governor King to be wary of Freemasonry. In 1803 "several officers of his Majesty's ships *Glatton* and *Buffalo*, together with some respectable inhabitants," petitioned Governor King to meet as a Masonic lodge. He refused the request. The men, including the wealthy Irish transportee Sir Henry Browne Hayes, ignored this instruction and held a clandestine lodge meeting at the public house of Thomas Whittle, an NCO in the New South Wales Corps. Catching wind of the meeting, the governor sent troops to break it up. A contemporary colonist recorded in his diary: "May 22nd, 1803. — A number of Masons, meeting at the house of Sergeant Whittel, in Sydney were arrested, and, after serious report, were discharged as having no willful intention to disturb the peace." Naval officers and local inhabitants attempted to hold another lodge meeting aboard a ship in the harbor, but King suppressed that meeting as well. Hayes was convicted and sentenced to further transportation (to Van Dieman's Land), though the government decided not to enforce his sentence, perhaps because of his status as a gentleman.[12]

Either unaware of or unconvinced by the concerted efforts of Freemasons in the British Isles and other parts of the empire to align the fraternity with the forces of loyalty and respectability, King associated the brotherhood with radicalism and troublemaking. He might have been concerned about Freemasonry's implication in the 'Ninety Eight, since most of the 780 Irish the colony received between 1800 and 1802 were political prisoners. Another concern was the possibility of the French recruiting disaffected Irishmen to help oust the British from New South Wales. King might also have seen a Masonic lodge as an internal political threat. Historian Alan Atkinson suggests that "such a lodge would have been a ritual meeting ground for the men among Sydney's elite, including soldiers like himself [Whittle], adding even further to the town's political voice." Whatever his reasons, King issued a General Order, published in the *Sydney Gazette* on 22 May 1803, officially banning Masonic meetings. If he refused to acknowledge Freemasonry's growing reputation for loyalism, he was nonetheless well aware of the brotherhood's popularity. King informed the Colonial Undersecretary that "every soldier and other person would have been made a Freemason, had not the most decided means been taken to prevent it."[13] Thus, because it had not received the governor's support, Freemasonry could not become established during the early decades of the colony's existence. It would take the arrival of a sympathetic governor — one who also happened to be a Freemason — for the brotherhood to flourish in New South Wales.

While a governor's approval was required for Freemasonry to take root in Australia, in India a governor's active participation in Freemasonry could make a significant difference in its fortunes from year to year. By the early nineteenth century, Freemasonry had enjoyed a long-running presence on the subcontinent. As we have seen, company servants (both civil and military) and merchants became Masons. Native and foreign inhabitants of the metropolises of Calcutta, Madras, and Bombay regularly witnessed public Masonic activities and read about them in the local press. To be sure, the fortunes of Masonry ebbed and flowed with the shifting pace of local politics, metropolitan directives, and imperial affairs in general. In 1803 a local Mason had reported that the "war in which our Government is engaged, with the Marathas, has been the cause of the temporary interruption to several of our subordinate lodges on this coast."[14] Yet the same wars that brought a temporary suspension in Masonic activity also ultimately led to the extension of Freemasonry into new parts of the subcontinent as first the East India Company and then the British Raj advanced during the nineteenth century.

High-ranking officials like governors-general Cornwallis and Wellesley had associated with Freemasonry in India at the end of the eighteenth century, but during the administration of Francis Rawdon-Hastings (then Earl of Moira, later Marquess of Hastings) the relationship between Freemasonry and the governing authorities became highly symbiotic. As we have seen, Moira was one of the most prominent Freemasons in England. In 1813 he completed a twenty-three-year term as English Grand Master, in which capacity he had achieved Freemasonry's exemption from the Unlawful Societies Act and the union between the Ancients and Moderns. Thanks to his administration, Freemasonry was well on its way to solidifying its reputation as a loyal, respectable institution supported by the government. His close friend and Masonic brother the Prince of Wales helped him secure the appointment as governor general of Bengal and commander-in-chief of India. The English Grand Lodge hosted a magnificent gala in honor of his service to the Craft on the eve of his departure.

Six royal dukes and dozens of other prominent Masons took part in the festivities, which included a public ceremony — with ladies in attendance — and a Grand Lodge meeting and banquet.

Moira's appointment to high office did not lessen his commitment to Freemasonry, which was in evidence even before he arrived in India. His transport stopped off at the Isle of France (Mauritius), captured from the French in 1810. He toured all parts of the verdant island and rested in preparation for the final leg of the trip. Yet he did not take a break from his Masonic duties. On 19 August Moira presided over a Masonic procession and ceremony to lay the "first stone of the re-edification" of the Catholic Cathedral of Port Louis, which French residents sympathetic to the Revolution had destroyed in the 1790s. Moira recorded in his journal that he had inspected the French lodges on the island prior to the ceremony and then, after a public procession, "laid the stone with all the solemnity that could make this act impressive." Noting the positive impact the event had on the French residents, he expressed his "great satisfaction to have officiated on this occasion." Moira probably considered such performances welcome preparation for the role awaiting him in India, where, in addition to serving as governor general, he would also take on the mantle of "Acting Grand Master of the Most Ancient and Honorable Society of Free and Accepted Masons in and over the whole of India and the Islands in the Indian seas."[15]

Moira's administration (1813–23) marked some important shifts in the nature of British rule. He was the first governor to administer India after the East India Company Charter Act of 1813 had scaled back the monopoly of the company and opened India to missionaries. He pursued land and educational reforms and also instituted freedom of the press. Through wars with the Gurkhas in Nepal (1814–16) and the Marathas in central India (1816), he brought immense swaths of territory under British rule; he also sent fellow Mason Stamford Raffles to purchase Singapore in 1819. As Britain's presence on the subcontinent solidified, increasing numbers of Britons made their way to India as soldiers, administrators, traders, evangelizers, and professionals. The social composition of Masonic lodges in the early 1800s reflected the growing diversity of this population. Once in India, Lord Moira observed that Freemasonry was a "Body spread throughout all classes of Society," a fairly accurate assessment, as long as one understood "all classes of Society" to mean British army personnel and resident European males. For example, Madras's Lodge Perfect Unanimity was composed of civil servants, advocates, merchants, attorneys, and army officers, as well as a chaplain, surgeon, member of council, deputy commercial resident, master of the ceremonies, and secretary.[16]

Like British North American Masons who eagerly accepted the leadership of prominent brethren, Masons in Bengal rejoiced at having an illustrious Mason in their midst. They realized Moira's presence would reflect positively on the brotherhood in their part of the empire. Evidence of Moira's commitment to Masonry came within a month of his arrival, when he constituted a new lodge in Calcutta, appropriately named "the Moira, Freedom and Fidelity Lodge." It soon boasted thirty-eight members. Moira welcomed opportunities to appear with the brotherhood. He received a deputation of local Masons in conjunction with a public levee at Government House in December 1813. As it did with all Masonic events, the *Calcutta Gazette* reported on the reception. At nine o'clock, 120 members of the Calcutta lodges marched into the appointed room and sat on crimson velvet cushions. The lodges' officers then "fil[ed] in a semicircle in front of His Lordship, who, decorated with the superb Masonic Lodges in England and various other jewels of the higher orders of Masonry, stood with his personal Staff." Members of the Provincial Grand Lodge, "as British Masons glorying in the mild and beneficent principles of our ancient and honourable institution," welcomed Moira and observed that his arrival portended "the highest prospects of encouragement and protection." The self-described "respectable body of Free Masons" then turned their attention to their new "Patroness of the Craft of India," Lady Moira. They did not fail to remind the audience that Countess Moira's grandfather, the fourth Earl of Loudon, had served as the English Grand Master in 1736. They expressed joy that "in your happy union with the Earl of Moira, the finest springs of our sublime institution have joined together in an ample current, to spread more widely, the luxuriant tide of benevolence, generosity, charity and social affection." She graciously accepted the Masons' "flattering mark of . . . good will."[17]

The lodges' sanguinity was not misplaced — during Moira's time in India, Freemasonry experienced a revival and solidified its reputation as a loyal and respectable brotherhood. One of the toasts at a Masonic banquet in 1813 referred to "the flourishing state of the Royal Art in Bengal." The city's most prominent lodge (Industry and Perseverance), which had ceased meeting between 1803 and 1812, welcomed six initiates and one joining member in 1813. Moira resuscitated the Provincial Grand Lodge of Bengal under the Hon. Archibald Seton (Resident of Delhi and shortly thereafter governor of Penang, 1811–12), though Moira himself did not participate in its day-to-day affairs. He also instructed local Masons to pay "a rigid attention to the established forms [rituals and procedures]" because "the uniformity of observances in Masonic Lodges satisfies all Governments that they are safe."[18]

Like his counterparts in other parts of the empire, Moira believed that Masonry served several useful purposes in the colonial setting. Moira reflected on his role in encouraging the Royal Art in India as he was preparing to depart for England in 1822. He acknowledged that he had always "felt a lively interest in the promotion of what I believe to be a highly beneficial Society." He viewed Freemasonry as a civilizing agent which had, in an earlier age, helped rescue Europe from "semi-barbarism." Its primary lesson was that "throughout the necessary gradations in a community, and amid the unavoidable destructions arising from talents or property, man was still the Brother of Man." This ideal of brotherhood and its corollaries (faith, charity, and loyalty), Moira asserted, had certainly influenced his actions as governor: "The doctrine imbibed in the Lodge became the rule of action for the man of might in his public sphere, and his example disseminated the principles of humanity and justice to the utmost extent of the circle." His participation in the brotherhood, he concluded, had helped him relieve "the despotism, the ferocity, the degradation of manhood in the Asiatic regions where no casual ray of Masonry has ever pierced the gloom." To bid farewell to their leader, Calcutta Masons marched in procession to Government House where, observed by 800 people, they presented him with an address. A few weeks later, Lord and Lady Moira attended the St. John's Day service at the Cathedral Church of Bengal and were feted at a banquet at the Town Hall, which was specially decorated with transparencies depicting Faith, Hope, and Charity.[19]

Moira's departure did lead to a temporary downturn in Masonry's fortunes in Bengal, but by the 1820s it was clear that the brotherhood had taken up a conspicuous place beside the company-state in the growing movement to spread British civilization through India. It regularly played a key role in the ceremonial life of the raj as it established institutions aimed at the betterment of the native population. In 1824 Calcutta Masons performed foundation stone laying ceremonies for the New Hindoo College and the New Mahommedan College (described at the beginning of this chapter). Speeches on both occasions revealed Freemasons' belief that their institution could contribute to the interventionist policies of new Utilitarianism-inspired governors. John Pascal Larkins, East India Company merchant, shipowner, and Provincial Grand Master, proclaimed: "We have the gratification of adding this evening another stone to the Grand Arch of Moral Improvement . . . and let us implore the Almighty Architect of the Universe to bless the structure which is about to be raised for the diffusion of knowledge." Institutions like schools, consecrated by British Freemasons, he observed, would help raise "the Native Inhabitants" from "the state of moral degradation into which the greater mass of the people confessedly are sunk" to "that state of amelioration, to which the efforts now making for their improvement must necessarily lead." The *Calcutta Gazette* congratulated the Masons on pulling off a scene that conveyed the "gratifying appearance of perfect union between the European and Native population of this City."[20]

Meanwhile, in Madras, local brethren also went about their Masonic business: attending regular lodge meetings, observing St. John's Days, practicing charity, and consecrating new buildings (in 1823 they marched in procession to "Black Town" where they laid the foundation stone of a Male Orphan Asylum).[21] Growing sporadically, Madras Masonry did not enjoy the patronage of a prominent brother until Lord Elphinstone arrived on the scene as governor of Madras in 1837. Membership in the oldest and most prestigious lodge, Lodge Perfect Unanimity, reached 102 in 1838; Elphinstone became Provincial Grand Master in 1840, and lodges began to multiply. One sign of prosperity was the decision to build a Masonic Temple. A fundraising campaign quickly amassed 14,000 rupees (including a 500 rupee pledge from the governor). As had been the case in Bermuda, the government granted a building site, and on 24 June 1839, Elphinstone laid the foundation stone. London's *Freemasons' Quarterly Review* monitored its progress and soon reported that "the Masonic Temple which has been gradually rising on the beach near Capper's, St. Thome, has of late assumed a peculiarly neat and imposing aspect as regards its exterior. To the masonic zeal of Lord Elphinstone we are much indebted."[22] When it was completed, Madras Masons used the site for their annual ball, which was "well known to the ladies of this presidency, for its brilliancy, and the gallant attention ever shown to them by the Brethren on this occasion."[23] As in other parts of the empire, the brotherhood had secured the sanction of the government, was patronized by important officials, and was instrumental in ceremonies and events designed to impress—upon local inhabitants as well as British women—the power of Britain and its empire builders.

Social Climbing in British North America

The eagerness with which men like Dalhousie, Moira, and Elphinstone participated in Freemasonry enabled the brotherhood to maintain a reputation as a loyal, respectable, and well-connected institution. Its associations with men of prominence—local elites as well as high-ranking military and government officials—made it attractive to men of more humble origins who had found material success in the colonies and craved status and power to accompany it. In lodge meetings, rising men became the brethren of prominent and powerful citizens. Their participation in the brotherhood might help them get contracts, secure promotions, or win elections. Some of Masonry's respectability could even rub off on them.

What gave rising men the confidence that they could join such a brotherhood was Freemasonry's claim to embrace not only men of various religious, political, and national backgrounds, but also men from across the social spectrum. As Margaret Jacob succinctly puts it, Masonry was designed to operate as "a social nexus that bridged profound class differences." Contemporaries made similar observations. The radical politician and prominent Freemason Lord Durham (who would become governor general of Canada in 1838) asserted that he encouraged Masonry "because it affords the only natural ground on which all ranks and classes can meet in perfect equality and associate without degradation or mortification, whether for purposes of moral instruction or social intercourse."[24]

Durham's assurance that highly placed men, like himself, could participate in Masonry without risking social degradation pointed to that fact that equality, as understood by Masons, was not a recipe for leveling society. When Masonic orators evoked equality, they were always careful to circumscribe its operation to the lodge. Outside lodge meetings, rank resumed its relevance. Moreover, Masons were very careful about whom they admitted to their lodges in the first place, keeping the inclusiveness promised by their ideology in check through a range of exclusionary strategies. Some were explicit regulations. The *Constitutions* had always forbidden the admission of women, eunuchs, slaves, disabled men, and scandalous characters. During the early nineteenth century, lodges confirmed these policies when disabled men, including some blind candidates, sought admission. Illiterate candidates and criminals were also consistently turned away. Moreover, this period witnessed the emergence of a category known as "serving brethren" (lower-status men who were allowed in the lodge to serve their betters but not given full membership) and new regulations preventing army lodges from admitting privates.[25]

But rather than drastically alter Masonic ideology to close off the brotherhood to men of humble origins, lodges adopted subtle strategies to ensure Freemasonry's prestige was not diluted. In the early-nineteenth-century empire — where the struggle to balance inclusiveness with the need to remain exclusive was particularly acute — local Masons could regulate Freemasonry by setting fees so high that membership was restricted to those who could afford the costs of brotherhood. Local power struggles also reveal how colonial Masons strategically deployed the language of respectability first to challenge lower-status Masons who could gain entrance into Scottish and Irish lodges and, second, the credentials of some men of humble origins to hold high Masonic office (and, by implication, such men's claims to social status and political power).

The act of balancing inclusiveness with exclusivity was clearly evident in British North America during the 1820s and 1830s, a period of tremendous growth for the settlement colonies. Between 1815 and 1850, 800,000 Britons settled in British North America. This population influx went hand in hand with a diversification of the British North American economy as well as its constituent social classes, as immigrants took advantage of increased opportunities for capital accumulation and social mobility. The expansion of the middle class produced newly prominent men who sought a voice in local and provincial politics. As tanners, brewers, and merchants achieved wealth and became civic-minded, they challenged established elites in the Maritimes and Lower Canada, which had long been part of the empire, and in the new colony of Upper Canada, whose "natural leaders" had quickly emerged with the arrival of Loyalists during the 1780s. Local oligarchies (referred to as the "Chateau Clique" in Lower Canada and the "Family Compact" in Upper Canada) remained powerful, but these shifts did result in an expansion of the colonial ruling establishment, symbolized by the achievement of responsible government in the 1840s. This broadening of the category of "men of property" who possessed the privileges of citizenship in British North America might be seen as the culminating moment of a wider, transatlantic "age of reform" that had begun with the abolition of the slave trade in 1807.

A period of great flux always produces anxieties on the part of traditional power brokers, the newly prominent, and aspiring men alike. Jockeying for social status and political power was a demanding and risky exercise. Such tensions were clearly evident in the world of Freemasonry, a brotherhood that had well-known connections to established elites but increasingly appealed to social climbers. Membership in Masonry regularly served as a springboard for rising men, who could, in turn, use the fraternity as a sifting device to identify who was and who was not "respectable" and thus had a legitimate claim to membership in the ruling establishment.

NOVA SCOTIA

As we have seen, through its long-running connection with the military and the colonial administration, Freemasonry had established itself as one of the preeminent institutions in Halifax, Nova Scotia. Masons in early-nineteenth-century Halifax were highly motivated to continue their brotherhood's associations with the ruling establishment. The respectable tenor of Nova Scotian Masonry was preserved primarily through the efforts of St. Andrew's and St. John's Lodges, the two oldest lodges in the colony. They provided all the officers of the Second Provincial Grand Lodge of Nova Scotia (1782–1829) and also took a leading role in building Halifax's Masonic hall and directing the fraternity's public appearances.[26] Through their dominance of the provincial grand lodge, prominent Halifax Masons hoped to control lodges throughout the colony. But their position caused resentment and came under challenge in the mid-1820s. This decade witnessed the first large-scale immigration of Scottish Highlanders, cleared from the Highlands by their profit-seeking landlords, and Lowlanders who sought to take advantage of opportunities across the Atlantic. As a result, the Grand Lodge of Scotland started setting up lodges in Nova Scotia. English lodges in Nova Scotia feared this influx because, they argued, Scottish lodges were willing to admit men who were not "of the best standing amongst Masons." Officials in the English Provincial Grand Lodge were worried that if the Scottish Grand Lodge kept warranting lodges, then men rejected for membership or suspended by their lodges would be admitted to Scottish lodges: "Consequently all regularity and harmony of the Fraternity would be superseded by Discord and Confusion." When some Nova Scotians did apply to Scotland for a warrant, the master of St. John's Lodge accused the Grand Lodge of being "in Error as to the Respectability of the Parties." In his opinion, St. John's Lodge was composed of "highly respectable" men, while those applying to the Grand Lodge of Scotland were "in Humble life." Masons affiliated with the English lodges asked English authorities to prevent the granting of Scottish warrants, but it had no power to do so. Scottish authorities organized several lodges and set up their own provincial grand lodge, with the result that ethnic tensions continued to trouble Masonry in Nova Scotia until the 1840s, when local Masons worked out a compromise.[27]

In addition to trying to prevent the establishment of Scottish lodges that would initiate humble men, Masons in Halifax sought to preserve their brotherhood's respectability through close monitoring of the office of provincial grand master. Back in 1786, at the installation of Governor Parr as Provincial Grand Master, the Grand Chaplain had proclaimed that "it is the fixed determination of this G. Lodge to put the Fraternity upon the most respectable footing possible, and to be always governed by the most worthy and honourable brother they can find in the Province." But his early-nineteenth-century successors were not in agreement about who among them was the most worthy and honorable. During the 1820s members of St. John's Lodge, and particularly newspaper publisher Edmund Ward, challenged the appointment of a highly dedicated Mason named John Albro as provincial grand master.[28] Their case against him hinged on the claim that he was insufficiently respectable to hold such an important Masonic office. Albro was one of those ambitious social climbers whose rise indicated the broadening of the merchantocracy governing Nova Scotia. As a young man in Halifax, he had started out as a tanner and a butcher. By 1812 he had become a merchant specializing in hardware. Successful in business, he gradually worked his way into the Halifax elite and became active in civic affairs. He erected two stone buildings near Sackville Street and rose through the ranks of the Halifax militia. Involvement in two key institutions — St. Paul's Church, where he served as a vestryman and churchwarden, and the Freemasons — certainly facilitated his rise to prominence and his election to the legislature (where he served between 1818 and 1822). Like social climbers in other colonies, Albro realized that membership in Freemasonry could offer an entrée to the upper reaches of society. By 1820 he had achieved sufficient prominence in Masonic circles to win election as Provincial Grand Master of Nova Scotia, a decision that members of St. John's Lodge (who backed the more prominent and politically connected attorney general, John Uniacke) came to resent.

The controversy surrounding Albro's election revealed how colonial Masons scrutinized a man's level of respectability to determine his suitability for high Masonic office. After an initial spat that resulted in the temporary suspension of St. John's Lodge and the intervention of the English Grand Lodge, members of St. John's decided to tolerate Albro. "If he is not in that elevated rank of Life that could be wished," they wrote to London, "he is nevertheless respectable and a Man of Property and has been emminently [sic] useful to the Fraternity." They noted his willingness to resign "whenever any Person of superior Rank or Attainment will take the situation" (they now had their eyes on Sir Howard Douglass, governor of New Brunswick). But when it later appeared to the master and members of St. John's Lodge that Albro might not so easily relinquish his office, they began to attack his character. They contrasted their own respectability with Albro's lack of it, describing him as a man who "does not hold that rank in society which is desirable for the head of a body so numerous and respectable." St. John's Lodge "contain[ed] the largest proportion of *respectable* inhabitants of Halifax together with officers of the Army and Navy." By contrast, Albro was not "a gentleman of rank and respectability"; he had even been seen, the master of St. John's claimed, "drinking in a Grog Shop." Concerns over Albro's administration had caused "respectable men" to shy away from the fraternity; members of Halifax's most prominent lodges "will never be satisfied with an individual of Mr Albro's rank and standing." The situation had become so desperate, according to Ward and St. John's, that Albro and his supporters had even opposed the selection of Governor Dalhousie as their leader.[29]

In the end, however, the Grand Lodge of England decided to reappoint Albro as its Provincial Grand Master. Metropolitan authorities were convinced he was sufficiently qualified for the office (his supporters had assured them that he was a "merchant of respectability," a member of the Legislative Assembly, a Justice of the Peace, and a public commissioner). He might not have the support of some prominent Masons in Halifax, but he still proved to be an active and reliable leader during a difficult time for the fraternity. Under his watch, Freemasonry maintained its strong public presence through ceremonial appearances: to lay the foundation stones of Dalhousie College (1820), to observe the completion of the Shubenacadie Canal (1826), and to honor Queen Victoria with a procession and loyal address to the lieutenant governor upon her accession to the throne (1837). Such occasions gave Masons the opportunity to demonstrate, through expressions of their "unshaken attachment to the Throne and peaceable submission to the laws," their alliance with the imperial state.[30]

By the time Alexander Keith (a Scottish brewer who rose to the rank of mayor and then legislative councilor) took over the office in 1839, it was no longer questioned that men of humble origins who had achieved wealth and prominence were suited to Masonic leadership. Keith led a revival of Masonry in the colony, resolved the tensions between English and Scottish lodges, and paved the way for the founding of an independent Grand Lodge of Nova Scotia later in the century. One highlight of his administration was Halifax Masons' hosting of a charity ball, attended by 600 people, including the lieutenant governor, in 1854. The band of the 72nd Highlanders provided the evening's music. Guests were also treated to a spectacle of global empire, presented by locals dressed as "flower girls and peasants of other climes, English squires, knights of Malta, the swarthy Indian, the dignified chief of the Snake tribe, the Spanish brigand, the Turk, the Portuguese muleteer, the sober Quaker, the sturdy Highlander, and the youthful Jockey, carefully watched over by a 'Mr. Pickwick' and 'the Wandering Jew.'" This proved, according to reports, "that the principles of Masonry knew no nation in particular."[31] It also proved the brotherhood's deep implication in empire.

LOWER CANADA

In the aftermath of Prince Edward's administration of Masonry in Lower Canada, Alexander Wilson, who was a surgeon in the Royal Artillery and acting head of the brotherhood, petitioned metropolitan authorities to name a provincial grand master for Quebec. According to Wilson, Freemasonry's prospects depended entirely on the brotherhood's ability to cast itself as a respectable institution. Lower Canadian Freemasons, Wilson informed the metropolitan authorities, wished "to have masonry cultivated amongst people in a superior rank of life" and "form a Grand Lodge and fill it with very respectable characters."[32] But, as in Nova Scotia, local Masons often disagreed over who was sufficiently respectable to hold high Masonic office, especially given the fluid social environment in which they lived.

The merchantocracy that ran Lower Canada in the early nineteenth century was limited but not entirely closed. If he possessed wealth, had friends in high places, and was unswerving in his loyalty to the crown, even a French Canadian merchant could work his way into elite circles. Being a Mason also opened doors. The man who took over from Prince Edward as Provincial Grand Master had just these credentials. Claude Dénéchau, the first civilian to hold the office of provincial grand master, was born into a middle-class French Canadian family in Quebec, where as a young man he entered into business. Within a few years, he had become a highly successful grain merchant. Eager to achieve prominence and respectability to accompany his wealth, he joined several institutions that helped him work his way into the English-dominated merchantocracy controlling the colony at the time. His first step was to become a Freemason. In 1800, under the sponsorship of his friend Prince Edward, Dénéchau joined the preeminent Masonic lodge in Montreal, St. Paul's, known for its loyalty to the British administration.[33] That year he was also initiated into the prominent Merchants' Lodge No. 40 at Quebec.

Membership in Freemasonry was not the only move that endeared Dénéchau to the Anglophone merchantocracy. From 1804, he served as an officer in the militia. In 1808 he was elected for the first time to the Lower Canadian House of Assembly, where he represented the interests of English Quebecers until 1820. By 1811 he was wealthy enough to purchase the seigneury of Berthier. Active in numerous organizations in and around Quebec, he took seriously what he perceived as the responsibilities of a respectable country squire. His success in securing government appointments (as a justice of the peace, commissioner of oaths, and commissioner for the relief of the insane and foundlings) indicated his rise to prominence. Meanwhile, Dénéchau's climbing up the ranks of Freemasonry both facilitated and confirmed his rise in the political and social circles of Lower Canada. In 1805 he was elected to office in the Provincial Grand Lodge under Edward. By 1812 he had effectively taken over the government of the Craft in the colony. As discussed in Chapter 4, Dénéchau was unequivocal in expressing support for the crown. The position of Provincial Grand Master gave him numerous public opportunities to demonstrate that he saw loyalty as the most important obligation of a Mason. One would come late in his career when, accompanied by Governor Dalhousie and the brethren of Quebec City, he orchestrated the ceremony to lay the foundation stone of the Wolfe and Montcalm Monument.[34]

Dénéchau's wealth, status, and impeccable credentials as a Loyalist, however, did not make him immune to attack from other Masons who questioned his suitability for high Masonic office. A power struggle that erupted in Lower Canadian Masonry in the early 1820s, like the dispute in Nova Scotia, shows rivals drawing on the discourse of respectability to discredit one another. Men on both sides did agree that having a prominent, respectable provincial grand master was crucial for solidifying Lower Canadian Masonry. One of Dénéchau's supporters urged metropolitan authorities to confirm Dénéchau as the Provincial Grand Master in 1819 (since 1812 members of the Provincial Grand Lodge had elected him even though English authorities insisted that the provincial grand mastership was an appointed position). If they failed to appoint him, the Provincial Grand Lodge, "which has been many years upheld by some of the most respectable persons here," would have no choice but to stop meeting. Without a governing authority, "it is obvious the Craft will fall into disorganization, ill repute and contempt." But Masons in the increasingly important and English-dominated city of Montreal felt that Dénéchau was not quite respectable enough. The very lodge that had initiated him, St. Paul's, led a campaign to circumscribe his jurisdiction by severing the Masonic province of Lower Canada into two administrative districts. "The fact is," they argued, "that Br. Denechau, though a very respectable man — that is, a good, quiet Canadian Country Gentleman without much talent or influence — is not exactly the man qualified to make an effective Provincial Grand Master. His station and influence in society are not sufficiently distinguished to bestow importance upon the office held by him." The Montreal brethren proposed the Grand Lodge replace Dénéchau with the Hon. John Hale, a legislative councilor and "one of the leading men in the Province." The English Grand Lodge capitulated by splitting the province of Lower Canada into two jurisdictions. Although it left the long-serving Dénéchau in charge of the Quebec region, the Grand Lodge drastically curtailed his sphere of influence by appointing William McGillivray as Provincial Grand Master of Montreal. In a subsequent correspondence, metropolitan authorities noted McGillivray's "high respectability and personal influence in the Province" and described him as a "Gentleman whose station and influence in the Province will confer importance on his mission."[35]

The Masonic power struggle offers a window onto broader issues and tensions evident in Lower Canada at the time. First, it shows the rise of Montreal in the early decades of the nineteenth century. Though Quebec remained the center of government, Montreal now challenged Quebec as the primary commercial center of Lower Canada.[36] Montreal's growing significance was due in large part to the activities of English merchants like William McGillivray. William and his brother Simon (who was Provincial Grand Master of Upper Canada) were nephews of North West Company founder Simon McTavish. McTavish and fellow Montrealers had established the fur-trading firm to rival the London-based Hudson's Bay Company in 1784. Working his way up from a clerkship in 1784, William took over the company when his uncle died in 1804 during a period of intense competition within the fur-trading industry (due to a declining beaver supply, manpower shortages, and inflation). Challenged by the Hudson's Bay Company and American rivals, the North West Company suffered a number of setbacks during the 1810s and was forced to merge into the Hudson's Bay Company in 1821. It was in the aftermath of this business crisis that William McGillivray launched his successful bid to take over Freemasonry in Montreal and its environs. He was certainly interested in solidifying his own social position in the wake of his company's collapse, and assuming a prominent role in Lower Canadian Masonry helped him to do just that.

The dispute between Dénéchau and McGillivray also reflected the growing ethnic tensions between the Anglophone and Francophone communities of Lower Canada and the first stirrings of French Canadian nationalism in the early decades of the nineteenth century. French Canadian seigneurs, professionals, and merchants were elected in increasing numbers to the House of Assembly, but the English-speaking bourgeoisie continued to dominate the mercantile, lumber, and ship-building sectors of the economy. Devoted to upholding the crown, the British connection, and the established churches, it was content with the oligarchic rule that concentrated power on the governor and his appointed advisors (men like McGillivray). Most members of the French community, on the other hand, resented the power of the English-dominated merchantocracy and began agitating for more representative institutions. Although Dénéchau was clearly on the side of the oligarchy, his French origins and Roman Catholicism made him suspect to elites. The documents are not explicit on this point, but an underlying anti-Catholic bias, couched in the language of respectability, was probably a factor.

For his part, Dénéchau continued to hope, even after his jurisdiction was limited to Quebec, that Freemasonry could serve as a bridge between the French and English communities and worked to establish lodges for this purpose. He noted in an optimistic 1822 letter that many recently initiated brethren were Catholics and anticipated the time "when our most ancient and honourable Institution will not be less revered by our Catholic Fellow Subjects in this quarter of the Empire, than by our Protestant Fellow Subjects in Britain and elsewhere." But in Lower Canada, as in Britain, Freemasonry was becoming increasingly associated with Protestantism. One year later, William McGillivray tried to explain to English authorities why in Montreal, a city of 25,000 people, there were only three Masonic lodges. "The reason is, that more than *threefourth* of the inhabitants are Roman Catholics, and their Priests absolutely forbid any of them becoming Free masons under the penalty of incurring the censures of the Church, which very few of them have the boldness to brave. Freemasonry," he continued, "is therefore almost exclusively confined to the British and American part of the inhabitants in the town and district." Dénéchau himself was soon forced to acknowledge that it was difficult to lead and foster the fraternity in the face of "almost overwhelming prejudices of my Countrymen (the Canadians) encouraged by the influence of our Catholic Clergy, who are decidedly hostile to our liberal Institutions." Whether under pressure from his family or concerned about his soul, Dénéchau renounced Freemasonry a few months before he died (after thirty-six years of service to the brotherhood). His departure from the fraternity in many ways marked British North American Freemasonry's last break with its relatively inclusive past. In the future, the brotherhood would be almost exclusively associated with the Anglophone, Protestant population.[37]

As Dénéchau struggled, McGillivray directed his attention to making sure Montreal Freemasonry remained on a respectable footing. Shortly after his appointment, he inspected the lodges in his district in order to find men to fill the offices of the provincial grand lodge. "[It] was no easy task," he complained to London, "as few characters of the Fraternity in this District were in all respects qualified to fill the station of Principal Officers." He had to resort to choosing "the most respectable Masons that could be found." One way to ensure the Provincial Grand Lodge's respectability was to demand its officers pay high fees (a strategy adopted elsewhere in the empire); they also had to provide their own regalia and were fined for not attending meetings. But four months later, he was able to report: "The Lodges in this Town have been industrious during the winter, and I have the pleasure to state . . . that they have improved in every respect — uniformity in Masonic clothing has been adopted, and they have increased their number of members from a more select class of the community."[38]

McGillivray's successor to the office of provincial grand master was indeed a member of the "more select class of the community." Emigrating to Montreal at the age of eighteen, John Molson was the orphaned son of a Lincolnshire landowner. He entered into partnerships with two butchers and a brewer upon his arrival in Montreal. Molson took over the brewing enterprise at the age of twenty-one and turned it into a highly profitable business. Meanwhile, he joined St. Paul's Lodge, where he associated with McGillivray and other Scottish merchants who dominated Montreal at the time. By the early 1820s, he had diversified his business interests (into steam shipping), been elected to the Legislative Assembly, and been made an officer in the Provincial Grand Lodge of Lower Canada. In this period, he was also the prime mover behind the building of the Montreal General Hospital, and he officiated, as Provincial Grand Master, in the laying of the foundation stone for its Richardson Wing in 1831. Finally, he was involved in the founding of the Bank of Montreal and served as president when it oversaw the liquidation of the brothers Simon and William McGillivray's North West Company. In these ways, Molson and his sons became firmly entrenched in the Anglophone community that dominated Montreal, supported proposals to unite Upper and Lower Canada (and thereby dilute the influence of French Canadians), and came under challenge from the Patriote Party in the 1830s.[39] Thanks to the involvement of men like John Molson, Freemasonry was able to secure explicit exemption from legislation designed to suppress seditious societies in the aftermath of the 1837 rebellion.[40]

Meanwhile, in Upper Canada, where Freemasonry was particularly attractive to rising men, comparable tactics on the part of Simon McGillivray also established the brotherhood's reputation as a respectable institution. Simon standardized lodge practices, encouraged prominent men to participate, and adopted measures to exclude "improper persons." One such measure was to demand the regular payment of dues from members. When some Upper Canadian Masons objected to this policy, McGillivray opined: "Any individual to whom the amount of the fee was an object was a very unfit person to be admitted a member of the lodge." Upper Canadian Freemasonry cultivated a strong public presence by conducting at least eleven foundation stone laying ceremonies between 1824 and 1856. And, as in Lower Canada, Freemasonry was explicitly exempted from legislation proposed to curb problematic associations, in this case the Orange Order.[41] The efforts of McGillivray and his successors thus set the stage for a long-term association between the institution and colonial elites, including some of the most prominent British Canadians of the second half of the nineteenth century (such as Allan Napier MacNab and John A. Macdonald).

Moving Up Down Under

New South Wales shared with Upper Canada the distinction of being a relatively young colony, built from the ground up in the aftermath of the American War. It too experienced population growth, though not on the scale of British North America (getting to Australia was of course a more daunting proposition than crossing the Atlantic). The overall numbers were smaller but the demographic shift underway was nevertheless profound. Arriving convicts outnumbered free immigrants by a ratio of ten to one in New South Wales during the 1810s. The ratio dropped to three to one in the next decade. Growing opposition to transportation and the effects of assisted migration schemes tilted the balance in the 1830s, with 40,300 settlers to 31,200 convicts. Imperial duty, the chance to be reunited with transported family members, and, increasingly, economic opportunity beckoned many. The influx of free settlers complicated an already unusual society. It remained an overwhelmingly male environment, though gender ratios began to balance as the century proceeded. And of course the well-established racial order that put Europeans in a position of dominance over Aborigines was only reinforced. It was in the makeup and dynamics of the "free white" population that the colony's atmosphere grew more complex and, as a result, divisive. A colonist living in New South Wales from the 1820s on was classified according to his legal status (exclusive vs. emancipist), social position (whether or not he was a landholder and, if not, his occupation), and place of origin ("sterling" vs. "currency").[42]

Conflicting interests created differing visions about the direction the colony should take: whether it would be an economy based on wool and dominated by large estate-owning magnates lording over convict and emancipist laborers, or a more diversified economy that presented opportunities for small-scale proprietorship and gave all white men a "fair go." The establishment of a free press allowed for the expression of discontent, especially from emancipists who sought more rights and opportunities. The 1823 Act for the Better Government of New South Wales set up civil courts to replace the military tribunals that had dispensed justice to this point, but did not grant emancipists the right to trial by jury. The act also established a Legislative Council appointed by the governor, which was only a tentative move toward representative government (a partially elected legislative council did not operate until 1842). As in British North America, a brotherhood that was initially identified with prominent men gradually broadened its appeal once rising men began to see membership as facilitating their upward mobility. But the penal settlements in the antipodes posed a problem that Masons in other parts of the empire would have found inconceivable: should former convicts be admitted to lodges? Not surprisingly, we see local Masons attempting to regulate their brotherhood by sifting not Scots and French Canadians, but Irishmen and emancipists.

Both emancipists and Freemasonry found an ally in the fourth governor of New South Wales, Lachlan Macquarie. Macquarie arrived in the aftermath of the disastrous administration of William Bligh, the infamous former captain of *The Bounty* who had gone head to head with the New South Wales Corps and found himself ejected from the colony. Macquarie restored the crown's authority and embarked on a thorough-going program of reform (by banning the use of rum as a currency and requiring church attendance) and development (by emphasizing urban planning and construction, road building, exploration and settlement, and cultivation and ranching). Like several of his fellow colonial governors, Macquarie realized the Masonic brotherhood could play an important role in the life of the colonial society under his charge. He had been initiated in Bombay in 1793 when serving in the British army. Historian of Australia Alan Atkinson describes him as "one of those Freemasons who liked polished manhood and good friends more than arcane knowledge."[43] Unlike his predecessor, Governor King, he made no effort to halt Freemasonry's spread to the colony.

Freemasons in New South Wales received a boost not only from having a brother in a position of power but also by the arrival of the 46th Regiment in 1814. The 46th Foot boasted one of the most important military lodges (No. 227), which had spread Freemasonry to several different parts of the empire since its founding in 1752. The lodge had a history of interacting with local colonists, as was the case in Sydney, though it was very selective in determining eligibility for membership. It would initiate only commissioned officers or high-status settlers and once refused to accept an Irish Mason (who was a past master of a lodge in Dublin) because his status as an emancipist would jeopardize "our Respectability both Military and Masonic." By 1816, it had initiated enough civilians to require the establishment of a stationary lodge, which met for the next several years under a dispensation from No. 227 rather than an official warrant.[44]

As in other parts of the empire, Freemasonry began taking a lead in the ceremonial life of the new Australian colonies; its public appearances both displayed and affirmed its status as a respected institution. In Hobart Town, Van Dieman's Land, the Reverend Knopwood recorded in his diary on 19 August 1814: "The Governor laid the first stone for the officers barrack on the hill; the masons attended him." Subsequently the *Hobart Town Gazette* reported on the foundation stone laying ceremony for St. David's Church (1817); Freemasons' participation in the Auxiliary Branch Bible Society (1819); the establishment of a tavern, the Freemason's Arms (1819); and the construction of a lodge building (1820). Likewise, the official newspaper of New South Wales, the *Sydney Gazette*, kept readers informed of regular lodge meetings and special Masonic occasions.[45] The first major public Masonic event took place in November 1816. Thirty-two brethren marched in procession, led by the band of the 46th Regiment and bearing the various ceremonial accoutrements (including candlesticks, globes, a basket of corn, pitchers of wine and oil, columns, the Bible, square and compasses, the lodge's charter, and a sword), to lay the cornerstone of John Piper's house at Elizabeth Point. Piper, who had been active in Masonry while serving on Norfolk Island, had recently moved to Sydney to take over as collector of customs and excise. The position provided him with over £400 a year, and by 1816, newly married, he was able to begin construction on Henrietta Villa. The governor had granted Piper the 190-acre site. Among Piper's brethren who participated in the event were the first judge of the Supreme Court of New South Wales, the lieutenant governor, a Solicitor of the Crown, a surgeon (who had been knighted by the king of Sweden), the naval officer and explorer John Oxley, and several officers of the 46th Regiment. When they completed the ceremony, "the Brethren embarked in boats prepared for the purpose, from the brother's house, and were saluted by seven guns from the merchant vessel *Wellesley* commanded by Brother Crosset [and named after another prominent brother], a Masonic ensign having been displayed at the main Top-Mast head."[46]

Whether Macquarie attended the ceremony at Elizabeth Point is unknown (he did lay the foundation stone of St. Mary's Catholic Church a few years later), but his relations with members of the lodge reveal shifts in the social geography of the colony. Macquarie's goals as governor included not only building the colony's infrastructure and extending its boundaries, but also upsetting its entrenched social structure. The colony was highly stratified, with exclusives lording over emancipists. Military officers and members of the colonial administration naturally gravitated toward the exclusives. Though the two groups conducted business transactions with one another, they did not interact socially. Macquarie sought to break down the barriers between exclusives and emancipists by making land grants to emancipists, appointing them to government offices, and even dining with them. Such a policy obviously did not endear Macquarie to members of the entrenched elite, several of whom belonged to the colony's Masonic lodge. Men like George Molle (the lieutenant governor), Jeffrey Hart Bent (the Supreme Court judge), and William Moore (the Crown Solicitor) all criticized Macquarie over his handling of the colony's affairs. Molle sought any opportunity to challenge emancipists, while Bent refused to allow them to plead cases in his courtroom. It is thus not surprising that the early bylaws of their lodge forbade the initiation of a "person who ever was a prisoner."[47]

By the time the Masons affiliated with No. 227 received their own warrant from Irish authorities in 1820, however, the social composition of their lodge was beginning to change. Australian Social Lodge met under its own warrant for the first time in August 1820. In December, the lodge joined the lodge of the 48th Regiment (which had replaced the 46th and taken over stewardship of the civilian lodge in 1817) in a procession through the streets of Sydney in observation of St. John's Day. Included in its early members were several emancipists who were attracted to Masonry as they negotiated their ascent from disrepute. Samuel Clayton was a member of a lodge in Dublin before arriving as a convict in 1816. He worked as a painter, engraver, and jeweler in Sydney and, despite a letter of recommendation from the Grand Lodge of Ireland, was refused admission into the lodge of the 46th Regiment. The more liberal lodge of the 48th Regiment did accept him in 1820. Another member of Australian Social Lodge was Francis Greenway, the talented architect who was transported for forging a contract in 1813. Equipped with a letter of recommendation from former governor Arthur Phillip, he was immediately put to work by Macquarie designing and overseeing the construction of Sydney's key public buildings, including a new Government House, the South Head light house, the Hyde Park barracks, several churches, and two hospitals. He was admitted into the lodge in 1823. Finally, William Bland, a naval surgeon transported from Bombay in 1813 on a murder conviction (for fighting a duel), was also admitted to the lodge.[48]

Although a few emancipists had found their way into Australian Social Lodge, its broader membership remained troubled by the issue of admitting former convicts and eager to preserve the respectability and legitimacy of Freemasonry. Whether genuinely unclear about the eligibility of emancipists or hoping for an excuse not to admit any more, the lodge wrote to the Grand Lodge of Ireland for a policy clarification shortly after receiving their warrant. Irish authorities ruled "that an individual becoming free by pardon or by expiration of sentence, possessing a good character may and would be eligible to become a Member of a Masonic Lodge." The ruling opened the way for emancipists to join Irish lodges in New South Wales and Tasmania, though they still faced resistance from the exclusives.[49]

The concern with respectability and procedure was also evident in Australian Social Lodge's approach to establishing new lodges in the colonies. Since a provincial grand lodge had yet to be formed, local Masons had to find an alternative way to facilitate Freemasonry's spread while closely monitoring its membership. Australian Social Lodge had received reports of "an unlawful assembly" of Freemasons in Van Dieman's Land as well as a request from "some very respectable Brethren" there for a dispensation. In a memorial to Dublin, they also observed that among many "respectable" brethren who were arriving in the colony, some were remaining aloof "on account of our Lodge being composed of some Brethren who had once the misfortune of falling under the Lash of the Law." Members of Australian Social Lodge were worried that such men would set up their own lodges and exclude emancipists, so they petitioned Dublin for the authority to create new lodges and use their power to unite "in one strong chain the poor man and the rich man; as well as keep all party distinctions from the Masonic walls in this infant Colony." Accompanied by a substantial donation of £10 to the Dublin Masonic Orphan School Fund, the petition received the assent of the Grand Lodge. Such an arrangement indicated the flexibility with which the Grand Lodge of Ireland approached colonial governance. Australian Social Lodge soon constituted another lodge, Leinster Marine in Sydney, although it informed the Irish Grand Lodge that the new lodge had itself passed an anti-emancipist bylaw. Grand Lodge authorities were quick to label the bylaw "un-masonic" and demand its expunging. Before English Freemasonry even secured a footing in New South Wales, the Irish had formed another lodge, this time in Hobart Town, Tasmania.[50]

While Irish lodges were proliferating, the Masons who formed the first English lodge in Australia were precisely the sort of middle-class social climbers who patronized the brotherhood in the other settlement colonies. Like the British North Americans we have already met, they adopted subtle means of regulating Freemasonry by deploying the language of respectability to challenge the social credentials of rivals, especially their Irish "brethren." John Stephen, the police magistrate whose words open this book, reported to the Grand Lodge of England on the desperate need for an English (read respectable) lodge in New South Wales. He surveyed the state of Masonic affairs for metropolitan authorities: "From all the information which I have been enabled to procure I am sorry to say that I cannot give a very flattering description of the Craft. The Lodges which are held here receive their authority from the Grand Lodge of Ireland; the business of them is not conducted in a pleasant agreeable manner or according to the forms of the Union. This is the more to be regretted as there are a great number of Brethren who are anxious to attach themselves to a Lodge but are unable or rather unwilling to connect themselves with such as now form the Lodges in this Colony." Stephen thought that the establishment of an English Provincial Grand Lodge would help bring credit and regularity to Masonry in the colony. Assuring them that New South Wales presented "a fine field . . . for cultivating the principles of the Craft," he included the names of seven Masons, whose certificates he had checked and were as anxious as he to establish a lodge: a Commissioner of the Court of Requests, a "settler of independent property," a government artist, a clerk of the peace, an army major, the Colonial Treasurer, and an army captain. Stephen explained that he could have gathered even more signatures from men who were already Masons, and he claimed: "There are at least 20 friends of mine who are anxious to be initiated into our mysteries, but cannot make up their minds to unite with such characters as now conduct the business of Masonry here, who really require some controlling power."

To back up his claim that the new lodge, if warranted, would include the most respectable inhabitants, Stephen closed his letter with a shopping list so impressive that metropolitan authorities must have felt his confidence was well placed. He asked for "complete and handsome gavels, squares, compasses &c," pillars, a Bible, swords, rough and perfect ashlars, tracing board, sixty aprons, six dozen gloves, a lodge book, three lodge candlesticks, and two dozen candles. The list not only indicated Stephen's confidence but also the flourishing material culture of early-nineteenth-century Masonry. And to assure metropolitan authorities he and his brethren were in the government's favor, he indicated that they were about to petition the authorities for a grant of land in Sydney "for the purpose of erecting a Temple on a liberal scale."[51] The Grand Lodge issued the warrant without hesitation and filled Stephen's order for lodge accoutrements; Lodge of Australia held its first meeting in 1829.

Another strategy the new lodge adopted to ensure its respectability was to set fees so high that membership was out of reach for most men. The initiation fee was £10, while the annual membership fee was £4. Its members also spent lavishly, perhaps in an effort to show off their status and wealth to the Irish lodges and the convicts, poor settlers, and emancipists in whose midst they lived. The lodge quickly amassed significant debts and had to assess the membership twice: first to pay for a tavern bill and an elaborately decorated canopy (£82) and then for the long-awaited shipment of Masonic paraphernalia worth almost £100. By the early 1830s, the lodge was clearly well established and had achieved a reputation for respectability. The governor, Sir Richard Bourke, agreed to serve as Patron of the lodge; the first mayor of Sydney, John Hosking, was initiated in the lodge; and Sir John Jamison, the prominent doctor and explorer who had joined Lodge No. 227 many years earlier, was installed as master in 1834 (he was appointed to the Legislative Council in 1837). The lodge had sufficient funds to construct its hall in 1839, and members regularly put themselves (and their imported regalia and jewels) on public display in Sydney.[52]

Although the new English lodge had fairly cordial relations with Sydney's two Irish lodges, it did not take long for jurisdictional rivalry to put the lodges at odds. We have already seen how the Masons under the English constitution looked down upon the "characters" who belonged to the Irish lodges. During the mid-1830s the actions of the English lodge posed a serious threat to the well-established, if not so respectable, Irish lodges. When Masons in Parramatta sought to establish a lodge in 1836, they bypassed the Irish provincial grand lodge and set themselves up under the English Lodge of Australia. The affronted Irish Masons wrote letters to both Irish and English authorities complaining about the "irregular and unconstitutional meetings" of the new lodges and inquiring about the "precedency of Irish and English lodges." Rather than acknowledge the precedence and authority of the long-standing Irish lodges, the Grand Lodge of England officially constituted the Parramatta Lodge in 1838 and appointed the master of its Lodge of Australia as District Grand Master of New South Wales the following year. With an active District Grand Lodge to coordinate them, the English lodges gained in confidence and popularity. Relations with Irish lodges continued to be tense, as exhibited by the refusal of Sydney lodges to admit Irish brethren as visitors.[53] Though Irish Masonry had clearly taken precedence in the early history of New South Wales, by 1888, when an independent Grand Lodge of New South Wales was officially recognized, no lodges in the colony were meeting under Irish warrants. Historian Beverly Kingston observes that by this point Freemasonry had come to reflect "the goal orientation and success ethic of male society, preaching brotherhood but practicing exclusivity."[54] And so, in these ways, the experiences of Freemasons in New South Wales paralleled those of their brethren in the other settlement colonies of the empire.

The Cape Colony

British Freemasonry first appeared in the Cape Colony during the wars with France in the 1790s, and it took root during the second British occupation (1805–14). Though the Dutch had been colonizing southern Africa since the mid-seventeenth century, the Vienna Settlement awarded the territory to Britain in 1815. It inherited a colony with 30,000 Dutch-Afrikaner, 15,000 Khoi-khoi, and 25,000 slave inhabitants. Almost immediately, the British started tinkering with the administration, introducing reforms to bring the Cape in line with other wage-based economies in the empire. Slavery, under attack in the climate of reform then gripping Britain, was abolished in 1834, though the shift in status did not actually translate into material improvements in the lives of most former slaves. Land expropriation and white settlement, begun under the Dutch, proceeded under the British. British settlers began arriving in the eastern Cape in 1820; the influx of Britons and their governing institutions provoked thousands of Dutch-Afrikaners to move further into the interior. The Colonial Office resisted the extension of its formal responsibilities, but continued settlement led to encroachment onto the lands of the Thembu and Xhosa in the east, the Griqua in the north, and eventually the Zulu in the far northeast. Warfare along the shifting borders was endemic. By the mid-1850s, the area under European settlement had doubled.[55]

As in the established colonies in the Caribbean and British North America, Freemasonry was closely associated with the army and the colonial administration and was thus considered a respectable institution from the outset. Masons in the Cape, unlike their brethren in New South Wales at the time, did not have to struggle to achieve legitimacy. The fact that a prestigious Dutch lodge (the Lodge de Goede Hoop) had been meeting in the colony since 1772 and welcomed British Masons helped ensure the brotherhood would receive official approval. The first permanent English lodge started working in 1799 when Richard Blake, Under Secretary of the colony and Examiner and Taster of Cape Wine and Brandy, made the masonically illegal decision to open a lodge under a lapsed warrant he had brought with him from Bristol. High-ranking officers of the garrison, such as the Aide-de-Camp Colonel James Cockburn, joined the lodge. That the Lodge de Goede Hoop sold property to the new lodge demonstrated its willingness to accept the existence of this "respectable English Lodge." In 1801, the Moderns named Blake as their Provincial Grand Master, but he returned to England before he was able to act upon his appointment.[56] The following year, the colony reverted to Holland, and the regimental lodges departed.

Despite the colony's passing back and forth between the Dutch and the British in this period, Dutch Masonry remained vibrant. The Cape was unique in the British Masonic world insofar as British Masons had to work alongside lodges thriving under a foreign jurisdiction. Dutch Masonry received a boost when Jacob Abraham de Mist, Commissary-General, arrived to take over the government of the Cape from the British in 1803. An active Mason, he encouraged Freemasonry among the permanent residents. The year of his arrival, de Mist was appointed Deputy Grand Master National of Dutch Freemasonry in the colony and oversaw a public ceremony to consecrate the Lodge de Goede Hoop's new temple, which was built at a cost of £10,000. Over 200 brethren and 100 ladies attended the festivities. English Freemasons continued to be welcomed in the Lodge de Goede Hoop and the Lodge de Goede Truow. When the British reoccupied the Cape in 1806, the members of de Goede Hoop, now under the leadership of prominent jurist Johannes Truter, convinced the commander-in-chief (Major General David Baird) to serve as their lodge's Protector. The lodge took the lead in Masonic affairs in the colony, setting up the Freemasons' Education Fund in 1813 to help address the deplorable state of education at the Cape and establishing a school two years later.[57]

Cape Freemasonry continued to maintain close associations with army officers and high-ranking colonial officials, but during the early nineteenth century it also began to attract members of the expanding imperial middle class, the same rising men who patronized the brotherhood in other colonies. Increasing numbers of British administrators, merchants, missionaries, entrepreneurs, and artisans began arriving during the second occupation. In 1811 a group of these lower-status Masons requested a warrant to set up a new lodge. Not insignificantly given the nationalistic climate in which they were living, they decided to call their lodge "The British Lodge," and Lord Moira readily issued its warrant. Richard Wrankmore, a local merchant, served as the lodge's first master, and founding members included a saddler, the Deputy Wine Taster, the Chief Searcher of Customs, a hotel-keeper, a cabinet maker, and several clerks. Reporting on Wrankmore's installation ceremony in 1812, the *Cape Town Gazette and African Advertiser* noted that Governor John Cradock, who was also a Mason, had sanctioned the proceedings. The officers of the city's two Dutch lodges and a number of "other respectable brethren" took part in the procession, church service, and dinner. By the end of the year, the lodge boasted thirty-six members.[58]

The Masonic lodge served a range of social functions for the Cape's new British inhabitants during the 1810s and 1820s. Its members contributed to government-sponsored subscriptions to improve colonial education, attended funerals of deceased Masons and supported their widows, and opened their "society rooms" to the general public. When military lodges were in the city, Masonic balls were organized for the entertainment of brethren and guests. The lodge's support for governor Lord Charles Somerset was put on public display when members contributed to a subscription to uncover the identity of someone who had libeled him. But the lodge also experienced downturns when members failed to attend and suitable meeting places were difficult to arrange (it met in eleven different places between 1818 and 1824). It was forced to rely on visitors and joining members, who hailed from farflung places like Halifax, Prince Edward Island, Dublin, and London, to bolster its numbers.[59]

Not coincidentally, British Masonry was established in the Cape at the moment the colony's Anglo-, male-dominated bourgeoisie emerged and the gradual shift to free trade was underway. In her comparative study of defamation cases in Sydney and Cape Town in this period, Kirsten McKenzie observes that clubs and lodges brought "men together for objects of mutual interest and lobbying as well as facilitating the provision of credit." Joining Masonry became a way for rising men to connect themselves to a broad network of fellow colonists and to assert their reputations as honorable, respectable men. As in other colonies, lodges became demarcated by the relative status and respectability of their members. The British Lodge, composed of low-level bureaucrats, clerks, and artisans, apparently did not appeal to Cape Town's wealthier merchants and professionals who set up The Hope Lodge in 1821. The lodge met in the newly completed Commercial Exchange, the site of regular auctions and business transactions. The lodge experienced some downturns but by the end of the decade included some of the Cape's most prominent citizens. In 1829 Clerke Burton, master of the Supreme Court, took over as master of the lodge; the Hon. John Edben, who belonged to the first Legislative Council, succeeded Burton. Architects, judges, clergymen, the Surveyor-General, and the royal Astronomer also joined the lodge. According to the *South African Commercial*

Members of British Lodge No. 334 (English Constitution), Cape Town, Cape Colony, ca. 1897 (copyright, and reproduced by permission of, the United Grand Lodge of England).

Advertiser, the "accession of a very considerable number of Brethren of such rank and importance in the Colony" would "ensure the best results to the laudable objects of the Institution." It expressed the hope that it would "ever maintain the character of high respectability which has now been given to it."[60]

The lodge was apparently able to sustain its reputation, offering an honorary mastership to Sir Benjamin D'Urban (governor, 1834–38). Back in London, the *Freemason's Quarterly Review* reported that the example set by D'Urban's participation had produced such a "beneficial effect" that "there is scarcely a leading person in Cape Town and places adjacent that have not associated amongst our Fraternity." Military and naval officers, professional men, the clergy, and "merchants of the first order and character" had joined the order. Another group whom Masonry attracted was the community of wealthy Anglo-Indians (English residents of India) who sojourned to the Cape for health reasons. Indians also seem to have participated in Masonry at the Cape. One local brother informed the English Grand Lodge that "the Indians generally appear to take a lively interest in Masonry" and that his lodge maintained a regular correspondence with one Indian who had returned to India. He requested lectures and

British Lodge Temple, Cape Town, Cape Colony, ca. 1897 (copyright, and reproduced by permission of, the United Grand Lodge of England).

books so that he could maintain "the regular proper system of working" not only at the Cape but also introduce it, via correspondence, to India.[61]

British and Dutch Masons in the Cape were as active in the ceremonial life of their colony as were their brethren in other parts of the empire. Masonic processions and ceremonies always attracted crowds and received detailed newspaper coverage. Two Dutch, four British, and one French lodge attended the ceremony to lay the foundation stone of the Scottish National Church in 1827. Two years later local Masons organized a major ceremony to constitute the English Provincial Grand Lodge (inactive since Blake's departure in 1802). Johannes Truter, the Dutch Deputy Grand Master, had agreed to serve simultaneously as the English Provincial Grand Master; by this point he had become the Chief Justice of the colony as well as the first South African to receive a knighthood on the basis of the valued legal advice he had given to Governor Cradock. The day-long ceremony to install Truter's officers was observed as a public holiday. About 200 English and Dutch Masons, representing five lodges, gathered at the Temple of the Lodge de Goede Hoop in the morning. At two o'clock, they welcomed into their temple the governor (Sir Galbraith Cole), other officials, and their wives, who had proceeded from Government House to the lodge along a street lined with soldiers. The paper reported that the governor's party "seemed highly pleased with the novelty of that truly Masonic assembly"; they heard a short oration and an anthem and departed the building to the strains of "God Save the King." Wearing formal regalia and carrying Masonic props (a cornucopia, golden ewars, a polished cubical stone, the Bible, lights, pillars, and banners), the assembled Masons then formed a long procession to the Dutch Reformed Church. The band of the 72nd Regiment led the march, and soldiers in the 98th Regiment were engaged "to keep off the press of the multitude." The governor's party rejoined the Masons at the church, and all took part in a divine service officiated by F. Fallows, H.M. astronomer at the Cape. Members of the new provincial grand lodge and other local Masonic dignitaries concluded the day with a grand banquet (though the newspaper noted "that the badness of the dinner and wines was generally complained of"). The following year, Governor Cole joined 400 Cape Masons in a comparable ceremony to lay the foundation stone of the English Episcopal Church. Several years later the Colonial Secretary, the Hon. John Montagu, was on hand to help Burton, now Provincial Grand Master, and local Masons lay the cornerstone of the Cape of Good Hope Gas Light Works. In these ways, Masonry played an instrumental role in the functioning — and public display — of what McKenzie describes as "the fraternal social contract" then under negotiation.[62]

The installation of a Provincial Grand Lodge in 1829 suggested that Cape Masonry was strengthening, but instead it experienced stagnation between the late 1820s and the late 1840s. (Only one new lodge emerged in this period — Albany Lodge established by settlers and traders in the eastern Cape outpost of Grahamstown in 1828.) A primary cause of the downturn was the instability generated by heavyhanded British administration. The status of free blacks and the movement to end slavery were especially controversial. British Masons publicly supported abolition. The British Lodge had contributed to a subscription "for the freedom of good and deserving Slaves" in 1828. In 1832, the lodge installed Thomas King, Assistant Protector of Slaves, as master and subsequently denied a petition for relief from a Brother Manuel Mergu because "being engaged in the Slave Trade, a profession inconsistent with the benevolent principles of Freemasonry, and prohibited by the law of God and man, he was not a proper object of relief from this or any other Masonic Lodge." But members of the Dutch-Afrikaner community disagreed with the ending of official discrimination against free blacks (1828), the abolition of slavery (1834), and other anglicizing reforms. Starting in 1834, thousands of Afrikaner farmers and their families began migrating out of the Cape Colony to establish interior settlements north of the Vaal and Orange Rivers. This significant population movement, combined with almost continuous frontier warfare and a stagnated economy, produced conditions unfavorable to the spread of Masonry. Moreover, Anglo-Dutch Masonic relations began to come under strain. The general tensions between the Afrikaner and British communities brought an end to the goodwill that had long characterized relations between Dutch and British lodges, and for two decades Cape lodges bickered with one another over relatively minor misunderstandings.[63]

By the 1850s, however, British lodges began multiplying as the population grew, the economy improved, and the frontier receded. Freemasonry came with settlers as well as the army (most of the regiments fighting on the eastern frontier had ambulatory lodges). Between 1851 and 1860 the English Grand Lodge issued warrants to six new lodges, like Zetland Lodge No. 884 at the frontier post of Fort Beaufort and Lodge of Goodwill at Port Elizabeth, which supplied the new settlers in the east. Freemasonry also appeared in the new eastern colony of Natal (originally settled by Boers in 1824 and annexed by the British 1843) when assisted migrants began arriving in the late 1840s and early 1850s. The minutes of the British Lodge in Cape Town note the large number of brethren migrating to Natal in 1848. The first lodges were established in the port city of Durban in 1858 and in the interior city of Pietermaritzburg in 1863. By this point, eight new lodges had emerged in the Cape Colony itself and Dutch Masonry was expanding under the capable leadership of Sir Christoffel Brand, Speaker of the Legislative Assembly and Deputy Grand Master National between 1847 and 1874.[64]

As Masonry's expansion mirrored the colonies' settlement geography, the brotherhood solidified its role as a key colonial institution. The new parliament, instituted to balance the autocratic powers of the governor in 1854, met in the banquet hall of the Lodge de Goode Hoep for two decades. The British Lodge

Gold Fields Lodge No. 2478 (English Constitution), Transvaal, South Africa, 1898 (copyright, and reproduced by permission of, the United Grand Lodge of England).

in Cape Town hosted annual balls, as well as concerts and dinners for members and their families (though men and women dined in separate rooms). In 1858, four Cape Town lodges assisted the governor, Brother Sir George Grey, in laying the foundation stone of the South African Museum and Library. Reporting on the event, the *Cape Argus* described the ceremony and informed readers that thirty "Kaffir convict laborers" who had worked on the building were treated "to an excellent dinner of roast beef, mutton, plum pudding with home brewed ale." Brother T. Maclear, the Astronomer Royal, sat at the head of the table and "illustrated the civilised mode of eating with knives and forks." Meanwhile, on the other side of the Cape, local Masons were among the dignitaries who welcomed Prince Alfred to Durban in 1860. Freemasonry's progress and prominence warranted the appointment of a high-ranking leader, so the Grand Lodge named the Hon. Richard Southey, Treasurer-General of the colony, to the post of "Provincial Grand Master for the Cape of Good Hope and Adjacent Colonies" in 1863. By the time of the discovery of diamonds (1867) and later gold

Fordsburg Lodge No. 2718 (English Constitution), Transvaal, South Africa, 1899 (copyright, and reproduced by permission of, the United Grand Lodge of England).

(mid-1880s), British Freemasonry was already expanding into the Boer Republics of the Transvaal and the Orange Free State.[65]

The Politics of Respectability

The Masonic brotherhood played an active, multifaceted role in all parts of the empire in this period. To be sure, local circumstances greatly affected the brotherhood, but sources suggest significant continuities across space. Wherever one went in the world of imperial Freemasonry between the 1790s and the 1830s, one was likely to find Masonic brethren taking part in public ceremonies that were often state-sponsored and viewed by colonial authorities as useful displays of imperial order and power. Freemasonry, despite being composed of men from across the social spectrum, was also typically associated with men of prominence: governors (Cotton in Barbados; Wentworth, Dalhousie, and Durham in British North America; Moira and Elphinstone in India; Macquarie and

Bourke in New South Wales; Cradock, D'Urban, and Grey in the Cape Colony); high-ranking colonial administrators (Bulkeley in Nova Scotia; Molle and Moore in New South Wales; Cockburn at the Cape); judges (Bent in New South Wales; Burton and Truter in the Cape Colony); mayors (Van Norden of Bermuda; Keith of Halifax; Hosking of Sydney); and businessmen from established families (the McGillivrays and Molson in the Canadas). Such high-ranking men saw participating in Masonry as a worthwhile pursuit, in part because it allowed them to put their prominence on public display.

One was also certain to observe the immersion of the brethren in what comparative historian Kirsten McKenzie describes as "the globalising culture of respectability then spreading throughout the British Empire."[66] Respectability has long been a concept of interest to historians of metropolitan Britain. Many argue that it functioned as a mechanism by which the upper and middle classes were able to control the working class;[67] others maintain that members of the working class deployed it strategically to enhance their position vis-à-vis the middle class.[68] Regardless of its effects on the working class, it seems clear that respectability was a central, if not entirely pervasive, value system for middle-class Britons, not only in the British Isles but also in the settlement colonies. Evidence presented here reveals that Freemasons in Nova Scotia, Lower Canada, Upper Canada, New South Wales, and the Cape spoke a common language of respectability. It shows that respectability carried meaning and performed similar functions across the colonized empire. Robert Ross, historian of South Africa, has gone so far as to describe "the establishment of respectable society, on terms essentially established in Great Britain," as "a global undertaking, an insidious, because totally informal, expression of cultural imperialism."[69]

In the extremely fluid and porous social environment of the early-nineteenth-century settlement colonies, respectability was a key factor in social mobility. Canadian historian J. K. Johnson has argued that to achieve prominence, a man in early-nineteenth-century Upper Canada had to secure a comfortable living (either through farming or the professions), become a commissioner of the peace and/or an officer in the militia, and skillfully exercise colonial patronage networks to his advantage. Johnson suggests that Freemasonry might have helped men achieve appointed or elected office, but he underestimates the extent to which membership in Freemasonry was also an important "ingredient of prominence."[70] Membership in the brotherhood helped men achieve prominence by functioning as a marker of respectability. After all, respectability—unlike gentility (into which a person was born)—could be acquired. One had only to adopt commonly agreed-upon markers of respectability to assert one's respectability. As Woodruff Smith puts it: "A person was respectable if he or she *acted* respectable."[71] By becoming a Mason (while gaining wealth, holding office, and plugging into patronage networks), men of humble origins like John Pyke, John Albro, Alexander Keith, Claude Dénéchau, James Fitzgibbon, William Campbell, Thomas Ridout, John Stephen, and Richard Wrankmore achieved respectability and prominence. The brotherhood thus contributed to the broadening of the early-nineteenth-century colonial ruling establishments by conferring respectability on rising men.

The world of imperial Masonry demonstrates another function of respectability, namely its use as a code to regulate this expanding class of powerful men. Local power struggles reveal Masons' attempts to sift the "respectable" from the "rough" in determining who was eligible for membership and leadership. Accusing a man of being insufficiently respectable was a common strategy for prominent Masons, whether they were attempting to exclude Scottish Masons in Nova Scotia, French Canadians in Quebec, or emancipists and Irish Masons in New South Wales. So while a man might be able to claim respectability by joining Freemasonry, his status ultimately depended on whether others accepted his claims. Some Masons, and some lodges, were clearly more respectable than others. A ship captain made this point in 1845 when, having traversed "the habitable Globe from the East to the West and from the North to the South in the capacity of commander of a Merchant Ship" and visited "the most respectable Lodges in the various countries my avocation led me to," he could confidently declare that English Masonry abroad was in a flourishing condition.[72]

SIX

A Spirit of Universal Fraternity

When British North American Freemasons took the first steps toward independence from metropolitan authorities in the 1850s, members of the brotherhood on both sides of the Atlantic celebrated their actions as evidence of their coming of age. The "alwise Parent Grand Lodges" rejoiced "to see their own offspring, in other lands . . . courageously taking upon themselves the duties of manhood, by the formation of Grand Lodges of their own . . . to imitate the virtues, and to strive to equal, and, if possible, to excel the glories of their illustrious parents." Meanwhile, on the other side of the world, the actions of Muslims, Parsis, and Hindus seeking entrance into the great imperial brotherhood of Freemasonry, though also interpreted through the idioms of kinship, were greeted with caution. Indians celebrated Freemasonry's ability to bring "the whole human race into one family," but the majority of British Masons in India refused to "hold out the hand of brotherhood" to indigenous candidates until forced by metropolitan authorities to do so. And even those who wanted to uphold "the great Masonic Doctrine of the Universal Brotherhood of man" by welcoming Indians into the Masonic family did so only on the grounds that their participation in Freemasonry would help raise up childlike natives "to the high level of European civilization and culture."[1]

These incidents represent just two of the countless examples of Freemasons' appropriating the language and idioms of families during the mid-nineteenth century. To be sure, the metaphor of the family had always held great explanatory power for Freemasons, not only as members of a cosmopolitan brotherhood but also as citizens of a global empire.[2] Yet it took on even greater significance in the mid-nineteenth century, when family functions seemed to be undergoing dramatic changes and a prescriptive domestic ideology concerning families was becoming increasingly pervasive. The metaphor played a key role not only in Masonic orations (where it had appeared with regularity during the eighteenth century), but also in Masons' correspondence, reports, minutes, and proceedings. Nineteenth-century Freemasons drew on their assumptions about, and experiences within, families in two ways. On a practical level, they modeled the organization and functions of their institution after those of families. Freemasons consciously used the idioms of kinship because they conveyed the fraternity's expectation that members would enjoy the rights and fulfill the obligations that supposedly characterized kin-based relations. On a more theoretical level, Freemasons also used the metaphor of the family as they negotiated local crises on the imperial periphery.

Developments across the mid-nineteenth-century empire demonstrate the centrality of the family metaphor to British Freemasonry. The middle decades of the nineteenth century constituted a period of great change in the British North America, the Caribbean, and India. In Canada, white male settlers, their numbers bolstered by the flood of immigrants from the British Isles, successfully demanded more autonomy within the imperial polity. Meanwhile, Caribbean colonies underwent the rocky transition from slavery through apprenticeship to freedom. So difficult was the shift that the British government agreed to the reassertion of direct colonial rule as the besieged planter minorities voted their legislative assemblies out of existence. In India, after an era of territorial expansion and bold programs of reform, the British faced an uprising that was unprecedented in its scope, costs, and implications for both imperial policymaking and the attitudes of the British and Indians toward each other.

These massive changes in the broader imperial context had implications not only for imperial governance but also for the idea of Masonic brotherhood. As we have seen, Masonic inclusiveness had been in retreat since the turn of the century. By the mid-nineteenth century, resembling less and less the cosmopolitan brotherhood its ideology continued to proclaim, it had become a club for loyalist, Protestant, respectable white men. Meanwhile, as more and more peoples converged under crown rule, demands for inclusion from free blacks, emancipated slaves, Muslims, Parsis, and Hindus began to put British Masonry to the test. These claims from "others" to be treated as "brothers" forced Freemasons to determine the extent to which the Masonic family was coterminous with the family of man.

The role of the British grand lodges proved crucial. Although traditionally unwilling to interfere with the admissions policies of local lodges, the British grand lodges did choose to intervene — albeit in a reactive rather than proactive manner — when local developments threatened the doctrine of universal brotherhood. They successfully overruled any stated admission policies that excluded particular groups on the basis of their skin color and religion, but in so doing met accusations of being insufficiently attuned to conditions on the ground. To help resolve the tension between their universal ideology and their duties as imperialists, colonial and metropolitan Masons consistently turned to the metaphor of the family. It enabled them to negotiate the disjuncture between their cosmopolitan, universalist ideology and the "rule of colonial difference" that underlay imperial power.[3] Recourse to the idioms of kinship is particularly evident in the movement to establish an independent Grand Lodge of Canada, the decision to admit former slaves into Freemasonry, and the debate over the admission of Parsis and Hindus, all of which took place between the 1840s and the 1870s. Examination of these key events sheds light on the complex interplay between "othering" and "brothering" that characterized this crucial period in the history of British imperialism.

The Model Family

During the late eighteenth and early nineteenth centuries — as industrial and gentlemanly capitalism, liberalism, evangelicalism, and imperialism transformed Britain — family structures and functions underwent important shifts, though it must be acknowledged that the so-called "modern" family continued to resemble early modern families in many significant ways.[4] "Family" during this period increasingly came to mean the private nuclear family, even though many nuclear families still lived within larger households, which included co-resident kin, servants, and lodgers.[5] Overall, there was a gradual restriction of family functions as other institutions took over its functions of production, education, social control, and welfare. Though the family remained the basic economic unit in the nineteenth century, the processes of industrialization and the relentless spread of capitalism had begun to chip away at the household-based economy.[6] Finally, the related notions of a sexual division of roles and the compartmentalization of lives into public and private spheres, though clearly evident in early modern assumptions about families, started gaining fuller elaboration and more

widespread currency at the turn of the nineteenth century. These ideals formed
an important part of the prescriptive domestic ideology of the Victorians, which
increasingly governed people's assumptions about, if not their actual experiences within, families and family relations.[7]

As these shifts were underway, the family emerged as the primary model and
metaphor for Freemasons when they referred to their institution. In 1852, the
Freemasons' Quarterly Review reminded its readers that "the Brethren of our
great family can never be uninterested in that which concerns each other." Such
comments were not unusual. Freemasons consistently described their institution as comprising a set of family-like relationships and borrowed the language
of family to convey expectations concerning the behavior of its members. Freemasons' expectations for the brotherhood were thus tied to their assumptions
about families and kin-based relations.[8]

First, Freemasons appropriated the idioms of kinship to organize the various
components of the brotherhood. While the individual member was identified as
a "brother," and the institution as a whole was described as a "fraternity," relations between lodges were typically couched in feminine terms. The metropolitan grand lodges were always known as "mother grand lodges," with the
Grand Lodge of England considered the grand mother of all lodges.[9] Similarly,
when a Mason discussed the lodge in which he was initiated, he referred to it as
his "mother lodge." Rudyard Kipling adopted the title "The Mother Lodge" for
his most explicitly Masonic poem. Along these lines, a grand lodge or a provincial grand lodge that had warranted a lodge to operate in its jurisdiction identified it as its "daughter lodge." In referring to one another, daughter lodges (as
well as grand lodges) described each other as "sisters."[10]

In addition to using the idioms of kinship to organize the brotherhood,
Freemasons drew on four key aspects of early Victorian ideology concerning families: loyalty and duty, mutual support, affective bonds, and patriarchal
authority. Masonry encouraged among the brethren the sense of loyalty and
obligation that was typically associated with familial relations in this period.
According to Leonore Davidoff, all-male institutions like Freemasonry "demanded from their members particular forms of loyalty and duty to the organization and its practices which are familial in their language and nature." A
Masonic manual from the mid-nineteenth century instructed newly initiated
Freemasons to prove their "obedience . . . by close conformity to our laws and
regulations." Like close kin, Freemasons were obligated to watch out for one
another, to help each other withstand life's vicissitudes. Thus, the manual explained that a Mason should extend the loyalty, duty, and "sentiments of benefi-

cence" he felt toward "those who are bound to him by the ties of kindred" to all members of the brotherhood. In this way Freemasonry ensured "that a Mason, destitute and worthy, may find in every clime a brother, and in every land a home." Quebec Masons could expect this benefit if they found themselves in France in the mid-nineteenth century. In 1851 Albion Lodge in Quebec established official relations with La Loge Clémente Amitie of Paris when it expressed a desire "to restore to Masonry its essential character of Cosmopolitanism, because it believes that Masons enjoy the benefits of family while travelling in a foreign land."[11]

Just as economic considerations were of utmost concern for families, the transmission of material resources was a significant concern of Freemasonry. As we have seen, the brotherhood functioned as a kind of global patronage network that helped men find employment, secure promotion, and cope with hardship. Such functions were traditionally performed by male family members and through extended kinship networks. As we have also seen, the *Constitutions* bound brethren to help one another find employment. Mutual assistance, or beneficence, according to the *Freemasons' Manual*, "forms the basis of the Masonic Institution, and Freemasonry has especial regard to the three stages of destitution — infancy, unavoidable misfortune, and extreme old age; for all these, when proved worthy, relief is at hand."[12]

By attending to the needs of sick brethren and members' dependents, Masonic lodges started taking over some of the functions typically fulfilled by families in earlier times.[13] This Masonic benefit was especially important for Masons who lived and worked in the empire, far from their blood relations in the metropole. Widows and orphans of deceased brethren received members' special attention. During the 1850s, a circular appealed to "all Free-Masons over the Globe" to raise money to support the widow and nine children of an Upper Canadian brother who died in destitution; Masons responded by granting the widow nearly £100. A man who joined the Freemasons could thus fulfill his role as provider even from beyond the grave. In another typical example of Masonic assistance, the District Grand Lodge of Madras aided one Brother Cottrell of Lodge Friendship No. 423 in Adelaide, South Australia. Cottrell had come to Madras to sell horses, but fell ill and ended up in the Vagrants' Home. Masonic authorities in Madras paid for his passage back to Australia and gave him ten rupees to recover the clothing he had pawned.[14]

Nineteenth-century Freemasons assumed that their institution, like the family, would also see to members' emotional needs. The domestic ideology of the early Victorians supposed that bonds of affection and love held together family members. It described the family home as an emotional haven from a harsh, foreboding world.[15] Like their eighteenth-century brethren, Victorian Masons saw love as a central tenet of Masonry. Masons endlessly repeated their mantra of "Brotherly Love, Relief and Truth" in their rituals, symbols, orations, and publications. Addressing Londonderry Freemasons in 1850, John Grant (who had just come from India) expounded on Masonry's "principle of universal love" and its "faith of universal brotherhood." Noting that neither religion nor politics stood in the way of brotherhood, he remarked that "the Jew, the Gentile, the Nomadic Arab, and the wild Indian" all acknowledged brotherly love as Freemasonry's underlying principle. The following year, as Masons from around the empire flocked to the imperial metropolis to attend the Great Exhibition, the *Freemasons' Quarterly Magazine* urged readers to welcome "brethren with whom we are linked in one great indissoluble bond, and whose arrival we must hail with the strongest emotions of brotherly love."[16]

Finally, Freemasons connected their assumptions about families with their expectations of their brotherhood by emphasizing the authority of a father figure, the lodge master. Early Victorian domestic ideology posited the father (the breadwinner) as the primary authority in the home, though patriarchal control might be mitigated or contested in a variety of ways. In Freemasonry, however, the master's authority could not be challenged. "The Charges" declared that the Master and his appointed officers "are to be obeyed in their respective stations by all the brethren . . . with all humility, reverence, love and alacrity." According to a Masonic lexicon, *The Master's power in his Lodge is absolute*. He is the sole decider of all questions of order, so far as the meeting is concerned, nor can any appeal be made from his decision, to the Lodge."[17]

Though Freemasonry drew on idealized notions of the family, the institution departed from "traditional" families in significant ways. Freemasonry was an unusual kind of family—it was a *fraternity* that privileged equality and masculine exclusivity. "The Charges" directly referred to the institution as a "brotherhood" and a "fraternity" and identified individual members as "brethren" or "fellows." Freemasonry distinguished itself from families at large by assuming the basic equality of all members, though this egalitarianism never compromised the ultimate authority of the master. The fraternity, a mid-nineteenth-century handbook explained, "esteems every man the peer of his fellow in nature and rights. Before her altars distinctions vanish, and all men meet on the level. The prince and the peasant stand alike in her presence." The master held authority during his tenure, but any member of a lodge who was sufficiently advanced in Freemasonry could be elected master. According to "The Charges,"

"All preferment among Masons is grounded upon real worth and personal merit only . . . therefore no Master or Warden is chosen by seniority, but for his merit."[18] Such a dynamic did not characterize broader family relations in the nineteenth century, when male heads of households exercised supreme authority over their dependents, whether female or male.[19] What also distinguished the Masonic family from other family units was its exclusion of women. British Freemasons continued to argue that the presence of women inside the lodge would irrevocably compromise their fraternal family. Thus, they defined their family not in terms of blood relations but rather in terms of mutual interest and shared experiences.

The absence of blood ties certainly did not stop nineteenth-century Masons from claiming (to an even greater degree than their eighteenth-century predecessors) that their institution operated like a vast extended family. In fact, Victorian Freemasons used the family not only as a model for the organization and functioning of their brotherhood but also as a metaphor that helped them respond to crises on the imperial periphery. Expansion and change in the broader imperial world brought new challenges as British North American Freemasons started demanding independence from metropolitan control, and free blacks, former slaves, Parsis, and Hindus sought inclusion into Freemasonry's theoretically universal brotherhood. As British Masons came face to face with these challenges and the tremendous diversity of the universal human family they claimed to champion, the family metaphor proved to have important ideological, as well as practical, uses.

Rebellious Adolescents

In the British North American case, Freemasonry offers a window onto the complex set of identities that emerged during a period of significant social, cultural, and political change. Two transatlantic forces drove these changes: first, the great migration flows of the post-1815 period, and, second, the increasing integration of the British imperial and British North American economies. The arrival of over a million Britons in British North America between 1815 and 1850 radically transformed the physical landscape of the colonies, especially Upper Canada as it developed from a backwater into a dominant colony. Altering the cultural landscape of the colonies, these migration flows and the spread of British social and political institutions led to the emergence of distinctly British societies, particularly in Upper Canada and the Maritime provinces. Finally, the period witnessed important shifts in the political landscape of British North America, with Anglophone settlers challenging the power of colonial oligarchies and making demands for a degree of autonomy within the extended imperial polity. These political movements culminated in Britain's grant of responsible government to the Canadian colonies in the mid-1840s and initial steps toward confederation in the 1850s.

As they experienced this age of dramatic change, Freemasons perceived themselves as belonging to a series of interrelated families at the local, national, imperial, and international levels. First, they belonged to their local lodge, which was the basic unit of Masonic governance and paralleled the nuclear family. Masons were also part of an extended family that corresponded to the jurisdiction (e.g., English or Scottish) under which their local lodge operated. For members of these lodges, the extended family involved a further level of association, the British or imperial Masonic family, which included members in all parts of the empire. Thus one Masonic official in Upper Canada described Freemasons in the British Isles and British North America as "branches of one common family."[20]

As is typical of most families, relations within the British Masonic family were not always happy and trouble free, a fact demonstrated by a rebellion that broke out in British North America during the 1850s. British North American Freemasons had been chafing under British grand lodge administration since the 1820s when they had first become frustrated with their fiscal and administrative dependence on the metropole. In 1845 the Provincial Grand Master of Nova Scotia notified the English Grand Lodge "that the inattention and neglect with which communications of importance in the Craft under my jurisdiction have been treated for many years is gradually producing a strong feeling of disaffection toward the Parent Grand Lodge." Meanwhile, Upper Canadians complained that they were being "taxed two-fold" by having to send their dues out of the colony while at the same time looking after needy British immigrants. Their charitable funds thereby depleted, British North American Masons did not have the resources to "follow the noble example set by our parent the United Grand Lodge of England" by establishing an institution for the widows and orphans of Masons.[21] These Masons felt that their extended familial duties compromised their ability to address the needs of their local families in the Canadian colonies.

One of the ways that Freemasons in British North America and other parts of the empire had attempted to deal with such problems was to play the British grand lodges against one another and thereby take advantage of a kind of Masonic sibling rivalry among them. The three grand lodges had agreed in 1814 to respect one another's jurisdictions at home, but the essentially British arena of the empire, where the boundaries between what was Irish, Scottish, and English were difficult to discern, posed challenges to their entente. Irish and Scottish authorities, who had a more relaxed attitude toward colonial brethren (in the settler colonies as well as India), did not hesitate to challenge the seniority of the Grand Lodge of England. Though the Grand Lodge of England had claimed itself as the Supreme Masonic Authority in British North America, Irish and Scottish lodges had been popping up with increasing regularity since the 1820s (the increase in lodges coincided with the growing numbers of Irish and Scottish migrants to British North America). The grand lodges started competing for members, influence, and control. When the English Grand Lodge suspended existing lodges or denied warrants for the formation of new ones, disgruntled petitioners often sought Irish warrants. The willingness of Irish authorities to comply with such requests prompted English Masons to complain about "the grievous injury done to the craft by almost indiscriminate issue of warrants from the Grand Lodge of Ireland."[22] Grand lodge rivalry could thus work to the benefit of some colonial Masons, but it also added to the level of overall frustration with the confused state of Masonic administration in British North America.

By the 1850s, these frustrations erupted into a full-fledged adolescent rebellion. Masons in Upper Canada asserted that they had grown up and were now capable of governing themselves. Under the leadership of Irish Masons, disaffected Upper Canadians formed the Independent Grand Lodge of Canada in 1855. They composed a formal farewell address to the Grand Lodge of England "from which the Masons of Canada, hailing from England, have for so many years been proud to hail, and from which Mother Lodge they now part with feelings of deep regret."[23] One by one, Irish, Scottish, and English lodges in the colony pledged allegiance to the new grand lodge, and the Canadians looked across the Atlantic for approval from the parents whose oversight they had just rejected.

The responses of the parent grand lodges varied, but it is clear that Masonic authorities on the other side of the Atlantic also saw it as a family affair. The Grand Lodge of Ireland was the first to recognize the fledgling Grand Lodge of Canada, and it did so graciously on the condition that any lodges or individual members who wished to "retain their present connexion with the Grand Lodge of Ireland" were free to do so. The Grand Lodge of Scotland did not extend immediate recognition, fearing that its lodges in Canada East (Quebec) would be pressured to join the new grand lodge, centered in Canada West. It extended its "fraternal wishes" to lodges that had remained loyal and praised the "*filial duty* of the Daughter Lodges in the Colonies." Likewise, the Grand Lodge of England also initially rejected the request for recognition. The Grand Master declared: "I cannot contemplate without the deepest concern the separation of so many lodges from the parent body."[24] But by 1858 both the Scottish and English Grand Lodges decided to follow the lead of the Irish in recognizing the Grand Lodge of Canada. Instrumental in changing metropolitan policy was the English Pro Grand Master, the Earl of Carnarvon (future Secretary of State for the Colonies) who presciently supported recognition on the grounds that it would enable English and Canadian Masons to nurture a closer affective connection with each other as the administrative ties dissolved.

The achievement of fiscal and administrative independence did in fact strengthen British North American Freemasons' sense of belonging to an extended British Masonic family. As with most rebellious adolescents, their ties to their parents remained strong even while they sought to assert their own identities and take control over their own affairs. After all, they had patiently endured three long decades of misadministration and neglect before finally declaring their independence. Once their frustrations were resolved, their sentimental ties remained and grew. They explicitly stated that they wanted to remain in the fold of the imperial Masonic family. At the Annual Communication of the Canadian Grand Lodge of Canada in 1857, Grand Master William Wilson assured concerned brethren that the new arrangement would "be the means of ensuring a still warmer feeling of fraternal regard" toward the "parent Lodge" from whom they would "ever proudly assert our descent."[25]

This rebellion within the world of British imperial Freemasonry brought to the fore a complex set of identities that were evolving in British North America during a period of widespread change. Historians of Canadian national identity have traditionally described national and imperial identities as antithetical: national identity developed in stages, growing stronger and stronger in inverse proportion to imperial sentiment.[26] Because of this assumption, they have focused on the processes of nation building during the years that immediately preceded and followed Confederation in 1867 or at the turn of the century (particularly the South African and First World Wars).[27] They have failed to identify the emergence of protonationalist sentiment before the 1860s and to appreciate the persistence of imperial identity long after that decade.

Examining Freemasons' response to the administrative crisis of the 1850s suggests a new interpretation of the history of Canadian national identity within the context of British imperialism. Masons involved in the affair were

Annual Communication of the Grand Lodge of Canada, London, Ontario, 1875 (Notman & Fraser, National Archives of Canada, PA-031495).

among the first British North Americans to reveal a sense of belonging to a nation they were calling Canada. Members of King Solomon's Lodge complained, for example, that though distressed brethren from England, Scotland, and Ireland claimed assistance, "comparatively few, if any, Canadian Brethren have claimed assistance from the Parent Grand Lodge." Similarly, Lodge No. 286 in York informed the Grand Lodge of Ireland that it had decided to join the new grand lodge by explaining: "We regret the severance from our Mother Grand Lodge but at the same time hope that it will not lessen the friendly connexion which has so long subsisted between us[,] and we as Canadian Masons will ever hail and receive you as Brethren and Masons."[28] In this way the independence movement demonstrates that some Irish, Scottish, and English settlers had developed a nascent sense of Canadianness at mid-century.

At the same time, their statements evinced a strong sense of belonging to the British Empire, which grew alongside this Canadian identity. Membership in Freemasonry, even after administrative links were severed, helped sharpen this sense of connection to the metropole and its vast empire. One of the leaders of the movement, Thomas Harington (a colonial administrator in Upper Canada), told the English Grand Lodge: "We have thought of England from first to last. We really do look upon the change as one more of *letter* than of *spirit*. We have made no sudden wrench, but have glided into our present position, and our *English* affection remains in strong force." Canadian Freemasons emphasized their continuing and growing fraternal love for their brethren across the Atlantic. At a public gathering in 1860, the Grand Master of Canada urged the audience to rejoice in the knowledge "that we form an integral part of that great empire" and to exert themselves "in rivetting still more closely the link which binds us to the land of our forefathers" to whom they were already united "in the bonds of affection and interest." A decade later, the grand master of the recently formed Grand Lodge of Quebec used the metaphor of the family to describe how achieving administrative independence enabled Freemasons to maintain their affective ties: "Although by the righteous orderings of God's Providence, children are separated from parents, for the more perfect fulfillment of the chief ends of their existence, yet, thereafter, neither do prudent parents nor dutiful children, have the less, but rather the more, interest in, and love for one another."[29] Such sentiments would develop, as we will see in the final chapter, into a full-fledged imperialist identity among Canadian Masons who willingly devoted their energy, money, and in some cases their lives to the "motherland" in its hours of need.

For British North American Masons and their brethren across the Atlantic, therefore, the family served as a primary frame of reference before, during, and after the rebellions of the mid-nineteenth century. The use of the metaphor demonstrates that British North American Masons viewed "imperial" and "national" as compatible rather than oppositional spheres. Britishness was a crucial component of Canadian identity.[30] To a great extent, early Canadians, like the Scots, Irish, and Welsh, "negotiated their cultural nationalism in relation to Empire," as John Mackenzie has recently argued. As he points out, these sub-nationalisms emerged not in the rejection of empire but in close interaction with it. It is therefore time for historians to heed Phillip Buckner's call to "place the imperial experience back where it belongs, at the centre of nineteenth-century Canadian history."[31]

The Family of Man

To conceptualize and describe their institution — as well as the empire and wider world in which they lived — mid-nineteenth-century Freemasons took the family metaphor a step beyond the nuclear (local lodge) and the extended (national-imperial grand lodge) families. Like their eighteenth-century brethren, they proclaimed their belief that all mankind belonged to one universal family. Indeed, Masonic ideology remained remarkably consistent on this point: Masons in both time periods professed belief in what they referred to as the common "fatherhood of God" and the "brotherhood of man." Speaking on the value and function of Freemasonry in New South Wales in 1849, Reverend Charles Woodward observed: "Mankind is but *one* family. Let us, then, cultivate more and more a spirit of Universal Fraternity." Eighteenth- and nineteenth-century Freemasons also agreed on the role their brotherhood should play in nurturing this family. Its cosmopolitan promise could transcend the religious, political, linguistic, and even racial differences that had, over time, come to divide the human family. According to the English periodical, the *Freemason's Quarterly Review*: "There never has yet been an institution calculated in an equal degree with Freemasonry to break down the artificial barriers which caste, creed, priestly ambition, and political rivalry, have created between different classes of the human family."[32] Masonic ideology taught members that such differences should never stand in the way of fraternity and charity.

But just how far did nineteenth-century British Masons take this idea of "universal fraternity" in practice? As Chapter 2 demonstrated, the brotherhood had admitted men of various religions and ethnicities during the eighteenth century. Even though the numbers of non-European candidates admitted was not statistically great, the institution itself was prominent and influential within the imperial establishment. Just having a reputation for crossing racial boundaries (ideologically if not always in practice) was significant. But if eighteenth-century exploration and colonization had widened the horizons of British empire builders, imperial expansion in the early nineteenth century brought an unprecedented diversity of peoples under the empire's purview. Meanwhile, the empire experienced fundamental changes that accompanied the ending of the slave trade and slavery, the shift toward free trade, and the massive migratory movements of the period. Once again, the imperial sphere became a practical testing ground for Freemasons' commitment to their ideology of universal brotherhood and the unity of the human family.

British Freemasons in the metropole and the colonies thus faced a dilemma. Their membership in Freemasonry asked them to consider as a brother any man, regardless of his race or religion, who professed to believe in the Great Architect of the Universe. But their role as imperialists typically required them to distinguish themselves from their subjects. When faced with requests for admission from free blacks, former slaves, Muslims, Parsis, and Hindus, British Masons thus deliberated very carefully about their claim to universal brotherhood. Sometimes lodges in the empire championed the rights of such men to join the brotherhood. More often, lodges—at both the local and the provincial level—implemented admissions policies that excluded candidates who belonged to these communities. Thus, by the early nineteenth century, a tension between the fraternity's inclusive rhetoric and its exclusive practice was increasingly evident and difficult to explain; it was a contradiction that made the metropolitan grand lodges uneasy.

In the early decades of the century, British Freemasons found themselves actually having to answer the rhetorical question posed by the caption of an abolitionist image of the slave in chains, "Am I not a man and a brother?" As we have seen, there were some instances of black men being accepted into the world of British Freemasonry during the previous century. The Grand Lodge of England had granted a warrant to Prince Hall to set up a lodge for black Masons in Boston in 1784. Although Hall made fairly regular returns to England until 1806, he complained of English authorities' failure to respond. In 1814, when it renumbered its lodges after the union, the Grand Lodge erased the warrant of African Lodge; by 1827, the brethren of African Lodge had declared, in a statement published in the *Boston Advertiser*, their independence from English authorities.[33] They were joined in their independence movement by two lodges Prince Hall had warranted in 1797.

As African Lodge and the Grand Lodge of England were parting company, free blacks in the Caribbean began testing Masonry's claims to universal brotherhood. In the early 1820s a black man, Lovelace Oviton, applied to visit a lodge in Barbados. Oviton produced a certificate indicating his status as a Master Mason (in 1807 he had been admitted into the third degree in Royal Clarence Lodge, No. 452, in Brighton), but the members of the all-white lodge refused, most unmasonically, to admit him. Oviton then applied to the English Grand Lodge for a warrant to establish a new lodge, presumably for black Masons on the island. It did not reject his petition outright but advised him to request a warrant from the Provincial Grand Master of Barbados.

Local Masonic authorities dashed off a frantic letter to the English Grand Lodge as soon as they learned "that some colored Men of this Island, had written to the Right Worshipful United Grand Lodge of England, to obtain a Warrant for establishing a Lodge of Free Masons on this Island." They hoped to prevent what they perceived as an impending disaster. "Should their request be complied with," the letter stated, "it will tend more materially to injure the Craft in the Western Hemisphere, than any other event that could possibly take place." The author of the letter urged the Grand Secretary (whom he described as a personal friend) to "use every exertion in [his] power, with His Royal Highness the Duke of Sussex, to prevent any such Warrant being granted." At the same time Provincial Grand Lodge authorities in Barbados also warned the Grand Lodge of Ireland about this "Lodge intended to be form'd of men of colour" and asked them to assist in preventing it.[34]

The metropolitan grand lodges apparently decided to leave the matter up to the men on the spot. The English Grand Lodge was prepared to back up its provincial grand master: if he outlined his objections to this particular lodge's being formed "there is no doubt but his Sentiments will have due weight." For its part, the Irish Grand Lodge declared itself unwilling to interfere in the affairs of another jurisdiction. Yet it is interesting to speculate how Irish authorities would have reacted had they received Oviton's petition for a warrant. The admission policies of the Irish were fairly liberal in comparison to those of the English. About this time it confirmed the rights of emancipists in Tasmania to seek membership in Irish lodges and in 1831 it allowed one of its lodges in Mauritius "to receive respectable people of colour."[35] Whether or not they would have granted a warrant to Oviton, Irish authorities would probably have had more difficulty than the English just ignoring the request.

The Grand Lodge was content to deal with free blacks on a case-by-case basis, but the abolition of slavery in 1833 presented a more daunting question: the admissibility of a substantial new class of people, former slaves. One strong supporter of both abolition and former slaves' admission into Masonic lodges was Robert Crucefix, editor of the *Freemason's Quarterly Review*. In 1836 he wrote a letter to Sussex in which he expressed his "feeling that it was a most singular thing that they should emancipate thousands of fellow-creatures, and not afterwards allow them to participate in the benefits of Free Masonry."[36] But the Grand Lodge of England refrained from making any major policy decisions until forced by colonial developments to do so. In this instance, as with Parsis and Hindus later in the century, "peripheral crises" seem to have dictated the timing of metropolitan action and policy making.

The first such incident occurred in 1840 when Lodge No. 277 in the Barbados asked the Irish Grand Lodge "how far the Legislative enactment giving liberty to the Slave population of the West Indies applies to their admissibility into the order of Freemasonry." Had they based their decision on the institution's ideological claims to sympathy with "all sections of the human family," admitting former slaves should not have been an issue. But—as those who were opposed to the admission of former slaves were quick to point out—a technicality in the wording of "The Charges" stood in the way of their inclusion.

Going back to 1723, "The Charges" had stated that "persons admitted members of a Lodge must be good and true men, *free-born*, and of mature and discreet age." The Grand Lodge decided to postpone its decision in order to form a committee to consider the matter and consult with the Grand Lodge of England. The following year, it also sent a representative to the French Grand Lodge to inquire, among other things, about its policy on freed slaves. It learned that "if any application was made to initiate them, they being proper characters, they would be made." In fact, the French had already sent warrants to Haiti "for the purpose of opening Lodges to make them."[37] Yet, as long as the word "free-born" remained in "The Charges," the letter of British Masonic law prevented British lodges from fully implementing the spirit of Masonic ideology and admitting former slaves as brethren.

In addition to these subtle legalistic arguments, outright racial prejudice erected barriers to the admission of black Masons, regardless of their labor status. In 1842 several black Masons in Hamilton, Upper Canada, repeatedly requested entrance into a local lodge. Edward Crumps and his brethren "used every means in their power to obtain the rights and benefits" of Masons, including presenting their legitimate certificates. Yet the members of Lodge No. 10 refused to admit them. The black Masons had difficulty understanding such a violation of "the genuine principle of Masonry": "All the information that your [petitioners] has got from them is thus that a portion of their members will not except [*sic*] us because that [*sic*] we are a colored race of people." So Crumps and the other decided to apply to English authorities for a warrant of their own. In their petition, they noted that "any regular lodge of free and excepted Masons" in the United States would willingly admit them (an interesting claim given that American Masonry was clearly segregated at this point) and assured the Grand Lodge of England that they were "a loyal people to the sovereign of great brittain [*sic*] and the coloneys [*sic*] belonging thereto."[38]

Once again, metropolitan authorities seem to have ignored Crumps' petition but, by the mid-1840s, the British grand lodges were realizing the need for a clear statement on blacks' eligibility for admission. At the level of policy, at least, they demonstrated an unwillingness to live with a contradiction between the theory of a race-blind brotherhood and the practice of excluding black men. Again, colonial developments were forcing their hands. In 1844 Lodge No. 622 in Barbados requested permission from the Irish Grand Lodge to admit two former slaves. Still unresolved in its decision about the wording of "The Charges," the Grand Lodge ruled that "no person who had been born in bondage is, *in the ordinary course* eligible to be admitted into the order." But it decided that a former slave could join a lodge by receiving special permission from the Grand Lodge (which it granted to the former slaves seeking to join No. 622).[39]

Though a bit slower to take action than their Irish counterpart, the English Grand Lodge ultimately developed a less ambiguous policy regarding the admissibility of former slaves. In 1847, the English Grand Master, Lord Zetland, brought the matter before the Grand Lodge. Letters that had arrived recently from Antigua and St. Vincent prompted Zetland and his fellow grand lodge officers "to obviate the difficulty felt on the proposition of such a person for initiation." Grand Lodge officials decided to revise the wording in the *Constitutions* to read "free man" rather than "free born." In making a change designed "to give relief to the colonies," the Grand Lodge demonstrated that its policies were subject to developments in the empire.[40] By shifting the wording of the *Constitutions* the grand lodges opened the way, theoretically at least, for former slaves to seek admission to the order. Yet the tension between Masonry's inclusive ideology and exclusive practices persisted and, as we will see, became a much-debated issue during the second half of the nineteenth century (and remains one even to this day).

The Debate over Parsis and Hindus

When it came to admitting men of different races and creeds, British Masonry had been, over time, most receptive to Muslims. In India, Freemasonry was for most purposes, if not for all intents, an exclusively European institution that flourished among East India Company servants, government officials, the merchant and professional classes, and army officers. But based on the precedent set in 1777 with the initiation of Umdat-ul-Umrah Bahadur, several early-nineteenth-century lodges did initiate Muslims. This precedent notwithstanding, Muslims' participation could cause controversy at the local level. The Marine Lodge in Bengal initiated Meer Bundeh Ali Khan in 1812. Two members of the lodge refused to attend the meeting on the grounds that "they were obligated not to be present at the Initiation of a Turk[,] Jew or Infidel, And they considered all Mahomedans, *Turks*." In the middle of the initiation ceremony, two other brethren who "were most unworthily and unmasonically employing themselves in ridiculing the Mahomedan Religion" were asked to leave. Within six months, the lodge was split over the issue; both sides presented their cases to the metropolitan authorities. Those advocating the Muslims' admission described the troublemakers as "three or four Ignorant Bros." who were not "able to appreciate the Meaning of what a Mason ought to be." The Muslim initiate was, on the other hand, "a man Universally respected" who could claim the Marquess Wellesley (a former governor general) as a reference. He also had the support of some prominent Masons in Bengal "as well as many other very worthy Brethren who have done us the Honor of visiting us, coming from all corners of the globe." Persuaded by these arguments, the Ancients allowed the initiation to stand.[41]

During the mid-nineteenth century, most of the Muslims initiated in British lodges in India belonged to the royal families of collaborating or recently conquered princely states. In 1836, the English Grand Lodge recognized the admission of the ambassador from the Kingdom of Oudh, which Wellesley had brought into the subsidiary alliance system in 1801. Early in the next decade, the Duke of Sussex took part in the initiation of several Indian princes. Such initiations demonstrated how useful the brotherhood could be in strengthening the power and influence of the expanding British Raj. Yet the inclusion of Muslims was not just a matter of political expedience, as demonstrated by the fact that lodges rejected some prominent Muslim candidates. One prince in Secunderabad sought admission but was turned away because he was a eunuch. Though Lodge St. John in Secunderabad admitted Meer Bundeh Ali Khan as a visiting brother, his son was initially rejected because he did not speak English. Moreover, Muslim initiates were invariably elites whose inclusion could be justified as politically beneficial to the empire; there is little evidence of middle-class Muslim professionals and merchants finding their way into lodges.[42] Despite the limited nature of this trend, it did set a precedent that led to a wider debate over native admissions during the 1840s. British Masons residing in India began discussing not only whether more Muslims should be admitted but also whether Parsis and Hindus were eligible. In 1840 the *Freemasons' Quarterly Review*, reporting on Masonic affairs in India, urged: "The question as to the propriety of admitting Mahomedans and Hindoos into the Order still occupies the attention of the Anglo-Indian Craft, and some intimation from headquarters is anxiously looked for." The time had come to determine the extent of Freemasonry's "sympathy with the whole family of man."[43]

Thankfully, the historical record has preserved a variety of perspectives—Scottish, English, Irish, and elite Indian—about the admission of indigenous candidates into Freemasonry. On one side of the debate stood a few vocal advocates, British and Indian, who were willing to include any Indian candidate, provided he gain acceptance into a local lodge. In making their case, they drew on the ideology of universal brotherhood and the family metaphor, which were by now commonly associated with Freemasonry. On the other side was the majority of English Masons in India, who did not want to welcome Hindus into their family. They deployed a range of arguments to justify their exclusion, and they conveniently avoided the language of brotherhood, except when they explicitly said that they could not imagine accepting the native Hindu as a brother. Yet all the British Masons involved in the controversy shared the perception that Hindus were culturally backward and in need of civilizing, and, especially after 1857, they expressed this opinion in the increasingly racialized discourse of imperialism.

Apparently taking the notion of the universal family of man more seriously than their English brethren, Scottish Masons in Bombay were the first to address the question of native participation. Dr. James Burnes, an East India Company medical officer who had arrived in 1821, was instrumental in this development. Scottish authorities had appointed Burnes Provincial Grand Master for Western India in 1836. He explained to a gathering of fellow Masons in 1840 that he was devoted to Masonry not only because it bound together educated Britons in the colonies but also because, for "the natives of this mighty empire," it could "extend, without awakening religious prejudice, a truer knowledge of the Great Architect of the universe, and more just notions of their duty to each other."[44] Burnes and his fellow Scottish Masons, it seems, were ready to open Freemasonry's doors to qualified Indians.

However, before they could formulate policies and procedures for native admissions, the actions of a prominent Parsi, Maneckji Cursetji, put the Scottish Masons on the defensive. In 1838, Cursetji became the first Indian appointed Assistant Collector of Customs in Bombay and he would later, after a successful career in the courts, become the first Indian sheriff of Bombay. In 1840 Cursetji sought admission into Burnes's own lodge in Bombay, the prominent Lodge of Perseverance. Rejected but unthwarted, Cursetji next attempted to join a lodge in England but once again was blackballed. Finally, in Paris, he found a lodge — La Gloire de L'Univers — that was willing to admit him into the mysteries of Freemasonry. In 1843 Cursetji returned to Bombay as a Master Mason, only to find the Lodge of Perseverance still unwelcoming. But the fact that he was already initiated put Scottish Masons in Bombay in a bind. They realized that Parsis and others could now find their way into Masonry through a back door. Better to control the process, they reasoned, than passively stand by while others made Masons of Parsi candidates. Thus, in 1843, twenty-seven brethren, including some members of the Lodge of Perseverance, petitioned Burnes to establish a new lodge that would oversee the admission of native members. The Lodge Rising Star of Western India came into being with four

Indian founding members, including three Muslims and a Parsi. The most important offices of the lodge, not surprisingly, remained in European hands, with Burnes himself serving as master and two other prominent Britons as Senior and Junior Wardens.[45]

It is significant that Parsis, a highly Anglicized community that played a dominant role in the economy and politics of nineteenth-century Bombay, were more readily accepted into Freemasonry than Hindus. The prominent Parsi families of western India had strong financial and political connections to European merchants and civil servants. The Parsi admitted as a founding member of the Lodge Rising Star of Western India, for example, was Ardeshir Cursetji Wadia, the Chief Engineer of the Bombay Dockyard and member of the Wadia shipbuilding family.[46]

The prosperity of Scottish lodges (at the expense of English lodges) in Bombay during the early 1840s suggests that Burnes's handling of the native admissions question met with approval. When Burnes took over as Scottish Provincial Grand Master, English Masons began deserting their lodges to join Scottish ones. By 1844, English Freemasonry in Bombay was dormant.[47] The brethren who had formerly belonged to English lodges may just have been happy to have a good administrator in their midst, but they certainly would not have forfeited their English warrants — the most prized warrants in the world of Masonry — had they disagreed fundamentally with his policy on the admission of Muslims and Parsis.

Viewing these activities from their base in Calcutta and motivated by the same sibling rivalry that characterized British Masonic relations in the Canadian colonies, English Masons realized they too needed a policy concerning the admission of indigenous candidates. The English Provincial Grand Master of Bengal during the 1840s, Dr. John Grant (Apothecary General of the East India Company and resident in India for over twenty-five years), was equivocal about admitting Indians into Freemasonry. He argued that the decision to admit "Musselmans and Hindoos" was the prerogative of the Provincial Grand Lodge rather than the right of individual lodges (which, according to Masonic law, had always had the right to determine their membership without interference from above). Grant also worried that needy British brethren would admit rich Indians in order to improve the condition of lodge coffers. But both the actions of the Scottish Masons in Bombay and Masonry's claims to universal brotherhood compelled him to make some concession toward Indians. He agreed to the admission, under the close supervision of the Provincial Grand Lodge, of "well educated and respectable natives and the advancement thereby not only of their moral position but the creation of a stimulus to the acquirement in some measure of an English education."[48]

Still, the prospect of admitting Indians in great numbers made Grant and his fellow "eminent and influential Masons in Calcutta" very anxious. It threatened white Masons' control over the brotherhood in a way that admitting the occasional Muslim never had. They turned to their "Grand Parent Lodge" for advice. Responding in 1842, the English Grand Master, the Duke of Sussex, pronounced: "The Question is one which has occupied [my] attention for many years, and formed a part of [my] Masonic creed; that provided a Man believe in the existence of the . . . Architect of the Universe, in fraternity, and extends that belief likewise to a state of Rewards and Punishments hereafter; such a person is fully competent to be received as a Brother." The duke cautioned against the "indiscriminate admission of Mahomedans and Hindoos" and warned Grant to be especially careful about ensuring the solemnity of the initiation ceremony, but he felt that "it is no doubt a great object to impress Brotherly and friendly feelings between Europeans and enlightened Hindoos." Such an open-ended policy decision caused Grant to recoil. He expressed horror that Hindus and Muslims might join the brotherhood en masse. Grasping for justifications to exclude Hindus specifically, he responded by arguing that properly obligating them was impossible and that the rules of caste precluded them from fraternizing with lower-caste Hindus. "After a residence of 26 years in this country . . . of all the natives whom I have ever known, two or three fingers would cover the names of those whom I could venture conscientiously to recommend for . . . Masonry." At this point, Grant put the question of native admissions on the back burner, and, in the aftermath of his administration, English Freemasonry in Bengal suffered from a lack of leadership and competition from Scottish Masons in Calcutta.[49]

Basically, therefore, during the 1840s, a handful of Indian Muslims and Parsis became a part of the Masonic family, though they had not received the warmest of receptions from British Masons resident in India at the time. The admission of Indians at this point depended on several factors: the candidate's religion and social status, the jurisdiction into which he sought inclusion, sibling rivalry between English and Scottish lodges, and the attitudes of provincial Masonic leaders. During the 1840s, admission was unlikely, but not impossible (unless, of course, the candidate was a Hindu). The unrest of the subsequent decade brought the limited trend toward inclusiveness to a standstill.

As with the Masonic independence movement in British North America, the debate over native admissions in India took place within a dramatically

Members of Alexandra Lodge No. 1065 (English Constitution), Jubbalpar, India, ca. 1870 (all Europeans) (copyright, and reproduced by permission of, the United Grand Lodge of England).

changing political and cultural context. At the beginning of the period, India was in the midst of a prolonged depression due, in large part, to the military and fiscal policies of the company-state. Over time, colonial rule led to the dismantling of indigenous commercial and investment institutions, deindustrialization, and an increasingly peasant-based economy; all these processes combined with the increasing strength of the colonial state to subordinate India ever further to metropolitan Britain. When the economy began to recover in the 1850s, India was under the highly interventionist administration of James Ramsay, Lord Dalhousie (1848–56). Dalhousie centralized and enhanced British power by annexing the Sikh state (1849) and part of Burma (1852) and deploying the "doctrine of lapse" to assume control over Satara, Jhansi, Nagpur, and Awadh. He also placed the kingdom of Oudh under direct British administration. The confident and energetic governor rationalized the revenue administration and reformed the military. His efforts to modernize and anglicize Indian society included a renewed commitment to mass education and missionary Christianity, as well as the introduction of transformative technologies: the railways, the telegraph, a postal system, and irrigation works.

Like several of his predecessors in the office of governor general (including Wellesley and Hastings), Dalhousie was an active Freemason and former Scot-

tish grand master, and he viewed the brotherhood as an asset to empire building. Immediately upon Dalhousie's arrival, the Masons of Bengal paid their
respects to the man they described as "so distinguished a Pillar, and Ornament
of the order." They deemed his arrival in India "an event full of promise for the
moral enlightenment and advancement of the country" and asked him to serve
as patron of the order. Expressing his gratitude at being "received with a hearty
welcome, on my arrival in this remote land by a body of Masons," Dalhousie
enthusiastically accepted the position of patron. He would "be ever ready to
promote the interest and benefit of the institution in this country" as long as its
lodges maintained strict discipline and purity. Such was his commitment to
Freemasonry that Dalhousie's first public appearance in Calcutta was to offici-
ate, in full Masonic regalia, at the foundation stone laying ceremony for the
city's new hospital.[50]

The policies of the mid-nineteenth-century governors like Dalhousie met
with various responses from Indians. Most accommodated the new colonial
order by adapting their survival strategies and reinventing their traditions in
light of British ideas, institutions, and technologies. The British found collaborators among native Indian princes, upper-caste Hindus, the so-called "martial"
communities that had made up the backbone of the company army, and merchant communities like the Parsis. But British policies, reforms, and cultural
arrogance also met with stiff resistance. The first half of the nineteenth century
witnessed a series of military mutinies and civil revolts, which culminated in the
Mutiny/Rebellion of 1857. The threatening combination of mutinous soldiers,
discontented peasants, and sympathetic landlords put the government into a
state of emergency for over a year. Though eventually suppressed, the Uprising
dealt the British a profound shock and compelled them to reassess their approach toward their Indian Empire.[51] Taking place in the midst of all these
developments, the Masonic debate over indigenous admissions therefore serves
as an inroad into the shifting attitudes and policies of the British, as well as the
responses of Indians to British rule, at mid-century.

Masons in both India and the British Isles responded to the events of 1857–
58. Though there is evidence of one lodge in Madras admitting "a native gentleman" named Runganadum Sastry, Masonry's leaders tried to put a stop to the
admission of indigenous candidates. The Provincial Grand Lodge of Bengal
revived and strictly enforced a bylaw (No. 55) requiring provincial grand masters personally to approve the admission of Indians on a case-by-case basis.
The majority of British Masons also lent their unquestioning support to the
government, though one daring brother shocked his brethren by suggesting

that "an enquiry be made into the conduct of the Lord Patron of Freemasons [Dalhousie] . . . owing to the awful crisis in which this country is now placed through the measures of his government." Lodge Industry and Perseverance gave up its banquets and contributed funds for "the Craftsmen, women and little children escaped from Cawnpore, Allahabad and other parts of the country, made desolate by the rioters." Back in the metropole, both the English and the Irish Grand Lodges considered "the numerous murders and barbarities committed by the Sepoys of Bengal upon the British inhabitants, and the great extent of distress and misery entailed upon their families, distress and suffering scarcely paralleled in history," and promptly contributed funds for their relief.[52]

If British lodges hesitated more than ever to welcome indigenous men into their lodges, the status of Eurasians (the offspring of mixed racial unions) was only slightly less tenuous. A fascinating letter from the master of one of the oldest Calcutta lodges sheds light on the state of Freemasonry in Bengal as it related to racial considerations in the aftermath of the Mutiny/Rebellion. The purpose of the letter was to recommend the ideal type of man to fill the open office of provincial grand master. P. Nubia, who worked in the Military Finance Department, observed that Bengal was characterized by "a great deal of *Class* distinction, *Caste* distinction, the former being military, civil, professional, and ceremonial, the latter, pure European, and Eurasian." Admitting that Europeans and Eurasians did work harmoniously together, he asserted that the "exclusiveness" of the Europeans was "carried to such an extent that some Lodges do not receive as Members, scarcely as visitors, any Brethren who have any hair of Asiatic descent; or who are not exclusively European." Nubia had difficulty conveying to the Grand Lodge the extent of the prejudice against Eurasians: "it requires to pass the equator to understand how wide is the gulf which separates, almost beyond the power of union in social life the two antagonistic classes." Thus, even though there were "many excellent and eminent" Eurasian Masons who might bring a lot of energy to the office, in no way could one serve as provincial grand master. Moving on to list the relative strengths and weaknesses of British residents in various occupations, Nubia concluded that the Grand Lodge should draw its next provincial grand master from the ranks of the civil service (rather than the military, professional, or mercantile classes). Metropolitan officials did exactly that when they appointed Hugh David Sandeman "of Her Majesty's Indian Civil Service" as Provincial Grand Master in 1862.[53]

Early in the Sandeman administration, a series of developments in local Masonic affairs forced officials in Bengal and the metropole to examine the growing disjuncture between Masonic claims to universal brotherhood and the exclusionary practices of Freemasons in India.[54] First, in Calcutta, a Hindu merchant named Prosonno Coomar Dutt challenged the English Masonic establishment in Bengal by boldly claiming the right to admission into the brotherhood. Dutt argued that the 55th By Law, which "debars so many of the human race from an Order which professes to be open to all, and to exclude no man on account of his religion," was highly objectionable. He petitioned Lodge Courage with Humanity, No. 392, for membership. Amenable, its master sought permission from Sandeman to initiate him. Sandeman decided to exclude Dutt by invoking the 55th By Law. He offered the vague explanation that Hindus' inclusion was "not desirable with reference to social considerations." He did not elaborate. But he did threaten to use his power of veto if any lodge chose to ignore the regulation.[55]

Meanwhile, another "Asiatic" candidate, a Muslim prince with support from British Freemasons in Kanpur, was testing English Freemasons' commitment to the doctrine of universal brotherhood. In 1863 Lodge of Harmony, No. 483, initiated Said-ud-Dowlah in direct contradiction of Sandeman's orders. Furious, Sandeman suspended two lodge leaders (Master Francis Jordan and Past Master M. O'Mealy) for their "contumacious and rebellious conduct." The master responded by putting his lodge into abeyance and taking possession of its warrant and books. This action provoked the Provincial Grand Lodge to expel Jordan and suspend O'Mealy. Members of the Provincial Grand Lodge applauded Sandeman when he threatened to suspend any Mason who challenged his ruling that "the initiation of an Asiatic in this Province without a Dispensation was illegal."[56]

Both cases provoked a great deal of letter writing, posturing, and heated debate over the boundaries of the Masonic family. As they reached Masonic authorities in the metropole, the discussions of the two incidents became intertwined. The objections voiced by Sandeman and members of the Provincial Grand Lodge fell into two categories. First, they argued that Hindus were polytheists who could not become Freemasons because they did not profess belief in a single supreme being. "Hindoos are a race of idolators," charged Brother Howe, "who worship not only graven images, but a variety of created things and beings, and whose superstitious and idolatrous rites are notorious, and in many instances abominable." According to Brother Howe and others, since Hindus did not demonstrate faith in "one true God" they could not be trusted and their admission would compromise Masonry's principles and secrets. English Masons also justified the exclusion of Hindus on the ground that the cultural differences between Hindus and Englishmen were just too great to bridge. Brother Abbott, a twenty-year resident of India, remarked of one of his most steady Indian employees (at the office of Ecclesiastical Registrar): "Yet he is a Hindoo and I am an Englishman, his tastes are not my tastes, his habits are not my habits, his God is not my God. Without entertaining any animosity, therefore, against Hindoos, I feel that there are few points of sympathy between us, and many points on which we cannot understand each other." Objectors also pointed out that questions of caste impeded the realization of true brotherhood between Indian and European: "How could [the Hindu] claim the right hand of fellowship with men whom he openly professes to scorn, and whose very touch is regarded by him as so contaminating, as to require ceremonies of ablution to obliterate?"[57]

In the face of these opinions (shared by a majority of Provincial Grand Lodge officers), one British voice stood out in support of the admission of Hindus. Charles Piffard, a Calcutta lawyer and active Freemason, implored the brethren to recognize the contradiction between Masonic ideology and the policy of excluding a group on the basis of its race. In making his argument, Piffard reminded the Provincial Grand Lodge of Freemasonry's central ideological pillar, "the great Masonic Doctrine of the Universal Brotherhood of man." "Our Order is composed of worthy men of many various races," he continued. "What reason has been given to call upon us to put a brand on one particular race"? He urged them to "hold out the hand of brotherhood" to any eligible Hindu candidates. Although the sole British voice supporting Hindus inclusion in Calcutta, Piffard might well have cited the argument of James Gibbs, a high-ranking officer in the English District Grand Lodge of Bombay, who had recently expressed the hope that "the Natives of this country" would join his "own countrymen" in "that sacred tie of Masonry, [through which] brotherly love may be engendered, relief to the distressed be practiced, and truth become the ruling principle of their lives."[58] Despite the force of their arguments, Piffard and Gibbs were clearly in a minority.

By 1864 both cases had made their way to the Grand Lodge of England, which readily decided in favor of both Dutt and Jordan and expressed faith in the civilizing, moderating power of Freemasonry. Metropolitan officials upheld the doctrine of universal brotherhood by confirming Masonry's fundamental purpose was "to serve as a meeting ground for men who might otherwise remain at a perpetual distance." The English Grand Lodge overturned the Provincial Grand Lodge's decision to expel Jordan and found the 55th By Law to be "in contravention of the main principles of the order." They argued that Hindus should be admitted into their fraternal family because Freemasonry would help introduce "true religion and enlightenment" and promote "large-hearted charity and brotherhood between man and man." The Irish Grand Lodge, and, notably, the Viceroy of India, Lord Mayo, also gave Dutt their immediate and unconditional support. Mayo reminded Bengal officials that there was "nothing in either the rules or spirit of Freemasonry which prevents persons who do not profess Christianity from being admitted to the order."[59] Under pressure from these metropolitan directives, Sandeman and the Provincial Grand Lodge were forced to capitulate. Dutt joined Lodge Anchor and Hope in 1872, after nine years of relentless petitioning.

Dutt and other South Asians who joined Freemasonry had forced British Masons to fulfill their institution's claims to cosmopolitan brotherhood. Of course, barriers to South Asians' complete participation in Freemasonry were still at work. Even though Muslims, Parsis, Hindus, and others found their way into lodges and multiracial lodges were increasingly common, Europeans continued to dominate the majority of lodges in India and elsewhere. While the grand lodges had lifted restrictions barring Hindus' admission, they could not —nor did they ever hope to—control the admissions practices of local lodges, which could still blackball candidates indiscriminately (or discriminately, as was probably often the case). Moreover, the emergence of lodges set up for particular religious or occupational groups (such as Parsi lodges in Bombay and army lodges composed primarily of officers) ended up reinforcing racial distinctions and compromising Masonry's inclusive, universalist ideology.

Nevertheless, Dutt's initiation marked the beginning of a new phase in the history of Freemasonry in India, a period in which it was not unusual to see multiracial lodges and widespread admission of indigenous candidates, regardless of their religion. Of the approximately 100 lodges at work in India during the early 1870s, at least one fifth included indigenous members. The Grand Lodge of All Scottish Freemasonry in India and the District Grand Lodges of Bombay, Bengal, and the Punjab had at least one Indian officer in their ranks. When the Lodge Rising Star of Western India met in 1877 to install Brother Rustomjee Merwanjee as master, *The Standard* reported that the Masonic hall was crowded with Parsi, Hindu, Muslim, and European brethren, "all happily assembled together for one common object—a social and fraternal band of Brotherhood." Meanwhile, in the Punjab, Lodge Light in the Himalayas, a primarily European lodge in Murree, elected Dhanjibhoy Camadore as its master. Back in Edinburgh the Scottish Grand Lodge regularly drew members' attention to and celebrated the "kaleidoscopic beauty" of its lodges in India. Brother Bhownagree, a Parsi, attended a Grand Lodge meeting in 1884 and

Prosonno Coomar Dutt (first Hindu admitted into an English lodge in Bengal, India), 1895 (copyright, and reproduced by permission of, the United Grand Lodge of England).

Members of the Lodge Rising Star of Western India No. 342 (Scottish Constitution), 1905 (British Library).

reported that Scottish lodges in India "thoroughly represent the noble principles of Masonry in refusing to make distinctions of caste or creed."[60]

Upper-class Indians joined the brotherhood for a variety of reasons. Like their Europeans brethren, they were attracted to the intellectual stimulation and spiritual cultivation that Freemasonry afforded. They enjoyed the convivial dinners that followed monthly lodge meetings and Masonry's public processions and ceremonies.[61] Indigenous members who were engaged in commercial pursuits or who traveled extensively welcomed access to the global network of lodges and brethren. Most significantly and radically, as we will see in the Conclusion, they embraced Masonry's ideology of fraternal cosmopolitanism.

Empire, Race, Family

Based on events examined here, it is tempting to argue that Freemasons' attitudes toward Indian candidates reflected a widespread trend historians typically associate with the high imperialism of the mid- and late nineteenth centuries: the growing prevalence of racial categorization as a way of understanding difference. Whereas the cosmopolites of the Enlightenment and the abolitionists of the late eighteenth and early nineteenth centuries had professed belief in the unity and perfectability of mankind (also described as historical evolution-ism),[62] mid-nineteenth-century observers started dividing mankind into many distinct, polygenetic, hierachically ordered races. Culminating in the emergence of social Darwinism, European attitudes toward indigenous peoples became less humanitarian and hardened into an imperialist ideology infused with as-sumptions about the rights and duties of superior master races over inferior subject races.[63]

Historians of Britain identify the moment of the shift to increasingly ra-cialized assumptions and attitudes quite precisely, during the 1860s, in the aftermath of imperial debacles in India and Jamaica. Catherine Hall has con-vincingly argued that the debate over Governor Edward Eyre's handling of the Morant Bay Uprising in Jamaica (which also coincided with the dramatic rise in popularity of Carlyle's *Occasional Discourse on the Nigger Question*) signaled the transition when new forms of overt racism challenged and eventually super-seded the "developmental notion of human nature" championed by John S. Mill and the abolitionist generation. She explains: "The debate over Eyre marked a moment when two different conceptions of 'us,' constructed through two different notions of 'them,' were publicly contested. Mill's imagined com-munity was one of potential equality, in which 'us,' white Anglo-Saxon men and women, believed in the potential of black Jamaican men and women to become like 'us' through a process of civilization. Carlyle's imagined community was a hierarchically ordered one in which 'we' must always master 'them.'" Other events in the empire — the Indian Mutiny/Rebellion, the Maori Wars, and Fenian violence — also contributed to this pervasive ideological shift. Ronald Hyam points out that writers, explorers, missionaries, politicians, and early ethnologists all shared these new assumptions about the deterministic character of racial heredity and its implications for Britain's imperial mission. "In these ways and with such words," Hyam asserts, "the optimistic eighteenth-century and early Victorian beliefs about the equality and perfectability of mankind were sharply reversed."[64]

Statements by Masons on both sides of the debate over Hindu admissions provide evidence of this broad shift in the way Europeans understood differ-ence and indicate the growing prevalence of racialized discourses. Opponents like Sandeman and Howe justified Hindus' exclusion by referring to the un-bridgeable cultural divide between Indians and Europeans, a gap they increas-ingly understood in terms of biological difference. Brother Fenn explained: "We never could know the Asiatic intimately, there was a wide and impassable gulf between us which nothing could bridge over. Men, though of the same blood, were not all alike, the word 'man' did not always bear the same signification; there were various races, various ranks and walks in life, and our race differed in every essential point from that of the Asiatic, so that we could never meet as Brothers." Likewise Brother Abbott "did not consider an Asiatic to be of our kind, and would never sit in Lodge with him." Although making the opposite argument, the United Grand Lodge and Piffard also conceptualized the difference between Indians and Britons in terms of racial categories. They would have agreed with the Grand Master of All Scottish Freemasonry who proclaimed a few years later that Freemasonry, as it penetrated "into the remotest corner of this Indian Empire," would help "raise up the natives of this country to the high level of European civilization and culture, and thus . . . establish an enduring bridge of sympathy and kind feelings over the gulf which now separates the governed from the governing races."[65] Dutt himself even used the category of race to argue for Hindus' inclusion, though, unlike the Britons who spoke in terms of multiple races (that should or should not be brought together under Freemasonry), he assumed the existence of a unitary human race.

However, events in the world of British imperial Freemasonry suggest that the shift from the historical evolutionism of the Enlightenment to a starkly racialized "new imperialism" was neither clear-cut nor complete by the 1860s and 1870s. Freemasons displayed a way of understanding difference that was more complex and subtle than historians of racial ideology have allowed. Masonic rhetoric from the period highlights the inconsistency and variability with which the category of "race" could be deployed. Some Masonic writers and orators remained committed to the idea of a unitary human race. A contributor to *The Craftsman* argued that "the belief in a common Divine Essence is the first great link that teaches man that the whole human race is a Brotherhood." A Masonic sermon idealistically observed: "More and more is the world recognizing the great fact that the human race is one family—the children of one parent." Other commentators drew on the metaphor of the family to reconcile racialist assumptions with their brotherhood's universalist ideology. While differences of all sorts (including race) did exist, Masonry taught that all men belonged to one family. The Reverend D. C. Moore, in a typical late-nineteenth-century Masonic sermon on brotherly love, drew on William Preston's *Illustrations of Masonry* when he proclaimed: "In the common brotherhood of man there is no distinction of race nor lineage. The proudest monarch on his throne, the humblest slave at his compelled labor—the white-skinned European—the Asiatic native of the 'red earth' as father Adam—or the 'swart Ethop' of the darken hue; all have the same right to claim GOD for their Father, and so comes the lovely, loving truth, 'all we are brethren.' 'We find a brother wher'er we find a man.' "[66] Although clearly influenced by widely circulating racialist ideas, Masons like Moore saw brotherhood rather than difference as the bottom line.

The majority of Masons celebrated their brotherhood's ability to bring the diverse races of the world together. A handbook published in Dublin in 1867 described Masonry's "tie of brotherly love" in the following terms: "Overlapping all geographical divisions, rising above all religious and political differences, and ignoring all diversities of race, it established a common bond of kindly intercourse among the Craft." On the other side of the empire, in Singapore, an audience gathered for a foundation stone laying ceremony learned that Freemasons "regard the whole human species as one family; all, without distinction of race or caste, the high and the low, the rich and the poor, as children of one Parent, and consequently bound to brotherhood." In sum, the Enlightenment language of universal brotherhood remained central to Freemasonry long after it had, according to most historians, disappeared from western European ideology during the "new imperialism" of the late nineteenth century.[67]

Even though the question of South Asians' admissibility had been resolved by the 1870s, the debate over "Prince Hall" Masonry was still putting British Freemasons' commitment to the ideology of universal brotherhood to the test in this period. As we have seen, the grand lodges had decided to substitute "free man" for "free born" in the wording of the *Constitutions*, thereby opening the way for former slaves to be initiated. Lodges in the Caribbean continued to be dominated by whites but men of various racial backgrounds, if deemed sufficiently respectable and worthy, were admitted. Meanwhile, in the United States, Freemasonry was starkly divided along the lines of race. Prince Hall and his successors had long warranted lodges for black Masons who wanted to participate in Freemasonry but were not welcomed by white American Masons. "Prince Hall Masonry" became so popular that two grand lodges, one to oversee the lodges of "regular" Masons and another to regulate African American Masons, emerged in many states. The Prince Hall grand lodges were keen to gain the approbation of the wider Masonic world through official recognition and the exchange of representatives and fraternal correspondence. Writing repeatedly to London in the late 1840s, the "National Grand Lodge of the United States of America of Colored Freemasons" sought an acknowledgment from the English Grand Lodge, a need they described as "a matter of life or death with us." They drew on the idea of a universal family to explain their exclusion from white lodges: "The portals are closed against us because our common parent has varied the shades of complexion." They also appealed to British Masons' pride in the inclusive traditions of their order: "To deprive us of our rights and privileges from this cause alone, we believe to be at war with the principles of our ancient order destroying the catholicity of the same and among freemen and Free and Accepted Masons should not be tolerated. . . . If there be no other bar, save an unrighteous and an American prejudice that excludes us from fellowship at home, may we not hope to be acknowledged in a land where worth and not the color of the skin makes the man."[68]

Despite such appeals, which came with regularity from many different states, the Grand Lodge of England was unwilling to extend the hand of brotherhood to Prince Hall Masons.[69] It had long recognized and exchanged correspondence with the original grand lodges and did not want to risk upsetting white American brethren. The English Grand Secretary explained his Grand Lodge's position to his Irish counterpart in 1871: "We have had many applications from 'Colored Grand Lodges' in America for recognition and exchange of Representatives. As, however, it is a rule of our Grand Lodge never to recognise more than *One* Grand Lodge in the same Country (Berlin excepted) and as we are on terms of amity with the Grand Lodges of almost all the States, it is manifestly impossible, setting aside every other consideration, that we could recognise the Colored Grand Lodges." Such legalistic arguments got the British grand lodges off the hook. They likely belied an underlying prejudice on the part of some, but this prejudice never had to be uttered. In fact, those discussing the issue claimed: "We dismiss, in the first place, as being unworthy a moment's consideration, the question of colour. . . . We see no objection whatever to their being Negro Masons, any more than to there being Mohammedan or Hindoo Masons. It would never occur to us to suggest that these American coloured Masons should be denied admission into our Lodges on the ground they are negroes."[70] Instead, they challenged the decision of the English Grand Lodge to grant Prince Hall a warrant in the first place. The legalistic arguments prevailed, and Prince Hall Masonry remained unofficially recognized until the end of the twentieth century.

Nevertheless, the issue was troublesome enough to British Masons that it remained a matter of considerable and regular discussion in their periodicals and official correspondence.[71] Advocates of upholding Masonry's doctrine of universal brotherhood in the case of Prince Hall Masonry could be found in other parts of the empire. Members of Lodge Albert Victor in Lahore viewed the issue of "Coloured Masonry" as "a subject for regret." Their proceedings for 1891 noted that "Colour 'per se' has never been a question raised under British or Irish, Masonic Government in this country." Referring to British Masonry's long tradition of initiating Muslims, they criticized "America" for failing to recognize the Masonic status of those "whom it spent many millions of dollars to emancipate." They perceptively concluded: "This disgraceful distinction of Black, Red or White in Masonry is happily exclusively American. It is one which ignores much of our symbolism, for it is certain that none of the ancient characters to which our Rituals refer were *white* men."[72] In 1901 Liverpool's *Masonic Journal* reported on Liberian Masons' being welcomed into a lodge in Birkenhead. It also noted that the English Grand Lodge had received the Grand Master of the Grand Lodge of Liberia, which had been warranted by a Prince Hall grand lodge in the United States, with "all the honors of a Sovereign Grand Master." Arguing in favor of recognition, the journal drew on the family metaphor: "If England acknowledged the daughter of Prince Hall, Liberia, as regular and constitutional, she cannot with any reason declare the parent and her American offshoots spurious and clandestine." Meanwhile, the operation of interracial lodges in India, the Caribbean, and eventually Africa indicated a blindness to race, even if only temporarily, in the lodge.[73]

Given, therefore, that many British Freemasons seem to have viewed the "other" as their brother, does the ideology of Freemasonry—centered as it was on the metaphor of brotherhood and family—provide evidence to support David Cannadine's argument that "the British Empire was at least as much (perhaps more?) about the replication of sameness and similarities originating from home as it was about the insistence on difference and dissimilarities originating from overseas"? Focusing on the issue of how Britons conceived of their empire as a sociological entity, Cannadine identifies ornamentalism—the "effort to fashion and tie together the empire abroad in the vernacular image of the domestic, ranked social hierarchy"—as the prevailing imperial ideology. Shared assumptions about status brought British and indigenous elites together into "one integrated, ordered, titular, transracial hierarchy."[74] While he acknowledges the importance of race, Cannadine challenges the extent to which it has become the central unit of analysis in British imperial studies. He thus argues that ornamentalism was a more prevalent ideology of empire than orientalism.

Were Freemasons more inclined to "brothering" than "othering"? It is here where taking simultaneous account of the metropole, dependent empire, and a settler colony proves so illuminating. The comparison with events in British North America demonstrates that differences of race and culture did have a significant effect on whether British Masons accepted colonial Masons as their equals. If Canadian Masons were adolescents whose independence movement assured their passage into adulthood, Indians and others (regardless of their status within their indigenous societies) were younger brethren, children, who were still very much in need of careful upbringing by patriarchal father figures. Imperial Britons admitted South Asians into their lodges with the understanding that they occupied a subordinate place within the family. Like children who observed their elders, indigenous members could use lodge meetings as opportunities to watch and imitate their betters. British Masons on both sides of the debate concurred that Indians "had not yet acquired a permanency of character, but were in a transition state from a low condition to a more English and Christian standard of civilization and morals." Even the Hindus' supporters, who claimed to be upholding "the great Masonic Doctrine of the Universal Brotherhood of man," described and treated them like younger brothers who still required extensive tutoring in the arts of civilization. Alluding to the Uprising of 1857, the Grand Lodge of England, which supported the admission of Hindus, inquired rhetorically: "How can western ideas make their way amongst a people whose superstitions so kindle their suspicions, that a greased cartridge may become the cause of a general rebellion? How can a man think of another as his brother, made like himself, after God's image, when to touch him is pollution?" Their answer was through the work of institutions like Freemasonry. Indians already enjoyed English laws and liberties, the Grand Lodge pointed out. Through education and institutions like Freemasonry they would also come "to adopt the faith and manners of Englishmen; until that day arrives, there can be but little hope of friendly intercourse between the dominant and the subject races." Similarly, according to an editor of a Masonic periodical published in India, Freemasonry was an institution "sufficient to bind and sustain the entire family of man in one vast chain of fraternity and love." Its mission was "to humanise, civilise and fraternise mankind." For British Masons who viewed indigenous members as their undercivilized younger brethren, the institution thus buttressed historicist discourses that, as Dipesh Chakrabarty explains, were European imperialists' "way of saying 'not yet'" to non-European peoples and keeping them indefinitely stuck in civilization's waiting room.[75]

To the extent that Freemasons posited indigenous members as their less civilized younger brethren, Masonic ideology offers a version of what Uday Mehta has described as a "liberal strategy of exclusion" (or, perhaps more precisely in this case, a liberal strategy of *inclusion*). The doctrines of English liberalism (with its emphasis on individual liberty, private property, and social contract), Mehta argues, actually served as an ideological buttress of imperialism. Liberalism's late-eighteenth- and nineteenth-century proponents based their ideology on the Lockean notion of freedom: like parents who retained authority over their children because they had not yet acquired reason, an imperial power like Britain justifiably held sway over childlike indigenes who lacked reason and thus the capacity to enter into consensual political arrangements.[76] British Freemasons — who perceived the global Masonic family not as an institution of equals, but one in which some children might grow into adulthood while others remained trapped in childhood — thus drew on the well-established ideas of English liberalism that had long justified imperialism.

In sum, as historians attempt to understand the subtleties of imperial ideology, we must factor both similarity and difference into the equation. After all, that is what the historical actors themselves did. As Thomas Metcalf points out: "Throughout the later nineteenth century, as they constructed their 'India,' the British always had to negotiate this disjuncture: between an acknowledgement of similarity, and an insistence upon difference. The task was never to be easy, nor was the result to be a coherent ideology of rule."[77] Freemasons had to negotiate a disjuncture between their universalist ideology, that taught Britons to acknowledge their basic similarities with their fellow men and brothers, and their duties and assumptions as imperialists, which required them to distinguish themselves from their subjects. Frequent recourse to the metaphor of the family helped them resolve this apparent contradiction: Masonry's familial model had plenty of room for the perpetuation of hierarchies based on racial and cultural differences even as it proclaimed that Britons and indigenous peoples belonged to the same universal family.

By failing to appreciate the ways that assumptions about social ranking *interacted with* assumptions about race, the idea of "Ornamentalism" therefore oversimplifies British ideologies of rule. Had British Masons really wanted to "eradicate the differences, and . . . homogenize the heterogeneities of empire,"[78] they would have taken the initiative to welcome indigenous candidates. Had they readily accepted the elements of Masonic ideology that encouraged them to appreciate the fundamental similarities between themselves and indigenous peoples, they would have foregone the two decades of hard-fought debate. Instead, the impetus had come from the Indians themselves.

SEVEN

Loyal Citizens of the Empire

In the midst of the South African War in 1900, members of the Grand Lodge of Nova Scotia marched in a procession, headed by the band of the 1st Regiment of Canadian Artillery, to St. Paul's Church in Halifax. There they heard an "instructive sermon" preached by the Reverend Reginald Bullock. He opened his lecture with a lengthy disquisition on Nehemiah's efforts to rebuild the walls of Jerusalem during the "troublous times" of the fifth century B.C.E. Emphasizing "a theme in fullest harmony with the spirit now dominating the Anglo Saxon race," he praised Nehemiah's "intense love of country, his fervid patriotism, his loyal attachment to the motherland." From there Bullock turned to his contemporaries' own "work of reconstruction": "the rebuilding of the Empire wall of England, causelessly and insolently broken down in Africa." Canada had dispatched to South Africa thousands of its "workmen," whose "work with sword and trowel has been crowned with high approval." Canadians' enthusiastic response proved the Dominion's value to the Motherland, the reality of imperial unity, and Canada's future promise as a great nation.[1]

Such views were representative of the widely held opinion that Masonry could play an instrumental part in building up the empire during a period of widespread insecurity about its future. Indeed, late Victorian Britons faced an entirely different situation than their early Victorian predecessors, the men of prominence and rising men who took for granted the Pax Britannica that had enabled them to succeed. First, there were concerns about Britain's slipping international position vis-à-vis formidable new rivals, nations that were industrialized, modernized, and hungry for empires of their own. During the 1870s the newly consolidated nations of Italy, Germany, and the United States (and later, in the 1890s, Japan) joined Britain's traditional rivals, France and Russia, as challengers to British global predominance. At the same time, the British Empire faced the threat of internal disintegration as rebellions, wars, and the emergence of colonial nationalism contributed to a growing sense of insecurity among the British. The response to both external and internal challenges was the same: Britons should do everything in their power to consolidate the empire that had for so long defined their national greatness. Thus, by the 1880s, enthusiasm for empire began reaching new levels and imperial matters came to occupy a central place in the domestic political agenda.

Efforts to turn the empire into an asset for Britain as it faced shifting geopolitical arrangements coalesced into a widespread, if uncoordinated and ill-defined, *imperialist* movement. The term "imperialist" was in widespread use at the time. Lord Milner explained in 1903 that "when we, who call ourselves Imperialists, talk of the British Empire, we think of a group of states, independent of one another in their local affairs, but bound together for the defence of their common interests and the development of a common civilization." Although imperialists disagreed widely over how best to bind together the empire's constituent parts, all shared a conscious sense of membership in the empire and an awareness of imperial developments, a commitment to imperial unity and (at the very least) preservation of the empire, and a plan for making imperial relations a source of strength for Britain and the colonies. To quote Milner again, "the maintenance and consolidation of what we call the British Empire should be the first and highest of all political objects for every subject of the Crown."[2]

Milner might have held up the Freemasons as exemplar imperial citizens. If the Masons of the early nineteenth century had identified themselves as loyalist Britons (as discussed in Chapter 4), their brethren at the end of the century clearly defined themselves as ardent imperialists who were not only loyal to the monarch and state but ready and willing to put their brotherhood in the service of the empire. Like the broader imperialist movement of which they were a part, Freemasons might disagree over tactics, but they were uniformly committed to pursuing the same strategy, namely preserving and strengthening imperial unity. Their attitudes and activities make clear the power of Freemasonry's fraternal ideology and practices to build empire citizens and cement imperial ties during the age of high imperialism.

TABLE 4. Lodges in South Africa

	English	Scottish	Irish	Dutch	Total
1875	22	—	—	21	43
1892	60	20	—	15	95
1951	239	81	38	49	407

Sources: *Coil's Masonic Encyclopedia*, 17; A. A. Cooper, "The United Grand Lodge Movement in South Africa."

Note: No independent grand lodges were established in South Africa. These figures therefore constitute a subset of the figures listed in Table 1.

TABLE 5. Lodges Belonging to Independent Grand Lodges in Canada

	Ontario	Nova Scotia	New Brunswick	Quebec	British Columbia	Prince Edward Island	Manitoba	Alberta	Saskatchewan	Total
1877	319	67	32	62	8	9	6	—	—	503
1889	354	67	32	59	10	12	40	—	—	574
1897	360	62	31	59	24	12	59	—	—	607
1918	458	75	39	66	80	15	79	102	135	1,049

Sources: Grand Lodge of Canada Proceedings, Grand Lodge of Nova Scotia Proceedings, Grand Lodge of Quebec Proceedings.

Note: Independent grand lodges were established in Ontario (1855), Nova Scotia (1866), New Brunswick (1868), Quebec (1869), British Columbia (1871), Prince Edward Island (1875), Manitoba (1875), Alberta (1905), and Saskatchewan (1906).

The imperialist efforts of Freemasonry as an institution and of individual Freemasons were multifaceted. First, Masonry's expansive network of lodges spread information, money, and people from one end of the empire to another. It fostered awareness of empire and facilitated movement through its widespread parts. Second, Freemasonry's meetings and ceremonies offered an outlet for imperialist energies and provided forums for the expression of imperialist sentiment. Intimately connected with the royal family, the brotherhood promoted the idea of the monarchy as an institution under which the diverse peoples of the empire could unite. Third, membership in the brotherhood proved especially useful to the cohort of high-level administrators and soldiers running the empire in this period. The *Canadian Craftsman* pointed out this fact when it posed the rhetorical question, "Did it ever occur to the brethren that in building up the British Empire to its present grand position in the world that the very leaders of the various achievements, that have made it such a mighty factor in the settling of the affairs of nations were members of the Craft."[3] Indeed, Masonry's homosocial culture seemed especially attractive to men who defined themselves first and foremost as imperial men.

Finally, the Masonic brotherhood was instrumental in solidifying relations between Britain and the white settlement colonies as they were developing into independent nations. (For the steady growth of Dominion lodges over time, see Tables 4–6.) Though neglected by many historians of imperialism, the Dominions of Canada, Australia, New Zealand, and South Africa were a primary focus of imperialist efforts to strengthen the empire in the face of its challengers. The cases of Canada and South Africa demonstrate the multiple ways Freemasonry actively nurtured Anglo-Dominion relations and how institutions like Freemasonry were more effective in uniting the empire, by nurturing ties of culture and sentiment, than were schemes for formal federation. The strength of these ties became apparent at the turn of the twentieth century when Britain's farflung citizens rallied to help in "the rebuilding of the wall of England," first in South Africa and then in the theaters of the First World War. It was at this point that the Masonic network, which had benefited so many expatriate Britons since the mid-eighteenth century, issued a remarkable payoff to Britain itself.

Imperialist Network

Under construction since 1728, the global Masonic network stretched to all parts of the empire (and, as we will see, back to the metropole) during the age of high imperialism. The network had always connected imperial men, but it

TABLE 6. Lodges Belonging to Independent Grand Lodges in Australia and
New Zealand

	New South Wales	Tasmania	Victoria	South Australia	Western Australia	Queensland	New Zealand	Total
1920	289	33	232	83	94	62	267	1,060
1950–54	767	64	710	175	256	415	357	2,743

Sources: Gould, *A Concise History of Freemasonry*; *Coil's Masonic Encyclopedia*, 81–82.

Note: Independent grand lodges were established in South Australia (1884), New South Wales (1888), Victoria (1889), New Zealand (1890), Tasmania (1890), Western Australia (1900), and Queensland (1903). Not all lodges in these colonies joined the grand lodges as soon as they were set up; the metropolitan grand lodges usually did not recognize a dominion grand lodge until a majority of lodges had joined it.

did so to an even greater degree from the 1870s on. Ideas, information, money, and people flowed with increased intensity across the Masonic network. The lessons learned in lodge meetings and the activities of Masonry encouraged brethren of all ranks to see the empire as an expansive yet discrete spatial entity through which they could move and to which they owed allegiance.

Whether living in Dublin, Montreal, or Calcutta, a man gained a keen awareness of the empire by belonging to Masonry. Masonic periodicals, which multiplied during this period, kept Masons in both the metropole and the colonies well informed about imperial developments. In fact, fostering imperial awareness was a chief aim of *The Craftsman*, a Canadian Masonic publication that was launched in 1866 "to promote the great interests of British America, as an integral part of the British Empire, by uniting Masons in every part of it more strongly in the bonds of brotherly love, relief and truth." Every issue contained news about imperial events. In March 1867, for example, *The Craftsman* informed readers about war breaking out in India, the birth of the daughter of Princess Alexandra, the British government's decision to pay for Governor Eyre's legal defense, the reported death of Dr. Livingston at the hands of "the Caffers," changes in the British Cabinet (including the retirement of brother Lord Carnarvon from the colonial secretaryship), the Fenians' plans to attack Canada, and the British North America Act. Later, the periodical kept readers abreast of the imperialist movement with reports on the Colonial Conferences in London. Its rival, the *Masonic Sun*, celebrated the advent of the imperial ocean penny postage service in 1899. In fact, the first letter to be sent via the service was a Masonic greeting from Canadian Freemasons to the English Grand Lodge. It concluded with an expression of hope that the new enterprise would "strengthen the kindly feeling we have for the Fatherland and for the myriad of brethren who look up to the great and good Grand Lodge of England as their 'Mother Grand Lodge.'" Comparable publications circulated in Britain, Ireland, and India. The *Indian Freemason* was founded in the hope that "we from the centre of Indian Freemasonry may read of the doings of our Brethren at the farthest points it reaches, East, West, South, or North in the Indian Empire." Many, like Dublin's the *Masonic Visitor*, even had specific sections devoted to "Colonial and Foreign Masonry," which included coverage of both Masonic and imperial topics.[4]

The periodicals were particularly fond of drawing attention to the imperial exploits of well-known brethren. *The Craftsman* praised Brothers Nelson, Wellington, Salisbury, Roberts, Kitchener "and hundreds of others . . . who have assisted in the upbuilding of the great fabric known as the British Empire, where equal Justice, freedom and imperishable glory exist." The *Freemason's Chronicle* (London) reported in 1899 that "members of the Masonic Brotherhood are foremost among the loyal citizens of the Empire, ready to serve the Queen and country wherever and whenever the occasion presents itself." It drew attention to lesser known figures like the Provincial Grand Master for East Lancashire, Lord Stanley, who was heading to South Africa, and other provincial grand masters who were ready to go "if the Empire can avail itself of their services." Readers were informed that Sir Henry Stafford Northcote, the Provincial Grand Master for Devonshire, was on his way to Bombay to serve as governor.[5] With reports celebrating the fact that many of Britain's most famous and accomplished empire builders belonged to their brotherhood, the Masonic periodicals affirmed, and asked their readers to share in, an imperialist identity.

Lodge meetings also channeled information about imperial affairs and encouraged members to feel a sense of belonging to an expansive, supranational polity. A member of Sydney's Trentham Lodge "aroused the enthusiasm of the gathering" by reciting the words of a song that urged Australians, who were "of British blood," to "keep the Empire one" and "link our hands from shore to shore, with hands across the sea. One God, one Flag, one Brotherhood, one Glorious Destiny." Local and grand lodges in the colonies, as we will see, observed the landmarks of Victoria's reign and took part in festivities marking the imperial tours of prominent men. At the same time, colonial matters were consistently on the agenda of the metropolitan grand lodges, which seemed to relish their role as governors of an expansive Masonic empire. The English Grand Lodge heard appeals from and listened to reports concerning colonial brethren on a regular basis. Whether they were debating the eligibility of an illiterate candidate seeking entrance into Royal Phoenix Lodge in Trinidad, the powers of the District Grand Master of British Burmah, or the un-Masonic conduct of a brother belonging to New Zealand Pacific Lodge, the empire figured centrally in the considerations of metropolitan Masons.[6]

Decisions about how to spend lodge funds, in response to requests pouring in from other nodes in the network, also kept Freemasons aware of imperial developments. Between the 1870s and the 1900s, members of the Grand Lodge of England voted grants of money to sufferers of famine in Persia, India, Kolapore, and Ireland; fires in New Brunswick and Jamaica; hurricanes in Curaçao and Barbados; floods in Queensland; a volcanic eruption in St. Vincent; and an earthquake in India. The regularity and liberality with which metropolitan Masons responded to the plight of victims — both Masons and others — in distant corners of the world indicated their sense of responsibility to and identity with the empire. Meanwhile, Freemasons in the colonies were asked to contribute to (and thus kept informed about) various imperial causes, like the Palestine Exploration Fund, Irish famine sufferers, and patriotic funds in wartime.[7]

In addition to channeling news, information, and money, Freemasonry encouraged members to think of themselves as empire citizens by facilitating their movements around the empire. Over the course of the nineteenth century, the British Empire had grown, through both formal acquisition and creeping colonialism, to vast and imposing proportions. Though the advent of travel by steamship and railroad had lessened the risks considerably, travel abroad could still pose challenges and produce anxiety. The ever-growing network of Masonic lodges (which kept pace with formal and informal imperial expansion) made existence in and movement through this space manageable. A Scottish Grand Lodge officer, noting that Masonic lodges could be found in "Africa, in Asia, in the Colonies, in India, and in every part of Europe," aptly described membership in the brotherhood as a "passport in all parts of the globe." So coveted was this passport that Freemasonry continued to be vulnerable to impostors. In the 1870s, Masonic officials in India issued warnings about "loafers — persons who have gained admission into the Order merely as a means of getting support, and who thus come upon the Craft, wherever they may wander, for assistance."[8]

Belonging to Masonry seems to have been particularly useful to lower-middle- and working-class people who got stuck somewhere in the empire and needed help moving on. Late-nineteenth-century India affords countless examples of lodges' readily granting "mobility assistance" to brethren and their families. The District Grand Lodge of Madras helped Masons from India, South Australia, Turkey, and Scotland. Brother Victor Dumas had gone to Madras to set up a veterinary practice. He had been initiated into Masonry in Mauritius and was also a member of Lodge Shanghai No. 106. When his veterinary practice failed to take off, he appealed to the District Grand Lodge for funds to go to Singapore. It paid for his passage aboard a French steamer and gave him money to cover "his immediate wants on his arrival." The Grand Lodge helped other men go to Bombay, Alexandria, and Rangoon. Masonic authorities in Madras seem to have been particularly active in assisting travel to Australia. In 1874, they sent Brother Cottrell (a horse trader) back to Adelaide and gave him money to reclaim the clothes he had pawned; Brother Saxton, who had fallen sick in Madras, to Calcutta so he could then get a passage to Australia; and, in 1896, the widow and two daughters of Brother Harry Stanley (of the Stanley Opera Company) to Calcutta where "she had friends intending to go to Australia." Across the ocean, Masons in Cape Town helped stranded brethren find their way home and offered other forms of assistance.[9]

Membership had privileges for Masons' dependents, especially as unfortunate circumstances forced them to adjust to imperial life without their husbands and fathers. The widows of brethren who had belonged to Madras lodges received regular aid. In 1886, for example, the District Grand Lodge was underwriting monthly pensions for Mrs. C. Sanderson, Mrs. Tholasy Ammul Naidoo (and her three sons), and Mrs. M. A. Lynn (and her three children). While the District Grand Lodge of the Punjab did see to the needs of living brethren, it was especially devoted to helping Masons' orphans. In the early 1870s, it established the Punjab Masonic Institution for the Education of the Children of Deceased and Indigent Masons; they were to receive relief "WITHOUT RE-GARD TO [THEIR] RACE OR RELIGION." In 1873, it was responsible for one boy and one girl. Ten years later, it oversaw fifteen boys and twelve girls. By 1893, the District Grand Lodge could boast of "educating 40 orphans who but for Masonic assistance must have been cast upon the world without means of earning a livelihood." Every Mason who belonged to an English lodge in the Punjab was assured that, even if he was outside the district, he and his family "may receive prompt and cheerful assistance when adverse circumstances compel them to put our well-known virtue of Charity to the test."[10]

Masons' assumptions that their charitable efforts would serve the empire by enhancing the productivity and respectability of its citizens revealed their immersion in the social and gender attitudes of the time. The Punjab Masonic Institution indicated its commitment to turning its wards into respectable imperial citizens: "the girls shall be taught what will make each of them fit to become a capable governess or useful wife," while the boys would be trained "for some definite calling or profession by which they will be able to earn an honest living in this their country of adoption." One of the institution's graduates, who became a teacher at a local girls' school, attributed her "good fortune," education, and "headway as an independent woman" to the benevolence of the District Grand Lodge. Meanwhile, South African Masonic authorities were committed to the education of Masons' children in order "to fit them, when entering the sphere of life, for the duties of their respective stations."[11]

Masonry clearly facilitated the movements of downtrodden brethren and their dependents as circumstances forced them from one part of the empire to another; it also assisted movement out of the British Isles. The effort involved all levels of the Masonic network from individual members to grand lodges and, initially at least, involved assisting the migration of individual families to the colonies on a case-by-case basis. In 1857 the Grand Lodge of England granted £10 to Brother Thomas Kirk, former member of the Royal Artillery and a Halifax lodge, who was residing in London but sought to migrate with his family to Australia. Similarly, the Irish Grand Lodge granted £15 to a brother "in a state of great destitution" to assist his passage to Australia. Meanwhile, Masons on both sides of the Atlantic cooperated to bring Irish women and children to Canada West. Alexander Abbott, a lodge secretary in London, Canada West, forwarded drafts "in aid of two girl orphans of a late worthy Mason who are endeavouring to make their way to this country" to the Grand Lodge. He prevailed upon Masonic officials in Dublin to make up any difference in the cost of the orphans' passage and told them they would be "promptly refunded with Masonic gratitude." In another case involving Abbott, we see Victorian gender attitudes at work once again. Abbott turned to the Masonic network to facilitate the migration of a brother's mother-in-law and her son, because he feared that if he mailed the money directly to the mother-in-law, Catherine Kelly, she would use it for other purposes.[12]

Such Masonic efforts to render assistance to British emigrants in the 1850s foreshadowed the wider emigration movement, fueled by private initiatives as well as government intervention, of the period between the late 1870s and the 1920s. Concerns about high unemployment and poverty combined with insecurity about Britain's geopolitical standing to lead many observers to conclude that empire migration was an effective strategy for shoring up Britain and its empire. It would promote stability in the metropole by relieving population pressures and strengthen the empire by helping the settlement colonies through their growing pains. Yet, as Andrew Thompson points out, Britain could not just dump its unwanted vagrants and "surplus" women on the Dominions. "Migrants had to be an asset rather than a liability to the societies receiving them."[13] While the government eventually became involved, initially the tasks of providing information about colonial settlement, offering financial assistance, and helping place the new arrivals in jobs were left to individuals and private institutions like Freemasonry.

The Masonic network proved especially useful in the effort to shift people around the empire and ensure the right sort of Britons went out to the colonies. The case of the Palmer family affords a representative example of the assistance offered to individual families. In 1878 Edmund Thomas Palmer, a Resident Medical Officer in Dublin, Ireland, died suddenly, leaving behind a penniless wife and three children. Palmer had been a member of lodges in Dublin and in St. John, New Brunswick, and upon his death his brethren on both sides of the Atlantic rallied to help his widow and "three orphan children." Freemasons in Ireland and Canada raised £112 for the family's passage to Bermuda, which was Fredericka Palmer's "native place" and site of her marriage to Edmund. On their journey across the Atlantic, the Palmers were shepherded by Masons in Halifax and Bermuda. In a note of appreciation Fredericka Palmer wrote: "I applied to you to assist me in my sad affliction, and to get me home to my people. You promptly took up my cause, and the result of your efforts has exceeded my most sanguine expectations, and more than realised my fondest hopes." She was especially thankful that the Masons had raised an extra £6 10s "to procure suitable mourning" and thereby guarded her respectability. Concluding that the Freemasons had saved the Palmers from the poorhouse, the principal sponsor of the drive remarked: "It is truly a happy thing to find that Freemasonry is not only universal, but that it is a practical system — a great reality — and not a matter of mere sentiment and words."[14]

British Freemasons also initiated more grandiose emigration schemes in this period. In the late 1860s Masonic officials in England and Howard Holbrook, a prominent Mason and legislator in British Columbia, opened discussions on a new emigration program. The English Grand Lodge proposed to organize and finance the emigration of female children from the Royal Masonic Institution for Girls in London to British Columbia. Masonic officials in London were motivated by both the need to create additional space in the institution and the current thinking of the day, which viewed female migration to the colonies as a good solution to the perceived problem of surplus women in Britain. On the other side of the Atlantic, Holbrook enthusiastically approved of the idea. He informed the Grand Lodge that he would discuss the matter with the highest-ranking Masonic authorities in British Columbia and assured them that they could overcome any difficulties. For Holbrook, the settlement scheme was a "means of rendering a boon to the colony of having introduced good religious girls well brought up and educated."[15]

As empire migration gained momentum with the proliferation of philanthropic emigration societies in the 1880s, Masonic initiatives also picked up steam. Freemasons on both sides of the Atlantic broadened their efforts to encourage the migration of men. During the 1880s lodges in the North of England helped needy brethren make their way to Liverpool, where the provincial grand lodge covered the cost of passage to the colonies. In 1886 Freemasons in New Westminster, British Columbia, set up an Immigration Committee, headed by Canon Cooper, Bishop of New Westminster and Grand Chaplain of the Grand Lodge of British Columbia. The committee communicated with lodges and emigration societies in England and distributed information about British Columbia to interested brethren. They even offered "to receive and welcome, and assist to the best of our ability all brethren, properly vouched for, on their arrival in New Westminster, and to pass them on to the care of other lodges if not intending to settle in our neighbourhood." Some years later, English Masons in Liverpool notified their brethren, through Masonic publications, that "we have been considering a scheme of Masonic emigration to Canada whereby the best class of men would be sent direct to employment in Canada. A mutual arrangement with the brethren on the Canadian side would be of very great advantage." To put the scheme in motion, a delegation of four Liverpool Masons journeyed to Canada on the SS *Empress of Britain*.[16] Like many of their fellow imperialists, Freemasons involved in such migration schemes viewed *people* as fundamental building blocks of a strengthened and rejuvenated empire.

The network of lodges that stretched across the empire and assisted needy Freemasons and their dependents had, by the 1880s, expanded to include a new kind of lodge for middle- and upper-class brethren with entirely different needs. These "imperial lodges" were located in London and served several purposes. Their membership comprised brethren from the colonies who were in London, British Freemasons who had spent their careers in the empire, and anyone who was particularly interested in imperial affairs. Men who joined imperial lodges benefited from the ready-made community they offered. Attending meetings where one could find brethren with similar interests and experiences certainly facilitated the repatriation process of British members and assisted colonial brethren during their temporary sojourns in the imperial metropolis.

Fostering imperial connections was the primary goal of the imperial lodges. The founding premise of the first imperial lodge — the Empire Lodge (1885) — was to strengthen "the bonds that unite the Dominions with the Mother Country, by bringing the Brethren from Overseas into close relationship with Freemasons in the Metropolis of the Empire." Within one year the membership had grown from 20 to 131 men representing twenty colonies and the Dominion of Canada. The English Pro Grand Master and former Colonial Secretary, Lord Carnarvon, gave his active support to Empire Lodge because in his opinion it "drew colonists in closer connection and sympathy with home matters." One highlight of the lodge's activities was its commemoration of Queen Victoria's Diamond Jubilee in 1897, when it hosted 300 brethren from throughout the empire, including five premiers of colonial governments. The Empire Lodge set a precedent for the founding of several other metropolitan lodges devoted to similar aims. The Empress Lodge was founded in 1885 "for the reception of Indian and Colonial Masons who may visit the Mother Country," while the Anglo-Colonial Lodge came into being in 1906 with the motto of "Hands across the sea." In 1912 the English Grand Lodge consecrated the Royal Colonial Institute Lodge "for the purpose of enhancing the ties of Empire and Craft and as an additional bond between the Resident and Non-Resident Fellows and Members" of the Royal Colonial Institute.[17]

Several of the empire lodges drew their memberships from men connected with a particular country, dominion, or colony, such as the Anglo-American Lodge, Anglo-Argentine Lodge, and Canada Lodge. The latter was founded in 1911 as "a bond of union between the Brethren of the Dominion and the Brethren of the United Kingdom." Its founders confidently hoped that Freemasonry would "assist in the great work of forming those bonds of 'indissoluble attachment' which shall forever unite the component parts of the British Empire." Participation in Canada Lodge, according to one observer, gave Britons and Canadians opportunities to know and understand each other — "thus laying that foundation of mutual respect and regard so necessary in the partnership of the British Empire." In 1914, the lodge did its part for the empire migration movement by using some of its funds to cover the passage money of a "deserving youth" who was related to a Mason and was willing to work on a farm in Canada.[18]

Composed of "earnest and energetic empire-builders" — Freemasons who could "think imperially" — the imperial lodges furnish evidence of the multidirectional proliferation of the Masonic network.[19] The network that had grown out from the British Isles since the 1730s was now reimposed on the metropole itself. As intended, the effect of this reinscription was to strengthen the connections among the component parts of the empire.

Royal Art, Royal Empire

The Masonic network raised consciousness of, and facilitated movement within, an imperial sphere of vast proportions and astoundingly diverse peoples. The primary goal of late-nineteenth-century imperialists was to create a reliable and durable unity within this multicultural entity. But what could bind together — in mutual respect and sympathy — a horsetrader from South Australia, a shipbuilder from Bombay, a Muslim prince, a businessman from Ontario, a West Indian merchant, an Irish army officer, and an English lord? For many imperialists, especially the Freemasons in their ranks, the answer was the British crown. Supporting the imperialist program was, therefore, not only a matter of expressing one's loyalty to the monarch, but also calling upon the monarchy as a crucial unifying institution.

By the 1870s the "imperializing" of the British monarchy was well underway. If the monarchy had been given a "face-lift" during the reign of George III, Victoria's reign witnessed the deliberate merging — at both a symbolic and a practical level — of the monarchy and the empire. It was apparent in the Imperial Titles Act that created Victoria Empress of India and the imperial tours of her sons. In all parts of the empire — settlement colonies, India, crown colonies — people associated Victoria and the empire; reverence for Victoria implied loyalty to the empire. The result was the proliferation, as Cannadine puts it, of the "day-to-day convergences between empire, monarchy and hierarchy: an amalgam of names, places, buildings, images, statues, rituals and observances that made it impossible for anyone to forget or ignore the fact that they were subjects of a sovereign rather than citizens of a republic." Freemasonry effected many of the "convergences" between empire and monarchy. Because Freemasonry — "The Royal Art" — had historic and contemporary connections with the royal family, it was well placed to promote this imperialist idea. Freemasonry's emphasis on ritual and ceremony also helped. The message of private lodge meetings and public Masonic ceremonials was consistent: Freemasons were unsurpassed in their loyalty to the Queen-Empress. One Canadian Masonic periodical explained that "we, as Freemasons, have been taught to . . . revere our Sovereign."[20] Membership offered, therefore, countless outlets for the expression of imperialist sentiment. Examining some of these ceremonies and the imperial/Masonic activities of Victoria's sons Edward (1841–1910, Prince of Wales) and Arthur (Duke of Connaught) demonstrates Freemasonry's role in furthering these imperialist goals.

Wherever they were in the empire, Freemasons sought to take a leading part in royal/imperial ceremonies of all kinds — ceremonies to observe the comings and goings of important imperial officials, to lay foundation stones of public buildings, to celebrate royal jubilees, and to mark the progress of British princes who toured the empire. For example, in 1869, George Bowen, governor of New Zealand, arrived in New Plymouth, Taranaki (on the western side of the North Island). He was greeted by a crowd of "the most loyal subjects in Her Majesty's dominions," which included local officials, Maoris "in their picturesque Native costume," and a guard of honor from the 18th Royal Irish Regiment. Indicating the centrality of Freemasonry's imperial role, the official levee took place at Freemasons' Hall, where the governor received deputations from various groups in the region. Among them were "loyal and faithful subjects" representing three local Masonic lodges who offered their enthusiastic congratulations to Bowen on his safe arrival. Noting that Masons in New Zealand and Queensland had presented him with similar greetings, he thanked "the members of that ancient, loyal, and charitable brotherhood, which embraces in its mystic tie all nations and languages, all political parties, and all social classes" for their blessings and prayed to the Great Architect of the Universe (GAOTU) to "build up here the fair fabric of Peace, Union, and Prosperity."[21]

If Freemasons in Taranaki occupied such a central place in ceremonies honoring a colonial governor, then their attentions to the Queen-Empress he represented had to be all the more impressive. Of course, Queen Victoria was not a Freemason. She lacked the essential qualification of being a man. But this did not prevent Freemasons from expressing their profound admiration for her. In fact, many felt she displayed the most important qualities of a Mason: faith in God, a philanthropic spirit, "fidelity to the constitution," and patriotism. She exercised the "virtues which should be exemplified in the life and character of every [Mason]." Moreover, as they constantly pointed out, almost all her male relatives were Masons: her father, her uncles, her sons, and even a grandson. It was not surprising that the Queen, "surrounded as she is by our atmosphere of Masonry, would seem to regulate her life and govern her actions by Masonic precepts." Celebrating Victoria's reign and expressing pride in the "long-enduring association of her family with our Fraternity of Freemasons" thus became a typical way for brethren throughout the empire to express imperialist sentiment.[22]

For her part, Victoria welcomed the close association between the royal family and the brotherhood. She agreed to serve as Patroness of English Freemasonry. After all, Victoria could always count on Freemasons to acknowledge — in their private meetings and also in public statements — important occasions and events like royal birthdays, jubilees, marriages and births, and assassination attempts. Victoria was well aware of the reciprocal relationship between Masonry and the empire. Observing that "the Society of Freemasons increases in numbers and prosperity in proportion as the wealth and civilization of my Empire increases," she expressed her "hearty" appreciation for their "charitable effort" and their "affectionate devotion to my throne and person."[23]

The event that occasioned these remarks from the Queen was her golden jubilee in 1887, an empire-wide celebration that put the interconnectedness of royalty, empire, and Freemasonry on public display. The jubilee afforded the ultimate venue for British Freemasons everywhere to rededicate their order to the imperialist agenda. Addresses of congratulations poured in from Freemasons throughout the British Isles, the settlement and crown colonies, and India. Local, district, and grand lodges held celebratory meetings. The efforts of the Grand Lodge of Nova Scotia were typical. It appointed representatives to the municipal committee charged with arranging the jubilee celebration in Halifax. In addition to taking part in public events commemorating the reign, all members of the Grand Lodge gathered for a public procession and a special church service. The Reverend David Moore, the Grand Chaplain, calculated that Victoria's reign had added 700 million square miles to the empire, quoted Disraeli at length on the "link[s] in the chain of Saxon thraldom," and gave thanks "for the Queen and Empress, not merely of Britain and Britain's dependencies, but Queen of our affections and Empress of our hearts." Meanwhile, the Grand Lodge of Scotland held a banquet, and Masons in Quetta, northern India, organized a jubilee ball. Others arranged for more lasting memorials. The District Grand Lodge of the Punjab established a Victoria Jubilee Scholarship in connection with the Punjab Masonic Institution; its counterpart in New Zealand set up the Jubilee Masonic Fund of Auckland for the relief of poor brethren and their dependents; and the Irish Grand Lodge founded the Victoria Jubilee Annuity Fund.[24]

Not surprisingly, Masons' most impressive jubilee event took place in London's Royal Albert Hall in June 1887. The celebration drew over six thousand Masons, including the grand master and officers of the Grand Lodges of England, Scotland, and Ireland, one Indian prince (the Maharajah of Kuch-Behar), and a Scottish Mason described as Major Proudfoot Dick (who presumably hailed from North America). Three of Victoria's sons—the Prince of Wales (Grand Master), the Duke of Connaught (Provincial Grand Master for Sussex and District Grand Master for Bombay), and Prince Albert Victor (Senior Grand Warden)—were in attendance. Prince Edward described the affair as one of the largest gatherings of Freemasons ever witnessed and led the assembled brethren in three enthusiastic cheers for the Queen. The Earl of Carnarvon observed that Masonic "representatives from every part of the civilised world" had journeyed to London to pay homage to the queen, whose reign witnessed the building of "an Empire greater than any over which the eagles of Rome ruled . . . accomplished and built up by the sturdy hands and hearts of Englishmen." Building on its tradition-inventing efforts at the turn of the century, the Grand Lodge reminded the Queen that Masonry was founded "on principles of unswerving loyalty" and assured her that the growth of imperial Masonry was "in unison with the welfare of the nation and the maintenance of the established Institutions of the land, which it will ever be our earnest desire to preserve inviolate."[25]

Like Carnarvon, brethren in all parts of the empire took note that the fortunes of Freemasonry and Victoria's empire were intertwined. Fifty years of rule under Victoria had allowed Freemasonry to make "astounding" progress, according to one brother who calculated that English lodges had increased from 475 in 1837 to 1,450 in 1887 and that the number of lodges in the empire had grown from 1,350 to 3,650. Likewise, the Grand Lodge of Canada attributed the prosperity of Freemasonry "to the liberty and toleration which have been so much fostered during the reign of our glorious sovereign." If Victoria's reign had fostered Freemasonry, then the brotherhood had strengthened Victoria's empire. Observing her birthday in 1900, one brother commented that Freemasons had "proved themselves to be the very bulwark of her throne." Masons like Nelson, Wellington, Salisbury, Roberts, and Kitchener were responsible for "building up the British Empire to its present grand position" and making it a "mighty factor" in international affairs. It "has been welded and is being more tightly welded together by men who have been reared and trained amidst Masonic influences."[26]

Masons were at the vanguard of subsequent commemorations honoring Victoria. South African Masons greeted the Diamond Jubilee of 1897 as an "eventful epoch of universal Jubilation throughout the enormous empire of

England." The Rev. C. W. Barnett-Clarke, Dean of Cape Town, reminded Masons gathered at a thanksgiving service of their profound obligation to their monarch—"so true a woman, so sagacious a Sovereign and so benevolent a mother to her vast Empire." Local authorities established the Queen Victoria District Masonic Pension Fund for Aged Freemasons and Widows in honor of their beloved queen. At the same moment Masons of Toronto raised money to endow a bed at the Hospital for Sick Children, and the District Grand Lodge of the Punjab helped finance a statue of the Queen-Empress in Lahore. More somber observations were held when Victoria died in 1901. Bloemfontein Masons, who had gathered only nine months earlier to celebrate Prince Edward's escape from an assassination attempt, reassembled to honor the queen and celebrate her long reign. The local Masonic temple overflowed to an extent never before seen, even though the South African War (which will be discussed shortly) was ongoing. Speakers remembered Victoria's many virtues and urged the assembled brethren to be obedient, remain loyal, and practice brotherly love. "Let us be true and steady," urged one, "so as to prevent jolting or disjointedness in this Colony and throughout the Empire."[27]

Victoria's sons embodied the convergence of royalty, empire, and Freemasonry and carried on these associations long after her death. One observer acknowledged that Victoria's reign had encouraged Freemasonry's "spread over that great empire of ours, as to some parts of which the sun is ever at its meridian." But he felt that her son Edward's tenure as Grand Master (1874–1901) was responsible for its roots' being struck "so deeply into the home and colonial life of the nation." The prince had seen "light in Masonry" on a visit to Scandinavia in 1868. The king of Sweden himself initiated Edward. All three British grand lodges conferred high Masonic rank on the prince.[28] When the Marquess of Ripon resigned as English Grand Master three years later (due to his conversion to Catholicism), Edward agreed to take over as the head of English Masonry. Eight thousand Masons descended upon London to attend the prince's installation ceremony in 1875 at Royal Albert Hall. At a time when provincial and district grand masters rarely attended grand lodge meetings, at least thirty-four, including the district grand masters for Jamaica, Bengal, Madras, Trinidad, and the Eastern Archipelago (Malaya), were present. Looking around a room that included at least two dozen members of Parliament, Edward's close friend Lord Carnarvon observed that Freemasonry had "allied itself with social order, with the great institutions of the country; and above all, with Monarchy, the crowning institution of all." This unprecedented assembly of Masons clearly touched Edward, who proclaimed that "as long as Freemasonry

Interior of Zoutpansberg Liberty Lodge No. 2486 (English Constitution), Transvaal, South Africa, 1898 (copyright, and reproduced by permission of, the United Grand Lodge of England).

keeps itself from being mixed up with politics, so long will, I am sure, this great and ancient order flourish, and its benign influences tend to maintain the integrity of this great Empire."[29]

Shortly after his installation, Edward embarked on a tour of India in advance of the 1877 durbar, an event Cannadine identifies as "the first climax of . . . this new 'culture of ornamentation.'" Cannadine describes how Edward received Indian princes, held public receptions, and took part in elaborately staged tiger hunts. What he neglects to point out is the prince's ceremonial role as Grand Master of English Freemasonry. During his visit to Bombay, the prince presided over an impressive Masonic ceremony to lay the foundation stone of the new Prince's Dock. English, Parsi, Muslim, and Hindu Masons were in attendance. The prince congratulated the 550 assembled Masons (in front of a crowd of over 10,000 spectators, including the governor, several "Native Chiefs," and local officials) on the flourishing condition of Freemasonry in India and their fulfilling the object of their institution — to "unit[e] men of various castes and creeds in the bonds of fraternal brotherhood." He was especially pleased to oversee a ceremony for a public work that would "tend to the protection of life and property, [and] to the extension of trade." In Calcutta and Madras, he received deputations from local Masons at Government House. The prince thanked Masons in Bengal for their loyal address and the beautiful casket that encased it, noting that "it is yet a greater pleasure to learn from you that in this distant part of the Empire the Craft upholds its ancient character by uniting Members in a Brotherhood of Charity and Loyalty, of good will to all, and of good works to benefit mankind." Back home, Carnarvon reported on the prince's Masonic activities throughout "the length and breadth of our Indian Empire." Pursuing imperialist objectives through Masonry, he had "cemented those blocks — those colossal blocks — of empire."[30]

Prince Edward clearly viewed the role of imperial booster and the role of Masonic ambassador as inseparable. After his first visit to India, he came to see himself as a spokesman for Freemasonry. He also agreed to serve as an intermediary between the brotherhood and the queen, an easy role for him since he viewed the Freemasons as her most loyal subjects. At the same time, he represented the monarchy and the empire when he was among Masons. For example, brethren gathered for an English Grand Lodge meeting in 1886 were made aware of his role in founding the Imperial Institute and encouraged to support it.[31] Other members of the royal family were similarly disposed. Edward's brother, the Duke of Connaught (whose Masonic-imperial activities are discussed in the next section), and his son Albert Victor (who toured India in 1889–90), simultaneously represented Freemasonry, the crown, and the empire at home and abroad.[32] The attitudes and activities of all three made it easy for Freemasons around the empire to express their loyalty and attachment to the British crown, especially when it was occupied by one of their "brothers." Edward's accession to the throne in 1901 provoked an outpouring of support from his Masonic brethren, who sang the praises of the man who had been "born to reign over a great Empire and a loyal people." For example, the Grand Lodge of Canada sent a congratulatory cablegram on behalf of "thirty thousand Freemasons and British subjects."[33]

Finally, the convergence of Masonry, empire, and monarchy is evident in ceremonies designed to honor the subsidiary rulers of the empire. The year 1905 marked the silver jubilee of the Nizam of Hyderabad, one of the richest men in the world. He ruled over the most important princely state in British India. Although the Nizam was not a Freemason, British lodges in the vicinity wanted publicly to recognize the success of his reign. The Freemasons were invited to attend a durbar and garden party in the Chow Mahala palace. Dressed in full regalia, they staged an impressive procession and read, in both English and Urdu, their official proclamation. The first order of business was to explain the purpose of their brotherhood, which they described as "a Great Empire that extends over the whole world." "We have nothing to do with worldly power, with wars, conquests or politics," they proclaimed. "Our main duty is the promotion of brotherly love and charity and we strive to form a bond of union amongst the whole of humanity regardless of Race, Religion or Nationality." They then offered their congratulations to the Nizam and thanked him for "the protection we have received in the discharge of our Masonic duties" in the state of Hyderabad. Lord Ampthill, the governor of Madras, could not attend the event, but sent, in his capacity as District Grand Master, a telegraph expressing his congratulations and appreciation.[34]

Proconsuls and Brothers

Freemasonry's multifaceted contribution to forwarding the imperialist agenda thus included encouraging awareness about the empire, facilitating movement around the empire, and rallying people to the crown as a symbol of imperial unity. These activities involved a broad range of people who were invested in the empire — destitute Masons and their dependents, middle-class brethren, elites, royal princes, and even the monarch. But Freemasonry's impact, at least as far as the imperialist agenda was concerned, seems to have been greatest on one class in particular, the empire's proconsuls. Contemporary Masonic observers claimed that Freemasonry played an especially important role in making men effective imperial governors. Prominent colonial governors, army commanders, and colonial secretaries agreed that Freemasonry was a valuable asset to the imperialist. It assisted them individually and collectively in the tasks of governing and defending the empire and in the imperialist mission of making the empire a source of national strength. In so doing, Freemasonry simultaneously reinforced the "hegemonic masculinity" of the late Victorian period that defined British manhood in terms of male comradeship, an unrelenting sense of duty to the state, willingness to sacrifice oneself, readiness and strong will, and the "cult of athleticism."[35] All were necessary attributes for empire builders.

Once again, it is instructive to look not only at Masonic rhetoric and activities, but also at the imperial/Masonic careers of prominent individuals, such as the Earl of Carnarvon. Carnarvon joined the Colonial Office in 1858; less than ten years later the Conservative Derby ministry appointed him Secretary of State for the Colonies (during his tenure he presided over the passage of the bill that established the Dominion of Canada in 1867). Carnarvon served again as Colonial Secretary under Disraeli between 1874 and 1878. By this point, he had taken over as Pro Grand Master of the English Grand Lodge, then under the leadership of his close friend the Prince of Wales. Carnarvon's career in the colonial office directly influenced his involvement in Masonry and vice versa. He drew on his experience as a colonial administrator when confronted with concerns from country and colonial lodges. Arguing that "English Freemasonry might be viewed as a kingdom, and its policy like that of a kingdom, had three great relations, foreign, colonial and domestic," he proposed turning the Grand Lodge into a parliament with representatives from all parts of "our federation." Carnarvon viewed his imperial and Masonic duties as interdependent. At the time that he was Under-secretary of State for the Colonies and promoting a degree of Canadian self-government, he was also supporting the position of Canadian lodges seeking more control over their own affairs. Lecturing the Grand Lodge on "the broad principles which I wish to see adopted in our Colonial policy," he warned against confusing "quantity" of imperial possession with "quality": "Extent of dominion is no test of real prosperity, unless accompanied by a living spirit breathing from the inmost centre to the outmost extremity." Later, as Colonial Secretary, Carnarvon advocated the establishment of a federation for the South African colonies of the Cape and Natal and the Boer republics. At the same time he pushed the English Grand Lodge to appoint a District Grand Lodge for the Transvaal and Orange Free State in the hope of subordinating Dutch Freemasonry to English Freemasonry. Writing some years later a District Grand Lodge officer in Bombay observed that Carnarvon "was able to apply the principles inculcated by Freemasonry in all the many and various duties which devolved on him."[36]

Freemasons believed their brotherhood had a profound influence on other prominent imperialists. In late 1898, Field-Marshal Kitchener (who had been initiated in La Concordia Lodge in Cairo in 1883 and belonged to five Cairo lodges by 1895) received a hero's welcome in Edinburgh. Only weeks before, Kitchener had successfully led an army of Anglo-Egyptian troops down the Nile into the Sudan (the British-officered Egyptian army had been inching south for much of the Jubilee year). With Britain's overwhelming victory over the Sudanese at Omdurman, Kitchener claimed the Sudan for the empire. That the British built a railroad line as the army proceeded indicated to the Sudanese, and the French, their intention to hold the Sudan once conquered. Commemorating these imperial achievements, the Scottish Grand Lodge took part in the festivities surrounding Kitchener's triumphant visit to Edinburgh. At a meeting of

"Freemasonry: Some prominent members of the Craft," *Pictorial World*, 8 May 1875. Left to right: Right Hon. Lord Mayor (Junior Grand Master), Lord Skelmersdale (Deputy Grand Master), Earl of Carnarvon (Pro Grand Master), H.R.H. Prince Leopold, H.R.H. Prince of Wales (Grand Master), John Hervey (Grand Secretary), H.R.H. Duke of Connaught (author's collection).

the Grand Lodge, the Grand Chaplain described Kitchener as a remarkable soldier, "diplomatist," statesman, civiliser, and "educationist." He then rhetorically inquired: "Now when we put all these things together and ask ourselves how does he possess them, how does it come about that one man can combine such qualities in himself, the answer surely is for us not far to seek. The reason surely is that Lord Kitchener is a Freemason. (Applause). Like Lord Wolseley, like Lord Roberts, like Sir William Lockhart at the present time . . . he is one of our brethren, and we can scar[c]ely wonder that he has attained to such eminence and distinction." Kitchener, according to John Tosh, was representative of a growing number of men who embraced imperial bachelorhood and envisioned the empire as "quintessentially a masculine arena, where men worked better without the company of women." The homosocial culture of Freemasonry (which, as Tosh points out, was rapidly proliferating in this period) attracted these men. A contemporary contributor to the *Canadian Craftsman* agreed: "This great institution of ours is pre-eminently a manly organization. . . . We want only men of individuality, of character, men who are willing to learn the lesson of obedience to lawful authority, and it is that which gives us power through this country of ours, and throughout this broad world."[37]

Prominent imperialists themselves agreed that Freemasonry rendered valuable assistance to them. Like other members of the brotherhood, they benefited as individuals from Freemasonry's ability to meet their social, spiritual, and material needs. But the institution also seems to have benefited them collectively, as a class of imperial proconsuls, in several ways. First, membership in Freemasonry helped Britons carry themselves as self-assured empire builders. Its mutual assistance network offered a sense of security in the face of the uncertainties that accompanied life in the empire. A member of Lodge Himalayan Brotherhood described Masonry as "a source of comfort and consolation to Englishmen of all ranks in India." He noted that many Englishmen who lived in isolated and perilous conditions valued highly "the feeling of confidence created by membership in our powerful organization for the relief of suffering and the support of friends and brothers." So important was Freemasonry's contribution, he argued, that the imperial state itself was obligated to Masonry "for its influence upon the conduct of public servants on all occasions of difficulty and danger." Another resident Englishman agreed that Freemasonry offered imperial servants "solace to all their woes" as they transferred from one station to another. It gave them comfort, spiritual guidance, and intellectual stimulation.[38]

This Masonry-inspired confidence seems to have extended all the way up the imperial ranks. When he was serving as commander-in-chief of the British army, Lord Frederick Roberts, army hero and Mason of long standing, observed that "wherever the craft exists throughout the Empire," it tended to strengthen British prestige. He also acknowledged "the benefits which its members obtain by the brotherly ties which knit them together." Roberts's fellow imperialist, Lord Ampthill, visited Simla in his capacities as acting viceroy of India, governor of Madras, and District Grand Master of Madras. The first body to offer him a public welcome was the Freemasons (English Freemasonry in the Punjab was under the leadership of Kitchener at the time). Ampthill told his brothers: "It was something to feel that although he stood there among a number of men who were complete strangers to him, yet he would rely on each and every one of them to regard him with more than ordinary friendliness and good will." "It was a great thing," he continued, "to be able to come among strangers with confidence like this." Being a Mason had never meant as much to him as it did then, when he was "in need of sympathy and support in the face of the arduous and responsible duties that lay before him."[39]

Second, Masonic social activities brought prominent and lower-ranking imperial administrators together and reinforced their identity as imperialists. Lodge Himalayan Brotherhood in Simla was particularly proud of the fact that its rolls included "the names of illustrious men who have in the past played an important part in the government of this Empire." Over seventy brethren attended the lodge's annual dinner in 1894. The honored guests included one ICS officer who had served on the Northwest Frontier and in Burma, a Major-General in the Army, and the Commandant of the Simla Volunteers. One brother's "comparison of the Masonic institution with the British Empire, on neither of which the sun ever sets," elicited enthusiastic applause. A few months later, Simla was the site of a week-long Masonic festival, some of the proceeds of which went to support the Punjab Masonic Institution. The week culminated in a Masonic ball that provided entertainment to 350 guests, including the viceroy and his wife (Lord and Lady Elgin) and the lieutenant governor and his wife. The Masons and their guests supped at midnight and danced until twilight. In this same period, Lodge Bolan in Quetta put on six balls, including jubilee balls in 1887 and 1897. It lived up to its claim of being "second to none in our loyalty to the Queen" by sending deputations to greet governors of Bombay who toured the region (Lord Sandhurst, who headed both English and Scottish Masonry, in 1898; Lord Northcote, the English Grand Master, in 1900; and Lord Lamington, the Scottish Grand Master, in 1905).[40]

Third, Masons concerned with colonial affairs believed that their brotherhood could help inculcate loyalty and foster imperial unity. When Lahore Freemasons raised funds for a statue of Queen Victoria in 1897, Sir Garnet Wolseley, commander-in-chief of the Punjab Army, applauded and encouraged their role in "the loyal movement in this district." Wolseley had joined the brotherhood as a young officer in Dublin in 1854 (motivated in part by the knowledge that Masonic membership might mean the difference between life and death for a military man). In 1897 he was District Grand Master of the Punjab, and he appointed another senior member of the army, General Sir E. H. H. Collen, as his deputy grand master.[41] The brotherhood's ability to serve as a meeting ground between ruler and ruled was billed as a great asset to the empire. The question of native participation in Masonry had certainly provoked heated debate at mid-century, but once it was resolved, Freemasons decided to put the policy to good imperial use. A Masonic official in Bombay explained to Queen Victoria that Freemasonry "has brought together, and united, men of various

races, castes and creeds, in one common Brotherhood, and, by its benign influence, has greatly tended to strengthen that feeling of devotion to your Throne."
Through institutions like Freemasonry, Europeans and Indians were getting
used to meeting together in public, and "the old isolation was gradually giving
place to a better understanding." The English, Scottish, Irish, and Indian members of Bombay's District Grand Lodge, it was claimed, were "as good citizens,
all animated by the same feelings of loyalty and devotion to our Sovereign Lady
the Queen-Empress." Further north, the master of Lodge Himalayan Brotherhood asserted in 1887 that "Masonry has shown itself to be a most powerful
influence for good in improving relations subsisting between the Englishman
and the Indian." Its inclusion of "the more advanced high-caste Indian" was
especially instrumental in "uniting the English and Indian subjects of Her Majesty in the 'firm and pleasing bond of fraternal love.' "[42]

For Freemasons, the ultimate proof that their brotherhood helped "to render the private life of India more reconciled to the rule of the British Empire"
was the attitude of India's princes toward Freemasonry. They could point to a
long history of Indian princely involvement stretching back to the eighteenth
century when the sons of the Nawab of Arcot had joined English lodges. During the nineteenth century, especially after the Mutiny/Uprising, the trend
increased. In 1893, the Maharajah of Cooch Behar was admitted to the District
Grand Lodge of the Punjab. By this point, he already held high Masonic rank in
the Grand Lodge of England and the District Grand Lodge of Bengal. He was
very active in the formation and working of Nripendra Narayan Lodge in the
mid-1890s and even paid for the construction of an elaborate hall for its use.
Sardar Muhammad Usman Khan, a member of Afghanistan's ruling family,
joined the Lodge Bolan in 1908. Though not a member of the order, the Nizam
of Hyderabad protected and encouraged Masonic lodges in his kingdom because, he believed, "it is calculated to improve good feelings and harmony
among the different creeds and classes in my Dominions." He assured Masons
in his kingdom that he would "not fail to give your Institutions all the encouragement that may be found necessary."[43]

The close relationship between empire, monarchy, and Freemasonry was
encapsulated at the turn of the century in the career of the Duke of Connaught,
whose life as a prominent army commander, proconsul, and Mason took him
throughout the Victorian/Edwardian empire. The third son (and seventh
child) of Queen Victoria and Prince Albert, Arthur was a dedicated army officer
and Freemason for all his adult life; he conceived of Freemasonry as a "public
service which has done so much to maintain our Empire in India." Embracing

any opportunity to travel and serve as an imperial citizen, Connaught was dispatched on several important proconsular missions to various parts of the empire. Fresh out of the Royal Military Academy at Woolwich, Arthur served in Canada during the Fenian invasion and the Red River Rebellion. When Queen Victoria created him Duke of Connaught in 1874, he was steadily rising through the ranks of the army. He served under Wolseley during the Egyptian expedition of 1882 and subsequently held commands in Bombay (1886–90), Ireland (1900–1904), the Mediterranean (1907–10), and Canada (1911–16).

As with so many others who belonged to Britain's imperial ruling class, Connaught's experience in Masonry and his imperial service intertwined. Connaught's career took him, in the aftermath of the Egyptian campaign, to India. In 1883, Freemasons in Bombay went to great lengths to include him in the foundation stone laying ceremony for the Pestonjee Hormusjee Cama Hospital. Although the duke initially agreed to take part, local Masons had to abandon their elaborate plans when it was discovered at the last minute that the duke's Masonic regalia was "on its way to Meerut." All parties regretted the change in plans but agreed that it was impossible for the duke to participate without the appropriate clothing. When Connaught returned to Bombay as commander-in-chief, his willingness to serve as District Grand Master more than made up for this disappointing incident. For local Masons, it was "a singularly auspicious circumstance that a Prince of the Blood Royal of England should come to reign over us." They wholeheartedly agreed with Connaught's estimation of Freemasonry as an ideal vehicle for uniting India's diverse populations behind the throne: "We are in an exceptional position of having amongst us men of all nationalities and all creeds," Connaught explained, "and I have always felt it to be a very great privilege to be enabled in any way, however small, to help in welding those different elements together in loyalty to our most Gracious Sovereign the Queen-Empress and in devotion to the Craft." The duke carried this message to Masons throughout India and, upon his departure, graciously received deputations from his brethren in Karachi, Quetta, Mhow, and Bombay.[44]

Representing Freemasonry, Connaught imbued loyalty and aroused imperialist sentiment not only in India but also in the settler colonies. The duke's next imperial sojourn took him to Toronto, where Canadian Freemasons were not to be outdone by their brethren in India. During this non-official visit, he met with 700 of his Masonic brethren in the Masonic Temple on Toronto Street. Brother Ryerson, head of the welcoming committee, noted that Connaught had always taken care to associate with Masons throughout "the greatest empire the world has ever seen," whether in "our northern land, in the wild plains of Egypt, in the cantonments of India, or in merry England herself." For the Masons of Toronto, Freemasonry played an especially important part in connecting them to Britain. "Of the ties which bind us to the mother country," they urged, "none are stronger than the bond which unites us to our brethren in Masonry in Great Britain." They expressed pride in their descent from "sturdy British stock" and praised their fathers for keeping Canada "for British hearts and British homes." Connaught was impressed with the "magnificence of the assembly" and assured his audience that he would convey to his mother and brother the affectionate loyalty of Canadian Freemasons.[45]

Connaught's activities as an ardent imperialist Freemason intensified during the early twentieth century. Returning to India in 1903 to serve as the king's representative to the Delhi Coronation Durbar, he attended a special communication of the District Grand Lodge of the Punjab. Over 4,000 brethren, representing English and Scottish lodges all over India as well as lodges in the United Kingdom and the United States, had gathered to install Field Marshal Kitchener as District Grand Master. The British dignitaries included Sir Michael Hicks Beach (former Colonial Secretary, Chancellor of the Exchequer, and Board of Trade President), Sir Henry Thoby Prinsep (District Grand Master Bengal), and Lord Ampthill. Sir M. M. Bhownaggrie (MP and high-ranking Scottish Freemason), the Maharajah of Cooch Behar, and the Rajah of Kapurthalla were among the prominent Indian Masons in attendance. During the installation ceremony, the duke expressed his pleasure at being among the Masons of India again and fondly recalled the time "when he was closely associated with the efforts that the Masons of India were doing to extend their principles in all parts of this great country."[46]

The duties of empire building could often impinge on the Masonic activity of prominent brethren like Kitchener and Connaught, but this did not seem to bother the brethren in their charge. On the contrary, they took pride in these distractions, which they interpreted as signs of their brotherhood's importance to the imperial mission. Kitchener had pledged to promote Freemasonry in his capacity as District Grand Master of the Punjab, but his military and administrative duties often precluded him from attending meetings. In 1906 the District Grand Lodge willingly excused Kitchener for being "at present deeply engaged in a work of construction that cannot but appeal to us as Freemasons — the repair and strengthening of the defences of this great Empire." The Duke of Connaught also received praise for his commitment to the empire, even when his proconsular roles prevented him from discharging his duties as English

Grand Master. In 1910, George V (the duke's nephew) sent Connaught to open the Union Parliament of South Africa. Members of the Grand Lodge of England were certain that his efforts had promoted the "peace and harmony which is necessary for the further development of the South African nation" and expressed pride in their Grand Master for being "so intimately concerned with the raising of the new Union to the full brotherhood of the Empire."[47] Here again we see Freemasons using kinship discourse, this time to welcome a settler colony as full member of the fraternal family of the British Empire.

South Africans might have looked to Canada as a model young nation that defined itself within the "brotherhood of the Empire." An effective integration of national and imperial identities was certainly what Connaught encountered in 1911 when he arrived in Canada as governor general and commander-in-chief of Canada. In 1912, he could not attend the annual meeting of the Grand Lodge of Canada but sent his wishes for the "continued success and prosperity" of Canadian Masonry. He was assured, in response, that during his time in Canada he would encounter "nothing but loyalty and devotion to the Empire," especially on the part of Freemasons. As European events began generating concern in 1913, the Grand Lodge of Canada described Connaught as a "link of silk stronger than forged steel in binding us to the Mother Country." The great strength of these bonds would become increasingly apparent as war broke out and dragged on for the next four years. As we will see, Canadians — inspired by men like Connaught and institutions like Freemasonry — would mount a "magnificent response" to empire in its hour of need.[48]

Brethren of British Connection

As Andrew Thompson argues in *Imperial Britain: The Empire in British Politics*, many imperialists of the late nineteenth and early twentieth centuries were particularly focused on the Anglo-Dominion relationship. Whereas at one time Britain could afford to ignore the "colonials" in Canada, Australia, New Zealand, and South Africa, the emergence of territory-amassing rivals like Russia and the United States provoked a reassessment: "There was at this time a profound transformation in the language of imperialism as the nature of imperial loyalty was reconceptualised, antiquated notions of colonial inferiority and subservience were abandoned, and a new agenda was constructed around the idea of a 'Greater Britain.'" Imperialists proposed a range of strategies for keeping the self-governing Dominions within the imperial fold. The most "constructive" among them advocated formalized constitutional, economic, and defensive unions. Others argued that Britain should encourage the already existing ties of sentiment that had naturally resulted from centuries of British migration to the settlement colonies. Meanwhile, the colonials themselves were keenly assessing their own interests, both as nearly independent nations in their own right and as central players in the world's greatest empire. Many in both the metropole and the Dominions had come to envision a mutually beneficial partnership. As the arch-imperialist Joseph Chamberlain put it in 1914: "We are sister States in which the mother country by virtue of her age, by virtue of all that has been done in the past, may claim to be first, but only first among equals."[49]

From the 1870s on, Freemasonry readily lent itself to the imperialist program of strengthening Anglo-Dominion relations. Individual brethren and the grand lodges contributed to a range of imperialist activities from constructive imperialist schemes (like the Imperial Federation League) to more informal efforts to unite the empire. Freemasonry not only offers a window onto the imperialist program but also a gauge of its success. While neither formal political unions nor an imperial zollverein (customs union) came about, it is clear that the ties of culture and sentiment, nurtured by Freemasonry and other institutions, were strengthening. In particular, Masonic rhetoric reveals that fraternalism remained a powerful concept for imperialists in this period. The master of Empire Lodge in London told a gathering of lodge members and 160 visiting Canadian soldiers in 1915 that "they all belonged to two Brotherhoods—those of Masonry and of the Empire." Conceiving of imperial relations in fraternal terms allowed dominion nationalism and imperialist identity to coexist in positive and mutually reinforcing interplay with one another. Canadian and South African Freemasons' response to the imperial crises of the late nineteenth and early twentieth centuries demonstrates both the supranational identity of empire citizenship and the strength of sentimental bonds.[50]

Masons in both the metropole and the Dominions actively supported the imperial federation movement of the 1880s through the 1910s. Imperial federation meant different things to different people, a fact that was plainly evident in the workings of the Imperial Federation League (1884–94). The idea to create a league devoted "to secure by Federation the permanent Unity of the Empire" had emerged out of the Royal Colonial Institute and at first merely involved the creation of a colonial council. The League played a role in staging the Indian and Colonial Exhibition in 1886 and bringing colonial statesmen to London for the first Colonial Conference in 1887 during the Queen's Golden Jubilee celebration. It even enjoyed enough support to establish branch chapters in the

Dominions. In addition to promoting general interest in the empire, the IFL specifically encouraged discussion of commercial federation between Britain and the Dominions. Proposals ranged from implementing reciprocal tariff agreements to the construction of a zollverein that spanned the empire.[51]

The connection between Masonry and the Imperial Federation League was evident in the activities of Lord Carnarvon. Pro Grand Master of English Freemasonry since 1874, Carnarvon had become a member of the League's council in 1885.[52] Three years later Carnarvon's constructive imperialist and Masonic agendas merged when he embarked on a three-month journey to South Africa and Australia to spread the word about imperial federation, drum up support for the cause of empire, and sort out Masonic affairs in New South Wales. As an official representative of the IFL, he delivered speeches on imperial federation, attended banquets and ceremonies, and raised money for the Imperial Institute. Every step along the way, he rallied Freemasons to the cause. In Victoria he succeeded in getting Masons to contribute to the Imperial Institute by informing them that their Masonic brother, the Prince of Wales, wanted the Institute to be a "great success" and assume a "central position in England." In Cape Town he opened a new Masonic temple and attended a ball held in his honor at the Commercial Exchange. Local Masons commended Carnarvon for visiting South Africa, which was usually not on the itineraries of illustrious Englishmen when they visited "Greater Britain." Such visits benefited both the visited and the visitor, because they "strengthen on the one side the bond of union with the imperial centre, on the other side they give a fair knowledge of distant parts of the empire in the place of vague imaginings." Carnarvon's visit to Kimberley occasioned "one of the largest and most imposing assemblages ever seen in the Diamond Fields." In his address to the assembled multitude, he expressed his hope that Masonry "would cement more strongly, if possible, the ties of union and brotherhood."[53]

While an enthusiastic ambassador for the Imperial Federation League, Carnarvon placed more importance on sentimental connections and a common identity than on federation itself. "Imperial federation may in future years assume a very different shape from that which its advocates either wish or expect," he claimed. "But so long as there is the common bond of sympathy and practical union between England and the colonies the nature of the formal tie will be a matter of secondary importance." Nothing was better suited to nurture such bonds, according to Carnarvon, than Freemasonry. Upon his arrival in New South Wales, he proclaimed: "Ever since I set foot on the shore of this great continent, wherever I have found Masonic brethren I have found a hearty welcome — (applause) — and everywhere I have found that one of the links that bind[s] this great continent, in feeling to the old mother-country is the link of English Freemasonry."[54]

By encouraging federation and Freemasonry, Carnarvon hoped to overcome two obstacles to imperial unity: the growing strength of local identities and the disruptive Irish element. In Victoria, he expressed concern that the younger generation of Australians did not share their parents' strength of attachment to England. "Our earnest desire in England," he proclaimed, "is that the younger generation shall not be allowed to let their hearts grow cold to the old country. (Prolonged cheering.)" His observations in Queensland were particularly troubling. He noticed "a marked feeling of antagonism between English and Australian interests" and detected the influence of the younger Australian generation growing stronger in Queensland than in other parts of Australia. Despite the colony's name, colonists had not celebrated the Queen's Jubilee, and he was worried that the leading politicians were not sufficiently friendly to the English connection. This former Lord Lieutenant of Ireland was equally apprehensive about the Irish: "It is a great question in my mind whether throughout Australia there is not a very wide and large feeling of disaffection on the part of the Irish only waiting the spark to kindle it into fire."[55]

Carnarvon was also worried about disintegrative forces at work within Masonry in New South Wales and had undertaken the journey, in part, to restore Masonic unity. Since 1847 Masonry in New South Wales had suffered from the same problems that had bedeviled lodges in Upper Canada: competing grand lodges, dissatisfaction with metropolitan administration, and a growing independence movement spearheaded by the Irish lodges. By 1885 some English lodges had joined the Grand Lodge of New South Wales, but most maintained their loyalty to the Grand Lodge of England. Matters became very complicated when the Grand Lodge of England appointed Sir Charles Wynn-Carrington, governor of New South Wales, as District Grand Master of New South Wales, even though they already had a district grand master in place. Calling on Carnarvon to serve as his official representative, the Prince of Wales wanted "the unity of the *Masonic* Empire maintained."[56]

To this end, Carnarvon advocated the same approach to New South Wales that he had to Canada during the 1850s: graciously bless the movement to achieve administrative self-government and watch the ties of sentiment and feelings of common identity intensify. (He seems to have learned the lesson of imperial history that the War of Independence had made "Americans" and not the other way around.) He acknowledged the emergent colonial nationalism of

Australia and growing obligations of Australians as Australians, but these did not necessarily entail a rejection of the imperial connection. After all, he told Victorians, Britons everywhere were "members of a great common family." In fact, South Australia offered a model. Masons there had created an independent grand lodge, but they remained closely attached to metropolitan Masons. "The severance of our connection with the Grand Lodges of Great Britain and Ireland," they reported to Carnarvon, has "no more diminished our fraternal feelings towards the members of the Craft under their respective jurisdictions . . . than the development of our political institutions has lessened our loyalty to the throne or our desire to continue united to the British Empire." Events like Carnarvon's visit only intensified these desires. They noted that his attentions had strengthened "the feelings of loyalty and affection which British colonies feel for the mother country" and they thanked him for all he had done for "the development, consolidation, and unity of her Majesty's colonial dominions."[57]

After Carnarvon's departure in 1887, Governor Carrington of New South Wales observed that the Pro Grand Master's role in settling Masonic matters had "done more to cement the good feeling which exists with England than the miles of Federation speeches." For many imperialists, relying on the sentimental ties that institutions like Freemasonry fostered was considered a smarter and safer way to keep the empire together than constructive imperialist proposals that might entail drastic changes to constitutional and commercial relations. As one contemporary Mason observed in 1897, by his attentions to Masons in various parts of the empire the Prince of Wales "has caused Freemasonry to do more than politics can." The observer continued, "He has brought together the Colonies nearer to the Mother Country, and has carried out an international federation it would have been impossible to carry out in any other way."[58] Indeed, imperial federation was proving to be a tricky issue, as evidenced by the dissolution of the IFL in 1894 when members could not arrive at a consensus on the kind or extent of federation to advocate. Freemasonry, by contrast, was proving itself quite effective in accomplishing similar goals by other means.

A Freemason could demonstrate his commitment to the empire by participating in ceremonies and festivities, assisting migration, joining "empire lodges," and supporting other imperial clubs and institutions. The prominent role Canadian Masons played in such activities led Toronto's *Masonic Sun* to conclude in 1904 that "mostly every movement of importance that has taken place during the past few years toward imperialism, or confederacy of the British Empire, has emanated from citizens of the Empire who have been Masons." But the ultimate manifestation of a Mason's imperialist ardor was the offer of his services, and even his life, in the empire's defense — as *The Freemason* put it in 1915, Canadian Masons were "offering themselves for the Empire."[59] Lending their support to the empire in its hours of need was a perfectly reasonable response for Masons who regularly boasted of the "British connection" and defined themselves as "British Canadians." At the institutional level, the Canadian grand lodges went to great lengths to promote overseas imperial service. They raised money for soldiers and their families as well as civilian victims of overseas wars. They encouraged enlistment in the armed forces and sang the praises of Canada's sons who took up arms in defense of the empire. They assisted and honored returning soldiers. Finally, in sermons, speeches, publications, circulars, and ceremonies, grand lodge officials drummed up imperial sentiment. Their members answered the call.

Litmus tests of imperialist identity, conflicts in India and Africa during the second half of the nineteenth century gave Canadian Masons the opportunity to prove their commitment to the empire they claimed to cherish so highly. Individual Masons became famous for their sacrifices, and lodges spread awareness of imperial affairs through their statements, commemorations, and fundraising efforts. Fifty years after the Indian Mutiny/Rebellion of 1857, Toronto Freemasons were still remembering the imperial service of Colonel John Inglis, who had been initiated in St. Andrew's Lodge in the city. Inglis had taken over the defense of Lucknow when Sir Henry Lawrence was mortally wounded. He coordinated the effort to fight off 8,000 Sepoys for eighty-seven days until the 78th Highlanders relieved the city. The Sudan campaign of 1885 also received Freemasons' attention. The *Canadian Craftsman* informed readers in August that the Grand Lodge of New South Wales had presented the Colonial Secretary with the sum of £500 for the relief of widows and orphans of soldiers who perished in the Sudan. A Masonic official in Quebec noted that, as Canadians, Freemasons took pride "in the achievements of our British Army in their efforts to crush the fanatical and cruel despotism of the 'Mahdi' on the Banks of the far-off Nile." He sang the praises of Kitchener as a military commander and a Mason and expressed sympathy for the brethren who "laid down their lives for the honor of the old flag and the brotherhood of man." One Manitoba Freemason, Colonel W. Kennedy, was honored for his gallant service to "his Queen" and the sacrifices he made "in defence of the mother country's rights" (on his way back to Canada from the Sudan, he had fallen victim to smallpox).[60]

The South African War of 1899–1902 was the first imperial war for which Canadians volunteered in significant numbers (over 7,000 eventually enlisted to fight in South Africa). The *Canadian Craftsman and Masonic Record* informed readers in 1899 that "the call to arms is being promptly responded to by thousands of Canada's hardy sons including many members of the Craft, from Cape Breton to Vancouver." Freemasons, as "citizens of the Great British Empire," had a duty to support the war effort. The periodicals and grand lodges constantly reminded Canadian Freemasons that several of their illustrious brethren (Roberts, Kitchener, and Wolseley) were representing them (and participating in lodge meetings) at the front. More significantly, the periodicals encouraged members to contribute to subscription funds "in aid of the dependents of our brave soldiers who are fighting the Empire's battles for liberty in South Africa" and defended the controversial use of concentration camps. Brothers Roberts and Kitchener, they claimed, should receive nothing but praise for their conduct of the war.[61]

Canadians viewed the South African War as a test of their commitment to the empire, of imperial unity, and of the worthiness of their nascent nation. According to Masonic observers at least, Canadians passed in all three regards. In a statement typical of Canadian grand lodge pronouncements in this period, the Grand Lodge of Ontario described the war as an "opportunity of proving to Great Britain and the Empire the loyal attachment of our people to the Throne and their willingness to have their loyalty submitted to a practical test." The preservation and demonstration of imperial unity was a consistent theme in Masonic rhetoric regarding the war. A prominent Mason in Ontario proclaimed in 1899: "We have despatched over two thousand of our gallant sons to that Dark Continent where, if grim necessity demand, they are willing to cement the bond of Imperial unity with their life's blood." The Grand Lodge of Nova Scotia observed that colonial response to the war proved that the Dominions (where "the red cross flag of St. George floats in the breeze and the English language is the mother-tongue") would treat any affront to Britain as an affront to themselves. The sacrifices of Canadian soldiers made "the quondam dream of Imperial unity a solid, splendid fact." The Grand Master of Quebec put it more succinctly: "No greater evidence could be shown of the Unity of the Empire than the magnificent events on the battlefields of South Africa."[62]

By defending the British Empire, Canadians were also proving their worth as an independent, if relatively young, nation. Once again we see Masonic rhetoric putting forward the idea of a fundamental relationship between imperialist and nationalist identity: acting on the former proved the latter. The Grand Master of the Grand Lodge of Ontario told fellow Masons at a banquet that Canada's stalwart soldiers had impressed Lord Roberts to the extent that he selected them for the most difficult duties. The performance of Canadian soldiers proved that Canada "had outgrown her swaddling clothes and is now a full-grown nation, about to take her station among the nations of the world." Brethren gathered for the annual meeting of the Grand Lodge of Canada (Ontario) in 1900 heard that in fighting the Boers, who were the enemies of justice and truth, the British Empire had "realized its strength and unity." The "whelps of the [British] lion" had rallied to her side. Because of their dutiful loyalty and noble sacrifice, Canada's sons had "placed Canada in the rank of nations."[63]

If the South African War provided Canadian Masons with opportunities to prove their loyalty to the empire, it presented South African Masons with an entirely different set of circumstances. Masons demonstrated their patriotism and bravery, but they also had to contend with war-time hardship. The Boers opened their offensive in October 1899 by besieging key cities in the Orange Free State, the Cape Colony, and Natal. Though certainly disrupted, Masonic activity did not come to a halt, even in the besieged cities. In Mafeking, Austral Lodge continued to hold meetings; one of its members, an auctioneer named Edward Ross, noted in his diary on 18 February that "during the time the lodge was working a volley of Mauser bullets fired into the town." The Masonic hall was the venue for a dance and later a concert. It also put on an exhibition of paintings, sketches, and photographs by Brother Robert Baden-Powell, who was in charge of the Mafeking garrison. When Mafeking was relieved in May (much to the joy of Britons back home), the Masonic hall served as a prison. Meanwhile, in Kimberley, the hall was converted into a hospital; a local Mason reported to London that "during the siege we practically closed up Masonry." (Cecil Rhodes, also a Mason, was in Kimberley during the siege.) Further south, in Bloemfontein, Lodge Rising Star was able to continue meeting with attendance averaging twenty-eight brethren. On 23 April 1900, the lodge met to celebrate Prince Edward's escape from an assassination attempt. Kitchener took part in this meeting. Lord Roberts, who could not attend the meeting, entrusted Kitchener with a resolution of thanksgiving, which the members and visitors of the lodge signed and forwarded to London. Subsequently the lodge held an emergency meeting to mourn Queen Victoria's death. Masonic historian George Kendall notes that several Boer brethren (including prisoners on parole) and probably both Arthur Conan Doyle and Rudyard Kipling were present. One local Mason who attended commented that "no greater factor in the reconciliation of the races . . . exists in South Africa than Lodge Rising Star." Back in London, the Grand Lodge set up a South African Masonic Relief Fund

Roodeport Lodge No. 2539 (English Constitution), Transvaal, South Africa, 1899 (copyright, and reproduced by permission of, the United Grand Lodge of England).

on the urging of George Richards, the District Grand Master for Transvaal. Over £10,000 was collected and distributed in the form of grants to widows and orphans, loans to brethren, and food and railway fares for refugees.[64]

Like the South African War, the First World War both interrupted Masonic activities in South Africa and afforded South African Masons the opportunity to demonstrate their loyalty and perform their duty as empire citizens. Once again, South Africans had to contend with war theaters in their own backyard. In September 1914 the Union government acceded to Britain's request to attack German South West Africa. The move did not endear the British to all sections of the South African community. Though Botha and Smuts supported the attack, some Boer army commanders in the Transvaal launched a rebellion in the closing months of 1914. Botha crushed the rebellion with primarily Afrikaner troops, but it created a climate in which English and Afrikaner Masonic relations came under strain. Both constitutions also faced financial crisis and lodge closures resulting from the general dislocation caused by the war and the large number of brethren volunteering for the operations in South West Africa, in other parts of Africa, and in Europe. At a meeting of the District Grand Lodge

Interior of Roodeport Lodge No. 2539 (English Constitution), Transvaal, South Africa, 1899 (copyright, and reproduced by permission of, the United Grand Lodge of England).

of Central South Africa in 1915, the District Grand Master expressed difficulty at "speaking cheerfully when so many of our members are serving their King and Empire on so many different battlefields." He looked forward to the day when the "dreadful War" concluded and all Masons could "help build up a universal brotherhood which will render it impossible for nation to rise against nation and the tenets and teaching of Freemasonry shall be world wide."[65] With these words he anticipated the vision of many Masons who, in the aftermath of the cataclysm, would see Masonry playing a critical role in regulating world affairs.

South African Freemasons who did not go to the front also displayed their imperialist credentials by contributing to the war effort. Masons practiced another Masonic virtue — relief — by raising money for suffering brethren and their families and entertaining wounded soldiers. District grand masters roused the patriotic sentiments of members through speeches extolling the Masonic virtue of loyalty and championing the "glorious cause" of the British Empire. They comforted their listeners by claiming the empire was engaged in a defense of the "very principles of Freemasonry": freedom, justice, righteousness, and civilization. The Grand Master of Natal commended Freemasons for "nobly show[ing] they are ever ready to take up arms to fight for our King and our Country, for our homes and for our loved ones and to stand up manfully and unflinchingly for Liberty, Freedom, Justice, and Honour." In December 1918 1,400 Masons attended a service of thanksgiving at Johannesburg's Town Hall to commemorate the conclusion of hostilities.[66]

The Great War also demonstrated the pervasiveness of imperialist sentiment among Canadian Freemasons, who believed that Masonry played a unique role in cementing the empire in times of crisis. In London, the imperial lodges opened their doors to Freemasons among the officer corps of the Canadian Expeditionary Force (whose initial force of 32,000 men included over 6,000 Masons). One of many examples of such lodge hospitality took place in December 1914 when Canada Lodge hosted a banquet for Canadian officers; an officer present commented that Canada Lodge was doing work equal to the Canadian Expeditionary Force "in binding together this wonderful Empire of ours through the bonds of Masonry." In January Empire Lodge hosted a banquet for 160 Canadian brethren on duty in England. The speeches of the English brethren reflected their feelings of respect and profound gratitude for the "cubs" of the British Lion. For their part, the Canadian Masons present assured their hosts of their heightened sense of duty to and identity with the British Empire. As one Freemason from New Brunswick put it: "All Masons were proud of having descended directly from the Mother Grand Lodges of Britain. These were no mean heritages, for they created and maintained a unity of Brotherhood and Empire which no international upheavals could sever." Two years later, Canada Lodge had one of the largest meetings in Masonic history, when they initiated nine Canadian soldiers and moved six others up to higher ranks. The post-lodge banquet was "almost entirely in khaki." Afterward, a member of Canada Lodge wrote to a Canadian brother: "If there is anyone in Canada who has the slightest doubt of the British Empire before this war finishes in their favour, they ought to have been at Canada Lodge last night, although it was sad to realise that of those Canadian soldiers who were our guests upon two occasions last year, nearly half of them have laid down their lives already, but we have the satisfaction of knowing that Canada Lodge was the essential link between the Dominion and this little Old Land."[67]

As they had done during the South African War (but on an even grander scale), the Canadian grand lodges launched a multifaceted campaign to assist the war effort and fan the flames of imperial patriotism. In their speeches, grand lodge officers justified Canadians' participation in a war being fought not for conquest but for the defense of freedom, truth, justice, and civilization.[68] They also exhorted the members of the brotherhood to fulfill their Masonic duty to be loyal. After hearing a sermon on their responsibilities as Canadian citizens, members of the Grand Lodge of Nova Scotia were told by their Grand Master that loyalty to the "great and glorious Empire" was part of the mission of Masonry. "It is our duty as Masons to be true to our principles and loyal to our country, and assist in upholding the dignity of its Crown and Government." Not everyone could volunteer for the army, he pointed out, but "we can serve our King and country as good and loyal citizens of this great and glorious Empire and fulfill the mission of Masonry" by taking care of wounded soldiers and the families of fallen soldiers. The grand lodges' efforts to raise funds for the war effort also revealed the extent to which loyalty to the empire had become synonymous with Freemasonry. In 1914 the Grand Lodge of Quebec issued a circular discussing the Canadian Patriotic Fund established by the Duke of Connaught and asking its members to donate "a subscription which would be distinctly Masonic, and be a striking testimony of that loyalty and allegiance to their Sovereign and of that attachment to the land of their birth and infant nurture." The Grand Lodge of Quebec alone contributed $2,000 to the fund in 1914. At the same time, the Grand Lodge of Nova Scotia sent circulars urgently reminding lodges of Freemasons' reputation for patriotism and urging them to support the Victory Loan; members of the fraternity responded generously.[69]

For Freemasons, Canadians' role in the Great War, as in the South African War, proved both the unity of the empire and Canada's worthiness as a nation. The "ready response" of Canada and other dependencies had demonstrated "the advantage and necessity for unity in an Empire scattered all over the earth." By responding so willingly and acquitting themselves so valiantly, Canadian soldiers had gained the gratitude and approval of the "chief nations" of the world. Speaking on behalf of Britons, who were profoundly grateful for the 350,000 "fine men" Canada had sent "of her own free will," the Duke of Connaught commended "the way in which Canada has shown her loyalty and her desire to do her duty to her Sovereign and to the Empire." The sacrifices of Canadian soldiers allowed Canada to take its place in their ranks. Yet Canada's hard-won status as a nation did not entail separation from the empire but rather maturity within it. Canadians were upholding Canada's honor, the Grand Master of Quebec explained, by upholding the flag of empire. According to the Grand Master of Canada, Canadians were fighting for the salvation of Canada "as a responsible and self-governing portion of the empire." Two years into the war, he proclaimed: "Today Canada stands before the world as a young and vigorous daughter in the Imperial family."[70]

Here, once again, we see Freemasons drawing on the metaphor of the family. Canada had grown up and proven itself capable of performing as Britain's partner in the work of empire building. Canadian nationhood had been realized *within* and *through* the empire, not in opposition to it. A Masonic official in Newfoundland demonstrated the centrality of the empire to Canadian identity as he bid farewell to the brethren of Newfoundland lodges who had volunteered for service with the first Newfoundland Regiment in 1914. He exhorted: "We . . . rejoice because a greater citizenship is ours, that of an Empire more great, more glorious, more rich, more righteous, more far-reaching in its beneficent influence than any that the world has known." Canadians were partners in the imperial mission. "Remember that you are fighting not only for your King, but for the Kingdom of Right and Justice — not alone for your country — your well-loved Newfoundland, but for the dear old Motherland, and for every section of the British Empire! Nor are you carrying arms for the Empire alone, but for the race."[71]

While Canadians perceived themselves as citizens of the empire, and were embraced by Britons as such, millions of other denizens of the British Empire were more accurately described as "subjects." They were still a part of the family but their status differed from those who had proven themselves as imperial citizens. It was a crucial distinction clearly evident in Masonic rhetoric of the postwar period, as the empire began unraveling and the idea of a British Commonwealth of Nations emerged.

Lodges East and West

The conflicts of the late nineteenth and early twentieth centuries revealed the empire's vulnerability to external threats and internal disintegration, but they also demonstrated multifaceted efforts on the part of Freemasons in the British Isles, Canada, Australia, New Zealand, and South Africa to preserve the empire for the present and the future. For the ordinary man as well as the imperial hero, belonging to the brotherhood was an indicator of one's identity as an empire citizen, a man who lived in, and pledged allegiance to, Britain's far-reaching empire. The ever-growing network of Masonic lodges helped men (and women) as they moved across the empire. It came to the assistance of downtrodden migrants, facilitated the careers of prominent proconsuls, and allowed businessmen and soldiers from the Dominions to feel "at home" in the metropole. Meanwhile, Masonic rhetoric and ceremonies conveyed the message that the diverse peoples of the empire could unite in their feelings of loyalty to the crown, well represented in Masonic circles by the Duke of Connaught and the Prince of Wales. Its message of fraternalism resonated with imperial administrators charged with the task of running a multicultural empire and soldiers who were committed to defending it. In all these ways, Masonry contributed significantly to the strengthening of imperial relations, especially between Britain and the Dominions, at a time when imperial confidence was beginning to waver.

Rudyard Kipling, perhaps the most famous imperialist and Mason of the era, recognized the empire was at a turning point. To commemorate Queen Victoria's jubilee in 1897 he composed a cautionary poem entitled "Recessional." Britons, "drunk with sight of power," had become irreverent. Their lack of humility and contrition had put Britain's "Dominion over palm and pine" in jeopardy. The poem can be read as a warning of the empire's impending demise rather than a death pronouncement. Britain and the empire could be spared if Britons remembered their moral and spiritual obligations and the "Lord God of Hosts" took mercy on them. Although he did not mention Masonry in this poem, Kipling would have certainly agreed that the brotherhood could assist in this process. He had been initiated in India in 1885. Throughout his career as a writer, Kipling drew on Freemasonry for inspiration. "Banquet Night," written for a lodge banquet in London, celebrates Masonic conviviality. *The Man Who Would Be King* tells the story of how two British vagabonds, Peachy Carnegan and Daniel Dravot, use Freemasonry to establish themselves as kings of Kafiristan. The hero of *Kim* escapes a Masonic orphan asylum to wander through India in search of adventure. A series of stories set during the South African War focuses on a mythical Masonic lodge that looked after wounded Freemasons returning from the front.[72] But the text most dedicated to the theme of Freemasonry is his poem "The Mother Lodge," in which Kipling recalls his experience of Masonry in India:

> There was Rundle, Station Master,
> An' Beazeley of the Rail,
> An' Achman, Commissariat,
> An' Donkin o' the Jail:
> An' Blake, Conductor Sergeent —

— Our master twice was 'e,
With 'im that kept the Europe shop,
Old Framjee Eduljee. . . .

There was Bola Nath, accountant,
And Saul, the Aden Jew,
An' Din Mohammed, draughtsman,
Of the Sursey office, too.
There was Babu Chicekerhitty,
An' Amir Singh, the Sikh,
An' Castro of the fitten'-sheds,
A Roman Catholic. . . .

Full oft on Guv'ment service
This rovin' foot 'ath pressed,
An' bore fraternal greetin's
To the Lodges east and west;
Accordin' as commanded,
From Kohat to Singapore,
But I wish that I might see them
In my Mother Lodge once more . . .

Outside — "Sergeant! Sir! Salute! Salaam!"
Inside — "Brother" an' it does n't do no 'arm.
We met upon the Level an' we parted on the Square,
An' I was Junior Deacon in my Mother Lodge out there.

These lines reveal the diverse membership of Masonic lodges in late-nineteenth-century Lahore, particularly the Lodge Hope and Perseverance that had initiated Kipling. They also capture the qualified nature of Masonic fraternity, which called for men to treat one another like brothers within the lodge while observing differences of rank and status (whether based on class or race) outside the lodge. Would British Masons continue successfully to navigate this tension between inclusiveness and exclusivity in the late imperial era? As will be seen, British and indigenous Masons alike began adjusting their notions of brotherhood to meet the needs of changing times. Not surprisingly, they came up with differing interpretations of what brotherhood meant.

CONCLUSION

The Cosmopolitan Order of the Ages?

In the years following World War I the British Empire grew with the acquisition of African, Pacific, and Middle Eastern territories (held in the form of League of Nations' mandates) that had formerly been parts of the German and Ottoman empires. Britons found themselves on the cusp of a profound shift: their empire had expanded to even greater proportions, but there were signs that it was beginning to tremble under its own weight. Not certain the empire had reached its zenith and certainly not yet willing to relinquish it, they were nonetheless forced to acknowledge it was going to take a lot to keep it together. Threats to the unity and longevity of the empire came from within and without. The Easter Rising in Ireland, followed by the Anglo-Irish War, a strengthening nationalist movement in British India, and increased self-confidence on the part of the Dominions — all made clear that British rule, in all its various guises, would have to adapt to the changing times. Meanwhile, rival imperial powers continued to encroach on British global dominance. The Germans and Ottomans were out of commission and the Russians distracted by internal matters, but France remained committed to its empire and the United States and Japan were only rising in their influence and ambitions.

Freemasonry was as imbricated in the empire of the postwar period as it had been since the eighteenth century. Its global network of lodges, first planted in the late 1720s with lodges in Gibraltar and Calcutta, continued to grow even in the interwar period, when the pace of globalization slowed somewhat (due to more protectionist trade policies, for example). As in previous eras, membership in the brotherhood connected men and facilitated their movements across the empire. The brotherhood kept women in their well-established place as observers of Masonry's public spectacles and objects of its charities. Masonic fraternalism still helped preserve and extend British power in both its material and ceremonial forms, as evidenced by the book's frontispiece. Here the Duke of Connaught, representing the English Grand Lodge and sporting a pith helmet, leads a Masonic procession down the dusty streets of Bulawayo, Rhodesia, in 1910. All the while, Masonry's ideology, born in the era of the Enlightenment, remained consistent in its instructions to the brethren to practice toleration and inclusiveness, acknowledge the fundamental unity of mankind, act as citizens of the world, and cultivate affection, sociability, and benevolence.

As we have seen, the extent to which British Masons' realized the cosmopolitan potential of their institution had varied over time and place. At times the contradictions between theory and practice were glaring. And even when Masonry was at its most inclusive, a tension between inclusiveness and exclusivity remained characteristic of the brotherhood. During the eighteenth century, Freemasonry had included in its ranks Catholics, Jews, and some Indian Muslim princes. Its membership was overwhelmingly white, but other groups, such as Native Americans, Atlantic Africans, and Asians were not completely excluded. Also significant was Freemasonry's fundamentally British nature; Scots, Irish, Welsh, and English joined, became brothers, and went about the business of maintaining and building the empire. Moreover, eighteenth-century Masonry was a relatively open institution when it came to the social status of members. The emergence and spread of Ancient Masonry broadened the social composition of the membership to such an extent that artisans, privates, and mariners rubbed shoulders in the lodge with their social betters. Finally Tories and Whigs, Jacobites and Wilkites, American loyalists and patriots, Irish "unionists" and nationalists — all found in Freemasonry an institution that suited their various social and political needs.

Though British, French, Dutch, and Danish Masons fraternized with one another in the Indian Ocean region in the second half of the eighteenth century, the warfare and national rivalry of the "imperial meridian" did take a toll on the brotherhood's ability to remain open. The crucible of the French Revolution and the Napoleonic Wars, combined with shifting class dynamics that accompanied industrialization, brought about a great reshaping of Masonry. By the 1820s, the brotherhood had become a primarily white, respectable, Protestant institution explicitly tied to the British monarchy. The period between the 1780s and the 1820s witnessed a concerted campaign to prove Masonry's credentials as a loyal association. In the process British Masons redefined the term "political," equating it with challenges to the state and excluding from its meaning any act designed to uphold the state (which allowed them to continue to claim they did not discuss political matters). Out in the empire, Masonry still provided both colonists and imperial functionaries with a means of navigating their careers. It also helped them build an identity that bound them together within the colony and linked them to Britain and the wider empire. By the 1880s, the fraternity was playing a significant role in the "imperialist" movement that sought to unify the empire under the symbol of the crown and make the empire, especially the settlement colonies, a source of strength to Britain. Its fraternal ideology — and frequent recourse to family idioms — helped ensure that Dominion nationalism remained compatible with imperialism.

Masonry's growing identification with the imperial center led to complicated outcomes. While it gained status and significance, the fraternity also ran into difficulties in defining brotherhood. The fraternity's ideology and rhetoric remained consistent from the eighteenth century through the nineteenth century. Its orators still claimed that Masons were "citizens of the world" and that Masonic cosmopolitanism "embrace[d] the great human family" and taught the "true principles of international toleration."[1] And so it is not surprising that the question of admitting indigenes grew increasingly pressing as the nineteenth century progressed. A number of Masons, often dominant at the local level, opposed such inclusion, preferring the fraternity to remain limited to whites. But the British grand lodges resisted this idea. The result was a slow and grudging acceptance of members who reflected the empire's diversity: free blacks, former slaves, emancipists, Parsis, Hindus, and Muslims (in more significant numbers). As a result, British Masonry's conception of brotherhood expanded, though, once again, not to the extent that it threatened imperial power.

The developments traced here had significant consequences for the brotherhood and the empire in the late imperial period (1910s–1930s). The question of whom to include in their brotherhood continued to provoke debate among Masons, but the grand lodges' decisions to declare previously excluded groups eligible for admission at least opened up the possibility of widescale participation of indigenous men in the brotherhood. In 1920 the English Grand Lodge confirmed that Masonry provided "a platform on which men of all conditions, classes, and creeds can work together for the common welfare."

Members of Sudan Chapter No. 2954, including Brother Lord Kitchener (seated in the middle), Sudan, 1910 (copyright, and reproduced by permission of, the United Grand Lodge of England).

Though systematic research is still required to determine the precise extent and nature of indigenous involvement, there is evidence that more and more indigenes were joining Masonry in the late imperial period. Much of the growth in British Masonry was, in fact, taking place in Britain's African and Asian colonies as well as in the Dominions. Expansion in African territories was significant enough to prompt the English Grand Lodge to set up District Grand Lodges in Nigeria, East Africa, Rhodesia, and Ghana between 1913 and 1930. The District Grand Lodges oversaw lodges for Europeans and lodges for elite indigenous men, but also some multiracial lodges. In 1926, the English Grand Lodge dispatched a deputation to visit lodges in Africa. Led by the Grand Secretary, the deputation traveled 21,000 miles between Cape Town and Cairo. Upon his return to London, the Grand Secretary told the members of the Anglo-Overseas Lodge that his party visited sixty-two lodges and met "more than 5000 native Brethren of their own Constitution, as well as in the Irish, Scottish, and the Netherlandic Constitutions, and in all of them the English language was used."[2]

The trend toward indigenous participation was even greater in South Asia. By 1930, the number of Scottish lodges had grown to 78 and the number of English lodges to 229. While many of these lodges remained exclusively European, an increasing number of Indians were joining either indigenous lodges or multiracial lodges, such as the Lodge Rising Star of Western India in Bombay or the Lodge Felix in Aden (administered under the District Grand Lodge of Bombay). The district grand lodges made a point of including both Europeans and Indians, and they regularly celebrated this fact. Indigenous men even held prominent leadership positions. During the 1920s, Indians served as officers in the English District Grand Lodges of Bombay, Madras, and Burma. Back in Britain, metropolitan authorities seemed to embrace their brotherhood's growing diversity. The year after the English Grand Secretary toured Africa, the Grand Lodge sent a deputation of high-ranking officers on an extended tour of India, Burma, and Ceylon. The deputation covered 25,754 miles and visited representatives of many of the 197 English lodges in the region. They happily reported on the generous hospitality they received from governors and maharajahs, as well as ordinary brethren, and the beautiful buildings they toured.

> But the most impressive feature, par excellence, was the assembly in Lodge of Brethren of varying nationalities, men of culture and distinction, working in amicable rivalry to render as perfectly as possible our beautiful Ritual. We have seen as many as five volumes of the Sacred Law in use at one and the same time, and Brethren of the following among other races, taken at random — Europeans, Parsis, Chinese, Burmans, Hindus, Americans, Ceylonese, Punjabis, Mohammedans, Sikhs, Armenians, Greeks, Bengalis, Jews, Aracanese, Madrassis, all participating in the Ceremonies. The Brotherhood of Man, in such circumstances, becomes a living reality.[3]

While the decisions taken in the mid-nineteenth century resulted in a more multicultural brotherhood in the twentieth, the tension between Masonry's inclusive ideology and its members' exclusive practices remained unresolved. It was arguably even more glaring in the postwar period because indigenous candidates who became Masons generally joined "native" lodges rather than lodges that included both European and indigenous brethren. Moreover, blackballing potential members on the basis of their religion or race undoubtedly continued to mark the practice of Masonry at the local level even if it no longer had the sanction of Masonic law.

Nonetheless, British Masons of the postwar period still had to respond to the growing diversity of their brotherhood, and they did so by developing new conceptions of Masonic brotherhood. Some responded by championing "Anglo-Saxon Freemasonry," which aimed to strengthen ties among white Masons in the British Isles, the United States, and the Dominions and posited "Anglo Saxons" as the appropriate guardians of the postwar world. Other British Masons responded by advocating "English-speaking Masonry," a conception of brotherhood that had room for indigenous members but still did not realize Masonry's full cosmopolitan potential. In elaborating and acting on these notions, contemporary Masons revealed their belief that their well-established institution remained firmly allied with the imperial state as it confronted the challenges of the late imperial era. In fact, they argued that the strengthening of these two forms of fraternalism would contribute to the empire's long-term preservation.

These distinct but overlapping conceptions of brotherhood were on display when the Grand Lodge of England hosted a commemoration at Royal Albert Hall in June 1919. Eight thousand Masons attended. Included in their ranks were representatives from Ireland, Scotland, Ontario, Newfoundland, New Brunswick, Quebec, New Zealand, Victoria, Queensland, and several U.S. states. English Masons representing districts in Gibraltar, Hong Kong, the Eastern Archipelago, Madras, Ceylon, and South America were also on hand. Overseeing the affair were two prominent imperial functionaries. The Duke of Connaught, who had concluded his duties as governor general of Canada and returned to Britain in 1916, was present in his capacity as Grand Master. At his side was Lord Ampthill, who had returned from India (where he had served as governor of Madras and acting viceroy) in 1906; from 1908 he occupied the second-highest position of English Freemasonry, Pro Grand Master. Ampthill proclaimed that "Freemasonry is one of the great forces of good" and exhorted the assembled Masons to remember that loyalty was their duty "as citizens of the world." Turning to Connaught, he read from an address that the Grand Lodge would be presenting to Connaught's nephew King George V: "It is our earnest hope that with the help of God our world-wide and antient Fraternity may become more extensively serviceable to mankind and may be of material assistance in promoting every effort to secure peace on earth and good will among men."

While Ampthill celebrated Freemasonry's worldwide mission, other speakers emphasized Masonry's role in promoting Anglo-Saxon unity. The Deputy Grand Master, Sir Thomas Halsey, proposed a resolution expressing thanks to the forces of the crown "who contributed to the victory for liberty, civilisation, and right." He claimed that "all the forces of the Empire, from the Dominions beyond the Seas, [had] shown to all time that though scattered throughout the world we are still one Great British nation." Acknowledging the representatives of American grand lodges, he then expressed his pride in "belong[ing] to the Anglo-Saxon race." W. H. Wardrope, the Ontarian Grand Master, agreed that "such Masonic unity will tend towards lasting friendship and goodwill between the English speaking races all over the world" and assured the assembly that Canadian Masons would go back to Canada "with a higher conception of our duty to the British Empire." The Grand Master of New York concurred that "the fundamental principles underlying Anglo-Saxon civilization found expression in Masonic principles."[4]

British Freemasons championed these new elaborations of Masonic fraternalism not only in response to the challenges of the postwar period but also in reaction to the internationalist aspirations of "Latin Masonry." "Latin Masonry" was the term twentieth-century British Masons used to describe European grand lodges and their offshoots with whom the English Grand Lodge had broken off communications in the late 1870s. The original cause of the rift was the decision on the part of the Grand Orient of France to admit atheists into the brotherhood in 1878. In 1879 the editor of the *Masonic Monthly Magazine* had claimed that the breakdown of relations between French and British Freemasonry had the effect of "throw[ing] Anglo-Saxons closer together, brother to brother, shoulder to shoulder, all over the world." British Masons and their allies throughout the world had therefore refused to take part in various internationalist movements undertaken by the representatives of "Latin Masonry" in the 1890s and early 1900s. In 1902 a conference at Geneva had led to the establishment of an International Bureau for Masonic Affairs, based at the Swiss Grand Lodge in Alpina, Switzerland. The young bureau faced several challenges to its goal of bringing unity to Masonry, most notably the isolationist attitude of British Masons.[5]

But the cataclysm of global war and the uncertainty of the postwar period renewed European Masons' zeal for building a truly international brotherhood. In 1919 they proposed the formation of a Masonic International Association (MIA). At the first congress, held in Geneva in October 1921, representatives from most European grand lodges, as well as the Grand Lodge of New York and the Grand Orient of Turkey, met to discuss their common aims. Freemasonry was the organization best qualified, they believed, to "further reconciliation between the peoples" and aid in the reconstruction of international relations in the aftermath of the war. Its declared principles included "toleration, respect for others and for self, liberty and conscience." The Association, the declaration went on, "holds it to be its duty to extend to all members of the human family the bonds of fraternity, which unite Freemasons the world over."[6]

The grand lodges of Britain, the empire, and the United States (except New York) refused to send representatives to the congress. To them "Latin Masonry" had moved too far away from the "ancient and essential landmarks" to even be considered Masonry. The fact that most of the European lodges admitted atheists was unforgivable. The British and American lodges also objected to the Congress because they perceived it as a political exercise. Finally, they expressed grave concerns that the Congress would be discussing "the woman question." And so the English Grand Lodge took the opportunity afforded by the invitation to reaffirm Masonry's landmarks, including the principle that "no woman can be a Freemason according to the original Plan of Freemasonry to which English Freemasons have from time immemorial adhered."[7]

In response to the internationalist movement of "Latin" Freemasons, British Masons also advanced an internationalist agenda, albeit one that was not as broadly conceived as the MIA. The idea was to establish a "Masonic League of Nations" that drew its members from the world of English-speaking Masonry. Receiving the support of Connaught, Lord Ampthill, and Freemasons throughout the empire, the proposal was the brainchild of Sir Alfred Robbins. Robbins was an English journalist and author who served as president of the English Grand Lodge's Board of General Purposes between 1913 and 1931. In this capacity, he coordinated much of the decision making that affected English Freemasonry at the local, national, imperial, and international levels. Robbins had long encouraged British Masons to "aim at the true universality of brotherhood." He believed that Masonry's eighteenth-century founders had infused the brotherhood with "that cosmopolitan spirit, that supreme touch of universality, that absolute freedom from dogmatic religious assertion which preserved the Craft from insularity and enabled it to spread throughout the world."[8]

Believing this global brotherhood with a cosmopolitan ideology had much to offer a war-torn world, Robbins issued his first call for a Masonic League of Nations in July 1918; he reissued the call during the boycott of the MIA in 1920–21. Robbins agreed that "English-speaking Masonry" and "Latin Masonry" were characterized by differences so fundamental that any attempts at "worldwide unity" would take British Masons onto "very dangerous ground." Rather than compromising on British Masonry's landmarks, he proposed British Masons work "to bring all English speaking Freemasonry closer together." English-speaking Masonry included any lodges that operated in British, American, or dominion jurisdictions, that used English in their meetings, and that defended the Ancient Landmarks (belief in a supreme being, renouncement of the political, and exclusion of women). Unifying this farflung brotherhood of over four million men, he predicted, would be a great contribution "to the peace and welfare of the world." To provide institutional support for English-speaking Masonry, Robbins proposed the formation of a new imperial-international Masonic body: "While Statesmen strive to establish a League of Nations, let us set up, for ourselves and the Brethren with whom we always in principle and practice have been allied, a League of Masons." The League would function as a superstructure "embracing, as in a house of many mansions, the vast Masonic family, independent as units, united as a whole. Britain and America, Australia and New Zealand, Canada and the Cape, India and the Isles beyond Seas can dwell together under that roof."[9]

Advocates of English-speaking Masonry thus promoted a fairly expansive conception of brotherhood that included indigenous brethren within the Masonic family. But like their nineteenth-century predecessors who had also turned to the family metaphor during the debates over the admission of Hindus, they accepted their inclusion on the grounds that it would strengthen — not undermine — the empire. Robbins and his fellow English Grand Lodge officers were particularly intrigued by the role Masonry could play in shoring up the British Raj. Even before the war, Robbins had expressed concern that "English Freemasonry, like the English Government, is in a very delicate position with regard to India." He closely monitored Grand Lodge decisions concerning India in an effort to maintain Masonry's reputation as "an impartial tribunal between the races of the Empire."[10] During his tenure as President of the Board of General Purposes, the Grand Lodge sent at least three missions to India. In 1921 the Duke of Connaught was back in India, this time representing George V at the opening of the legislative councils of Madras, Bengal, and Bombay. Once again, his imperial and Masonic missions converged. Connaught visited the district grand lodges and reported that Masons in India were "devoutly loyal," "keen and alert," and steadily increasing in numbers. "I know of no part of the British Empire," he proclaimed, "where Masonry can be of greater use in cementing those good feelings which should exist among the different nationalities, casts and creeds than the great Empire of India." Upon Connaught's return the English Grand Lodge, apparently still confident in the permanence of the Raj, commended him for brilliantly performing his duties as a "citizen of the world" and completing "a task of such vital importance to the Empire."[11] Connaught and other members of the Grand Lodge were firmly convinced of the value of such visits: "Nothing will do more to increase the loyalty of our lodges to the

Sovereign, to the Empire, and to the Craft than visits like the one which has just been completed." And so, six years later, when metropolitan Masons determined that the affairs of India were at a "highly critical juncture," they sent an even bigger deputation to the east. It was this deputation, described above, that had reached the conclusion that "the Brotherhood of Man" had become "a living reality" in India under the Raj.[12] Of course, it was a conception of brotherhood that fell far short of more cosmopolitan interpretations of Masonic ideology. The inclusion of indigenous brethren was celebrated not as evidence of their equality with Britons but in the belief that Freemasonry, by encouraging indigenous members to be loyal, would help keep India subordinated within the empire.

At the same time that advocates of English-speaking Freemasonry posited a brotherhood that had room for indigenous brethren, they also actively supported exclusively Anglo-Saxon conceptions of brotherhood. Their efforts to reinforce their fraternity's Anglo-Saxon foundations at the moment it was becoming increasingly multiracial put Masonry's inherent tension into bold relief. New "imperial lodges," founded in London at the end of the war, gave pride of place to the relationship shared by Britain, the United States, and the Dominions. A "feeling of mutual aid and friendship which has drawn together the Motherland, the Dominions Overseas and the United States in a common struggle for liberty and civilization" led to the establishment of Motherland Lodge. Its declared object was "to weld together in closer union all the English-speaking people in all parts of the world, and more particularly in all parts of their Imperial Commonwealth." Robbins and James Stephen assisted at its consecration; four of its early masters were Canadians; Kipling was a member. Consecrating the Overseas Lodge in 1920, Ampthill told its new members that he "looked to Freemasonry to maintain the idealism of the British race." Brigadier General Sir Newton Moore picked up on this theme when he spoke at a meeting of the lodge the next year, characterizing Masonry "as one of the living monuments that welded together the Anglo-Saxon race." Robbins was present at the consecration of another imperial lodge in 1926, the Anglo-Overseas Lodge, which was founded because existing "imperial lodges" could not keep up with all the visitors coming from overseas and looking for a Masonic home in London. In his oration on the occasion, the Reverend F. Gillmor observed that he had always felt "a sacred and indissoluble attachment to those in Anglo Overseas Dominions and Colonies." Noting that it had been 343 years since England had acquired its first colony, Newfoundland (Gillmor's birthplace), he urged, "Surely the qualities which enabled Britishers of the past to form or

Freemasons Hall, Great Queen Street, London (author's collection).

found our Colonies and our Dominions are what we need to-day to make Freemasonry a living force, a spiritual power."[13]

High-level visits undertaken by British, American, and Canadian Masons also served to strengthen Anglo-Saxon brotherhood. Robbins commended the American and Canadian grand lodges for sending representatives to English Freemasonry's bicentennial observances in June 1917 and the Masonic Peace Celebration of 1919. He encouraged British brethren, lodges, and grand lodges to reciprocate. In fact, before they ventured to Africa in 1926 and Asia in 1927, grand lodge officials had already journeyed to Canada and the United States. In 1923 Lord Ampthill and other officers represented the English Grand Lodge on a tour of Canada. The deputation visited Quebec, Nova Scotia, Newfoundland (where the governor gave an official dinner party), and Ontario. They attended the annual meeting of the Grand Lodge of Canada in Ontario and then were the honored guests at a banquet in Toronto's Massey Hall. The 4,000 people who attended were treated to imperialist songs, toasts, and poems by Kipling. Grand Lodge leaders, Ampthill, and the secretary of London's Canada Lodge all addressed the same themes in their speeches: the valiant performance of Canadian troops during the war; the "filial affection" between the Mother Grand Lodge and the "daughter Grand Lodges to which she gave birth"; and Freemasonry's mission in the postwar world. "If you who are of our stock, who are joint partners with us in the great heritage of the British Empire," Lord Ampthill exhorted, "will stand shoulder to shoulder with us," then Freemasons could take the lead in directing the world "once more towards progress and the restoration of a higher feeling of humanity." Such efforts would make the brotherhood "serviceable to our fellow-countrymen and the Empire and to humanity at large." The reception Canadian Masons had given their British brethren convinced Ampthill and his party that "constant and personal intercourse is . . . essential." Upon their return to England, they urged grand lodge officers who traveled to the Dominions "in pursuance of their own personal business" to visit local lodges.[14]

Ampthill's visit had been inspired, in part, by a request from Colonel William Ponton, a Canadian Mason who took empire citizenship and Anglo-Saxon fraternalism to the extreme. Ponton was a Belleville lawyer and long-term member of the Belleville Board of Commerce (in this capacity he regularly attended meetings of the Congress of Chambers of Commerce of the Empire). He was Grand Master of Ontario during Ampthill's visit, an event that, according to Ponton, had "strengthened the Imperial ties" and convinced him "more than ever . . . that we belong to a radiant race." Ponton was one of the most prominent and influential Canadian Masons of the period. In a speech before the Grand Lodge in Ontario, he proclaimed: "The pulse of Canada beats strongly responsive to the heart of the Empire, wherein are the title deeds of liberty and the cement of unity which holds together as one great family of sister states — the British League of Nations; of which the centre is and ever will be to us as Masons of the Mother tongue and Mother Lodge, the dear old Motherland." A spirit of Anglo-Saxon race patriotism suffused Ponton's writings, speeches, and correspondence. A letter from a Masonic officer in Massachusetts encouraged Ponton to stress in his speeches the point that "English-speaking peoples and organizations [are] the saviour of the world and more than ever needed at this time." The correspondent described cooperation between British and American Freemasons as "a contribution to world civilization." Not coincidentally, a primary theme of Ponton's speech before the Grand Lodge the following year was the "International Anglo-Saxon vision":

> One bulwark of the right;
> One front in every fight;
> One life of liberty;
> One noble destiny;
> One glorious memory;
> Anglo Saxons one.

Using poems like this, Ponton expressed his profound attachment to the empire and "Anglo-Saxon civilization" to receptive Masonic audiences through the 1920s.[15]

The efforts of men like Ampthill, Robbins, and Ponton to build up English-speaking Masonry and reinforce its Anglo-Saxon core during the late 1910s and 1920s coincided with a turning point in Anglo-Dominion relations. The Balfour Declaration of 1926 officially recognized what had been clear for several years: that the Dominions were independent nations tied to Britain only through cultural and historical connections and a shared affiliation within a now formalized "British Commonwealth of Nations." Masonic orators approved of the formalization of the British Commonwealth and even seemed to anticipate it in their proposals. As we have just seen, Ponton embraced the idea of a "British League of Nations" and felt Masonry had a crucial role to play in its realization. On the other side of the empire, a Masonic official in New Zealand proposed the formation of an Empire Grand Lodge based on the same ideas and principles that would underlay the British Commonwealth. "Citizens of the British Empire," he observed, were held together not by "territorial sentiments" but by their loyalty to the king. Through this common allegiance, "the United Kingdom, the Dominions of Canada and New Zealand, the Commonwealth of Australia, the Union of South Africa, and the Empire of India together form the British Empire." The Empire Grand Lodge would bring together Masons from all parts of the empire to standardize practices and discuss issues "of constitutional importance," but it would not interfere with the administration of Masonry at the local level. He acknowledged the strong "spirit of independence" evident among "the peoples of the several parts of the British Empire." Through the operation of an Empire Grand Lodge, the Masons among them would learn to balance domestic and imperial interests. Applying these lessons "out of the

K. R. Cama (1831–1909), Parsi, Orientalist, and Freemason, ca. 1907 (British Library).

Lodge" would "add unity and strength to the British Empire."[16] Brandon's
inclusion of India in his proposed Empire Grand Lodge marked a significant
departure from the British Commonwealth, whose membership was initially
restricted to the Dominions. India and the crown colonies might be excluded
from the early British Commonwealth on the basis of their dependent status,
but an Empire Grand Lodge could hardly confine itself to the Dominions. It
would have to accommodate representatives from any part of the empire in
which Masonry was well established. (Here we see Freemasonry, once again,
anticipating wider trends, in this case the shift to a multiracial commonwealth
in the late 1940s.)

As the age of late empire gave way to the era of decolonization, British Freemasons were left with several unresolved issues. Which grand lodges through-

Freemasons Hall, Park Street, Calcutta, built 1911 (copyright, and reproduced by permission of, the United Grand Lodge of England).

out the world (such as Prince Hall Grand Lodges in the United States) would they recognize as legitimate? Just how cosmopolitan—how integrated—should their brotherhood become? Perhaps not surprisingly, the Empire Grand Lodge never materialized. But the very idea of an Empire Grand Lodge suggested that notions like Anglo-Saxon Freemasonry would become increasingly untenable, if not downright embarrassing. They existed very uncomfortably alongside more cosmopolitan visions of brotherhood, such as those Indian brethren had long promoted. Indian Masonic commentators had, at times, celebrated the civilizing power of Masonry and its role in fostering loyalty to the crown.[17] But they were more likely to emphasize elements of its fraternal cosmopolitanism that seemed to undermine the "rule of colonial difference," such as the idea of a universal human family. P. N. Wadia, a past master of a Scottish Lodge in India and Masonic author, described Masonry as "the most wonderful institution on the face of the earth" because it "embodies men of every clime, country, and religion" and teaches them to practice virtue, fear God, and love their brother man. "It does more," he continued. "It brings the whole human race into one family." They also praised the tolerant atmosphere of the Masonic lodge, which allowed for Indians of various communities and Europeans to fraternize. Dr. S. P. Sarbadhikari, surveying the seventy-five brethren of Calcutta's Lodge Anchor and Hope (of which he was master), celebrated "the distinct gain that the sons of the East and West should forget all racial distinctions, all distinction of caste, colour, and creed, and give a practical effect to the Grand teachings of our Order."[18]

Most significantly, Indian members celebrated the cardinal Masonic teaching that all brethren "met upon the level." As prominent Bombay Mason and prolific Masonic author K. R. Cama observed: "One of the happy results attained by introducing natives into Masonry has been that of bringing them to closely associate, socially, with their European brethren — I was almost going to say, masters." Cama had to think twice about referring to Europeans as his brethren because the concept was such a radical one. While the lessons taught in British lodges would have never encouraged indigenous men to defy the Raj, they did present Indians with the possibility that they were not just the younger brethren of European Masons but in fact their equals. It was but a short step from there to demand equality outside the lodge. The extent to which colonial nationalists and British Masons both found in Freemasonry resources for dealing with the era of decolonization remains a matter in need of further investigation.[19] What is clear, however, is that the same ideology that had long been used to build and maintain the empire could also be used to destroy the foundations upon which it rested.

APPENDIX

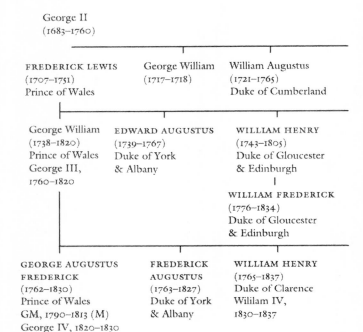

George II
(1683–1760)

FREDERICK LEWIS
(1707–1751)
Prince of Wales

George William
(1717–1718)

William Augustus
(1721–1765)
Duke of Cumberland

George William
(1738–1820)
Prince of Wales
George III,
1760–1820

EDWARD AUGUSTUS
(1739–1767)
Duke of York
& Albany

WILLIAM HENRY
(1743–1805)
Duke of Gloucester
& Edinburgh

WILLIAM FREDERICK
(1776–1834)
Duke of Gloucester
& Edinburgh

GEORGE AUGUSTUS
FREDERICK
(1762–1830)
Prince of Wales
GM, 1790–1813 (M)
George IV, 1820–1830

FREDERICK
AUGUSTUS
(1763–1827)
Duke of York
& Albany

WILLIAM HENRY
(1765–1837)
Duke of Clarence
Wiliam IV,
1830–1837

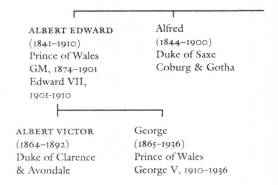

ALBERT EDWARD
(1841–1910)
Prince of Wales
GM, 1874–1901
Edward VII,
1901–1910

Alfred
(1844–1900)
Duke of Saxe
Coburg & Gotha

ALBERT VICTOR
(1864–1892)
Duke of Clarence
& Avondale

George
(1865–1936)
Prince of Wales
George V, 1910–1936

Royal Freemasons

THOMAS DUNCKERLEY
(1724–1795)
(Illegitimate son)

HENRY FREDERICK
(1745–1790)
Duke of Cumberland
& Strathearn
GM, 1782–1790 (M)

Frederick William
(1750–1765)

EDWARD AUGUSTUS
(1767–1820)
Duke of Kent
& Strathearn
GM, 1813 (A)

Victoria
(1819–1901)
Queen Victoria
1837–1901

ERNEST AUGUSTUS
(1771–1851)
Duke of Cumberland
King of Hanover
1837–1851

GEORGE
(1819–1878)
Duke of Cumberland
King of Hanover, 1851–1878

AUGUSTUS FREDERICK
(1773–1843)
Duke of Sussex
GM, 1813–1843

ARTHUR
(1850–1942)
Duke of Connaught &
Strathearn
GM, 1901–1934

LEOPOLD
(1853–1884)
Duke of Albany

Capital letters indicate Masonic membership
GM = Grand Master
M=Moderns; A=Ancients

NOTES

ABBREVIATIONS

AQC	*Ars Quatuor Coronatorum*
BL	British Library
CCMR	*Canadian Craftsman and Masonic Record*
CP	Carnarvon Papers, Add MS 60757–61100, BL
DCB	*Dictionary of Canadian Biography*
DGL	District Grand Lodge
DGLB	District Grand Lodge of Bengal
DGLBom	District Grand Lodge of Bombay
DGLM	District Grand Lodge of Madras
DGLP	District Grand Lodge of the Punjab
DGM	District Grand Master
DGSCF	Deputy Grand Secretary's Correspondence Files (Grand Lodge of Ireland)
FC	*Freemason's Chronicle*
FHL	Freemasons' Hall Library and Archives, London
FMMM	*Freemasons' Magazine and Masonic Mirror*
FQMR	*Freemasons' Quarterly Magazine and Review*
FQR	*Freemasons' Quarterly Review*
GLASFI	Grand Lodge of All Scottish Freemasonry in India
GLC	Grand Lodge of Canada (Ontario)
GLE(A)	Ancient Grand Lodge of England
GLE(M)	Modern Grand Lodge of England
GLI	Grand Lodge of Ireland
GLNS	Grand Lodge of Nova Scotia
GLQ	Grand Lodge of Quebec
GLS	Grand Lodge of Scotland
IF	*Indian Freemason*
IMI	*Irish Masonry Illustrated*
MG	Manuscript Group
MH	*Masonic Herald*
MMM	*Masonic Monthly Magazine*
MS	*Masonic Sun*

MV	*Masonic Visitor*
NAC	National Archives of Canada
NAI	National Archives of Ireland
OIOC	Oriental and India Office Collection (British Library)
PANS	Public Archives of Nova Scotia
PGL	Provincial Grand Lodge
PGLB	Provincial Grand Lodge Bombay
PGLCW	Provincial Grand Lodge Canada West
PGLLC	Provincial Grand Lodge Lower Canada
PGM	Provincial Grand Master
TF	*The Freemason*
TS	*The Standard*
UGL	United Grand Lodge of England
UGLHC	United Grand Lodge Historic Correspondence (FHL)
WNPP	William Nesbit Ponton Papers, MG30 E96, NAC

INTRODUCTION

1. John Stephen to UGL, 1 September 1827, UGLHC 21/C/1.
2. GLS, Proceedings, 30 November 1888, 157.
3. *FQR* (September 1841): 360.
4. Carnarvon quoted in Hardinge, *Life of Henry Herbert*, 225.
5. Spark, *Oration*, 10.
6. Marshall, "Britain without America," 576. For this period, see Bayly, *Imperial Meridian*.
7. Sinha, *Colonial Masculinity*, 9, and "Britishness, Clubbability, and the Colonial Public Sphere," 491. See also Bayly, *Imperial Meridian*; Burton, "Rules of Thumb," 484; Cooper and Stoler, *Tensions of Empire*, 4; Hall, *Cultures of Empire*; Cannadine, *Ornamentalism*; Hall, *Civilising Subjects*; Wilson, *Island Race*.
8. For Masonry, see Money, "Freemasonry and the Fabric of Loyalism" and "Masonic Moment"; Jenkins, "Jacobites and Freemasons"; and Stevenson, *Origins of Freemasonry*. For "British history," see Pocock, "British History: A Plea for a New Subject" and "Limits and Divisions of British History"; Clark, "English History's Forgotten Context"; Colley, "Britishness and Otherness"; Samuel, "British Dimensions"; Armitage et al., "American Historical Review Forum: The New British History in Atlantic Perspective."
9. For two examples of British historians' shying away from Ireland, see Colley, *Britons*, 8, and Thompson, *Imperial Britain*, xi.
10. Colley, "What is Imperial History Now?," 138.
11. This is not to deny the existence of vibrant historiographies concerning Canada, New Zealand, Australia, and South Africa, but rather to argue for their inclusion in the

"new imperial history." For concerns about Canadian historians' neglect of the imperial context, see Buckner, "Whatever Happened to the British Empire?"

12. For provocative analyses along these lines, see Burton, "Who Needs the Nation?"; Duara, *Rescuing History from the Nation*; Burton, *After the Imperial Turn*, especially Stuart Ward, "Transcending the Nation: A Global Imperial History?," 44–56.

13. Roberts, "Freemasonry: Possibilities of a Neglected Topic," 326; Hyam, *Britain's Imperial Century*, 297; Prescott, "The Study of Freemasonry as a New Academic Discipline."

14. For continental Europe, see Jacob, *Radical Enlightenment* and *Living the Enlightenment*; Burke and Jacob, "French Freemasonry, Women, and Feminist Scholarship"; Weisberger, *Speculative Freemasonry and the Enlightenment*; Beachy, "Recasting Cosmopolitanism." For colonial America and the United States, see Bullock, *Revolutionary Brotherhood*; Clawson, *Constructing Brotherhood*; and Carnes, *Secret Ritual and Manhood*. For Russia, see Smith, *Working the Rough Stone*.

15. Rich, *Elixir of Empire*, 83. Assumptions about Freemasonry's history being draped in secrecy and the inaccessibility of Masonic archives have also contributed to historians' neglect of Freemasonry. My research experiences on both sides of the Atlantic revealed, however, that Masonic institutions are extremely welcoming to professional researchers.

16. See the "Oceans Connect" special issue of the *Geographical Review* 89 (1999).

17. Hopkins, *Globalization in World History*, 13, 17.

18. Ballantyne, "Empire, Knowledge, and Culture," 117.

19. For "extensity," see Held and McGrew, *Global Transformations Reader*.

20. See Bayly, *Imperial Meridian* and *Birth of the Modern World*.

21. For insights into identities, see Hall, "William Knibb," 303–4, and "Imperial Man," 132–33; Wilson, *Island Race*, 1–5.

22. Thorne, *Congregational Missions*, 92; Wilson, *Island Race*, 2–3; Wilson, "Empire, Gender, and Modernity," 14; Hall, "Imperial Man," 133.

23. Kennedy, "Imperial History and Post-Colonial Theory," 357.

24. Melton, *Rise of the Public*, 255, highlights the appeal of Masonry to merchants, but much work needs to be done on the role of the brotherhood in commercial networks.

25. Stockwell in Marshall, *Cambridge Illustrated History of the British Empire*, 166; Francis, *Governors and Settlers*, 30; Rich, *Elixir of Empire*, 73.

26. See Peers, "'The Habitual Nobility of Being,'" 569.

27. Francis and Rich demonstrate some limited consultation with evidence from the world of Masonry, while Cannadine overlooks the brotherhood entirely.

28. GLC, *Book of Constitution*, 73–76.

29. On imperial collaboration, see Robinson, "Non-European Foundations of European Imperialism"; Porter, *Lion's Share*, 27–47; Burroughs, "Imperial Institutions and the Government of Empire," 178–83. None mentions the role of cultural institutions like Freemasonry in the process of gaining collaborators.

30. Levine, "Introduction," 2. See also Hall, *Civilising Subjects*, 16; Roper and Tosh, *Manful Assertions*, 11.

31. Tosh, "What Should Historians Do with Masculinity?" 179–80.

32. Representatives of this literature include Mangan, *Athleticism in the Victorian and Edwardian Public Schools*; Mangan and Walvin, *Manliness and Morality*; Rich, *Elixir of Empire*; Dawson, *Soldier Heroes*.

33. Tosh, "What Should Historians Do with Masculinity?," 183. Rutherford's *Forever England* and McDevitt's *"May the Best Man Win"* are exceptions.

34. Roper and Tosh, *Manful Assertions*, 2–4; Tosh, "What Should Historians Do with Masculinity?," 183–84. See also Sedgwick, *Between Men*, 5; Hall, *White, Male, and Middle Class*, 13.

35. Hall, "Of Gender and Empire," 72.

36. This reformulates the question Levine poses in her introduction to *Gender and Empire*, 6.

37. Tosh, "What Should Historians Do with Masculinity?," 186; Sedgwick, *Between Men*, 1.

38. Tosh, "What Should Historians Do with Masculinity?," 184. On the integral role women played in the public celebrations of a contemporary empire, see Davidson, "Women at Napoleonic Festivals."

39. Anderson, *New Book of Constitutions*, 148; Roper and Tosh, *Manful Assertions*, 12; Barker and Chalus, *Gender in Eighteenth-Century England*, 7. These hegemonic masculinities, of course, shift over time.

40. Clawson, *Constructing Brotherhood*, 4.

41. Hyam, *Britain's Imperial Century*, 297. One study that takes fraternalism into account is Atkinson's *Europeans in Australia*.

42. Bullock, *Revolutionary Brotherhood*, 39, 74. For a discussion of this tendency within fraternal organizations in general, see Clawson, "Early Modern Fraternalism," 368.

43. For an argument in favor of introducing some flexibility to our understanding of the family as an institution, see Barker and Chalus, *Gender in Eighteenth-Century England*, 16.

44. Under the influence of Irish and Ancient Masonry, the United Grand Lodge of England also recognized the Royal Arch degree in 1813. But to this day it administers no other degrees.

45. How, *Freemason's Manual*, 76–85. Several historians, like Clawson, Carnes, and Bullock, provide detailed examinations of this and other key rituals.

46. Bullock, *Revolutionary Brotherhood*, 17; Clawson, *Constructing Brotherhood*, 42–43.

47. Inwood, *Sermons*, 11.

48. Anderson, *Constitutions of the Free-Masons*. Bullock argues persuasively that the tension between inclusiveness and exclusivity was the central dynamic in Freemasonry. See *Revolutionary Brotherhood*, 4, 150, 214, 224–25, 234–37. See also Clawson, *Constructing Brotherhood*; Jacob, *Living the Enlightenment*; Smith, *Working the Rough Stone*.

49. See, for example, Cooper and Stoler, *Tensions of Empire*; Wilson, "Empire, Gender,

and Modernity," 14; Levine, "Introduction," 3. The historiography of imperial mas-culinities has also been focused on masculinity defined against others. See Sinha, *Colonial Masculinity*. Hall argues that affinity-building identities were important but only up until the 1860s. See *Civilising Subjects* and "Of Gender and Empire," 72.

50. Cannadine, *Ornamentalism*, xix.

51. Samson, "Are You What You Believe," 2. For a related argument, see Metcalf, *Ide-ologies of the Raj*; Burroughs, "Imperial Institutions and the Government of Empire," 182–83; O'Brien, *Narratives of Enlightenment*. Conklin, "Colonialism and Human Rights," explores the interplay of universalism and racialism in French imperial rhet-oric during the turn of the twentieth century.

CHAPTER I

1. Weeks, *Sermon*, 23; GLE(M) Proceedings, 23 November 1786. For evidence of an English lodge assisting an "Arabian Mason" in 1764, see Gould, *History of Freema-sonry*, 4:436.

2. Historians interested in the origins of Freemasonry vigorously dispute the relation-ship between *speculative* Freemasonry (the term used to describe the fraternal organi-zation of men who adopted masonry for spiritual and intellectual purposes) and its *operative* antecedent (the actual craft of building with stones). It is clear, however, that the Freemasonry explored here — the modern fraternal institution that spread across the British Empire — was a product of the eighteenth century.

3. Hamill, *Craft*, 42–44.

4. For more on the emerging Masonic bureaucracy, see Harland-Jacobs, "Essential Link," 34–40, 53–63.

5. Crawley, "Irish Constitutions," 14. For an example of a lodge in Bengal request-ing a Book of Constitutions from metropolitan officials to ensure the uniformity of their "working," see Hugh Honycomb to GLE(M), 27 December 1784, UGLHC 17/A/15.

6. Anderson, *Constitutions of the Free-Masons*.

7. Lepper and Crossle, *History of the Grand Lodge*, 232–34; Gould, *History of Free-masonry*, 5:53, 62; Laurie, *History of Free Masonry*, 120.

8. Minutes of Lodge no. 241 reprinted in Graham, *Outlines*, 88; John Ross to GLE(A), 20 June 1792, UGLHC 20/B/7. A Masonic certificate dated 1796 is in the Hodgson Papers, Add MS 36995 f.65, BL.

9. Weeks, *Sermon*, 20–23.

10. Hamill, *Craft*, 50; Clarke, "Formation," 92; Lepper and Crossle, *History of the Grand Lodge*, 231–32; Harland-Jacobs, "Essential Link," 80–84.

11. The fine for non-attendance was 2s. 6d. A return was the list of members sent to the grand lodge every year with a lodge's annual dues. Clarke, "Formation," 94–95; Sadler, *Masonic Facts and Fictions*, 70–77. On Dermott, see also Jacob, *Living the Enlightenment*, 60–62; Bullock, *Revolutionary Brotherhood*, 89.

12. Clarke, "Formation," 98–99, 106–7; GLE(M) Proceedings, 18 April 1777 and 8 April 1778. For later counterattacks, see GLE(A) Proceedings, 27 December 1802 and 2 March 1803.

13. Hamill, *Craft*, 47–49; Clarke, "Formation," 105–13. The incorporation movement was a controversial and ultimately failed attempt on the part of the Moderns to be rid of the Ancients. See Clark, *British Clubs and Societies*, 340–41.

14. Bullock, *Revolutionary Brotherhood*, 42; Jacob, *Radical Enlightenment*, Chapter 4; Weisberger, *Speculative Freemasonry*, 26.

15. Dermott, *Ahiman Rezon* (1756), 21, 16; Jacob, *Living the Enlightenment*, 60; James Heseltine to Grand Master, 1 April 1775, GLE Letterbook II, fo. 126–28; GLE(M) to Terence Gahagan, 4 April 1786, GLE Letterbook III, fo. 173–74. On the Ancients' social composition, see Clark, *British Clubs and Societies*, 313; Bullock, *Revolutionary Brotherhood*, 87–90. On their more democratic approach, see Hamill, *Craft*, 51.

16. Dermott, *Ahiman Rezon* (1778), ii. The phrase "Ahiman Rezon" is of Hebrew origin and is usually translated as "help to a brother."

17. Gould, *History of Freemasonry*, 4:446; GLE(A) to GLS, 1771 and 1772, quoted in Laurie, *History of Free Masonry*, 124–25; GLI Minutes, 6 November 1783.

18. For the neglect of the Ancients, see Sadler, *Masonic Facts and Fictions*; Bullock, *Revolutionary Brotherhood*, 343.

19. Parkinson, *History of the Grand Lodge*, 268–69. For a Mason's frustrations on not being able to assemble a lodge because his warrant had been lost in wartime, see Gahagan to GLE(M), 12 October 1784, UGLHC 18/A/5. Sometimes warrants were illegally sold. See GLI Minutes 5 July 1781; Parkinson, *History of the Grand Lodge*, 299; and Smyth, "Master-Mason," 225.

20. Ruling of PGLLC, 1772, quoted in Gould, *Military Lodges*, 127.

21. Parkinson, *History of the Grand Lodge*, 290–93; Milborne, "Overseas Development," 260.

22. Gould, *Military Lodges*, 41, 126; Gould, *History of Freemasonry*, 5:53–54.

23. Gould, *Military Lodges*, 41; Sheppard, "Details."

24. Gould, *Military Lodges*, 139–41; Parkinson, *History of the Grand Lodge*, 294–95; Saul, *Historical Sketch*, 5–10; Crawley, "General George Washington," 96.

25. Harris, "Maritime Provinces," 33–35; Gould, *Military Lodges*, 133–34.

26. Graham, *Outlines*, 36–37; Parkinson, *History of the Grand Lodge*, 304–5; McLeod, *Whence Come We?*, 12–13.

27. Anias Sutherland et al. to GLI, 11 April 1759, reprinted in Case, "American Masonic Roots," 1395–96.

28. Cranstoun-Day, *British Lodge*, 3–4; Butterfield, *Centenary*, 10–11. The Grand Lodge National of the Netherlands warranted its first lodges in Bengal in 1759 and in Batavia in 1763. J. C. M. Rademacher, a high-ranking VOC merchant, was the moving force behind these lodges as well as the first lodge at the Cape, the Lodge de Goede Hoop, in 1772. At least six British lodges were active in regiments involved in the first occupation. See Penman, "Freemasonry in South Africa," 280–81.

29. "List of Lodge in the East Indies and Ceylon, compiled from *Lane's Masonic Records*," 3; Hugh Honycomb to GLE(A), 27 December 1784, UGLHC 17/A/15.

30. John Chamier to GLE(M), 10 September 1791, UGLHC 18/A/22; PGL officers to GLE, 10 February 1798, UGLHC 18/A/44.

31. Milborne, "Overseas Development," 260; Newton, "Brethren Who Made Masonic History," 52–54; Smyth, "Master-Mason," 223–24.

32. Smyth, "Master-Mason," 226; Milborne, "Overseas Development," 261; Gould, *Military Lodges*, 119; GLE(A) Proceedings, 15 December 1773, quoted in Gould, *Military Lodges*, 128. Milborne, "Overseas Development," 260, estimates 42 percent of regimental lodges were Irish, 26 percent Ancient, 14 percent Scottish, and 11 percent Modern. For statistics, see also Smyth, "Master-Mason," 226; Sheppard, "Details"; Brereton, *British Soldier*, 111; Crawley, "First Military Lodge," 2.

33. Provincial grand masters were appointed for Montserrat, "South America," Gambia, the Cape Coast, Cape Breton/Louisbourg, and Bermuda, but no lodges were active in these places until later. *The Institutes of Free Masonry* (1788) listed forty-one provincial grand masters under the Moderns.

34. Gould, *History of Freemasonry*, 5:53; Laurie, *History of Free Masonry*, 121. Drummond constituted the first foreign Scottish lodge at Aleppo in 1748. Coil, *Coil's Masonic Encyclopedia*, 73.

35. Jackson, "William Mathew," 203; McLeod, *Whence Come We?*, 9, 24; Milborne, "Overseas Lodges," 250–51; John Jones to GLE(M), 12 April 1789, UGLHC 16/H/31.

36. Francis Robson et al., Proclamation, 13 August 1797, UGLHC 21/B/1; petition from St. Helena Masons to GLE(M), 27 January 1798, UGLHC 21/B/3; petition from St. Helena Masons to GLE(M), 11 November 1799, UGLHC, 21/B/4; Robson to GLE(M),11 November 1799, UGLHC 21/B/5; petition from St. Helena Masons to GLE(M), 27 January 1798; petition from St. Helena Masons to GLE(M), 11 November 1799; Robson to GLE(M), 11 November 1799, UGLHC 21/B/1–5 (emphasis in originals).

37. Hamill, *Craft*, 87; GLNS, "Rise and Progress," 5; GLI Minutes, 4 October 1787, and 3 September 1789.

38. Hopkins, *Globalization in World History*, 4. Hopkins, 12–44, reviews many of the theories arguing for and against the novelty of globalization. Works that present globalization as an outcome of the modern period include Harvey, *Condition of Postmodernity*; Giddens, *Consequences of Modernity*; and Appadurai, *Modernity at Large*.

39. Hopkins, *Globalization in World History*, 29.

40. Ibid., 4. Those presenting sweeping phases include Held and McGrew, *Global Transformations Reader*, and Robertson, *Globalization: Social Theory and Global Culture*.

41. On the 1760s as a key "globalizing decade," see Ballantyne, "Empire, Knowledge, and Culture," 118–20, and Osterhammel and Petersson, *Globalization*, 57–62.

42. Edward Ward to GLE(M), 1 September 1767, GLE Letterbook I, fo. 82; James Gawler, Quebec, quoted in Milborne, "Overseas Development," 263. For other exam-

ples of the ritual "healing" ceremonies both Ancients and Moderns required converts to undergo, see Graham, *Outlines*, 20; Firminger, *Second Lodge of Bengal*, 35.

43. Leybourne Lloyd to PGL Calcutta, 1 February 1785, UGLHC 17/A/16; John Burnett to GLE(M), 1785, quoted in Milborne, "Overseas Development," 230.

44. Lloyd to PGL Calcutta, 1 February 1785, UGLHC 17/A/16.

45. Lodge No. 152 to GLE(A), 12 March 1778, UGLHC 19/A/3; Malden, *History of Freemasonry*, 132-33.

46. PGL Madras to GLE(A), 7 July 1785, UGLHC 19/A/23; PGL Madras to GLE(A), 13 September 1785, UGLHC 19/A/28; Gahagan to GLE(M), 9 October 1786, UGLHC 18/A/9.

47. Milborne, "Overseas Development," 229-30; William Leake to GLE(M), 20 July 1786, and 22 December 1786, UGLHC 20/A/2-3; Gould, *History of Freemasonry* 6:313; J. W. Ross to GLE(A), 18 September 1789, UGLHC 20/B/3 and 15 August 1792, UGLHC 20/B/8. By the early 1790s the Ancient lodges outnumbered the Moderns' by three to one and all but one Modern lodge had disappeared by the 1810s. Charles Este to GLE(M), 3 September 1790, UGLHC 20/A/20.

48. GLE(A) Proceedings, 20 January 1792; PGL Jamaica to GLE(A), 4 May 1799, UGLHC 22/C/11; GLE(A) circular, 2 June 1802, vol. 2157, MG 20, GLNS Papers, PANS; Gould, *History of Freemasonry*, 6:357, 364, 369.

49. John Selby to GLE(A), 9 July 1793, UGLHC 16/G/52; James Thompson to B. J. Peters, 1785, quoted in Milborne, "Overseas Development," 263; address to Edward, 2 January 1794, reprinted in Graham, *Outlines*, 99; William Jarvis to James Agar, 10 March 1798, UGLHC 16/G/1. For Jarvis's disastrous tenure, see Harland-Jacobs, "Essential Link," 203-7.

50. Bullock, *Revolutionary Brotherhood*, 51, 85-86, 90-98, describes the transformation of American Masonry into a broader organization as a result of the Ancients' ascendancy. For the Ancients' more liberal policy in providing relief to petitioners, see Lepper and Crossle, *History of the Grand Lodge*, 232.

51. Williamson to Earl of Effingham, 17 October 1785, UGLHC 17/A/20; return of Lodge No. 4 at Fort St. George, 1790, UGLHC 18/A/17; return of Lodge No. 419 Perfect Harmony at St. Thomas's Mount, Coast of Coromandel, 1796, UGLHC 18/A/32.

52. Joseph Dunbar to GLE(M), 30 December 1769, UGLHC 23/A/1; Thomas Lynch and Francis Massell to GLE(M), 1 June 1782, UGLHC 23/A/4; Alexander MacPherson to GLE(M), 26 April 1790, UGLHC 23/A/10; returns of Mt. Sinai Lodge, St. Johns, 1780s, UGLHC 23/A/11-12. One member of Mt. Sinai lodge was listed as living in Philadelphia.

53. Hewitt, "Grand Lodge of England," 85; Errington to GLE(M), 11 November 1769, UGLHC 23/B/2; Laurie, *History of Free Masonry*, 121; Milborne, "Overseas Development," 244; J. Thompson to GLE(M), 8 November 1788, UGLHC 16/H/30 (emphasis in original).

54. Lodge No. 249 to GLE(A), 26 December 1791, UGLHC 16/G/72. See also GLI

Minutes, 4 August 1785. The connection with Scotland was clearly demonstrated in the last third of the century when certain Scottish grand masters (e.g., the 2nd and 3rd Dukes of Atholl) also served as grand masters of the Ancients.

55. John Burnett to GLE(M), 1785, quoted in Milborne, "Overseas Development," 230.

56. Irregular lodges could emerge when local Masons copied or purchased warrants. For the activities of a typical lodge, see *Sesquicentennial History of St. George's Lodge*. The most important annual ceremony took place on the Festival of St. John the Evangelist every 27 December.

57. Lodge return, 2 February 1770, UGLHC 17/A/1; lodge return, 27 December 1772, UGLHC 17/A/10a; Williamson to GLE(M), 17 October 1785, UGLHC 17/A/19; Malden, *History of Freemasonry*, 147; Robert Cooper to GLE(M), 9 October 1789, UGLHC 20/A/17; Royal Lodge of Freemasons, Proceedings, 5 November 1778 and 6 May 1779, Add MS 29970, BL.

58. Proceedings of the land board, Niagara, 24 June 1791, quoted in Ormsby, "Building a Town," 27; Carnochan, *History of Niagara*, 106, 120–21; Power, "Religion and Community," 112–13.

59. Riddell, *Life of John Graves Simcoe*, 452, 458–61; Harris, "John Graves Simcoe," 1170, 1174–75; Simcoe quoted in Errington, *The Lion, the Eagle, and Upper Canada*, 31.

60. Scott, *John Graves Simcoe*, 80–85; Simcoe's speech before the first session of the Parliament of Upper Canada, 17 September 1792, reprinted in Read, *Life and Times of . . . Simcoe*, 149–50; Talman, "Early Freemasonry in Ontario," 378.

61. Johnson was Superintendent of Indian Affairs until his death in 1774. His papers are peppered with references to his Masonic activities. On the younger Johnson's activities as PGM, see Graham, *Outlines*, 70. On the patronage networks of these prominent Niagara Freemasons, see Power, "Religion and Community," 123–24, and Wilson, "Patronage and Power," 50–54.

62. Gould, *History of Freemasonry*, 6:328; Malden, *History of Freemasonry*, 151; Lady Anne Barnard to Earl of Macartney, 4 January 1801, reprinted in Cranstoun-Day, *British Lodge*, 5.

63. James Thompson to GLE(M), 23 October 1787, UGLHC 16/H/26. For descriptions of Masonic processions in colonial British North America, see Hamilton, *Papers of Sir William Johnson*, 6:576, and Bullock, *Revolutionary Brotherhood*, 52–56, 78–82. For an example of a manual that provided instructions on ceremonies, see Turnough, *Institutes*, 43–79.

64. Gahagan to GLE(M), 9 October 1786, UGLHC 18/A/9 (emphasis in original); GLE(M) to Gahagan, 24 March 1787, GLE Letterbook III, fo. 203; Graham, *Outlines*, 94; *Upper Canada Gazette*, 4 January 1797, quoted in Power, "Religion and Community," 125; Middleton, *Municipality of Toronto*, 414. See also *Upper Canada Gazette*, 30 June 1798, quoted in Talman, "Early Freemasonry in Ontario," 376–77.

65. Firminger, *Second Lodge of Bengal*, 8, 10, 28, 47. Masons in Antigua built their own hall as early as 1744, and Barbadian Masons constructed theirs in 1772. See Turnough, *Institutes*, 265–66.

66. Knox, *Historical Journal* 1: 182–83; Clarke, *History of the Minden Lodge*, 29.

67. Laurie, *History of Free Masonry*, 124. For friendly societies in this period, see Wallace, "Needs of Strangers," and Clark, *British Clubs and Societies*. Masons' use of the idioms of kinship is discussed in Chapter 6.

68. Milborne, "Overseas Development," 248; memorial of Quebec Lodges to GLE(M), 8 November 1762, reprinted in Wright, *Gould's History*, 6:85–86; GLE(M) Proceedings, 12 November 1777; John Ordeson to GLE(M), 22 May 1782, UGLHC 23/B/9.

69. Thompson to GLE(M), 23 October 1787, UGLHC 16/H/26; Joseph Peters to John McCormick, 29 November 1790, UGLHC 16/G/48.

70. Talman, "Early Freemasonry in Ontario," 376; Firminger, *Second Lodge of Bengal*, 99; R. W. Eastwick to Lodge Industry and Perseverance, 13 July 1799, reprinted in Firminger, 90; Anderson, *Constitutions of the Free-Masons*. For examples of the assistance William Johnson rendered to Masonic brethren, see Hamilton, *Papers of Sir William Johnson*, 6:732, 757; 8:40–41, 1040–41.

71. John Miller to GLE(M), 11 February 1793, UGLHC 17/B/14; Williamson to GLE(M), 10 January 1799, UGLHC 17/B/31; Milborne, "Freemasonry in Bermuda," 14–19; Badger's certificate quoted in full in Graham, *Outlines*, 108. Stuart became PGM of Bengal in 1791. See Petition to the GLE(M), 12 January 1791, UGLHC 17/B/4.

72. W. M. Leake to GLE(M), 12 December 1788, UGLHC 20/A/10.

73. Hamilton, *Papers of Sir William Johnson*, 12:1075 (emphasis in original); Firminger, *Second Lodge of Bengal*, 58–59.

74. Gahagan to GLE(M), 9 October 1786, UGLHC 18/1/9; GLE(M) to Gahagan, 24 March 1787, GLE Letterbook III, fo. 203.

75. Firminger, *Second Lodge of Bengal*, 19; *Upper Canada Gazette*, 28 June 1797, quoted in Talman, "Early Freemasonry in Ontario," 375.

76. Graham, *Outlines*, 96; Clarke, *History of the Minden Lodge*, 22. For a fictional example of this, see Rudyard Kipling's *Kim*.

77. Malden, *History of Freemasonry*, 144–45.

CHAPTER 2

1. Anderson, *Constitutions of the Free-Masons*; Anderson, *New Book of Constitutions*, 144.

2. Jacob, *Living the Enlightenment*, 121.

3. Tosh and Roper, *Manful Assertions*, 12.

4. Kleingeld, "Six Varieties," 506n.3; Schlereth, *Cosmopolitan Ideal*, xii; Jacob, *Living the Enlightenment*, 147–48.

5. Kleingeld, "Six Varieties," 507.

6. For the tensions, ambivalences, and limitations in the rhetoric and practices of toleration in this period, see Grell and Porter, *Toleration in Enlightenment Europe*. For the

imperial context, see Carson, "The British Raj and the Awakening of Evangelical Conscience."

7. Schlereth, *Cosmopolitan Ideal*, 93; Porter, *Creation of the Modern World*, xxi, 203; Kleingeld, "Six Varieties," 515.

8. Anderson, *Constitutions of the Free-Masons*; Jacob, *Living the Enlightenment*, 66–67; Turnough, *Institutes*, 4.

9. Jacob, *Living the Enlightenment*, 66. Like the "antiphilosophes" who objected to toleration because of its threat to the idea of one true faith, Masonry's detractors were not comforted by the idea that in the lodge a Muslim or Jew was equally respected as a Christian. For antiphilosophes' attitudes, see McMahon, *Enemies of Enlightenment*, 44–45, 78, 131–33. For discussions of religious toleration within Freemasonry, see Katz, *Jews and Freemasons*, 14–15, and Schlereth, *Cosmopolitan Ideal*, 86–88.

10. Anderson, *Constitutions of the Free-Masons*; Turnough, *Institutes*, 124; GLE(A), Address to the King, *Times*, 7 March 1793; GLI Minutes, 3 January 1793.

11. Mehta, "Cosmopolitanism and the Circle of Reason," 623.

12. For monogenesis and imperialism, see Hyam, *Britain's Imperial Century*, 74–77; Metcalf, *Ideologies of the Raj*, 5–6, 28–34; and Pagden, *Peoples and Empires*, 138–40.

13. Davenport, *Love to God and Man*, 6, 8; Browne, *Master-Key*, 28. See also Dodd, *Oration*, 7; Preston, *Illustrations*, 14–15; Turnough, *Institutes*, 3; Inwood, *Sermons*, 8–9. For German Freemasons' evocations of this idea, see Beachy, "Recasting Cosmopolitanism," 266.

14. Schlereth, *Cosmopolitan Ideal*, 191n.3; Heater, *World Citizenship*, 71; Hannerz, "Cosmopolitans and Locals," 239.

15. Smith, *Working the Rough Stone*, 91; Preston, *Illustrations of Masonry*, 15. For how worldly citizenship could play out in a local context, see Atkinson, *Europeans in Australia*, 241–43.

16. Bullock, *Revolutionary Brotherhood*, 56–57, quoting William Brogden, *Freedom and Love*, 10, 12; Weeks, *Sermon*, 20; A Free and Accepted Mason, "Dissertation on Free-Masonry," 78. See also Turnough, *Institutes*, 2–3.

17. Schlereth, *Cosmopolitan Ideal*, 90; Preston, *Illustrations of Masonry*, 26–27; Dodd, *Oration*, 16; Turnough, *Institutes*, 3–4; A Free and Accepted Mason, "Dissertation on Free-Masonry," 78.

18. Wilson, "Empire, Gender, and Modernity," 20–22.

19. Smith, *Working the Rough Stone*, 92; Preston, *Illustrations of Masonry*, 75–76, 5; Anderson, *Constitutions of the Free-Masons*. On stadialism and imperialism, see Wilson, *Island Race*, 8–10, 72–78. For a contemporary sermon focused on the qualified nature of Masonic equality, see Weeks, *Sermon*. See also Jacob, *Living the Enlightenment*, 60–65, 147, and Bullock, *Revolutionary Brotherhood*, 4–5, 33, 39–40.

20. Browne, *Master-Key*, 28; Jacob, *Living the Enlightenment*, 34–35, 120–30. See also Bullock, *Revolutionary Brotherhood*, 150–53, and Smith, *Working the Rough Stone*, 91–135.

21. *Freemasonry for the Ladies*, dedication page.

22. Turnough, *Institutes*, 4, 124; Langford, *Polite and Commercial People*, 242; Power, *Land, Politics and Society*, 228–29. For continental lodges, see Jacob, *Living the Enlightenment*, 153, 181–83.

23. Clarke, "Freemasonry and Religion," 213; Crawley, "Old Charges," 14; Lepper and Crossle, *History of the Grand Lodge*, 423. On the Catholic middle class, see Whelan, *Tree of Liberty*.

24. GLI Minutes, 5 July 1787 and 3 January 1793; Lepper and Crossle, *History of the Grand Lodge*, 422–27.

25. GLI Minutes, 7 November 1799; Crawley, "Old Charges," 14.

26. Graham, *Outlines*, 33; McLeod, *Whence Come We?*, 11–12. The meetings of Merchants' Lodge were advertised in the first issue of the first Canadian newspaper, *Quebec Gazette* 1 (21 June 1764), quoted in Graham, *Outlines,* 42.

27. Edward Antill to GLE, 25 August 1768, quoted in MacTaggart, Smith, and Bond, *Old St. Paul's Lodge*, 7; La Loge des Coeurs-Unis, "Histoire," n.p. Two prominent French members of the first Executive Council, Sir Charles Tarrieu and Charles Picotte, were members of Lodge Les Frères Canadiens and St. Peter's Lodge, respectively, during the 1770s.

28. Colley, *Britons*, 20–25. For a counterargument, see Whelan, *Tree of Liberty*, 102–6.

29. Katz, *Jews and Freemasons*, 15–16; Dermott, *Ahiman Rezon, 1778,* 43–44; Sadler, *Masonic Facts and Fictions*, 118–19; Clarke, "Freemasonry and Religion," 211; Bullock, *Revolutionary Brotherhood*, 33; Stevenson, "James Anderson," 224; UGL Proceedings, 3 December 1845 and 3 June 1846.

30. Katz, *Jews and Freemasons*, 17–20. See also Jacob, *Living the Enlightenment*, 154–55, 173–74.

31. Katz, *Jews and Freemasons*, 17; Bullock, *Revolutionary Brotherhood*, 59; Lazarus, "Experiences in Caribbean Masonry." Katz points out that some Jews in English lodges may have been Ashkenazic. For returns of lodges in Jamaica that included Jews, see C. Mendes to GLE(A), 7 September 1810, UGLHC 22/C/16. The Friendly Lodge in Kingston, founded in the 1790s, had a majority of Jewish members. See Leon, *History of The Friendly Lodge.*

32. GLE(M) Proceedings, 12 November and 5 December 1777; GLE(M) to Umdat-ul-Umrah Bahadur, 12 April 1780, GLE Letterbook III, fo. 93; Umdat-ul-Umrah Bahadur to GLE(M), 29 November 1778, in Proceedings, 2 February 1780; Gahagan to GLE(M), 9 October 1786, UGLHC 18/A/9. For English Masons' attempts to persuade the nawab to contribute to their charities, see Gahagan to GLE(M), 9 April 1799, UGLHC 18/A/48; Prince of Wales to Umdat-ul-Umrah Bahadur, 29 May 1799, UGL HC 18/A/49; Malden, *History of Freemasonry*, 43–44, 144–46.

33. *Encyclopedia of Native American Biography*, 51–53.

34. White, *Middle Ground*, x, 433.

35. Cannadine, *Ornamentalism*, 43; GLI Minutes, 6 May 1784; GLE(M) Proceedings, 23 November 1786.

36. Hall's place of birth remains unknown, but scholars do agree he was a freed slave. See Draffen, "Prince Hall Freemasonry," 71; Coil and Sherman, *Documentary Account*, 19–23; Bullock, *Revolutionary Brotherhood*, 158–60; Brooks, "Early American Public Sphere," 16.

37. Draffen, "Prince Hall Freemasonry," 72–73; Kaplan and Kaplan, *Black Presence*, 202–14; Coil and Sherman, *Documentary Account*, 29–31.

38. Hall to William Moody, 30 June 1784, reprinted in Draffen, "Prince Hall Freemasonry," 75; Hall to GLE, 16 May 1787, UGLHC 28/A/5 and 23 May 1788, UGLHC 28/A.

39. Hall to GLE(M), 9 November 1789, UGLHC 28/A/8; Wesley, *Prince Hall*, 77–81.

40. Hall to GLE(M), 10 May 1787, UGLHC 28/A/4; Bullock, *Revolutionary Brotherhood*, 159; Draffen, "Prince Hall Freemasonry," 72; Hall, *Charge*, 10; Kaplan and Kaplan, *Black Presence*, 211–13; Brooks, "Early American Public Sphere," 14; Wesley, *Prince Hall*, 62–76.

41. For white Masons' attitudes toward African Lodge, see Wesley, *Prince Hall*, 44–54. For Hall's contacts with black Masons in Rhode Island and Philadelphia, see Wesley, *Prince Hall*, 124–29. Hall's successors wrote as late as 1824 seeking a renewal of their charter under the English Grand Lodge. Draffen, "Prince Hall Freemasonry," 76–78; Brooks, "Early American Public Sphere," 16; Voorhis, "Negro Masonry in the United States," 364–68.

42. Bullock, *Revolutionary Brotherhood*, 67–68; Stemper, "Conflicts and Development," 199–200; Schlereth, *Cosmopolitan Ideal*, 58–59.

43. Lemay, *Reappraising Benjamin Franklin*, 21, 116; Lopez, "Was Franklin Too French?," 145–47. On Franklin's involvement in the lodge, see also Schoenbrun, *Triumph in Paris*, 105, 195–96. On his role as a spy, see Baigent and Lee, *Temple and the Lodge*, 233–38; Srodes, *Franklin*, 313.

44. Samuel Parsons to Lodge Unity, No. 18, 23 July 1779, reprinted in Milborne, "British Military Lodges," 37–38. See also Bullock, *Revolutionary Brotherhood*, 128–29.

45. Gould, *History of Freemasonry*, 6:326; Butterfield, *Centenary*, 7–10.

46. Address of the Lodge Triple Hope, Isle of France, to the Lodge of Perfect Unanimity, 18 October 1788, reprinted in Malden, *History of Freemasonry*, 137–39; John Macdonald to GLE(M), 19 March 1793, UGLHC 21/E/13; Gould, *History of Freemasonry*, 6:333.

47. List of members of the PGL on the coast of Coromandel ca. 1789, UGLHC 18/A/13; Gould, *History of Freemasonry*, 6:328; Firminger, *Second Lodge of Bengal*, 71–72; PGL Bengal to GLE(M), 11 February 1798, UGLHC 17/B/15; PGL Bengal to GLE(M), 25 April 1798, UGLHC 17/B/28.

48. Lodge minutes quoted in Firminger, *Second Lodge of Bengal*, 22; Horne to GLE(M), 16 January 1785, UGLHC 18/A/8; PGL Madras to Wm. Randall, 7 July 1785, UGLHC 19/A/23.

49. Jacob, *Living the Enlightenment*, 69.

50. Jacob, "Freemasonry," 82.

51. Ibid., 72, 80–81; Jacob, *Living the Enlightenment*, 120–42.

52. Jacob, *Living the Enlightenment*, 139; Burke and Jacob, "French Freemasonry," 520, 540, 537; Jacob, "Freemasonry," 72–73; Robison, *Proofs of a Conspiracy*, 3. See also Burke, "Leaving the Enlightenment." For Russia, see Smith, *Working the Rough Stone*, 28–30.

53. Ridley, *Freemasons*, 42–43; Jacob, "Freemasonry," 72; Jacob, *Living the Enlightenment*, 121; Anderson, *Ancient Constitutions*, 45; Atkinson, *Europeans in Australia*, 242.

54. Gould, *History of Freemasonry*, 5:43, 6:397–98.

55. Dermott, *Ahiman Rezon* (1778), 29; Whytehead, "Women in Freemasonry," 18.

56. Cohen, "Manliness," 59; Bullock, *Revolutionary Brotherhood*, 34; Jacob, *Living the Enlightenment*, 124.

57. Dodd, *Oration*, 1; Smith, *Use and Abuse*, 361–64 (emphasis in original).

58. Turnough, *Institutes*, 5–6, 68; Hutchinson, *Spirit of Masonry*, 126 (emphasis in original); "Dissertation on Free-Masonry," 79 (emphasis in original). See also Smith, *Use and Abuse*, 351.

59. *Oriental Masonic Muse*. On conviviality, see Hamill, *Craft*, 80–81.

60. Preston, *Illustrations of Masonry*, 11; Browne, *Master-Key*, iv, 28; A Free and Accepted Mason, *Dissertation on Free-Masonry*, 78; Bryson, *Duties of Masonry*, 17, 25. See also Dodd, *Oration*, 5–16, and Turnough, *Institutes*, 5, 126. On the role of lodges in fostering sociability and politeness, see Porter, *Creation of the Modern World*, 22.

61. On this trend, see Tosh, *Man's Place*, 123. For a text that addresses separate spheres explicitly, see Smith, *Use and Abuse*, 354.

62. Davidoff and Hall, *Family Fortunes*, 13; Tosh, "Old Adam and the New Man," 229–30.

63. Hamill, *Craft*, 82–83; *Oriental Masonic Muse*, 148–49.

64. Turnough, *Institutes*, 67–68; Smith, *Use and Abuse*, 354; Anderson, *Constitutions of the Free-Masons*; Dodd, *Oration*, 16 (emphasis in original). See also Jacob, *Living the Enlightenment*, 56.

65. For an example of the tendency to use "cosmopolitan" as a synonym for "diverse," see Bowen, *Elites, Enterprise and . . . Empire*, esp. Chapter 7. Two exceptions to this trend are Pagden, *Peoples and Empires*, and Bayly, "'Archaic' and 'Modern' Globalization," 5.

66. Newman, *Rise of English Nationalism*, 1. Schlereth, *Cosmopolitan Ideal*, and Heater, *World Citizenship*, both adopt the tracking approach.

67. Cheah and Robbins, *Cosmopolitics*, 2. See also Breckenridge and Pollock, *Cosmopolitanism*, and O'Brien, *Narratives of Enlightenment*.

68. Post-colonial studies scholars and historians of science and exploration have long made the connection between imperialism and the Enlightenment, but it still does not receive the attention it deserves in work on the history of cosmopolitanism and, more generally, eighteenth-century Europe.

69. Jacob, *Living the Enlightenment*, 147. For another argument against the "straightforward antinomies of patriotism and cosmopolitanism," see O'Brien, *Narratives of Enlightenment*, 4.

70. Jacob, "Freemasonry," 82.

CHAPTER 3

1. Anderson, *Constitutions of the Free-Masons*.

2. UGL, *Constitutions*.

3. Money, "Freemasonry and the Fabric of Loyalism," 255. Over the course of two important pieces, Money tracks what he describes as Freemasonry's shift "from the free and easy cosmopolitanism of the past, toward a more serious association with Church, King, and Protestant Constitution." He sees Freemasonry as evolving "at an angle to the overt structure of power rather than in alignment with it" and corresponding "more to the populism of patriot politics than to the hierarchy of king, church, and aristocracy" through the 1750s. But after mid-century, he argues, its "underlying direction" was undoubtedly loyalist. "Masonic Moment," 377, 372; "Fabric of Loyalism," 256, 265.

4. Dickinson, *Politics of the People*, 6; Hobsbawm, *Primitive Rebels*, 153, 163–64; Brewer, *Party Ideology*, 195–97; Whelan, *Tree of Liberty*, 86; Jacob, *Radical Enlightenment*, 121.

5. Lepper and Crossle, *History of the Grand Lodge*, 292; Jacob, *Living the Enlightenment*, 50–51, 56. Jacob does describe English Freemasonry as having a radical underside but argues that it never seriously challenged the more dominant tendency within English Freemasonry toward supporting order, loyalty, and oligarchy. See particularly her discussion of how Freemasonry expressed the tension between "court" and "country" in Chapter 2.

6. Melton, *Rise of the Public*, 270. Money, "Fabric of Loyalism," 259, agrees with this point, but only for the 1750s and 1760s. See also Wilson, *Sense of the People*, 70; York, "Freemasons and the American Revolution," 329.

7. Jacob, whose unrivaled scholarship pioneered the academic study of English and Continental European Freemasonry, is careful to emphasize Masonry's "international character," but her discussion focuses on English rather than British Freemasonry writ large. Weisberger's books also look at Freemasonry in multiple national contexts but adopt neither an explicitly connective nor comparative approach.

8. Jenkins, "Jacobites and Freemasons," 406.

9. For clubs and associations, see Money, *Experience and Identity*; Morris, "Clubs, Societies, and Associations"; Wilson, *Sense of the People*; Clark, *British Clubs*; Porter, *Creation of the Modern World*.

10. For the eighteenth century, see Breen, "An Empire of Goods"; Colley, "Britishness and Otherness"; Bowen, *Elites, Enterprise and . . . Empire*; Gould, "Virtual Nation"; Greene, "Empire and Identity"; and Wilson, *Island Race*.

11. Jenkins, "Jacobites and Freemasons," 406. On Masonic toleration in the face of political divisions, see Morris, "Clubs, Societies, and Associations," 401.

12. Jacob, *Living the Enlightenment*, 32. See also Newman, "Politics and Freemasonry," 33, 41, and Brewer, *Party Ideology*, 149.

13. Jacob, *Radical Enlightenment*, 127; Newman, "Politics and Freemasonry," 36. A portrait of Walpole from late in his life reveals him wearing Masonic insignia.

14. Williams, "Masonic Personalia," 231, 235; Jacob, *Radical Enlightenment*, 131–32; Weisberger, *Speculative Freemasonry*, 59–61.

15. Jacob, *Living the Enlightenment*, 46; Weisberger, *Speculative Freemasonry*, 37, 59.

16. Monod, *Jacobitism*, 305; Jenkins, "Jacobites and Freemasons," 402; Devine and Young, *Eighteenth-Century Scotland*, 83; Wilson, *Sense of the People*, 70. See Monod for a discussion of the issues involved in defining Jacobitism.

17. Monod, *Jacobitism*, 12. For details of Wharton's Masonic coup d'état, see Blackett-Ord, *Hell-fire Duke*, 88–90.

18. Newman, "Politics and Freemasonry," 36; *London Journal*, 16 June 1722, quoted in Blackett-Ord, *Hell-Fire Duke*, 89.

19. Jenkins, *Making of a Ruling Class*, 153; Jenkins, "Jacobites and Freemasons," 393.

20. Jenkins, "Jacobites and Freemasons," 392; Jenkins, *Making of a Ruling Class*, 153; Newman, "Politics and Freemasonry," 37.

21. McLynn, *Jacobites*, 140; Jacob, *Living the Enlightenment*, 89; Monod, *Jacobitism*, 301. For Russia, see Smith, *Working the Rough Stone*, 18–19, and Milborne, "Overseas Development," 232–33.

22. Devine and Young, *Eighteenth-Century Scotland*, 83–84; Monod, *Jacobitism*, 302. On Ramsay, see Jacob, *Radical Enlightenment*, 129, 257–58. On the Strict Observance, see Monod, *Jacobitism*, 302–3, and Szechi, *Jacobites*, 107.

23. London papers cited in Gooch, *Desperate Faction*, 39, 111; Jacob, *Living the Enlightenment*, 89–90; Devine and Young, *Eighteenth-Century Scotland*, 83–84; McLynn, *Jacobites*, 140; Gould, *Military Lodges*, 39–40. Kilmarnock's other sons were loyal to the king: the eldest was an officer in the 21st Foot (which took part in the Battle of Culloden) and became Scottish Grand Master in 1751; the youngest was in the navy.

24. Jacob, *Living the Enlightenment*, 27, 89–90. See Jacob, 4–6, on the French authorities' suspicions of Freemasonry during the 1740s. On relations between Jacobite Masons and the Church, see McLynn, *Jacobites*, 140, and Gooch, *Desperate Faction*, 111.

25. Szechi, *Jacobites*, 25; Monod, *Jacobitism*, 305. Philip Jenkins makes a similar argument: that Welsh Masonic lodges of the 1760s were the "clubbable" successors to the political societies that had supported Jacobitism in the 1720s. Jenkins, "Jacobites and Freemasons," 393–94.

26. Money, "Masonic Moment," 372; Weisberger, *Speculative Freemasonry*, 61–62; Newman, "Politics and Freemasonry," 36; Jenkins, "Jacobites and Freemasons," 401–2.

27. Treloar, *Wilkes and the City*, 73; Newman, "Politics and Freemasonry," 38. Wilkes belonged to several Masonic lodges (both Ancient and Modern) as well as a number of quasi-masonic organizations. He frequented the Horn Tavern, where the Joiners Company, a free and easy club, and three Masonic lodges met. Brewer, *Party Ideology*, 149, 194–95.

28. Brewer, *Party Ideology*, 196, 181; Newman, "Politics and Freemasonry," 38; Jenkins, "Jacobites and Freemasons," 392. See Jenkins, 399–402, for numerous examples of Welsh radicals who descended from Jacobite families and belonged to Freemasonry. See Money, "Freemasonry and the Fabric of Loyalism," 257–58, for a critique.

29. Hamill, *Craft*, 47; Brother Fench to Brother Banks, 31 October 1768, Industry and Perseverance, No. 109, Calcutta Lodge File, FHL.

30. Money, "Freemasonry and the Fabric of Loyalism," 260–61; Jacob, *Radical Enlightenment*, 120–21, 130–31, and *Living the Enlightenment*, 54, 56.

31. The regiment was the 77th Foot or Atholl Highlanders, raised in 1778 (disbanded in 1783); it was named after the Duke of Atholl, Grand Master of England and later of Scotland. The practice was apparently widespread because the GLS felt it necessary to issue a circular "forbidding the practice of offering bounties to military recruits, together 'with the freedom of Masonry.'" Gould, *History of Freemasonry*, 5:63.

32. Burgoyne quoted in Gould, *Military Lodges*, 172.

33. For an argument about Freemasons' willingness to engage in rebellion on the basis of the belief that government was no longer consensual, see York, "Freemasons and the American Revolution," 328–29.

34. Bullock, *Revolutionary Brotherhood*, 109. For an introduction to the concept of Atlantic history, see Armitage, "Three Concepts of Atlantic History."

35. Bullock, *Revolutionary Brotherhood*, 114; *Sesquicentennial History: St. George's Lodge*, 15. Work on the Masonic affiliations of prominent revolutionaries is well developed. In addition to Bullock, see Cerza, "Colonial Freemasonry"; Baigent and Leigh, *Temple and the Lodge*; Heaton, *Masonic Membership*.

36. Bullock, *Revolutionary Brotherhood*, 113; Baigent and Leigh, *Temple and the Lodge*, 224; York, "Freemasons and the American Revolution," 322–25.

37. Thomas, *John Paul Jones*, 26, 37, 216–17, 221.

38. Bullock, *Revolutionary Brotherhood*, 109, 122–24, 129, 109; Tatsch, *Freemasonry in the Thirteen Colonies*, 202–22. For Masonry's role in shaping corps identity among Massachusetts officers, see Kaplan, "Veteran Officers."

39. Bullock, *Revolutionary Brotherhood*, 121; Stemper, "Conflicts and Development," 200–201. For another argument on the ideological uses to which Freemasonry was put, see Albanese, "Whither the Sons (and Daughters)?"

40. Parramore, *Launching the Craft*, 54–60; Cerza, "American War of Independence," 172. See also the discussion of John Van Norden in Chapter 5.

41. Master and officers of Lodge No. 1, Halifax to GLE(M), 17 August 1778, UGLHC 16/H/8.

42. Cerza, "American War of Independence," 171; Bullock, *Revolutionary Brotherhood*, 61, 74, 79.

43. Cerza, "Colonial Freemasonry," 229; DeSaussure, "Address on the History of Freemasonry in South Carolina."

44. Bullock, *Revolutionary Brotherhood*, 112–13.

45. Davidson, *Propaganda*, 331, quoting Moore, *Diary of the Revolution*, 2:443; Cerza, "Colonial Freemasonry," 227.

46. Cerza, "American War of Independence," 173; McLeod, *Whence Come We?*, 9–10.

47. Voorhis, *Freemasonry in Bermuda*, 4; George Errington to GLE(M), n.d., UGLHC 23/B/4; Walter Davidson to GLE(M), 10 June 1782, UGLHC 22/B/6.

48. The Defenders were a Catholic secret society that combined the techniques of agrarian agitation with the goals of republicanism.

49. Lepper and Crossle, *History of the Grand Lodge*, 247–48; Smyth, "Freemasonry and the United Irishmen," 168–70; Whelan, *Tree of Liberty*, 86. On the Defenders and the Orange Order, see Musgrave, *Memoirs of the Irish Rebellion*, 58; Smyth, "Freemasonry and the United Irishmen," 169.

50. Most scholars of the United Irishmen describe the movement as occurring in two phases, one constitutional (until 1794) and another revolutionary. Curtin argues that Freemasonry's influence was much more significant in the second phase. Yet it is important not to underestimate its influence in the first phase, particularly in the ideological origins of the movement. See Curtin, *United Irishmen*.

51. "Declaration of a Society, calling themselves a Society of United Irishmen in Dublin, 9th November 1791," House of Commons, *Report from the Committee of Secrecy*, 59 (hereafter cited as *Report*); "Address from the Society of United Irishmen in Dublin to the Delegates for the promoting Reform in Scotland," 23 November 1792, *Report*, 76–78.

52. Whelan, *Tree of Liberty*, 120; Stewart, *Deeper Silence*, 177.

53. Drennan to William Bruce, 7 February 1784, cited in Stewart, *Deeper Silence*, 137; "Idem Sentire, Dicere, Agere," June 1791, *Report*, 67–72. See also Drennan to Samuel McTier, 21 May 1791, in Chart, *Drennan Letters*, 54–55. Stewart, *Deeper Silence*, 174–76, makes an argument that Drennan was a Mason; for a counter argument, see Knox, *Rebels and Informers*, 31–32.

54. "Constitution" and "Test," *Report*, 34–36.

55. *Belfast Newsletter*, 11 December 1792; *Northern Star*, 16 January 1793; *Belfast Newsletter*, 18–22 January 1793. All NS and BNL articles pertaining to Freemasonry are available in Cochrane, *Irish Masonic Records*. On the instrumental role of James Reynolds (a Presbyterian physician) in linking Volunteering with Freemasonry and organizing the convention of lodges at Dungannon, see McBride, *Scripture Politics*, 174.

56. Whelan, *Tree of Liberty*, 75, 86. For the names of prominent United Irishmen who were also Freemasons, see Smyth, "Freemasonry and the United Irishmen," 172–75. For the role of Masonic lodges, Defender cells, Volunteer companies, and reading societies in the underground phase of the United Irish movement in Ulster, see McBride, *Scripture Politics*, 180.

57. James Paterson to General Knox, 25 December 1797, Rebellion Papers 620/28/14, NAI (hereafter cited as Rebellion Papers); William Taylor to Pelham, 17 March 1798, Rebellion Papers, 620/36/17; *Freemasons' Repository*, 1797, quoted in Caillard, "Australia's First Lodge Meeting," 225. The United Scotsmen followed the United Irishmen's lead in the use of lodges as covers. See McFarland, *Ireland and Scotland*, 159.

58. Letter from Thomas Higginson, 15 February 1797, Rebellion Papers 620/28/275; examination of Richard Boynham, 19 April 1797, Rebellion Papers 620/29/282. On the circulation of information, see Whelan, *Tree of Liberty*, 80.

59. Pelham to Donoughmore, 24 October 1797, Rebellion Papers 620/32/184. See also

Pelham to Joseph Pollock, 27 February 1798, Rebellion Papers 620/35/156; Knox to Edward Cooke, 3 May 1798, Rebellion Papers 620/37/3; report of T. Waring, 25 May 1798, Rebellion Papers 620/37/160 (Smyth, "Freemasonry and the United Irishmen," 173, also cites this evidence).

60. *Freeman's Journal*, 22 December 1792, and *Northern Star*, 23 January 1793, cited by Curtin, *United Irishmen*, 56; report of Francis Higgins, 19 November 1796, Rebellion Papers, 620/36/226; Berry, "Some Historical Episodes," 5. For other examples, see Clifford, *Freemasonry and the Northern Star*.

61. GLI, Circular, 3 January 1793, reprinted in Lepper and Crossle, *History of the Grand Lodge*, 298.

62. Declaration of the General Committee of all the Free and Accepted Masons of the County of Armagh, 21 June 1797, Rebellion Papers, 620/31/155.

63. Whelan, *Tree of Liberty*, 86. Correspondence between Pelham and Donoughmore described by Berry, "Some Historical Episodes," 6.

64. Miller, *Irish Immigrants in the Land of Canaan*, 631–35; Uriah Tracy to Oliver Wolcott, 7 August 1800, quoted in Wilson, *United Irishmen, United States*, 1.

65. E. Collins et al. to GL(M), 18 July 1799, UGLHC 18/A/45 (emphasis in original).

CHAPTER 4

1. GLE(M), "Address to his Majesty" in Proceedings, 6 February 1793. For the loyal address movement of 1792, see Dozier, *For King, Constitution, and Country*, 1–2, and Eastwood, "Patriotism and the English State," 154–55.

2. GLE(A), address to the King, *Times*, 7 March 1793. The use of the term "unionist" before 1800 is admittedly anachronistic, but it is nonetheless useful for referring to those who wanted to maintain the connection with Britain rather than set up an independent republic (as eventually became the goal of the United Irishmen).

3. Whelan pinpoints this moment to 1797 and 1798 when the spread of Orange Lodges (encouraged by General Knox to stem the tide of republicanism) neutralized Freemasonry's ability to serve as a vector of radical thought. Whelan, *Tree of Liberty*, 120. For Freemasonry's role in the increasing nationalist climates of Europe and the United States in this period, see also Jacob et al., "Forum: Exits from the Enlightenment: Masonic Routes."

4. GLE(M), *Proceedings*, 7 February and 28 November 1787, 10 February 1790; Hamill, "Earl of Moira," 33; Abbott, *Royalty and Freemasonry*, 15–18; UGL, *Proceedings*, 3 March 1819.

5. The Duke of Clarence was also active in Freemasonry while serving overseas with the navy. According to Voorhis, *Freemasonry in Bermuda*, 14, he attended at least one lodge while in Bermuda.

6. Harris, "H.R.H. Prince Edward Augustus," 308–13; Woodham-Smith, *Queen Victoria*, 9.

7. Minutes of Lodge No. 241, 18 December 1791, reprinted in Graham, *Outlines*, 90;

petition from Lodges No. 9, 40, and 241 to GLE(A), 27 December 1791, UGLHC 16/G/13; warrant appointing Prince Edward PGM of Lower Canada, 7 March 1792, reprinted in Abbott, *Royalty and Freemasonry*, 22–23; Graham, *Outlines*, 93–94; Harris, "H.R.H. Prince Edward Augustus," 315; list of lodges constituted by Edward, 1793, UGLHC 16/G/25. For Galloway, see Chapter 1.

8. John Selby to GLE(A), 9 July 1793, UGLHC 16/G/52; Wilson to GLE(A), 5 November 1792, 16/G; Keable Sarjeant to GLE(A), 19 February 1796, UGLHC 16/G/32.

9. PGL(A) Nova Scotia to Edward, 27 May 1794, and Edward to PGL(A) Nova Scotia, May 1794, reprinted in Harris, "H.R.H Prince Edward Augustus," 319–21; Harris, "H.R.H. Prince Edward Augustus," 325; Blakeley, *Glimpses of Halifax*, 73–74.

10. On addresses, see Dozier, *For King, Constitution, and Country*, 2, and Dickinson, *Politics of the People*, Chapter 8; on parliamentary petitions, see Colley, *Britons*, 329–34, 342–43.

11. *Calcutta Gazette*, 11 June 1793, and PGL Bengal, Address to the Prince of Wales, 27 December 1793, reprinted in Firminger, *Second Lodge of Bengal*, 103–4 (emphasis in original).

12. "Address to His Majesty," GLE(M), *Proceedings*, 6 Feb. 1793; Malden, *History*, 146.

13. Colley, "Apotheosis of George III," and *Britons*, especially Chapter 5; GLE(A), Circular, 4 June 1800, vol. 2157, MG 20, GLNS Papers, PANS; Laurie, *History of Free Masonry*, 162–63. Colley mentions that Freemasons typically occupied a prominent place in royal celebrations. She also notes that the monarchy's reputation fluctuated greatly, even after George's apotheosis. Colley, *Britons*, 230.

14. Colley interprets ridiculing members of the royal family as a sign of veneration for the monarchy. Colley, *Britons*, 210. See also Bayly, *Imperial Meridian*, 109–15.

15. 39 George III, c. 79 in House of Commons, *Sessional Papers of the Eighteenth Century*.

16. Robison, *Proofs*, 11. For Barruel, see Jacob, *Living the Enlightenment*, 10–12.

17. GLE(A) Proceedings, 6 May 1799 and 5 June 1799; Hamill, "Earl of Moira," 33–34; Hamill, *Craft*, 154–55.

18. GLE(M), Circular, 30 July 1799 (appears after 10 April 1799 Proceedings); Laurie, *History of Free Masonry*, 152–54; GLE(A), Circular, 4 June 1800; GLE(A) Proceedings, 6 May 1799 and 27 December 1800.

19. GLI Minutes 1 November 1798, 6 December 1798, 14 February 1799; Lepper and Crossle, *History of the Grand Lodge*, 296–99; Crawley, "Irish Constitutions," 14–15.

20. GLE(M), "Address to his Majesty," Proceedings, 6 February 1793; Proceedings, 3 June 1800.

21. GLE(M) Proceedings, 3 June 1800; GLE(A), Circular, 4 June 1800, vol. 2157, MG 20, GLNS Papers, PANS; Laurie, *History of Freemasonry*, 162–63. Like countless other metropolitan lodges, the Royal Lodge of Freemasons in London also sent a loyal address in 1800. See Proceedings of the Royal Lodge of Freemasons, 5 June 1800, Add MS 29970, BL.

22. Petition from Ancient Lodges in Barbados to the Duke of Atholl, n.d., and Petition to the King, 18 October 1800, UGLHC 23/B/17 and 17c.

23. GLI Minutes, 6 July 1837.

24. C. Dénéchau to PGLLC, 27 December 1821, reprinted in Graham, *Outlines*, 157–58 (emphasis in original); printed circular of PGLLC, 27 December 1822, UGLHC 16/C/7.

25. Hobsbawm and Ranger, *Invention of Tradition*, 1.

26. Moira to Sheriff Depute, 1808, quoted in Hamill, "Earl of Moira," 33.

27. Lepper and Crossle, *History of the Grand Lodge*, 422–27; Donoughmore to GLE, n.d. (after 24 June 1813), reprinted in GLI Minutes, 3 February 1814.

28. Lepper and Crossle, *History of the Grand Lodge*, 407–8, 315.

29. For centralization efforts and the Seton Affair, see GLI Minutes, 5 March 1807–5 March 1812, passim, and Lepper and Crossle, *History of the Grand Lodge*, 321–400.

30. See GLE(A) Proceedings, 7 March 1810.

31. Moira to PGLM, reprinted in Malden, *History*, 67–68. For the negotiations between 1811 and 1813, see Hamill, "Earl of Moira," 35–36.

32. Woodham-Smith, *Queen Victoria*, 7.

33. For changes in grand lodge administration under Sussex, see UGL Proceedings for 1814 and Hamill, *Craft*, 54–55.

34. UGL Proceedings, 2 March 1814; volume of early printed communications of GL, 1803–1830, FHL.

35. GLI Minutes, 6 November 1783; correspondence between John Boardman to Thomas Harper 1801–1806, UGLHC 15/A/2–5, 13. See also GLI Minutes, 6 March 1788.

36. GLI Minutes, 9 June 1808, 3 November 1808. See also Moira to GLI, 12 November 1808, reprinted in GLI Minutes, 1 December 1808.

37. "International Masonic Compact," 27 June–2 July 1814, reprinted in Parkinson, *History of the Grand Lodge*, 21–23.

38. Burns, "3rd Duke of Leinster," 206–39. For further discussion of these developments, see Harland-Jacobs, "Essential Link," 160–73.

39. GLI Minutes, 7 April 1814; Samuel Boyd to Robert Peel, 1 April 1824, reprinted in Berry, "Some Historical Episodes," 8. In the aftermath of the rebellion the Archbishop of Dublin published the papal bulls against Freemasonry. Crawley, "Old Charges and the Papal Bulls," 15.

40. Augustus Hely Hutchinson to Dr. O'Reilly, 5 February 1814, in GLI Minutes, 3 March 1814 (emphasis in original).

41. GLI Minutes, 6 May 1819, 3 June 1830.

42. GLI Minutes, 2 December 1824, 6 January 1825.

43. GLI Minutes, 1 August 1823; Parkinson, *History of the Grand Lodge*, 40–49.

44. Free Masons of Ireland petition to the House of Commons, 1824, Robert Peel Papers, Add MS 40361, vol. CLXXXI, f. 22, BL; Samuel Boyd to Peel, 1 April 1824, reprinted in Berry, "Some Historical Episodes," 8; *Hansard Parliamentary Debates*, 11:16–18.

45. GLI Minutes, 5 September, 3 October, and 7 November 1822, 5 August 1824, 3 July 1828, 7 August 1828, 5 March 1829, 6 August 1829, 3 June 1830, 18 August 1831, 1 September 1831, 3 November 1831. For police reports regarding Masonic processions in 1825, see Berry, "Some Historical Episodes," 9–11.

46. UGL Proceedings, 1 June 1836, 7 September 1836; GLI Minutes, 2 June 1836, 14 July 1836, 6 July 1837, 14 July 1837, 16 June 1838, 14 July 1838, 17 August 1838. See also Parkinson, *History of the Grand Lodge*, 93, 96, 114.

47. GLI Minutes, 16 June 1837. O'Connell joined the brotherhood in 1799 while he was a barrister in Dublin. He served as a legal advisor to the grand lodge during the Seton affair. Parkinson, *History of the Grand Lodge*, 105–7.

48. Foster, *Modern Ireland*, 305.

49. Clark, *British Clubs*, 325; Harling, "Duke of York Affair," 965. For patriotism, see note 53 below. For loyalism, see Dozier, *For King, Constitution, and Country*; Dickinson, *Politics of the People*, especially Chapter 8. For nationalism, see Newman, *Rise of English Nationalism*, and Colley, *Britons*.

50. The tendency in the historiography has been to conflate these terms. Eastwood is an exception. Dozier attempts to distinguish them but his explanation is confusing and unsatisfactory.

51. For the political contests over and changing meanings of patriotism in this period, see Cunningham, "Language of Patriotism," 9–15; Jordan and Rogers, "Admirals as Heroes," 201–2, 211–24; Colley, "Radical Patriotism," 169–87, and *Britons*, 1–7, 177–87, 237–319; Eastwood, "Patriotism and the English State," 146–68, and "Robert Southey and the Meanings of Patriotism," 265–71; and Harling, "Duke of York Affair."

52. Loyalist sentiment can also focus on a constitution. See Dozier, *For King, Constitution, and Country*, 2, 104, 176, and Eastwood, "Patriotism and the English State," 149. Jacobitism might be seen as an intriguing example of a "radical loyalism" but it was a spent force by the end of the eighteenth century.

53. Dickinson, *Liberty and Property*; Dozier, *For King, Constitution, and Country*; Christie, *Stress and Stability*; Dickinson, "Popular Conservatism and Militant Loyalism"; Dickinson, "Popular Loyalism in Britain in the 1790s"; Dickinson, *Politics of the People*.

54. See chapters by Dinwiddy, Philp, and Eastwood in Philp, *French Revolution and British Popular Politics*.

55. GLE(M), "Address to his Majesty," in Proceedings, 6 February 1793; Inwood, *Sermons*, 5–7, 46.

56. GLE(A) Proceedings, 4 December 1805, 5 March 1806; GLE(M) Proceedings, 3 June 1800 (emphasis added); printed circular of PGLLC, 27 December 1822, UGLHC 16/C/7; *Freemason's Guide*, 302.

57. Colley, *Britons*, 210, 216.

58. Challenging Colley, Jordan and Rogers, in "Admirals as Heroes," 224, argue that naval heroes like Admiral Nelson "proved a more compelling symbol of national unity than the cult of George III." But Freemasons seem to have reserved their patriotic senti-

ments for the king. In another critique, Philip Harling, "Duke of York Affair," 966, calls for a more balanced assessment of the relationship between royalty and war-time patriotism. But Freemasons did not publicly chastise either the Duke of York at this point or the Prince of Wales over the Queen Caroline affair some years later. Even scandal does not seem to have changed Freemasons' mind about the value of their associations with the royal princes.

59. PGL(A) Nova Scotia to Prince Edward, 27 May 1794, reprinted in Harris, "H.R.H. Prince Edward Augustus," 319–20; Moira, "Address to the Right Honourable the Lord Provost and Magistrates," 25 October 1809, reprinted in Laurie, *History of Free Masonry*, 178–79; "Masonic Festival," Thursday, 18 July 1811, *Selections from the Calcutta Gazette*, 255–56. Though Colley, *Britons*, 227, mentions the Freemasons as willing participants in royal celebration, she underestimates their contribution to the very processes she describes.

CHAPTER 5

1. "New Hindoo College," *Calcutta Gazette*, 1 March 1824, and "New Mahommedan College," *Calcutta Gazette*, 22 July 1824, in Das Gupta, *Days of John Company*, 7–11 and 23–31. See also Cohn, "Representing Authority," 177–78.

2. Bayly, *Imperial Meridian*, identifies the period between 1780 and 1830 as a crucial phase of British imperialism characterized by an enhancement in the power of the colonial executive and an increasingly exclusive British nationalism.

3. Harper, "British Migration," 75.

4. Davidoff and Hall, *Family Fortunes*; Hall, *White, Male and Middle Class*.

5. Cannadine, *Ornamentalism*, xxiv. Examples of works on specific colonies include Fingard, "Race and Respectability in Victorian Halifax," and Ross, *Status and Respectability in the Cape Colony*. In "Of Convicts and Capitalists" Kirsten McKenzie compares New South Wales and the Cape Colony.

6. Melton, *Rise of the Public*, 254.

7. GLNS, "Rise and Progress," 6.

8. John Dabzoll to Leslie, 31 December 1798, UGLHC 22/A/2; Milborne, "Freemasonry in Bermuda," 14–19. Academic studies of Freemasonry in the Caribbean are sorely lacking.

9. GLNS, "Rise and Progress," 6–7.

10. Pyke quoted in Longley and Harris, "Short History of Freemasonry in Nova Scotia"; GLNS, "Rise and Progress," 7; Weeks, "Charge," xii–xiii.

11. New South Wales Government, "Index to the Colonial Secretary's Papers"; GLI Minutes, 6 July 1797.

12. Hayes to Lord Hobart, 6 May 1803, reprinted in Cramp and Mackaness, *History*, 7; *Sydney Gazette and New South Wales Advertiser* 1, 2 (22 May 1803), reprinted in *Freemason* 36, no. 1 (February 2004): 15; colonist quoted in Cramp and Mackaness, *History*, 9. Hayes, a knighted sheriff of Cork City, had abducted a woman (whom he

tried to force into marriage) and was sentenced to death. He belonged to a Cork lodge and within a few months of his sentence his lodge addressed a memorial to the PGM of Munster in favor of their "esteemed but unfortunate Brother." His sentence was commuted to transportation. See Parkinson, *History of the Grand Lodge*, 306.

13. Caillard, "Australia's First Lodge Meeting," 226; Gascoigne, *Enlightenment*, 25; Atkinson, *Europeans in Australia*, 278, 246; King quoted in Lamonby, *Some Notes*, 3. By contrast, those in charge of the Norfolk Island penal settlement encouraged Masonry. See GLSA, "Some events," and Linford, "First Australian . . . Lodge."

14. T. Gahagan to UGL(M), 19 October 1803, UGLHC 18/B/19.

15. Entry for 19 August 1813, Private Journal of Francis Rawdon-Hastings, Hastings Papers, Special Collections, Duke University.

16. Hastings's reply to the Freemasons of Calcutta, 22 December 1822, UGLHC 17/D/4; list of members of Lodge of Perfect Unanimity, 20 February 1801, UGLHC 19/B/2. On this "second age of expansionary imperialism," see Washbrook, "India," 399–404.

17. Gould, *History of Freemasonry*, 6:329–30; addresses of Lodges Star in the East, Industry and Perseverance, and Moira Lodge to Lord and Lady Moira, 11 December 1813, in Sandeman, *Selections*, 339–45. For a similar address from Madras Masons and Moira's reply, see *Calcutta Gazette*, 21 October 1813, in Sandeman, *Selections*, 321–23.

18. *Calcutta Gazette*, 1 July 1813, in Sandeman, *Selections*, 304; Firminger, *Second Lodge*, 127; Moira's address to the Freemasons of Bengal in Sandeman, *Selections*, 342–43.

19. Reply of Marquis of Hastings, 22 December 1822, UGLHC 17/D/4; Hamill, "Earl of Moira," 40. For squabbles over the suitability of Moira's successor, which reveal that Masons in Bengal were as obsessed with respectability as their brethren in the settlement colonies, see UGLHC 17/D and Firminger, *Second Lodge of Bengal*, 100, 131–32.

20. Das Gupta, *Days of John Company*, 25–29, 10.

21. On the asylum, see R. H. Kerr to PGL, 26 August 1800, reprinted in Malden, *History*, 148–50, 155. In 1822, Lodge Unity, Peace and Concord raised £50 to send to distressed Masons in Ireland. Gribble, *History*, 13.

22. Malden, *History of Freemasonry*, 88–89, 154–60; *FQR* (1841) 121, quoted in Malden, 89. A member of Perfect Unanimity paid over Rs. 300 in annual dues. A certificate from the Lodge Friendship No. 6, London, 20 September 1836, is in the Elphinstone Papers, MSS Eur F87 5/E, OIOC.

23. *FQR* (September 1840): 540.

24. Jacob, *Radical Enlightenment*, 115; Lord Durham, 1834, quoted in *MH* (August 1874): 155. See also Reel C, Durham Papers, NAC. On Masonry's ability to bring men of various social classes together, see Money, *Experience and Identity*, 99; Clark, *British Clubs*, 319–25; Melton, *Rise of the Public*, 253–54, 265.

25. For serving brethren, see *Mason's Manual*, 23–24; Firminger, *Second Lodge of Bengal*, 91–93. The proceedings of the GLI and the UGL in this period both contain references to disabled and illiterate men being turned away.

26. Likewise, in Bengal, membership in the PGL was drawn from the two oldest lodges (Industry and Perseverance and Star in the East) and, in Madras, all the PGL officers belonged to Lodge Perfect Unanimity.

27. Keith to UGL, 19 December 1826, and Ward to UGL, 24 September 1827, UGLHC 16/I/13–14. For the influx of Scottish lodges, see Harris, "Maritime Provinces," 48–49.

28. Weeks, "Charge," xiii.

29. Ward to UGL, 24 September 1827; memorial of St. John's Lodge to UGL, 14 December 1827; Lawes to UGL, 24 March 1829; Ward to UGL, 6 December 1828, UGLHC 16/I.

30. "Despatch from Lieutenant-General Sir Colin Campbell" and "Address of the Members of the Masonic Body resident in Halifax, in Provincial Grand Lodge convened," 4 July 1838, *Sessional Papers*, 10:387–88; Harris, "Maritime Provinces," 39. During the 1820s, English Freemasonry in Nova Scotia suffered not only from the arrival of Scottish Freemasonry but also significant changes in metropolitan policies and the fallout from the Morgan affair (a scandal involving New York Freemasons that resulted in a highly damaging anti-Masonic backlash in the United States and Canada).

31. *Freemasons Quarterly Magazine* 2 (1854): 163.

32. Alexander Wilson to GLE(A), 30 October 1791, UGLHC 16/G/71.

33. Graham, *Outlines*, 121; MacTaggart, Smith, and Bond, *Old St. Paul's Lodge*, 12.

34. Yves Beauregard, "Claude Dénéchau," *DCB*, 7:241–43; Graham, *Outlines*, 143–44. For an analysis of Dalhousie's use of this ceremony as a "display of authority," see Francis, *Governors and Settlers*, 41–48.

35. W. H. Snelling to UGL, 20 August 1819, UGLHC 16/C/6; Simon McGillivray, "Circumstances in regard to the formation of a new Provincial Grand Lodge at Montreal," ca. 1823, UGLHC 16/C/8; UGL to Dénéchau, 7 June 1823, UGLHC 16/C/9. McGillivray held several government commissions, served in the Lower Canadian House of Assembly, and was a militia officer. In 1814, he was appointed to the Legislative Council, a position Dénéchau never achieved.

36. Ouellet, *Lower Canada*, 162; McNaught, *Pelican History of Canada*, 63–64.

37. PGLLC, printed circular, 27 December 1822, UGLHC 16/C/7; McGillivray to UGL, 20 January 1824, UGLHC 16/E/3 (emphasis in original); Dénéchau to Duke of Sussex, 1 September 1824, UGLHC 16/C/15; Beauregard, "Claude Dénéchau," 242. There was only one French-Canadian among the provincial grand officers for Quebec in 1825. For the Quebec Church's opposition to Freemasonry in this period, see *Mandement de Monseigneur L'Évêque*.

38. McGillivray to UGL, 20 January 1824 and 14 May 1824, UGLHC 16/E/3 and 6. The rates were: Deputy Grand Master, £10; Wardens, £8; Grand Treasurer, £5; all other officers, £3. Graham, *Outlines*, 167.

39. Alfred Dubuc, "John Molson," *DCB*, 7:616–21; Graham, *Outlines*, 170–71. Molson's successor, Peter McGill, was a social climber who became a legislative councilor in the years leading up to the transition to responsible government. See Robert Sweeny,

"Peter McGill," *DCB*, 8:540–44. For a fascinating discussion of how Molson, McGill, and other Montrealers used Freemasonry in their pursuit of science and patronage of geological surveys, see Zeller, *Inventing Canada*, Chapter 2.

40. "Despatch from Lieutenant-general Sir John Colborne, G.C.B. to Lord Glenelg," with enclosures, 28 November 1838, in *Sessional Papers*, 10: Paper 35, 265.

41. Simon McGillivray, report of his proceedings as Provincial Grand Master for Upper Canada in the year 1822, 28 February 1823, UGLHC 16/D/22; McLeod, *Whence Come We?*, 207. For an extended discussion of the politics of respectability in Upper Canadian Masonry, see Harland-Jacobs, "Essential Link," 203–24.

42. Vamplew, *Australians, Historical Statistics*, 4. In the 1840s, 76,650 free settlers ("exclusives") and 3,340 convicts arrived. "Sterling" colonists had been born in Britain, "currency" in Australia.

43. Ellis, *Lachlan Macquarie*, 43; Atkinson, *Europeans in Australia*, 324.

44. Cook, "Irish Connection"; Cramp and Mackaness, *History*, 29.

45. GLSA, "Some events"; for *Sydney Gazette* reports, see Henley, *History*, 162–77.

46. Cramp and Mackaness, *History*, 19–22; GLSA, "Some Events."

47. Cramp and Mackaness, *History*, 12; Cook, "Irish Connection"; bylaws quoted in Cramp and Mackaness, *History*, 34. For Macquarie's attitude toward emancipists, see Atkinson, *Europeans in Australia*, 339–40.

48. GLI Minutes, 6 January 1820; Cook, "Irish Connection."

49. GLI ruling quoted in Cramp and Mackaness, *History*, 34.

50. Memorial of Lodge No. 260, 12 November 1821, quoted in Cramp and Mackaness, *History*, 37–38; GLI Minutes 2 May 1822, 4 July 1822, and 6 August 1829; GLI, "Communications from or relating to Masonic Lodges in NSW"; Cramp and Mackaness, *History*, 42–43. Lodge No. 260 effectively worked as a provincial grand lodge. In 1842 it granted a dispensation for the first British lodge to meet in New Zealand. The previous year, the *New Zealand Herald and Auckland Gazette* had reported that local Masons had laid the foundation stone of St. Paul's Church. See Northhern, *History*, 5–6.

51. John Stephen to UGL, 1 September 1827, UGLHC 21/C/1.

52. "History of Lodge of Australia No. 3 U.G.L. of N.S.W."

53. GLI Minutes, 5 March 1835; Fowler to UGL, 21 December 1836, enclosing copy of letter from Australian Social Lodge no. 260, UGLHC 15/A/48; UGL Proceedings, 3 December 1856; GLI Minutes, 7 August 1856; "History of Lodge of Australia." Lodge of Australia had initiated seventy members by 1838. The UGL warranted a further ninety lodges in NSW by 1888. Cramp and Mackaness, *History*, 57. The new English provincial grand lodge established the first English lodge in New Zealand in 1842. English lodges emerged throughout the islands as British settlement proceeded. By the 1870s, English, Irish, and Scottish provincial grand lodges were in operation. See Northhern, *History*, 6–8.

54. Kingston, *Oxford History of Australia*, 89. For Freemasonry in Western Australian in this period, see Brown, *Merchant Princes of Fremantle*, 1, 133.

55. Saunders and Smith, "Southern Africa," 597–604.

56. GLE(M) Proceedings, 9 May 1804. Cockburn was the Mason who offended Lady Anne Barnard by not inviting husbands to the Masonic ball (discussed in Chapter 1).

57. Cooper, *Freemasons of South Africa*, 18, 39–40; Butterfield, *Centenary*, 11. In 1814 the lodge boasted over 200 members. Chief Justice Sir Henry de Villiers, Sir Charles Brand, Speaker of the House of Assembly, and Sir John Brand, president of the Orange Free State, would later join. *South African Freemasonry*, 9.

58. Cranstoun-Day, *British Lodge*, 14–15; Mills, *Bicentenary of English Freemasonry*, 20–23.

59. Cooper, *Freemasons of South Africa*, 40–43; Cranstoun-Day, *British Lodge*, 11, 22, 35, 38–39.

60. McKenzie, "Of Convicts and Capitalists," 203; Cranstoun-Day, *British Lodge*, 33; *South African Commercial Advertiser*, 11 March 1829, excerpted in Cranstoun-Day, 32. On the Commercial Exchange, see McKenzie, "Of Convicts and Capitalists," 206, 214–15.

61. *FQR* (1835): 231; William Egye to UGL, 5 March 1833, UGLHC 21/A/1; Cranstoun-Day, *British Lodge*, 33.

62. Cooper, *Freemasons of South Africa*, 46; Cranstoun-Day, *British Lodge*, 39–46, 57; Penman, "Freemasonry in South Africa," 282; McKenzie, "Of Convicts and Capitalists," 202.

63. Gould, *History of Freemasonry*, 6:345; Cranstoun-Day, *British Lodge*, 42, 53; *South African Freemasonry*, 13; Cooper, *Freemasons of South Africa*, 19–21.

64. Cooper, *Freemasons of South Africa*, 21; Gould, *History of Freemasonry*, 6:345; Cranstoun-Day, *British Lodge*, 59; Butterfield, *Centenary*, 22–35.

65. Cooper, *Freemasons of South Africa*, 43–47; Butterfield, *Centenary*, 32–33. The Masons officiated at the foundation stone laying ceremony of the new Houses of Parliament in 1875.

66. McKenzie, "Of Convicts and Capitalists," 1. See also Hall, "Of Gender and Empire," 70–71.

67. Best, *Mid-Victorian Britain*; Thompson, *Rise of Respectable Society*. For an alternative but related argument, see Kirk, *Growth of Working Class Reformism*.

68. Harrison, *Peaceable Kingdom*; Bailey, "'Will the Real Bill Banks Please Stand Up?'"; Cordery, "Friendly Societies and the Discourse of Respectability."

69. Ross, *Status and Respectability*, 5. For the role of respectability in late-nineteenth-century Canada, see Fingard, "Race and Respectability in Victorian Halifax," and Bouchier, "Idealized Middle-Class Sport." For South Africa, see Goodhew, *Respectability and Resistance*, and Ross, *Status and Respectability*. For respectability's limitations, see Huggins, "More Sinful Pleasures?"

70. Johnson, *Becoming Prominent*. The relationship between Freemasonry and respectability receives limited attention in Johnson, Fingard, and Bouchier. Ross, McKenzie, and Goodhew make no mention of Masonry.

71. Ross, *Status and Respectability*, 4; Smith, *Consumption and the Making of Respectability*, 204–7.

72. C. L. Van Zuilecom to GLI, 25 July 1845, Lodge No. 301 File, DGSCF.

CHAPTER 6

1. GLQ Proceedings, 19–20 October 1870, 33; Wadia, *Poetry of Freemasonry*, 20; DGLB Proceedings, 22 September 1863; Annual Report of the GLASFI, 1875, reprinted in *TS* 1, no. 2 (May 1876): 55.

2. Jacob, *Living the Enlightenment*, 117–18; Bullock, *Revolutionary Brotherhood*, 26, 39.

3. Chatterjee, *Nation and Its Fragments*, 10.

4. O'Day, *Family and Family Relationships*, 197–98; Davidoff et al., *Family Story*, 16–50; Shoemaker, *Gender in English Society*, 90. See also Davidoff and Hall, *Family Fortunes*; Hareven, "History of the Family"; Tadmor, "Concept of the Household-Family in Eighteenth-Century England."

5. Hareven, "History of the Family," 99–100, 120, and Davidoff et al., *Family Story*, 31–39.

6. Hareven, "History of the Family," 119–21; Davidoff and Hall, *Family Fortunes*, 32.

7. Key works on separate spheres include Davidoff and Hall, *Family Fortunes*; Hall, "Early Formation of Victorian Domestic Ideology," in Hall, *White, Male, and Middle Class*, chap. 3; Rose, *Limited Livelihoods*; Vickery, "Golden Age to Separate Spheres"; Clark, *Struggle for the Breeches*; Shoemaker, *Gender in English Society*.

8. *FQMR* (March 1852): 119; Clawson, *Constructing Brotherhood*, 25.

9. For examples of this discourse, see Harland-Jacobs, "All in the Family," 453.

10. Kipling, *Collected Verse*, 318–20; Alexander Keith to Clarke, 15 August 1867, Robert Burnaby to UGL, 8 February and 31 May 1869, 14 July and 6 November 1871, and UGL to Burnaby, 10 May 1869, UGLHC Miscellaneous Correspondence Box.

11. Davidoff et al., *Family Story*, 8; Clawson, *Constructing Brotherhood*, 25; How, *Freemason's Manual*, 83, 78; Leblanc de Marconnay to Albion Lodge, No. 17, Quebec, 31 February 1851, reprinted in Graham, *Outlines*, 182–83.

12. Anderson, *Constitutions of the Free-Mason*; How, *Freemason's Manual*, 78.

13. Clawson, *Constructing Brotherhood*, 222; O'Day, *Family and Family Relationships*, 75.

14. Goderich-Union Lodge circular, 13 February 1852, UGLHC 16/A/17; DGLM Proceedings, 30 January 1874, 3.

15. Hall, "Early Formation of Victorian Domestic Ideology," 82–90; Shoemaker, *Gender in English Society*, 32, 34, 101–13, 121; Davidoff et al., *Family Story*, 39–45.

16. *FQR* (September 1850): 415–19; *FQMR* (31 March 1851): 1–2.

17. GLNS, *Constitution*, 13; Morris, *Pocket Lexicon*, 35 (emphasis in original). See also How, *Freemason's Manual*, 83–84. On patriarchy, see Clawson, *Constructing Brotherhood*, 25–33; Clark, *Struggle for the Breeches*, 248–63; Davidoff et al., *Family Story*, 135–57.

18. Anderson, *Constitutions of the Free-Mason*; Clawson, "Early Modern Fraternalism," 371; Coppin, *Handbook*, xix.

19. Shoemaker, *Gender in English Society*, 112; Clawson, *Constructing Brotherhood*, 205–10.

20. John Dean to UGL, 30 November 1821, UGLHC 16/D/11. For a fuller discussion of these developments, see Harland-Jacobs, "Essential Link," 234–52.

21. Keith to UGL, 3 March 1845, UGLHC 16/I/50; UGL Proceedings, 16 June 1858; PGLCW Proceedings, 20 May 1853, 5.

22. PGLCW Proceedings, 25 October 1854.

23. PGLCW Minutes, 9–10 September 1857, UGLHC 16/A/7.

24. GLI Minutes, 3 April 1856 and 1 October 1857; GLS Proceedings, 5 May 1855, in Laurie, *History of Free Masonry*, 314 (emphasis in original); UGL Proceedings, 3 March 1858.

25. GLC Proceedings, 1857, 161.

26. Russell, *Nationalism in Canada*; Bumsted, *Peoples of Canada*, 326–27; Stacey, *Canada and the British Army*.

27. Penlington, *Canada and Imperialism*; Page, "Canada and the Imperial Idea," 33–38; Miller, *Painting the Map Red*.

28. Lodge No. 222 to GLI, 29 November 1854, Lodge No. 222 File, DGSCF; Edward Brownwell to GLI, 8 September 1856, Lodge No. 286 File, DGSCF.

29. UGL Proceedings, 3 March 1858 (emphasis in original); GLC Proceedings, 13 July 1859, 432; GLQ Proceedings, 1870, 33.

30. Carl Berger does see imperialism as one variety of Canadian nationalism, but he looks only at the post-1867 period and sees imperialism as merely a means to an end—the creation of a separate Canadian nation. See Berger, *Imperialism and Nationalism* and *Sense of Power*.

31. Mackenzie, "Empire and National Identities," 221, 229; Buckner, "Whatever Happened to the British Empire?" 32.

32. Woodward, *Oration*, 11–12 (emphasis in original); *FQR* (December 1846): 411.

33. See Draffen, "Prince Hall Freemasonry," 78, and Coil and Sherman, *Documentary Account*, 36–38.

34. James Cummins to UGL, 10 January 1823, UGLHC 23/B/24; GLI Minutes, 6 March 1823.

35. UGL to Cummins, 18 April 1823, UGL Letterbook C; Parkinson, *History of the Grand Lodge*, 46; GLI Minutes, 3 March 1831.

36. UGL Proceedings, 1 September 1847. For opposition to the slave trade, see *FQR* (December 1843): 548; (March 1845): 39; (March 1847): 172.

37. GLI Minutes, 2 July 1840 and 4 February 1841; *FQR* (31 December 1846): 415; Anderson, *Constitutions* (emphasis added). Further research is required to determine the extent to which former slaves and free blacks participated in British Freemasonry.

38. Edward Crumps to GLC and GLE, 17 January 1842, UGLHC 16/A/5d.

39. GLI Minutes, 5 February 1844 (emphasis in original); Parkinson, *History of the Grand Lodge*, 130.

40. UGL Proceedings, 2 June and 1 September 1847. The GLI followed suit.

41. Correspondence reprinted in Walker, "250 Years," 177 (emphasis in original).

42. UGL Proceedings, 1 June 1836; UGL to Grant, 30 July 1842, UGLHC 17/D/28; St. John's Lodge, No. 434 Minutes, 24 June 1832 and 27 December 1832, in Gribble, *History of Freemasonry*, 42. For reports of Muslims admitted in 1839, see Walker, "250 Years," 177. In 1840 Lodge Industry and Perseverance in Calcutta voted to accept Muslims but not Hindus. See Firminger, *Second Lodge of Bengal*, 183.

43. *FQR* (December 1840): 533; John Grant quoted in *MH* (January 1871): 9.

44. *FQR* (September 1840): 535.

45. For Cursetji, see Walker, "250 Years," 178; Finan, *History of the Grand Lodge*, 37–38; Gupta, *Freemasonic Movement*, 12–13; Musa, "First Indian Freemason." Cursetji was the first Indian admitted to the Royal Asiatic Society in England; he established the Alexandra Girls' English Institution in Bombay in 1863. He was elected master of the lodge in 1857.

46. On the Parsis, see Luhrmann, *Good Parsi*, 84–125.

47. Gould, *History of Freemasonry*, 6:335.

48. Grant to UGL, 30 November 1840, UGLHC 17/D/24, and 17 April 1841, UGLHC 17/D/25.

49. Augustus to Grant, 2 July 1842, UGLHC 17/D/28; Grant quoted in Walker, "250 Years," 179. See also PGLB, extracts of the Proceedings, 27 December 1841, UGLHC 17/D/26, and Grant to UGL, 10 May 1842, UGLHC 17/D/27.

50. PGLB Minutes, 22 May 1848, UGLHC 17/D/35; program from the Ceremony of Laying the Foundation Stone of the New Surgical Ward of the Medical College Hospital, Calcutta, 3 February 1906, Owen Wynne Cole Papers, MSS Eur D958, OIOC.

51. Washbrook, "India, 1818–1860," 395–421; Metcalf, *Ideologies of the Raj*, 28–65.

52. Malden, *History of Freemasonry*, 166; DGLB Proceedings, 22 September 1863; Firminger, *Second Lodge of Bengal*, 228–29. The Irish contributed £100 and the English £1,000. GLI Minutes, 1 October 1857; UGL Proceedings, 2 December 1857.

53. P. Nubia to UGL, 8 July 1862, UGLHC 17/D/47; DGLB, Special Communication, 29 October 1862. On the diversity and stratification of the European population of Bengal, see Misra, *Business, Race, and Politics*, 35–38.

54. Despite the reservations of Masonic leaders, some lodges had begun admitting Hindus without attracting much notice. Other instances of Hindu admissions (including the Lodge of the Rock's welcoming of seventeen Hindus between 1863 and 1877) are recorded in Walker, "250 Years," 178, 182; Gupta, *Freemasonic Movement*, 10–11; and *FMMM* 62 (8 September 1860): 192 and 67 (13 October 1860): 291.

55. *Brother Prosonno Coomar Dutt* (hereafter cited as "Dutt pamphlet"); DGLB Proceedings, 22 September 1863.

56. DGLB Proceedings, 22 September 1863, 5 November 1863, 28 December 1863; UGL Proceedings, 6 June 1866.

57. DGLB Proceedings, 22 September 1863 and 24 June 1865.

58. DGLB Proceedings, 22 September 1863; DGLBom Proceedings, 1862.

59. UGL Proceedings, 6 June 1866; Report of the Colonial Board; Duke of Leinster to Dutt, 1 November 1869; Earl of Mayo to Dutt, 24 February 1869, in Dutt pamphlet, 10–11.

60. *TS* 2, no. 1 (January 1877): 4; Sidhwa, *District Grand Lodge of Pakistan*, 27; GLS Proceedings, 1 December 1890 and 1 December 1884. See also GLS Proceedings, 5 August 1880; 30 January 1890; 30 November 1894, 30 November 1897. Statistics compiled from lodge reports in *TS* 1, no. 6 (September 1876).

61. Both Kharshedji Rustamji Cama and Jivanji Jamshedji Modi, for example, published works on the connection between the ancient history of Freemasonry and Zoroastrianism. Late-nineteenth-century Masonic periodicals reported on the widespread participation of indigenous members. See Modi, *The K. R. Cama Masonic Jubilee Volume*.

62. To be sure, they posited that members of that family displayed varying levels of civilization. But, believing in the idea of a universal human family (monogenesis), they argued that lower civilizations could, if their unfavorable environments were improved, rise along the "scale of civilization." See Chapter 2.

63. According to the ideas of social Darwinism, the advancement of less civilized races was not possible without biological contact with superior races. See Bolt, *Victorian Attitudes to Race*, and Lorimer, *Colour, Class and the Victorians*. McClintock suggests that the Victorians merged the discourses of social Darwinism with the metaphor of the family of man to create the "evolutionary Family of Man" through which "hierarchical (and, one might add, often contradictory) social distinctions could be shaped into a single historical genesis narrative." McClintock, "Family Feuds," 63.

64. Hall, *Civilising Subjects*, 25; Hyam, *Britain's Imperial Century*, 155–60. Bayly, *Imperial Meridian*, 147–55, argues that the shift took place much earlier.

65. DGLB Proceedings, 24 June 1865; *TS* 1, no. 2 (May 1876): 55.

66. *Craftsman* (15 August 1869): 168; Halford, *Oration*, n.p.; GLNS Proceedings, 23–24 June 1869, 80. William Hull, writing in New South Wales in the 1840s, also used Masonry to resist early racialist theories of the origins and nature of Aboriginal society. See Turnbull, "Forgotten Cosmogony."

67. Coppin, *Handbook*, xxii; Read, *Ceremony of Laying the Foundation Stone*, 18–19; Hall, "Imperial Man," 156; Hyam, *Britain's Imperial Century*, 76; Metcalf, *Ideologies of the Raj*, x, 59, 66–112.

68. John Hilton to UGL, 1848, 1849, 1850, UGLHC 28/A/12. See also Coil and Sherman, *Documentary Account*.

69. For similar petitions UGLHC 28/A.

70. UGL to Charles Walmisley, 23 August 1871, DGSCF, GLI; *FC* 4, no. 95 (21 October 1876): 257–58.

71. See GLNS Proceedings, 24–30 June 1870; *FC* 4, no. 87 (26 August 1876): 130–33; *CCMR* 10, no. 2 (1 February 1876), 38–43; *CCMR* 34, no. 2 (August 1899): 38–39; *MS* 3, no. 6 (23 February 1900): 46.

72. Lodge Albert Victor, *Minutes of Proceedings*, 24 (emphasis in original).

73. Reported in the *MS* 4, no. 2 (28 January 1901): 11. For West Africa, see Casely-Hayford and Rathbone, "Politics, Families, and Freemasonry." For the Caribbean, see Bryan, *Jamaican People*, 204–5; Lazarus, "Experiences in Caribbean Masonry"; Voorhis, "Freemasonry in Bermuda"; Smith, *Creole Recitations*, 31; Creighton and Prescott, "Black Freemasonry."

74. Cannadine, *Ornamentalism*, xix, 90.

75. DGLB Proceedings, 22 September 1866; "Report of the Colonial Board"; *MH* 1 (August 1871): 130–32; Chakrabarty, *Provincializing Europe*, 8. Supporters of indigenes' admission basically viewed Masonic lodges as factories for building collaborators, the need for which was especially acute after 1857. On collaborators, see Metcalf, *Aftermath of Revolt*, 219–48, and Gopal, *British Policy in India*, 8–15, 34–40.

76. Mehta, *Liberalism and Empire*, Introduction and Chapter 1.

77. Metcalf, *Ideologies of the Raj*, 66. See also Burroughs, "Imperial Institutions," 182–83.

78. Cannadine, *Ornamentalism*, 10.

CHAPTER 7

1. GLNS Proceedings, 13 June 1900, 6–15.

2. Milner quoted in Gollin, *Proconsul in Politics*, 123; Milner, *Nation and the Empire*, 135–52.

3. *CCMR* 34, no. 12 (June 1900): 364.

4. *Craftsman* 1, no. 1 (October 1866): 8; 1, no. 6 (15 March 1867): 96; *CCMR* 22 (15 May 1888): 135; *MS* 12 (10 February 1899): 90; GLC Proceedings, 19–20 July 1899, 48–49; *IF* 1, no. 1 (January 1894): 1; *MV* 1, no. 2 (15 February 1895): 25.

5. *CCMR* 34, no. 12 (June 1900): 364; *FC* 1202 (30 December 1899): 301.

6. *CCMR* 34, no. 4 (October 1899): 119; UGL Proceedings, 28 July 1869, 5 December 1877, 7 June 1882.

7. UGL Proceedings, 6 December 1871, 3 June 1874, 5 September 1877, 3 March 1880, 3 March 1897, 5 September 1877, 7 March 1883, 6 March 1878, 15 October 1898, 6 September 1893, 4 June 1902, 7 June 1905. On Masonic involvement in the Palestine Exploration Fund, see GLC to John A. Macdonald, 25 November 1869, vol. 537, John A. Macdonald Papers, NAC; "Palestine Exploration Fund" file, MG 20, vol. 2147, GLNS Papers, PANS; *CCMR* 10, no. 11 (1 November 1876): 381; UGL Proceedings, 1 December 1875. For contributions to Ireland from Masons in Calcutta, New Brunswick, and British Columbia, see GLI Minutes, 2 April 1846; Francis Clerke to GLI, 27 February 1847, Lodge No. 301(A) File, DGSCF; Edgar Baker to GLI, 4 March 1880, Misc. File, DGSCF.

8. GLS Proceedings, 30 July 1896; DGLM Proceedings, 5 February 1876, 181.

9. DGLM Proceedings, 1869–1896; DGL South Africa (Western Division), *Queen Victoria Commemoration*, 10.

10. DGLM Proceedings, 30 July 1886, n.p.; Jamiat Rai, *Brief History*, 59 (emphasis in

original); Davies, *Handbook*, 183; DGLP Proceedings, 11 February 1893, n.p., and 27 December 1893, 169–70.

11. Davies, *Handbook*, 186; DGLP Proceedings, 2 March 1893, 17; DGL South Africa (Eastern Division) Proceedings, 7 June 1882, 8–9.

12. GLE to GLI, 2 March 1857, DGSCF; GLI Minutes, 5 June 1862; Alexander Abbott to GLI, 21 April 1855, Abbott to Charles Murphy, 26 May 1855, and undated note, Lodge No. 209 File, DGSCF. For another example of help to emigrants, see GLI Minutes, 3 December 1885.

13. Thompson, *Imperial Britain*, 137. See also Harper, "British Migration and the Peopling of the Empire."

14. Fredericka Palmer to William Wilkinson, 12 October 1878; circular letter from Wilkinson, 14 October 1878, with printed attachment, "Palmer Fund"; Wilkinson to Committee of Charity and Inspection, 21 October 1878, Foreign Grand Lodges File, DGSCF.

15. Howard Holbrook to UGL, 29 January 1869, UGLHC Correspondence Box — British Columbia, Montreal, Newfoundland, Prince Edward Island, Nova Scotia (1860–1906). Founded in 1788 to support the daughters of indigent or deceased members, the RMIG had over 200 girls enrolled in the 1880s. Its centenary was lavishly celebrated in Royal Albert Hall in 1888 when £50,000 was raised for the institution. For child and female migration, see Parr, *Labouring Children*; Bush, " 'The Right Sort of Woman' "; Chaudhuri, " 'Who Will Help the Girls?' "; Thompson, *Imperial Britain*, 146–51.

16. UGL Proceedings, 6 December 1882; *TF* 19, no. 914 (September 11, 1886): 537; *MS* 10, no. 11 (May 1908): 228.

17. "History of Empire Lodge, No. 2108," Empire Lodge No. 2108 File, FHL; *TF* 18, no. 873 (28 November 1885): 578; *TF* 19, no. 904 (3 July 1886): 398; *FC* 42, no. 1084 (19 October 1895): 166; Royal Colonial Institute Lodge, *History*.

18. Program from the Installation Banquet of the Canada Lodge No. 3527, 26 June 1917, vol. 2148, MG20, GLNS Papers, PANS. See also Program from the Installation Banquet of the Canada Lodge No. 3527, 6 July 1920, vol. 12, WNPP; Installation Banquet of the Canada Lodge, No. 3527, 17 June 1914, Canada Lodge No. 3527 Lodge File, FHL; Program from Installation Meeting, 6 June 1914, Canada Lodge No. 3257 File, FHL.

19. *TF* 53, no. 2313 (5 July 1913): 7–8.

20. Cannadine, *Ornamentalism*; Thompson, *Imperial Britain*, 7; *CCMR* 34, no. 12 (June 1900): 366.

21. Address from the Masonic body to Sir George Ferguson Bowen and His Excellency's reply, 27 September 1869, *Sessional Papers*, 16:164–66.

22. GLC Proceedings, 13–14 July 1887, 35–36, 209; Sussex Lodge, *Lodge of Sorrow*, 8; *CCMR* 34, no. 12 (June 1900): 365–66; *CCMR* 20 (15 November 1886): 346.

23. UGL Proceedings, 7 September 1887. For an address congratulating the queen on escaping an assassin, see UGL Proceedings, 15 March 1882.

24. GLNS Proceedings, 22 June 1887, 20–21, 69, 83–89; GLS Proceedings, 30 November 1886; Davies, *Handbook*, 40, 45; Parkinson, *History of the Grand Lodge*, 227–28. For Quebec Masons' observations, see GLQ Proceedings, 26 January 1887, 14, and Proceedings, 26 January 1898, 22, 16–17. For South Africans', see DGL SA (Eastern Division) Proceedings, 15 June 1887, 6.

25. *Diamond Fields Advertiser* (Kimberley), 26 September 1887, Add MS 60940, CP; UGL Proceedings, 13 June 1887. For India, see DGLBom Proceedings, 12 November 1887, 21.

26. CCMR 22 (15 February 1888): 56–57; GLC Proceedings, 14–15 July 1886, 49; CCMR 34, no. 12 (June 1900): 363–64.

27. DGL SA (Western Division), *Queen Victoria Commemoration*, 5; *MS* 3, 7 (10 March 1900): 52; DLGP Proceedings, 13 September 1897, 178; Rising Star Lodge, *Mourning Lodge*, 1–8. For similar observations in other parts of the empire, see UGL Proceedings, 14 June 1897; Brazier, "Freemasonry during the Queen's Reign"; GLS Proceedings, 30 November 1897; *CCMR* 34, no. 12 (June 1900): 365–66.

28. *MS* 1, no. 1 (August 1897): 1; UGL Proceedings, 2 June 1869, 1 September 1869, 1 December 1869; GLI Minutes, 3 July 1871.

29. UGL Proceedings, 28 April 1875. There were twenty-three MPs in attendance.

30. Cannadine, *Ornamentalism*, 46; "Ceremony of Laying the Foundation-Stone of the Prince's Dock, Bombay, with Masonic Honours, by HRH Albert Edward, Prince of Wales, on Thursday, 11th November, 1875," in DGLBom Proceedings, 11 November 1875; DGLB Proceedings, 21 March 1876, 5; DGLM Proceedings, 11 December 1875, 5; *TS* 1, no. 6 (September 1876): 182; *CCMR* 10, no. 6 (1 June 1876): 216–17. See also UGL Proceedings, 3 January 1877.

31. UGL Proceedings, 15 March 1882, 1 December 1886.

32. On Albert Victor's initiation, see *CCMR* 19 (15 April 1885): 113; on his visit to India, see Sidhwa, *District Grand Lodge*, 41; on his death, see UGL Proceedings, 27 January 1892. For a gender analysis of the prince's reputation as a clothes horse, see Breward, *Hidden Consumer*, 63–75. Edward's second son, George, Duke of York, was not a Freemason. On a visit to India in 1906 as Prince of Wales, he nonetheless participated in the ceremony to lay the foundation stone of the Victoria Technical Institute. See Ampthill to Sir Walter Lawrence, 18 December 1905, Mss Eur E233/22, Ampthill Papers, BL. On royal tours, see Cannadine, *Ornamentalism*, 114–15.

33. UGL Proceedings, 4 March 1885; GLC Proceedings, 17–18 July 1901, 311. Of course, at the same time they expressed their deep sadness over the death of Victoria. See GLC Proceedings, 1901, 32–34; GLNS Proceedings, 12 June 1901, 17–18; GLQ Proceedings, 31 January 1901, 24–25, 114–15; *MS* 5, no. 3 (29 April 1902): 20, and 5, no. 6 (30 June 1902): 41, 44.

34. Gribble, *History of Freemasonry*, 230–33, includes address from the Masons of Hyderabad to His Highness Assaf Jah....Mir Mahoob Ali Khan Bahadur Fateh Jung, G.C.S.I, G.C.B and his speech in reply.

35. For late Victorian masculinity, see Mangan, *Games Ethic and Imperialism*; Mangan and Walvin, *Manliness and Morality*; Roper and Tosh, *Manful Assertions*; Dawson, *Soldier Heroes*; Sinha, *Colonial Masculinity*; Rutherford, *Forever England*; Tosh, *Man's Place*; Windholtz, "Emigrant and a Gentleman"; Breward, *Hidden Consumer*; Mc-Devitt, *"May the Best Man Win"*; Tosh, *Manliness and Masculinities*.

36. Carnarvon's speech to UGL, 30 March 1857, quoted in Hardinge, *Life of Henry Herbert*, 1:224–25; Cooper, "United Grand Lodge Movement in South Africa," 115; DGLBom Proceedings, 21 March 1890, 6.

37. GLS Proceedings, 30 November 1898; Tosh, *Man's Place*, 174, 186; *CCMR* 20 (15 May 1886): 135. For Kitchener's Masonic career (he became DGM of the Sudan in 1899), see Pollock, *Kitchener*, 54, 86, 228–29.

38. Communication of Lodge Himalayan Brotherhood, No. 459, 10 September 1887, in Davies, *Handbook*, 47–48; W. H. Hildesley, Address, 1887, in Davies, 52.

39. *MS* 6, no. 9 (15 October 1903): 87; DGLP Proceedings, 29 April 1904, 121–22.

40. DGLP Proceedings, 10 September 1894, 256–58; *IF* 1, no. 7 (July 1894): 142, and 1, no. 9 (September 1894): 170; Jamiat Rai, *Brief History*, 1–26, 42–46, 59, 98.

41. *IF* 2, no. 23 (November 1895): 409; Sidhwa, *District Grand Lodge*, 50; DGLP Proceedings, 13 September 1897, 178; Wolseley, *Story of a Soldier's Life*, 81. Sir Charles Napier also attributed his good treatment as a French POW to his membership in Freemasonry. See *CCMR* 20 (15 May 1886): 135.

42. DGLBom Proceedings, 12 November 1887, 17, 30–31; meeting of the DGLBom, 23 August 1895, reported in *IF* 2, no. 21 (September 1895): 388; E. W. Parker's address to Lodge Himalayan Brotherhood, 10 September 1887, in Davies, *Handbook*, 47–48. See also Robertson, *History of Freemasonry in Canada*, 1; DGL Turkey Proceedings, 6; Riley, *Modern Freemasonry*, 8–9; Brazier, *Freemasonry during the Queen's Reign*.

43. UGL Proceedings, 2 March 1892; DGLP Proceedings, 11 September 1893, 122; *IF* 2, no. 17 (May 1895): 304, and 3, no. 30 (June 1896): 90; Jaimiat Rai, *Brief History*, 25; Gribble, *History of Freemasonry*, 230–33.

44. DGLBom Proceedings, 7 December 1883, 4, 19–23, and 12 November 1887, 21–31, and 21 March 1890, 28–40. On his visits to lodges in the Punjab, see Davies, *Handbook*, 45, 47. On his life, see Frankland, *Witness of a Century*.

45. GLC Proceedings, 16–17 July 1890, 42, 152; *FC* 31, no. 805 (14 June 1890): 370–71. When his brother became king, Connaught took over as English Grand Master.

46. *CCMR* 34, no. 4 (October 1899): 93; DGLP Proceedings, 7 January 1903, 1–7.

47. DGLP Proceedings, 14 September 1903, 58; 29 April 1904, 121; 7 April 1906, 361–62; UGL Proceedings, 7 December 1910.

48. GLC Proceedings, 19–20 July 1912, 45–46; UGL Proceedings, 3 March 1915. For the GL's reaction on his appointment as governor general of Canada and the "great service he has rendered to the Empire," see UGL Proceedings, 1 March 1911. Five hundred Masons welcomed Connaught at a Masonic reception during a trip to New-foundland in 1914. See *TF* 54, no. 2371 (15 August 1914): 97–98. For his role in inspiring Canadian loyalty, see *TF* 54, no. 2391 (2 January 1915): 348.

49. Thompson, *Imperial Britain*, 37; Chamberlain quoted in Green, "Political Economy of Empire," 356.

50. *TF* 54, 2391 (2 January 1915): 347. See also UGL Proceedings, 4 June 1890, and *TF* 49, no. 2123 (13 November 1909): 305.

51. Hyam, *Britain's Imperial Century*, 50. The League had some significant parallels with Freemasonry: it was conceived as a supposedly apolitical institution that sought to bring together men separated by vast distances and circumstances but sharing a sense of belonging to an overarching global entity. See Green, *Crisis of Conservatism*, 35–41, and Reese, *History of the Royal Commonwealth Society*, 67–68.

52. For Carnarvon's colonial office career, see Knox, "Earl of Carnarvon."

53. *Argus*, 15 November 1887; *Cape Argus*, 17 September 1887; *Cape Times*, 1 October 1887; *Diamond Fields Advertiser*, 26 September 1887, clippings in Add MS 60940, CP.

54. "Earl Carnarvon with the Freemasons," unidentified clipping, December 1887; *Sydney Morning Herald*, 18 January 1888, Add MS 60940, CP. See also *Brisbane Courier*, 5 January 1888, Add MS 60940, CP.

55. *Argus*, 15 November 1887; *Brisbane Courier*, 5 January 1888, Add MS 60940, CP; Carnarvon's Notebook on travels in South Africa and Australia, 1887–1888, Add MS 60809, CP.

56. Shadwell Clerke to Carnarvon, 15 August 1887, Add MS 60807 f. 153, CP (emphasis in original). For Carrington's credentials as a Freemason and an imperialist, see GLS Proceedings, 30 November 1888, 157. For the movement to establish an independent grand lodge in New South Wales, see Cramp and Mackaness, *History*, Chapter 10. For English Masons' debates on the issue, see UGL Proceedings, 2 September 1885, 6 June 1886, 5 December 1888, and 6 September 1899.

57. *Argus*, 15 November 1887; *South Australian Advertiser*, 3 December 1887, Add MS 60940, CP. When he returned to London, he succeeded in convincing the English Grand Lodge to support the creation of an independent Grand Lodge of NSW. The GLS also supported Masonic self-government movements within the empire on the grounds that ties would be strengthened. See GLS Proceedings, 30 November 1888 and 2 December 1889.

58. Carrington to Carnarvon, 20 September 1888, quoted in Hardinge, *Life of Henry Herbert*, 1:229; UGL Proceedings, 3 March 1897.

59. *MS* 6, no. 17 (15 February 1904): 72; *TF* 54, no. 2391 (2 January 1915): 348; *MS* 1, no. 16 (15 March 1898): 122.

60. *MS* 10, no. 7 (January 1908): 143; *CCMR* 19 (15 August 1885): 255 and (15 September 1885): 282; GLQ Proceedings, 25 January 1899, Report on Foreign Correspondence, 1; *CCMR* 19 (15 May 1885): 145; GLNS Proceedings, 2 June 1886, 231.

61. *CCMR* 34, no. 6 (December 1899): n.p.; *CCMR* 34, no. 9 (March 1900): 281; *MS* 3, no. 12 (11 June 1900): 90; GLNS Proceedings, 1900, 266; GLC Proceedings, 18–19 July 1900, 335; GLQ Proceedings, 1901, 23; *FC* 1202 (30 December 1899): 301; *CCMR* 34, no. 7 (January 1900): 189; *CCMR* 34, no. 12 (June 1900): 364; *MS* 5, no. 5 (14 June 1902): 36. For the GLC's fundraising efforts and a list of Masons who

volunteered for service, see GLC Proceedings, 1900, 68–70. On Canadians' response to and experiences in the war, see Page, "Canada and the Imperial Idea"; Miller, *Painting the Map Red*.

62. GLC Proceedings, 1900, 335; *MS* 3, no. 5 (6 February 1900): 34; GLNS Proceedings, 1900, 9–10; GLQ Proceedings, 1901, 21, 115.

63. *CCMR* 34, no. 12 (June 1900): 351; GLC Proceedings, 1900, 67–68, 335. See also GLNS Proceedings, 1900, 9–15, and GLQ Proceedings, 1901, 21, 115.

64. Kendall, "Freemasonry during the Anglo-Boer War," 20–22; Edward Ross quoted in Cooper, *Freemasons of South Africa*, 74; John Reid quoted in Kendall, "Freemasonry during the Anglo-Boer War," 24; UGL Proceedings, 7 March 1900; Butterfield, *Centenary*, 119–20. Readers of Canadian periodicals were kept informed of the activities of their brethren in South Africa; see *MS* 3, no. 2 (24 November 1899): 11, and 3, no. 3 (12 December 1899): 22. Several Boer leaders, like General Louis Botha, Commandant General Petrus Jacobus Joubert, General Piet Cronje, General Ben Viljoen, and Captain B. G. Verselewel de Witt Hamer, were Masons. Many were granted parole to participate in Masonic meetings while being held as POWs on St. Helena. See Cooper, *Freemasons of South Africa*, 77–78.

65. DGL Central South Africa Proceedings, 22 September 1915, 7; Cooper, *Freemasons of South Africa*, 122–25.

66. Masonic officials quoted in Cooper, *Freemasons of South Africa*, 127, 130.

67. *TF* 54, no. 2391 (2 January 1915): 347; past master of Canada Lodge to Ponton, 26 July 1916, vol. 11, WNPP. Among the concrete ways that Canada Lodge helped the imperial cause was by raising funds for the "Queen's Canadian Military Hospital" in 1914. See "Canadian Freemasons and the War. Canadian Officers at the Canada Lodge Banquet," 5 December 1914, vol. 12, WNPP; F. Williams Taylor to Ponton, 12 September 1914, vol. 11, WNPP.

68. GLNS Proceedings, 9 June 1915, 18; GLQ Proceedings, 10 February 1915, 21. For a lengthy justification of the war in terms of its threat to British institutions and liberties (both in Britain and the empire), see GLC Proceedings, 21–22 July 1915, 78–80. For expressions of the idea that Britain's wars were Canada's wars, see GLNS Proceedings, 1915, 18–19, and GLC Proceedings, 1915, 76.

69. GLNS Proceedings, 1915, 18–19; *TF* 54, no. 2381 (24 October 1914): 228; GLNS, Circulars, 1 November 1917 and 26 October 1918, vol. 2147, MG 20, GLNS Papers, PANS. The master of the GLC noted a significant growth in membership during the war. See GLC Proceedings, 17 July 1918, 34–35.

70. GLC Proceedings, 19–20 July 1916, 40; GLNS Proceedings, 1915, 18; UGL Proceedings, 6 December 1916, 97; GLQ Proceedings, 1915, 21; GLC Proceedings, 1915, 76, and 1916, 386–87. For imperial unity, see also GLC Proceedings, 1915, 74–75; GLQ Proceedings, 1915, 21; GLNS Proceedings, 14 June 1916, 21.

71. *TF* 54, no. 2383 (7 November 1914): 243–44.

72. On Kipling's use of Masonic themes, see Mason, *Kipling*, 25, 83–85, 280–81, 304; Wilson, *Strange Ride of Rudyard Kipling*, 314–15. For his imperialist credentials, see

Mason, *Kipling*, 193–199; Wilson, *Strange Ride*, 250–252; and Harrison, *Rudyard Kipling*, 2, 17, 20–21.

CONCLUSION

1. *FC* 1, no. 3 (16 January 1875): 33–34. The quote in the chapter title is from *MS* 5 (28 November 1902): 110.

2. UGL Proceedings, 1 September 1920 and 4 June 1924; *FC* 104, no. 2711 (25 December 1926): 404; *FC* 104, no. 2689 (24 July 1926): 47. On African participation, see Casely-Hayford and Rathbone, "Politics, Families, and Freemasonry."

3. *FC* 3, no. 2869 (4 January 1930): 4–5; "Report of the Deputation Appointed by the M. W. the Grand Master to Visit the District Grand Lodges in India, Burma, and Ceylon," reprinted in *FC* 106, no. 2788 (16 June 1928): 372–73; UGL Proceedings, 7 December 1927.

4. UGL Proceedings, 27 June 1919. The rather unmasonic concept of "Anglo-Saxon Freemasonry" was not a new idea when invoked by postwar Masons. See UGL Proceedings, 7 June 1871; *MMM* 6, no. 63 (September 1878): 128–29; GLQ Proceedings, 25 January 1899, Report on Foreign Correspondence, 1–2. Charles Dilke, author of *Greater Britain* (1868) and one of the best-known proponents of Anglo-Saxon unity, was himself a Mason. See his certificate in the Dilke Papers, Add MS 43910, f. 217, BL.

5. *MMM* 6, no. 67 (January 1879): 290; Cooper, *Freemasons of South Africa*, 134–37. In 1910 the Earl of Onslow (who had served as governor of New Zealand between 1888 and 1892) noted in a speech that the strong connection between Freemasonry and the Royal Family was due to English Masons' acknowledging "existence and guidance of the Supreme Being, whereas in Continental countries it was the contrary." Address of the Earl of Onslow to Mark Master Masons of Surrey, 11 November 1910, Onslow Papers 5337/5/9, Surrey History Centre.

6. *Builder Magazine* 11, no. 3 (March 1925): n.p., and 8, no. 4 (April 1922): n.p.

7. UGL Proceedings, 2 March 1921. Recently returned from Africa in 1922 General Sir Reginald Wingate (governor general of the Sudan between 1899 and 1916, High Commissioner for Egypt from 1917 to 1919, District Grand Master of Egypt and Sudan from 1901 to 1920) noted the existence of many lodges that worked in Arabic and "various European languages." Describing some of these lodges as "centres of sedition and even of revolution," he happily reported that "British Freemasonry is entirely free from any such taint." Wingate address, 2 May 1922, Wingate Papers, 240/5/5–31, Sudan Archive, Durham University Library.

8. Robbins, *English-Speaking Freemasonry*, 54.

9. *Builder Magazine* 10, no. 6 (June 1924): n.p.; *TF* 60, no. 2690 (25 September 1920): 158.

10. UGL Proceedings, 5 June 1912.

11. UGL Proceedings, 1 June 1921. By this point, India was inching toward responsible

government. The British, who never set a timetable and clearly intended to control the pace of change, had calculated that the move would preserve the empire. The Montagu-Chelmsford Reforms of 1919 were aimed to implement the principles of dyarchy — the granting of limited responsible government at the local and provincial levels while control of finance and law and order and central administration remained in British hands. These reforms were followed by the Government of India Act (1921), which set up a bicameral parliament (the majority of whose members were elected), required the Viceroy's Executive Council to have at least three Indian members, and expanded provincial councils and made them responsible to local electorates. Meanwhile, the Raj had passed the repressive Rowlatt Acts and Gandhi had launched his first all-India satyagraha campaign.

12. GLC Proceedings, 1929, Report on Fraternal Correspondence, 38; UGL Proceedings, 7 December 1927.

13. Barnett, *First Seventy Five Years*, 4; *TF* 65, no. 2953 (10 October 1925): 214; program for the consecration of Lodge Motherland, No. 3861, 28 June 1918, MG 20 vol. 2148, GLNS Papers, PANS; *TF* 60, no. 2715 (19 March 1921): 472; *FC* 104, no. 2711 (25 December 1926): 404–5; *TF* 66, no. 3016 (25 December 1926): 367.

14. GLC Proceedings, 18–19 July 1923, Appendix II; UGL Proceedings, 4 June 1924, Appendix A. Victoria de Grazia argues that the Rotarians were the first voluntary organization to produce a "mass-manufactured sociability" in the service of empire (the twentieth-century U.S. empire). But, as we have seen here, the Freemasons had clearly set the precedent. De Grazia, *Irresistable Empire*, 31–32.

15. UGL Proceedings, 4 June 1924, Appendix A; GLC Proceedings, 19 July 1922, 63; John Thomas to Ponton, 4 February 1922, MG30 E96 vol. 12, WNPP; GLC Proceedings, 18–19 July 1923, 70–71.

16. *TF* 65, no. 2946 (22 August 1925): 115–16. More and more Masons started alluding to the Commonwealth in their speeches and reports; see GLC Proceedings, 20 July 1927, 57; 18–19 July 1928, 201; 17 July 1929, 384.

17. Wadia, *Poetry of Freemasonry*, 19.

18. Ibid., 13–20; S. P. Sarbadhikari in *How Hindus Were Admitted*, 19–20, quoted in Fozdar, " 'Imperial Brotherhood,' " 2. See also Ghose, "What Is Freemasonry," 41.

19. Cama, *Discourse on Freemasonry*, 5. Historian Vahid Fozdar describes Masonry as an "unstudied fount of Indian nationalism." Fozdar, " 'Imperial Brotherhood,' " 15. Frank Karpiel examines the role of Freemasonry in Hawaiian and Filipino nationalism in "Freemasonry, Colonialism, and Indigenous Elites."

BIBLIOGRAPHY

MANUSCRIPT COLLECTIONS

British Library, London, England
    Carnarvon Papers
    Charles Dilke Papers
    Hodgson Family Correspondence
    Robert Peel Papers
    Ripon Papers
    Royal Lodge of Freemasons, Proceedings

British Library, Oriental and India Office Collections
    Ampthill Papers
    Owen Wynne Cole Papers
    Elphinstone Papers
    Stamford Raffles Papers
    Richard Temple Papers

Duke University Special Collections, Durham, North Carolina
    Percy Butler Papers
    John Easthope Papers
    Francis Rawdon-Hastings, journal

Durham University Archives, Durham, England
    Reginald Wingate Papers

Library and Archives, Freemasons' Hall, Dublin, Ireland
    Deputy Grand Secretary's Correspondence Files
    Minutes

Library and Archives, Freemasons' Hall, London, England
    Historic Correspondence
    Letterbooks
    Lodge Files

National Archives of Canada, Ottawa, Canada
    Durham Papers

John A. Macdonald Papers
Mt. Zion Lodge No. 28 Papers
William Nesbit Ponton Papers

National Archives of Ireland, Dublin, Ireland
1798 Rebellion Papers

Public Archives of Nova Scotia, Halifax, Nova Scotia
Grand Lodge of Nova Scotia Papers
Virgin Lodge No. 3 Papers

Surrey History Centre, Surrey, England
Onslow Papers

BRITISH PARLIAMENTARY PAPERS

Hansard Parliamentary Debates. 2nd ser., vol. 11 (30 March–25 June 1824).
House of Commons. *Report from the Committee of Secrecy, 21 August 1798*. London: J. Debrett and J. Wright, 1798.
——. *Sessional Papers* vol. 10 (Colonies, Canada) and vol. 16 (Colonies, New Zealand). Shannon: Irish University Press, 1968.
——. *Sessional Papers of the Eighteenth Century*. Vol. 120. Wilmington, Del.: Scholarly Resources, Inc., 1975.

CONSTITUTIONS

Anderson, James. *The Ancient Constitutions of the Free and Accepted Masons*. 2nd ed. London: B. Creake, 1731.
——. *The Constitutions of the Antient and Honourable Fraternity of Free and Accepted Masons*. London: J. Scott, 1756.
——. *The Constitutions of the Free-Masons*. London: John Senex and John Hooke, 1723.
——. *The New Book of Constitutions of the Antient and Honourable Fraternity of Free and Accepted Masons*. London: Caesar Ward and Richard Chandler, 1738.
Charges and Regulations . . . Extracted from Ahiman Rezon. Halifax: John Howe, 1786.
Dermott, Laurence. *Ahiman Rezon: Or, A Help to a Brother; Showing the Excellency of Secrecy, And the First Cause, or Motive, of the Institution of Free Masonry*. London: James Bedford, 1756.
——. *Ahiman Rezon; or a Help to all that are, or would be Free and Accepted Masons*. London: James Jones, 1778.
Grand Lodge of Nova Scotia. *Constitution of the Ancient Fraternity of Free and Accepted Masons*. Halifax: Edmund Ward, 1819.
Grand Lodge of Canada. *The Book of Constitution of the Grand Lodge of A F and A M of Canada*. Hamilton: GLC, 1866.

United Grand Lodge. *Constitutions of the Ancient Fraternity of Free and Accepted Masons*. London: W. P. Norris, 1815.

LODGE MINUTES AND PROCEEDINGS (PUBLISHED)

Note: unless otherwise indicated, all minutes and proceedings are available at FHL.
District Grand Lodges
All Scottish Freemasonry in India (available in the *MH*, 1875–77)
Bengal (available at OIOC)
Bombay
Canada West
Central South Africa
Madras
Natal
Punjab (available at BL)
South Africa, Eastern Division
Turkey (available at BL)
Grand Lodges
British Columbia (available at NAC)
Canada in the Province of Ontario (available at NAC and GLC Library, Hamilton, Ontario)
England, Ancients
England, Moderns
Ireland (available at Freemasons' Hall, Dublin)
Nova Scotia (available at PANS)
Scotland (available at Iowa Masonic Library, Cedar Rapids, Iowa)
Quebec (available at Iowa Masonic Library, Cedar Rapids, Iowa)
United Grand Lodge of England

MASONIC PERIODICALS

Canadian Craftsman and Masonic Record (Toronto)
The Freemason (London)
The Freemason (Toronto)
Freemason's Chronicle (London)
Freemasons' Magazine and Masonic Mirror (London)
Freemasons' Quarterly Review (London)
Indian Freemason (Calcutta)
Indian Freemason's Friend (Calcutta)
Irish Masonry Illustrated (Dublin)
Masonic Herald (Calcutta)
Masonic Monthly Magazine (London)

Masonic Sun (Toronto)
Masonic Visitor (Dublin)
South African Freemason (East London)
The Standard (Bombay)

NEWSPAPERS

Clifford, Brendan. *Freemasonry and the United Irishmen, Reprints from the Northern Star,*
    1792/3. Belfast: Athol Books, 1992.
Das Gupta, Anil Chandra. *The Days of John Company: Selections from Calcutta Gazette, 1824–*
    1832. Calcutta: West Bengal Government Press, 1959.
Seton-Karr, W. S. *Selections from the Calcutta Gazette of the Years 1806–1815 Inclusive*. Calcutta:
    Bibhash Gupta, 1987.
Sandeman, Hugh David. *Selections from Calcutta Gazettes 1816–1823*. Calcutta: Bibhash
    Gupta, 1987.
The Times (London)

PAMPHLETS, SERMONS, ORATIONS, MANUALS, MEMOIRS, PUBLISHED
LETTERS

The Antient Constitutions of the Free and Accepted Masons . . . 2nd ed. London: B. Creake,
    1731.
Brazier, J. J. *Freemasonry during the Queen's Reign*. Bournemouth: n.p., 1897.
Brother Prosonno Coomar Dutt. N.p.: n.p., 189?. [available at FHL]
Browne, J. *The Master-Key through all the Degrees of a Free-mason's Lodge*. London: n.p.,
    1798.
Bryson, James. *The Duties of Masonry Briefly Stated. A Sermon delivered before the Orange
    Lodge, Belfast, 24 June 1782*. Belfast: Henry and Robert Joy and Co., 1782.
Cama, K. R. *A Discourse of Freemasonry among the Natives of Bombay*. Bombay: Times of
    India Steam Press, 1877.
Chart, D. A. *The Drennan Letters*. Belfast: HMSO, 1931.
Clarke, John. *History of the Minden Lodge of Ancient Free and Accepted Masons No. 63*.
    Kingston, Bermuda: Argus, 1849.
Coppin, John. *A Handbook of Freemasonry: Its History, Traditions, Antiquities, Rites, and
    Ceremonies*. Dublin: William McGee, 1867.
Davenport, Thomas. *Love to God and Man inseparable, A Sermon preached before a respectable
    Ancient and Honourable Society of Free and Accepted Masons, on the 27th Day of December,
    1764 . . .* Birmingham: Thomas Davenport, 1765.
DeSaussure, Wilmot Gibbes. *Address on the History of Freemasonry in South Carolina*.
    Charleston: D. L. Alexander, 1878.
DGL South Africa (Western Division). *Queen Victoria Commemoration*. Cape Town: "Cape
    Times" Printing Works, 1897.

Dodd, William. *An Oration delivered at the Dedication of Freemasons' Hall . . . on Thursday, May 23, 1776.* London: Grand Lodge, 1776.

A Free and Accepted Mason. "A Dissertation on Free-Masonry, addressed to HRH George PoW, Grand Master of England." *Attic Miscellany* 2 (1790): 73–80.

The Freemason's Guide Intended for the Use of the Brethren in India, Selected from Approved Works on the Royal Art. Bombay: R. W. Walker, Telegram Press, 1812.

Freemasonry for the Ladies. London and Dublin: Thomas Wilkinson, 1791.

Ghose, P. C. "What Is Freemasonry." In *The K. R. Cama Masonic Jubilee Volume*, edited by J. J. Modi, 38–41. Bombay: Fort Printing Press, 1907.

Grand Lodge of Nova Scotia. "Rise and Progress of Freemasonry in Nova Scotia." In *Constitution of the Ancient Fraternity of Free and Accepted Masons*, 5–8. Halifax: Edmund Ward, 1819.

Halford, John. *An Oration delivered . . . on the occasion of the consecration of the Commercial Lodge, No. 1391.* Birmingham: W. G. Moore, 1872.

Hall, Prince. *A Charge Delivered to the African Lodge, June 24, 1797.* Boston: n.p., 1797.

Hamilton, Milton, comp. *The Papers of Sir William Johnson.* 13 vols. Albany: State University of New York Press, 1921–1962.

How, Jeremiah. *The Freemason's Manual; or, Illustrations of Masonry.* London: Jeremiah How, 1865.

How Hindus Were Admitted Into the Mysteries of Freemasonry and a Short Masonic Career of the First Hindu Mason. Calcutta: Victor Printing Works, 1900.

Hutchinson, William. *The Spirit of Masonry in Moral and Elucidatory Lectures.* 2nd ed. Carlisle: F. Jollie, 1796.

Inwood, Joseph. *Sermons; in which are explained and enforced the religious, moral, and political virtues of Freemasonry.* London: J. Delahoy, 1799.

Kipling, Rudyard. *Collected Verse of Rudyard Kipling.* New York: Doubleday, Page & Co., 1907.

Knox, John. *An Historical Journal of the Campaigns in North America for the Years 1757, 1758, 1759, and 1760.* 3 vols. 1769; Freeport, N.Y.: Books for the Libraries Press, 1970.

Lodge Albert Victor. *Minutes of the Proceedings of Lodge Albert Victor, No. 2370 EC of a Regular Meeting held on the 31st January 1891.* Lahore: n.p., 1891.

Mandement de Monseigneur L'Évêque de Montreal contre Les Sociétés Secrètes. Montreal: L. Perrault, 1846.

Milner, Alfred. *The Nation and the Empire.* London: Constable and Company, 1913.

Modi, Jivanhi Jamshedji, ed. *The K. R. Cama Masonic Jubilee Volume.* Bombay: Fort Printing Press, 1907.

Morris, J. *Pocket Lexicon of Canadian Freemasonry.* Perth: Walker Brothers, 1889.

Murray. *The Rise and Purposes of Speculative Freemasonry, Being an Address Delivered to the Brethren of Zetland Lodge, No. 525, Hong Kong.* Hong Kong: A. Shortrede & Co., 1866.

Musgrave, Richard. *Memoirs of the Irish Rebellion of 1798.* 1801; reprint, Fort Wayne, Ind.: 1995.

New South Wales Government. "Index to the Colonial Secretary's Papers, 1788–1825." <http://www.records.nsw.gov.au/indexes/colsec>. 22 June 2004.

The Oriental Masonic Muse: Containing a Collection of Songs, Odes, Anthems, an Oratio, Prologues, Epilogues, and Toasts. Calcutta: Joseph Cooper, 1791.

Preston, William. *Illustrations of Masonry.* London: William Preston, 1772.

Provincial Grand Lodge of Lower Canada. *The Mason's Manual Comprising Rules and Regulations for the Government of the Most Ancient and Honorable Society of Free and Accepted Masons, in Lower Canada.* Quebec: T. Cary, 1818.

Read, W. H. *District Grand Lodge, Eastern Archipelago. Ceremony of Laying the Foundation Stone of the Clyde Terrace Market, at Singapore, the 29th Day of March, 1873.* Singapore: Straits Times Press, 1873.

Richards, Frank. *Old Soldier Sahib.* N.p.: Harrison Smith and Robert Haas, 1936.

Riley, J. Ramsden. *Modern Freemasonry as a Social and Moral Reformer.* Hull: n.p., 1888.

Rising Star Lodge. *A Mourning Lodge . . . in memory of Her Most Gracious Majesty Queen Victoria.* Bloemfontein: Barlow Bros. and Co., 1901.

Robbins, Alfred. *English-Speaking Freemasonry.* New York: Macoy Publishing, 1930.

Robertson, James. *Freemasonry: Sketch of its Origins and Early Progress. . . .* Dublin: John Fowler, 1862.

Robison, John. *Proofs of a Conspiracy against All the Religions and Governments of Europe, Carried on in the Secret Meetings of Free Masons, Illuminati, and Reading Societies.* London: T. Cadell and W. Davies, 1798.

Smart, William. *Address, Delivered before the Provincial Grand Royal Arch Chapter of Upper Canada.* Kingston: H. C. Thompson, 1823.

Smith, George. *The Use and Abuse of Free-Masonry; A Work of the greatest Utility to the Brethren of the Society, to Mankind in General, and to the Ladies in Particular.* London: George Smith, 1783.

Spark, Alexander. *An Oration Delivered at the Dedication of Free-Mason's Hall in the City of Quebec.* Quebec: William Brown, 1787.

Spence-Gray, H. J. *The Spirit of English Freemasonry, A Sermon Preached in Lahore Cathedral . . . before the Freemasons of the Punjab.* Lahore: News Printing Press, 1893.

Speth, George William. *What is Freemasonry? A lecture delivered . . . on the 7th November, 1892, at the Church Institute, Margate.* London: George Kenning, 1892.

Sussex Lodge, No. 7, Free and Accepted Masons (Saint Stephen, N.B.). *Lodge of Sorrow in Memory of our late Sovereign Her Most Gracious Majesty Queen Victoria Patroness of the Masonic Order.* N.p.: Courier Press, 1901.

The Textbook of freemasonry: a complete handbook of instruction to all the workings in the various mysteries and ceremonies of Craft Masonry. London: Reeves and Turner, 1881.

Turnough, John. *The Institutes of Free Masonry; To which are added, A Choice Collection of Epilogues, Songs, & c. Addressed to the Sea Captains' Lodge.* Liverpool: Thomas Johnson, 1788.

United Grand Lodge of England. *Report of the President and Vice-President of the Colonial*

Board to the Colonial Board on the eligibility of Parsees and Hindoos to be admitted to the Mysteries and Privileges of Freemasonry. London: United Grand Lodge, 1864.

Wadia, P. N. "The Admonitions of Freemasonry." In *The K. R. Cama Masonic Jubilee*, edited by J. J. Modi, 74–82. Bombay: Fort Printing Press, 1907.

———. *The Poetry of Freemasonry*. Bombay: Hehangir Bejanji Karani & Company, 1893.

Weeks, Joshua Wingate. *Sermon presented at St. Paul's Church in Halifax being the Festival of St. John . . .* Halifax: John Howe, 1785.

———. "A Charge Delivered on St. John's Day, at Halifax, when His Excellency Governor Parr, was Installed as Grand Master." In *Charges and Regulations*, xii–xv. Halifax: John Howe, 1786.

Wellson, J. E. C. *The Gay and Grave Sides of Fm, being an address delivered . . . at Simla, on the 25th July, 1900*. Simla: The "Simla Courier" Press, 1900.

Whytehead, T. B. "Women in Freemasonry. Read Before the Eboracum Lodge, No. 1611." In *Occasional Papers in the History of Freemasonry. Reprinted from the Freemason's Chronicle*. London: W. W. Morgan, 1882.

Wolseley, F. M. *The Story of a Soldier's Life*. New York: Charles Scribner's Sons, 1904.

Woodward, Charles. *Oration delivered on the 10th of May, 1849, at the consecration of a Prov GL . . .* Sydney: William John Row, 1849.

SECONDARY SOURCES

Note on Masonic sources: several key Masonic sources lie somewhere in between the realms of primary and secondary sources, insofar as their authors include facsimile reproductions of important Masonic documents. The most significant works in this category are those by Henry Coil and John Sherman, Chetwode Crawley, Walter Firminger, Robert Gould, John Lepper and Philip Crossle, C. H. Malden, and John Ross Robertson.

Abbott, G. Blizard. *Royalty and Freemasonry*. London: George Kenning, 1900.

Albanese, Catharine. "Whither the Sons (and Daughters)? Republican Nature and the Quest for the Ideal." In *The American Revolution: Its Character and Its Limits*, edited by Jack Greene, 362–87. New York: New York University Press, 1987.

Appadurai, Arjun. *Modernity at Large: Cultural Dimensions of Globalization*. Minneapolis: University of Minnesota Press, 1996.

Armitage, David. "Three Concepts of Atlantic History." In *The British Atlantic World, 1500–1800*, edited by David Armitage and Michael J. Braddick, 11–30. New York: Palgrave, 2002.

Armitage, David, et al. "American Historical Review Forum: The New British History in Atlantic Perspective." *American Historical Review* 104 (1999): 426–500.

Atkinson, Alan. *The Europeans in Australia, A History*. Vol. 1, *The Beginning*. Melbourne: Oxford University Press, 1997.

Baigent, Michael, and Richard Leigh. *The Temple and the Lodge*. New York: Arcade Publishing, 1989.

Bailey, Peter. "'Will the Real Bill Banks Please Stand Up?' Towards a Role Analysis of Mid-Victorian Working-Class Respectability." *Journal of Social History* 12 (Spring 1979): 336–53.

Ballantyne, Tony. "Empire, Knowledge, and Culture: From Proto-Globalization to Modern Globalization." In *Globalization in World History*, edited by A. G. Hopkins, 116–40. New York: W. W. Norton, 2002.

Barker, Hannah, and Elaine Chalus, eds. *Gender in Eighteenth-Century England*. London: Longman, 1997.

Barnett, Rex A. *The First Seventy Five Years, Motherland Lodge No. 3861, 1918–1993*. Privately published, 1993. [available at FHL]

Bayly, C. A. "'Archaic' and 'Modern' Globalization in the Eurasian and African Arena, ca. 1750–1850." In *Globalization in World History*, edited by A. G. Hopkins, 45–72. New York: W. W. Norton, 2002.

——. *The Birth of the Modern World*. London: Blackwell, 2004.

——. *Imperial Meridian: The British Empire and the World, 1780–1830*. London: Longman, 1989.

Beachy, Robert. "Recasting Cosmopolitanism: German Freemasonry and Regional Identity in the Eighteenth Century." *Eighteenth-Century Studies* 33 (2000): 266–74.

Berger, Carl. *Imperialism and Nationalism, 1884–1914: A Conflict in Canadian Thought*. Toronto: Copp Clark, 1969.

——. *The Sense of Power: Studies in the Ideas of Canadian Imperialism, 1867–1914*. Toronto: University of Toronto Press, 1970.

Berry, Henry. "Some Historical Episodes in Irish Freemasonry, 1790–1830." *Transactions of Quatuor Coronati Lodge* 26 (1913): 3–12.

Best, Geoffrey. *Mid-Victorian Britain, 1851–1870*. Glasgow: Collins, 1982.

Blackett-Ord, Mark. *Hell-Fire Duke*. Windsor Forest, Berks: Kensal Press, 1982.

Blakeley, Phyllis. *Glimpses of Halifax 1867–1900*. Belleville: Mika Publishing, 1949.

Bolt, Christine. *Victorian Attitudes to Race*. London: Routledge and K. Paul, 1971.

Bouchier, Nancy. "Idealized Middle-Class Sport for a Young Nation: Lacrosse in Nineteenth-Century Ontario Towns, 1781–1891." *Jounral of Canadian Studies* 29 (1994): 89–110.

Bowen, H. V. *Elites, Enterprise and the Making of the British Overseas Empire 1688–1775*. New York: St. Martin's, 1996.

Breckenridge, Carol, and Sheldon Pollock, eds. *Cosmopolitanism*. Durham: Duke University Press, 2002.

Breen, T. H. "An Empire of Goods: The Anglicization of Colonial America, 1690–1776." *Journal of British Studies* 25 (1986): 467–99.

Brereton, J. M. *The British Soldier: A Social History from 1661 to the Present Day*. London: The Bodley Head, 1986.

Breward, Christopher. *The Hidden Consumer: Masculinities, Fashion and City Life 1860–1914*. Manchester: Manchester University Press, 1999.

Brewer, John. *Party Ideology and Popular Politics at the Accession of George III*. Cambridge: Cambridge University Press, 1976.

Brooks, Joanna. "The Early American Public Sphere and the Emergence of a Black Print Counterpublic." *William and Mary Quarterly* 62, no. 1 (2005): 67–92.

Brown, Patricia. *The Merchant Princes of Fremantle: The Rise and Decline of a Colonial Elite, 1870–1900*. Perth: University of Western Australia Press, 1996.

Bryan, Patrick. *The Jamaican People 1880–1902: Race, Class, and Social Control*. London: Macmillan, 1991.

Buckner, Phillip. "Whatever Happened to the British Empire?" *Journal of the Canadian Historical Association* 4 (1994): 3–32.

Bullock, Steven C. *Revolutionary Brotherhood: Freemasonry and the Transformation of the American Social Order, 1730–1840*. Chapel Hill: University of North Carolina Press, 1996.

Bumsted, J. M. *The Peoples of Canada: A Pre-Confederation History*. Don Mills, Ont.: Oxford University Press, 1992.

Burke, Janet. "Leaving the Enlightenment: Women Freemasons after the Revolution." *Eighteenth-Century Studies* 33 (2000): 255–65.

Burke, Janet, and Margaret Jacob. "French Freemasonry, Women, and Feminist Scholarship." *Journal of Modern History* 68 (1996): 515–49.

Burns, J. F. "The 3rd Duke of Leinster." *Transactions of the Lodge of Research, No. CC, Ireland* 16 (1975): 206–39.

Burroughs, Peter. "Imperial Institutions and the Government of Empire." In *Oxford History of the British Empire*, vol. 3, *The Nineteenth Century*, edited by Andrew Porter, 170–97. Oxford: Oxford University Press, 1999.

Burton, Antoinette. "Rules of Thumb: British History and 'Imperial Culture' in Nineteenth- and Twentieth-Century Britain." *Women's History Review* 3, no. 4 (1994): 483–500.

———. "Who Needs the Nation? Interrogating 'British' History." *Journal of Historical Sociology* 10 (1997): 227–49.

———, ed. *After the Imperial Turn: Thinking with and through the Nation*. Durham: Duke University Press, 2003.

Bush, Julia. "'The Right Sort of Woman': Female Emigrators and Emigration to the British Empire, 1890–1910." *Women's History Review* 3 (1994): 385–409.

Butterfield, Paul. *Centenary: The First 100 Years of English Freemasonry in the Transvaal 1878–1978*. Johannesburg: Ernest Stanton Publishers, 1978.

Caillard, Bernard. "Australia's First Lodge Meeting." *Ars Quatuor Coronatorum* 100 (1987): 224–27.

Cannadine, David. *Ornamentalism: How the British Saw Their Empire*. London: Allen Lane, 2001.

Carnes, Mark. *Secret Ritual and Manhood in Victorian America*. New Haven: Yale University Press, 1989.

Carnochan, Janet. *History of Niagara*. Belleville, Ont.: Mika Publishing, 1973.

Carr, Harry, ed. *The Collected Prestonian Lectures*. 2 vols. London: Lewis Masonic, 1965, 1983.

Carson, Penny. "The British Raj and the Awakening of the Evangelical Conscience: The Ambiguities of Religious Establishment and Toleration, 1698–1833." In *Christian Missions and the Enlightenment*, edited by Brian Stanley, 47–70. Grand Rapids, Mich.: William B. Erdmans Publishing, 2001.

Case, James R. "American Masonic Roots in British Military Lodges." *Papers of the Canadian Masonic Research Association* 2 (1986): 1393–1401.

Casely-Hayford, Augustus, and Richard Rathbone. "Politics, Families and Freemasonry in the Colonial Gold Goast." In *Peoples and Empires in African History: Essays in Memory of Michael Crowder*, edited by J. F. Ade Ajayi and J. D. Y. Peel, 143–60. London: Longman, 1992.

Cerza, Alphonse. "American War of Independence and Freemasonry." *Ars Quatuor Coronatorum* 89 (1976): 169–75.

——. "Colonial Freemasonry in the United States of America." *Ars Quatuor Coronatorum* 90 (1977): 218–30.

Chakrabarty, Dipesh. *Provincializing Europe*. Princeton: Princeton University Press, 2000.

Chatterjee, Partha. *The Nation and Its Fragments: Colonial and Post-colonial Histories*. Princeton: Princeton University Press, 1993.

Chaudhuri, Nupur. "'Who Will Help the Girls?': Maria Rye and Victorian Juvenile Emigration to Canada, 1869–1895." In *Imperial Objects: Essays on Victorian Women's Emigration and the Unauthorized Imperial Experience*, edited by Rita S. Kranidis, 19–42. New York: Twayne, 1998.

Cheah, Pheng, and Bruce Robbins, eds. *Cosmopolitics: Thinking and Feeling beyond the Nation*. Minneapolis: University of Minnesota Press, 1998.

Christie, Ian R. *Stress and Stability in Late Eighteenth-Century Britain: Reflections on the British Avoidance of Revolution*. New York: Oxford University Press, 1984.

Clark, Anna. *The Struggle for the Breeches: Gender and the British Working Class*. Berkeley: University of California Press, 1995.

Clark, J. C. D. "English History's Forgotten Context: Scotland, Ireland, and Wales." *Historical Journal* 32 (1989): 211–28.

Clark, Peter. *British Clubs and Societies 1580–1800: The Origins of an Associational World*. Oxford: Clarendon Press, 2000.

Clarke, H. G. M. "Freemasonry and Religion." In *Grand Lodge 1717–1967*, edited by A. S. Frere, 92–128. Oxford: Oxford University Press, 1967.

Clarke, J. R. "The Formation (ii) 1751–1813." In *Grand Lodge 1717–1967*, edited by A. S. Frere, 92–128. Oxford: Oxford University Press, 1967.

Clawson, Mary Ann. *Constructing Brotherhood: Class, Gender, and Fraternalism*. Princeton: Princeton University Press, 1989.

——. "Early Modern Fraternalism and the Patriarchal Family." *Feminist Studies* 6 (1980): 368–91.

Cochrane, Keith, comp. *Irish Masonic Records*. CD-ROM. Second CD Edition. Belfast: Grand Lodge of Ireland, 2002.

Cohen, Michele. "Manliness, Effeminacy and the French: Gender and the Construction of National Character in Eighteenth-Century England." In *English Masculinities, 1660–1800*, edited by Tim Hitchcock and Michele Cohen, 44–62. London: Longman, 1999.

Cohn, Bernard. "Representing Authority in Victorian England." In *The Invention of Tradition*, edited by Eric Hobsbawm and T. O. Ranger, 165–210. Cambridge: Canto, 1983.

Coil, Henry Wilson. *Coil's Masonic Encyclopedia*. New York: Macoy Publishing, 1961.

Coil, Henry Wilson, and John Sherman. *A Documentary Account of Prince Hall and Other Black Fraternal Orders*. N.p.: Missouri Lodge of Research, 1982.

Colley, Linda. "The Apotheosis of George III: Loyalty, Royalty, and the British Nation, 1760–1820." *Past and Present* 102 (February 1984): 94–129.

———. "Britishness and Otherness: An Argument." *Journal of British Studies* 31 (1992): 309–29.

———. *Britons: Forging a Nation, 1707–1837*. New Haven: Yale University Press, 1992.

———. "Radical Patriotism." In *Patriotism: The Making and Unmaking of British National Identity*, edited by Raphael Samuel, 169–87. London: Routledge, 1989.

———. "What is Imperial History Now?" In *What is History Now?* edited by David Cannadine, 132–47. New York: Palgrave, 2004.

Conklin, Alice L. "Colonialism and Human Rights, A Contradiction in Terms? The Case of France and West Africa, 1895–1914." *American Historical Review* 103, no. 2 (April 1998): 419–42.

Cook, Ron A. "The Irish Connection." <http://www.geocities.com/Athens/Thebes/6779/irish.html>. 17 June 2004.

Cooper, A. A. *The Freemasons of South Africa*. Cape Town: Human & Rousseau, 1986.

———. "The United Grand Lodge Movement in South Africa." *Ars Quatuor Coronatorum* 99 (1986): 115–19.

Cooper, Frederick, and Ann Laura Stoler, eds. *Tensions of Empire: Colonial Cultures in a Bourgeois World*. Berkeley: University of California Press, 1997.

Cordery, Simon. "Friendly Societies and the Discourse of Respectability in Britain, 1825–1875." *Journal of British Studies* 34 (January 1995): 35–58.

Cranstoun-Day, Thomas. *The British Lodge No. 334 and English Freemasonry at the Cape of Good Hope 1795–1936*. Cape Town: District Grand Lodge of Cape Town, 1936.

Cramp, Karl, and George Mackaness. *A History of the United Grand Lodge of Free and Accepted Masons of New South Wales*. Sydney: Angus and Robertson, 1938.

Crawley, Chetwode. "The First Military Lodge, 1732." In *Caementaria Hibernica*, vol. 2. Dublin: William McGee, 1895–1900.

———. "General George Washington and Lodge No. 227 (I.C.)." *Ars Quatuor Coronatorum* 23 (1910): 95–97.

———. "The Irish Constitutions." In *Caementaria Hibernica*, vol. 1. Dublin: William McGee, 1895–1900.

——. "The Old Charges and the Papal Bulls." *Transactions of Quatuor Coronati Lodge* 24 (1911): 47–65, 107–17, 251–67.

Creighton, Sean, and Andrew Prescott. "Black Freemasonry." Centre for Research in Freemasonry Paper. <http://freemasonry.dept.shef.ac.uk/?q=papers_black_freemasonry>. 30 October 2005.

Crossle, Philip. *Irish Masonic Records*. Dublin: Grand Lodge of Ireland, 1973.

Cunningham, Hugh. "The Language of Patriotism, 1750–1914." *History Workshop Journal* 7 (1981): 8–33.

Curtin, Nancy. *The United Irishmen: Popular Politics in Ulster and Dublin, 1791–1798*. Oxford: Oxford University Press, 1994.

Davidoff, Leonore, Megan Dolittle, Janet Fink, and Katherine Holden. *The Family Story: Blood, Contract and Intimacy, 1830–1960*. London: Longman, 1999.

Davidoff, Leonore, and Catherine Hall, eds. *Family Fortunes: Men and Women of the English Middle Class, 1780–1850*. London: Routledge, 1987.

Davidson, Denise. "Women at Napoleonic Festivals: Gender and the Public Sphere during the First Empire." *French History* 16, no. 3 (September 2002): 299–322.

Davidson, Philip. *Propaganda and the American Revolution*. Chapel Hill: University of North Carolina Press, 1941.

Davies, J. J. *Handbook of the District Grand Lodge of the Punjab with Proceedings of District Grand Lodge*. Lahore: W. Ball & Co., n.d.

Dawson, Graham. *Soldier Heroes: British Adventure, Empire and the Imagining of Masculinities*. London: Routledge, 1994.

de Grazia, Victoria. *Irresistable Empire: America's Advance through 20th-Century Europe*. Cambridge: Harvard University Press, 2005.

Devine, T. M., and J. R. Young. *Eighteenth-Century Scotland: New Perspectives*. East Lothian, Scotland: Tuckwell, 1999.

Dickinson, H. T. *Liberty and Property: Political Ideology in Eighteenth-Century Britain*. London: Weidenfeld and Nicolson, 1977.

——. *The Politics of the People in Eighteenth-Century Britain*. New York: St. Martin's Press, 1995.

——. "Popular Conservatism and Militant Loyalism." In *Britain and the French Revolution*, edited by H. T. Dickinson, 103–26. New York: St. Martin's Press, 1989.

——. "Popular Loyalism in Britain in the 1790s." In *The Transformation of Political Culture: England and Germany in the Late Eighteenth Century*, edited by Eckhart Hellmuth, 503–33. Oxford: Oxford University Press, 1990.

Dickson, David, Daire Keogh, and Kevin Whelan, eds. *The United Irishmen: Republicanism, Radicalism and Rebellion*. Dublin: Lilliput, 1993.

Dinwiddy, John. "Interpretations of Anti-Jacobinism." In *The French Revolution and British Popular Politics*, edited by Mark Philp, 38–49. Cambridge: Cambridge University Press, 1991.

Dozier, Robert. *For King, Constitution, and Country: The English Loyalists and the French Revolution*. Lexington: University Press of Kentucky, 1983.

Draffen, George. "Prince Hall Freemasonry." *Ars Quatuor Coronatorum* 89 (1976): 70–91.

Duara, Prasenjit. *Rescuing History from the Nation: Questioning Narratives of Modern China*. Chicago: University of Chicago Press, 1995.

Eastwood, David. "Patriotism and the English State in the 1790s." In *The French Revolution and British Popular Politics*, edited by Mark Philp, 146–68. Cambridge: Cambridge University Press, 1991.

———. "Robert Southey and the Meanings of Patriotism." *Journal of British Studies* 21 (July 1992): 265–71.

Ellis, M. H. *Lachlan Macquarie: His Life, Adventures, and Times*. 1947; reprint, London: Angus and Robertson, 1978.

Encyclopedia of Native American Biography. New York: Henry Holt, 1997.

Errington, Jane. *The Lion, the Eagle, and Upper Canada: A Developing Colonial Ideology*. Montreal: McGill-Queen's University Press, 1987.

Finan, A. *History of the Grand Lodge of All Scottish Freemasonry in India, 1837–1924*. Bombay: Thacker & Co., 1928.

Fingard, Judith. "Race and Respectability in Victorian Halifax." *Journal of Imperial and Commonwealth History* 20 (May 1992): 169–95.

Firminger, Walter K. *The Second Lodge of Bengal in the Olden Times*. India: K. A. Korula, 1954.

Firth, Edith, ed. *The Town of York, 1815–1834: A Further Collection of Documents of Early Toronto*. Toronto: The Champlain Society, 1966.

Foster, Roy. *Modern Ireland*. New York: Penguin, 1988.

Fozdar, Vahid. "'Imperial Brotherhood': Indian Freemasonry and Global Networking during the British Raj." Paper presented at "How Empire Mattered: Imperial Structures and Globalization in the Era of British Imperialism," Berkeley, California, 4–5 April 2003.

Francis, Mark. *Governors and Settlers: Images of Authority in the British Colonies, 1820–60*. London: Macmillan, 1992.

Frankland, Noble. *Witness of a Century: The Life and Times of Prince Arthur Duke of Connaught 1850–1942*. London: Shepheard-Walwyn, 1993.

Frere, A. S., ed. *Grand Lodge, 1717–1967*. Oxford: Oxford University Press, 1967.

Gascoigne, John. *The Enlightenment and the Origins of European Australia*. Cambridge: Cambridge University Press, 2002.

Giddens, Anthony. *The Consequences of Modernity*. Stanford: Stanford University Press, 1990.

Glazebrook, George P. *The Story of Toronto*. Toronto: University of Toronto Press, 1971.

Gollin, Alfred. *Proconsul in Politics*. London: Garden City Press, 1964.

Gooch, L. *The Desperate Faction?: The Jacobites of North East England, 1688–1745*. Hull: University of Hull, 1995.

Goodhew, David. *Respectability and Resistance: A History of Sophiatown*. Westport, Conn.: Praeger, 2004.

Gopal, Sarvepalli. *British Policy in India, 1858–1905*. Cambridge: Cambridge University Press, 1965.

Gould, Eliga. "A Virtual Nation: Greater Britain and the Imperial Legacy of the American Revolution." *American Historical Review* 104 (April 1999): 476–89.

Gould, Robert F. *A Concise History of Freemasonry*. London: Gale & Polden, 1920.

——. *The History of Freemasonry: Its Antiquities, Symbols, Constitutions, etc.* 6 vols. London: Caxton Publishing Company, 1886.

——. *Military Lodges: The Apron and the Sword or Freemasonry under Arms*. London: Gale and Polden, 1899.

Graham, John H. *Outlines of the History of Freemasonry in the Province of Quebec*. Montreal: John Lovell, 1892.

Grand Lodge of Ireland. "Communications from or relating to Masonic Lodges in NSW preserved in the correspondence files of the Deputy Grand Secretaries of the Grand Lodge of Ireland, 1821–1888." [available at Freemasons' Hall, Dublin]

Grand Lodge of South Australia. "Some events in the early history of Freemasonry in Australia and the SW Pacific to 1848." <http://www.freemasonrysaust. org.au/his toryearly.html>. 17 June 2004.

Green, E. H. H. *The Crisis of Conservatism: The Politics, Economics and Ideology of the British Conservative Party, 1880–1914*. London: Routledge, 1995.

——. "The Political Economy of Empire, 1880–1914." In *The Oxford History of the British Empire*, vol. 3, *The Nineteenth Century*, edited by Andrew Porter, 346–70. Oxford: Oxford University Press, 1999.

Greene, Jack. "Empire and Identity from the Glorious Revolution to the American Revolution." In *The Oxford History of the British Empire*, vol. 2, *The Eighteenth Century*, edited by P. J. Marshall, 208–31. Oxford: Oxford University Press, 1998.

Grell, Ole Peter, and Roy Porter, eds. *Toleration in Enlightenment Europe*. Cambridge: Cambridge University Press, 2000.

Gribble, James. *History of Freemasonry in Hyderabad*. Madras: Higginbotham, 1910.

Gupta, G. S. *Freemasonic Movement in India*. New Dehli: Indian Masonic Publications, 1981.

Hall, Catherine. *Civilising Subjects*. Chicago: University of Chicago Press, 2002.

——. "Imperial Man: Edward Eyre in Australasia and the West Indies, 1833–66." In *The Expansion of England*, edited by Bill Schwartz, 130–70. London: Routledge, 1996.

——. "Of Gender and Empire: Reflections on the Nineteenth Century." In *Gender and Empire: The Oxford History of the British Empire Companion Series*, edited by Philippa Levine, 46–76. Oxford: Oxford University Press, 2004.

——. *White, Male and Middle Class: Explorations in Feminism and History*. London: Routledge, 1992.

——. "William Knibb and the Constitution of the New Black Subject." In *Empire and Others*, edited by Martin Daunton and Rick Halpern, 303–24. Philadelphia: University of Pennsylvania Press, 1999.

———, ed. *Cultures of Empire; A Reader; Colonizers in Britain and the Empire in the Nineteenth and Twentieth Centuries*. New York: Routledge, 2000.

Hamill, John. *The Craft*. Leighton Buzzard, England: Crucible, 1986.

———. "The Earl of Moira, Acting Grand Master 1790–1813." *Ars Quatuor Coronatorum* 93 (1980): 31–48.

Hannerz, Ulf. "Cosmopolitans and Locals in World Culture." In *Global Culture: Nationalism, Globalization, and Modernity*, edited by Mike Featherstone, 237–51. London: Sage, 1990.

Hardinge, Arthur. *The Life of Henry Herbert, Fourth Earl of Carnarvon*. London: Oxford University Press, 1925.

Hareven, Tamara K. "The History of the Family and the Complexity of Social Change." *American Historical Review* 96 (1991): 95–124.

Harland-Jacobs, Jessica. "All in the Family: Freemasonry and the British Empire in the Mid-Nineteenth Century." *Journal of British Studies* 42 (October 2003): 448–82.

———. "'The Essential Link': Freemasonry and British Imperialism, 1751–1918." Ph.D. diss., Duke University, 2000.

———. "'Hands Across the Sea': The Masonic Network, British Imperialism, and the North Atlantic World." *Geographical Review* 89 (April 1999): 237–53.

Harling, Philip. "The Duke of York Affair (1809) and the Complexities of War-time Patriotism." *Historical Journal* 39 (December 1996): 963–84.

Harper, Marjory. "British Migration and the Peopling of Empire." In *The Oxford History of the British Empire*, vol. 3, *The Nineteenth Century*, edited by Andrew Porter, 75–87. Oxford: Oxford University Press, 1999.

Harris, Reginald V. "H.R.H. Prince Edward Augustus, Duke of Kent and his Canadian Masonic Career." *Papers of the Canadian Masonic Research Association* 1 (1986): 308–31.

———. "John Graves Simcoe, Freemason, Soldier, Statesman 1752–1806." *Papers of the Canadian Masonic Research Association* 2 (1986): 1169–76.

———. "Maritime Provinces." In *Gould's History of Freemasonry throughout the World*, vol. 4, edited by Dudley Wright, 26–62. New York: Charles Scribner's Sons, 1936.

Harrison, Brian. *Peaceable Kingdom: Stability and Change in Modern Britain*. Oxford: Clarendon Press, 1982.

Harrison, James. *Rudyard Kipling*. Boston: Twayne, 1982.

Harvey, David. *The Condition of Postmodernity: An Enquiry into the Origins of Cultural Change*. Oxford: Blackwell, 1989.

Heater, Derek. *World Citizenship and Government: Cosmopolitan Ideas in the History of Western Political Thought*. New York: St. Martin's Press, 1996.

Heaton, Ronald E. *Masonic Membership of the Founding Fathers*. Silver Spring, Md.: Masonic Service Association, 1974.

Held, David, and Anthony McGrew, eds. *The Global Transformations Reader: An Introduction to the Globalization Debate*. Cambridge: Cambridge University Press, 2003.

Henley, W. *History of Lodge Australian Social Mother, No. 1*. Sydney: Gibbs, Crey & Co., 1920.

Hewitt, A. R. "The Grand Lodge of England." In *The Collected Prestonian Lectures*, vol. 2, edited by Harr Carr, 74–93. London: Lewis Masonic, 1983.

"History of Lodge of Australia No. 3 U.G.L. of N.S.W." [available at FHL]

Hobsbawm, Eric. *Primitive Rebels: Studies in Archaic Forms of Social Movement in the 19th and 20th Centuries*. New York: W. W. Norton, 1965.

Hobsbawm, Eric, and T. O. Ranger. *The Invention of Tradition*. Cambridge: Canto, 1983.

Hopkins, A. G., ed. *Globalization in World History*. New York: W. W. Norton, 2002.

Huggins, Mike J. "More Sinful Pleasures? Leisure, Respectability, and the Male Middle Classes in Victorian England." *Journal of Social History* 33 (Spring 2000): 585–600.

Hyam, Ronald. *Britain's Imperial Century, 1815–1914: A Study of Empire and Expansion*. 1976; reprint, Lanham, Md.: Barnes & Noble Books, 1993.

Jackson, A. C. F. "William Mathew: A Governor of the Leeward Islands and His Connection with Estienne Morin." *Ars Quatuor Coronatorum* 103 (1990): 202–7.

Jacob, Margaret. "Freemasonry, Women, and the Paradox of the Enlightenment." In *Women and the Enlightenment*, edited by Margaret Hunt et al., 69–93. New York: Institute for Research in History, 1984.

———. *Living the Enlightenment: Freemasonry and Politics in Eighteenth-Century Europe*. New York: Oxford University Press, 1991.

———. *The Radical Enlightenment: Pantheists, Freemasons and Republicans*. London: George, Allen, and Unwin, 1981.

Jacob, Margaret, Janet M. Burke, Robert Beachy, and Steven C. Bullock. "Forum: Exits from the Enlightenment: Masonic Routes." *Eighteenth-Century Studies* 33 (2000): 251–79.

Jamiat Rai, Rai Bahadur. *A Brief History of Freemasonry in Quetta*. Bombay: Times Press, 1908.

Jenkins, J. P. "Jacobites and Freemasons in Eighteenth-Century Wales." *Welsh Historical Review* 9 (1979): 391–406.

———. *The Making of a Ruling Class: The Glamorgan Gentry, 1640–1790*. Cambridge: Cambridge University Press, 1983.

Johnson, J. K. *Becoming Prominent: Regional Leadership in Upper Canada, 1791–1841*. Kingston: McGill-Queen's University Press, 1989.

Jordan, Gerald, and Nicholas Rogers. "Admirals as Heroes: Patriotism and Liberty in Hanoverian England." *Journal of British Studies* 28 (July 1989): 201–24.

Kaplan, Sidney. "Veteran Officers and Politics in Massachusetts, 1783–1787." *William and Mary Quarterly*, 3rd ser. 9 (January 1952): 29–57.

Kaplan, Sidney, and Emma Nogrady Kaplan. *The Black Presence in the Era of the American Revolution*. Amherst: University of Massachusetts Press, 1989.

Karpiel, Frank. "Freemasonry, Colonialism, and Indigenous Elites." Paper presented at "Interactions: Regional Studies, Global Processes, and Historical Analysis," Library of Congress, Washington, D.C., 28 February–3 March 2001. <http://www.history cooperative.org/proceedings/interactions/karpiel.html>. 1 November 2005.

Katz, Joseph. *Jews and Freemasons in Europe, 1723–1939*. Cambridge: Harvard University Press, 1970.

Kendall, George. "Freemasonry during the Anglo-Boer War 1899–2002." *Ars Quatuor Coronatorum* 97 (1984): 20–33.

Kennedy, Dane. "Imperial History and Post-Colonial Theory." *Journal of Imperial and Commonwealth History* 24 (1996): 345–63.

Kingston, Beverly. *The Oxford History of Australia: Glad, Confident Morning, 1860–1900*. Melbourne: Oxford University Press, 1993.

Kirk, Neville. *The Growth of Working Class Reformism in Mid-Victorian England*. Urbana: University of Illinois Press, 1985.

Kleingeld, Pauline. "Six Varieties of Cosmopolitanism in late Eighteenth-century Germany." *Journal of the History of Ideas* 60, no. 3 (1999): 505–34.

Knox, Bruce. "The Earl of Carnarvon, Empire, and Imperialism, 1855–90." *Journal of Imperial and Commonwealth History* 26 (1998): 48–66.

Knox, Oliver. *Rebels and Informers: Stirrings of Irish Independence*. New York: St. Martin's Press, 1997.

Lamonby, W. F. *Some Notes on Freemasonry in Australasia: From the Earliest Times to the Present Day*. London: Warrington and Co., 1906.

Lane, John. *Masonic Records 1717–1894*. London: Freemasons' Hall, 1895.

Langford, Paul. *A Polite and Commercial People: England 1727–1783*. Oxford: Clarendon Press, 1989.

Laurie, W. *The History of Free Masonry and the Grand Lodge of Scotland*. Edinburgh: Seton & Mackenzie, 1859.

Lazarus, Afeef. "Experiences in Caribbean Masonry: The Jamaican Perspective." *The Philalethes Magazine* <http://www.freemasonry.org/psoc/jamcia.htm>. 1 November 2005.

Lemay, J. A. Leo, ed. *Reappraising Benjamin Franklin: A Bicentennial Perspective*. Newark: University of Delaware Press, 1993.

Leon, Emmanuel. *The History of the Friendly Lodge, No. 239, Dist. No. 2, Kingston, Jamaica*. Jamaica: Mortimer De Souza, 1898.

Lepper, J., and P. Crossle. *History of the Grand Lodge of Free and Accepted Masons of Ireland*. Dublin: Lodge of Research, CC, 1925.

Levine, Philippa. "Introduction: Why Gender and Empire?" In *The Oxford History of the British Empire Companion Series Gender and Empire*, edited by Philippa Levine, 1–13. Oxford: Oxford University Press, 2004.

Linford, R. "The First Australian Stationary Masonic Lodge? Norfolk Island and New South Wales (Australia)." <http://www.geocities.com/Athens/Thebes/6779/linford1.html>. 1 November 2005.

Lodge Anchor and Hope. *Light of Freemasonry: Bi-Centennial Souvenir of Lodge Anchor and Hope No. 1 of the Grand Lodge of India, 1773–1973*. Calcutta: Naba Mudran P. Ltd, 1973.

Loge des Coeurs-Unis. "Histoire." <http://www.coeurs-unis45.org/CoeursUnis.html>. 12 February 2005.

Longley, Ronald, and Reginald Harris. "A Short History of Freemasonry in Nova Scotia." <http://www.grandlodgens.org>. 28 February 2005.

Lopez, Claude-Anne. "Was Franklin Too French?" In *Reappraising Benjamin Franklin: A Bicentennial Perspective*, edited by Leo J. A. Lemay, 143–53. Cranbury, N.J.: Associated University Presses, 1993.

Lorimer, Douglas. *Colour, Class and the Victorians: English Attitudes to the Negro in the Mid-Nineteenth Century*. Leicester: Leicester University Press, 1978.

Luhrmann, T. M. *The Good Parsi: The Fate of a Colonial Elite in a Postcolonial Society*. Cambridge: Harvard University Press, 1996.

McBride, I. R. *Scripture Politics: Ulster Presbyterians and Irish Radicalism in the Late Eighteenth Century*. Oxford: Oxford University Press, 1998.

McClintock, Anne. "Family Feuds: Gender, Nationalism, and the Family." *Feminist Review* 44 (Summer 1993): 61–80.

McDevitt, Patrick. *"May the Best Man Win": Sport, Masculinity, and Nationalism in Great Britain and the Empire, 1880–1935*. New York: Palgrave Macmillan, 2004.

McFarland, E. W. *Ireland and Scotland in the Age of Revolution*. Edinburgh: Edinburgh University Press, 1994.

Macinnes, Allan. "Scottish Jacobitism: In Search of a Movement." In *Eighteenth-Century Scotland: New Perspectives*, edited by T. M. Devine and J. R. Young, 70–89. East Lothian, Scotland: Tuckwell Press, 1999.

McKenzie, Kirsten. "Of Convicts and Capitalists: Honour and Colonial Commerce in 1830s Cape Town and Sydney." *Australian Historical Studies* 118 (2002): 199–222.

McLeod, Wallace, ed. *Whence Come We? Freemasonry in Ontario 1764–1980*. Hamilton: Grand Lodge of Canada, 1980.

McLynn, Frank. *The Jacobites*. London: Routledge, 1985.

McMahon, Darrin. *Enemies of Enlightenment: The French Counter-Enlightenment and the Making of Modernity*. Oxford: Oxford University Press, 2001.

McNaught, Kenneth. *The Pelican History of Canada*. Harmondsworth: Penguin, 1982.

MacTaggart, D. D., Pemberton Smith, and W. L. Bond. *Old St. Paul's Lodge*. N.p.: n.p., 1924. [available at FHL]

Mackenzie, John M. "Empire and National Identities: The Case of Scotland." *Transactions of the Royal Historical Society* 8 (1998): 215–31.

Malden, C. H. *A History of Freemasonry (Under the English Constitution) on the Coast of Coromandel*. Madras: Addison & Co., 1895.

Mangan, J. A. *Athleticism in the Victorian and Edwardian Public Schools: The Emergence and Consolidation of an Educational Ideology*. London: F. Cass, 2000.

———. *The Games Ethic and Imperialism: Aspects of the Diffusion of an Ideal*. Cambridge: Cambridge University Press, 1981.

Mangan, J. A., and James Walvin, eds. *Manliness and Morality: Middle-Class Masculinity in Britain and America, 1800–1940*. Manchester: Manchester University Press, 1981.

Marshall, P. J. "Britain without America — A Second Empire?" In *The Oxford History of the British Empire*, vol. 2, *The Eighteenth Century*, edited by P. J. Marshall, 576–95. Oxford: Oxford University Press, 1998.

———, ed. *Cambridge Illustrated History of the British Empire*. Cambridge: Cambridge University Press, 1996.

Mason, Philip. *Kipling: The Glass, the Shadow and the Fire*. New York: Harper and Row, 1975.

Mehta, Pratap Bhanu. "Cosmopolitanism and the Circle of Reason." *Political Theory* 28 (2000): 619–39.

Mehta, Uday Singh. *Liberalism and Empire: A Study in Nineteenth-Century British Liberal Thought*. Chicago: University of Chicago Press, 1999.

Melton, James. *The Rise of the Public in Enlightenment Europe*. Cambridge: Cambridge University Press, 2001.

Metcalf, Thomas. *The Aftermath of Revolt: India 1857–1870*. Princeton: Princeton University Press, 1964.

———. *Ideologies of the Raj*. Cambridge: Cambridge University Press, 1997.

Middleton, Jesse. *The Municipality of Toronto: A History*. Vol. 1. Toronto: Dominion Publishing Co., 1923.

Milborne, A. J. B. "British Military Lodges in the American War of Independence." *Transactions of the American Lodge of Research* 10 (1966): 22–85.

———. "Freemasonry in Bermuda." *Ars Quatuor Coronatorum* 74 (1961): 11–31.

———. "Overseas Development and the Military Lodges." In *Grand Lodge 1717–1967*, edited by A. S. Frere, 224–64. Oxford: Oxford University Press, 1967.

Miller, Carman. *Painting the Map Red: Canada and the South African War, 1899–1902*. Montreal: McGill-Queen's University Press, 1993.

Miller, Kerby. *Irish Immigrants in the Land of Canaan: Letters and Memoirs from Colonial and Revolutionary America, 1675–1815*. New York: Oxford University Press, 2003.

Mills, Stephen. *The Bicentenary of English Freemasonry in South Africa*. N.p.: District Grand Lodge of South Africa, Western Division, 2001.

Mirala, Petri. "'A Large Mob, Calling Themselves Freemasons': Masonic Parades in Ulster." In *Crowds in Ireland, c. 1720–1920*, edited by Peter Jupp and Eoin Magennis, 117–38. New York: St. Martin's Press, 2000.

Misra, Maria. *Business, Race, and Politics in British India c. 1850–1960*. Oxford: Clarendon, 1999.

Money, John. *Experience and Identity: Birmingham and the West Midlands, 1760–1800*. Montreal: McGill-Queen's University Press, 1977.

———. "Freemasonry and the Fabric of Loyalism in Hanoverian England." In *The Transformation of Political Culture: England and Germany in the Late Eighteenth Century*, edited by Eckhart Hellmuth, 235–74. Oxford: Oxford University Press, 1990.

———. "The Masonic Moment; Or, Ritual, Replica, and Credit: John Wilkes, the Macaroni Parson, and the Making of the Middle-Class Mind." *Journal of British Studies* 32 (1993): 358–95.

Monod, Paul. *Jacobitism and the English People, 1688–1788*. New York: Cambridge University Press, 1989.

Morris, R. J. "Clubs, Societies, and Associations." In *The Cambridge Social History of Britain, 1750–1850*, edited by F. M. L. Thompson, 395–444. Cambridge: Cambridge University Press, 1990.

Musa, Fraser B. "The First Indian Freemason Rt. Wor. Bro. Manockjee Cursetjee." *Ars Quatuor Coronatorum The Supplement* 81 (1968): 317–21.

Newman, Aubrey. "Politics and Freemasonry in the Eighteenth Century." *Ars Quatuor Coronatorum* 104 (1991): 32–41.

Newman, Gerald. *The Rise of English Nationalism: A Cultural History 1740–1830*. New York: St. Martin's Press, 1987.

Newton, Edward. "Brethren Who Made Masonic History." In *The Collected Prestonian Lectures*, vol. 2, edited by Harry Carr, 46–57. London: Lewis Masonic, 1983.

Northhern, F. G. *History of the Grand Lodge of Ancient, Free and Accepted Masons of New Zealand 1890–1970*. Gisborne: Te Rau Press, 1971.

O'Brien, Karen. *Narratives of Enlightenment*. Cambridge: Cambridge University Press, 1997.

O'Day, Rosemary. *The Family and Family Relationships, 1500–1900: England, France, and the United States of America*. New York: St. Martin's Press, 1994.

Ormsby, Joy. "Building a Town: Plans, Surveys, and the Early Years of Niagara-on-the-Lake." In *The Capital Years: Niagara-on-the-Lake, 1792–1796*, edited by Richard Merritt, Nancy Butler, and Michael Power, 15–44. Toronto: Dundurn Press, 1991.

Osterhammel, Jürgen, and Niels P. Petersson. *Globalization: A Short History*. Princeton: Princeton University Press, 2005.

Ouellet, Fernand. *Lower Canada, 1791–1840: Social Change and Nationalism*. Toronto: McClelland & Stewart, 1980.

Pagden, Anthony. *Peoples and Empires: A Short History of European Migration, Exploration and Conquest from Greece to the Present*. New York: Modern Library, 2001.

Page, Robert. "Canada and the Imperial Idea in the Boer War Years." *Journal of Canadian Studies* 5 (1970): 33–49.

Parkinson, Raymond. *History of the Grand Lodge of Free and Accepted Masons of Ireland*. Dublin: Lodge of Research, CC, 1957.

Parr, Joy. *Labouring Children: British Immigrant Apprentices to Canada, 1869–1924*. London: Croom Helm, 1980.

Parramore, Thomas. *Launching the Craft: The First Half-Century of Freemasonry in North Carolina*. Raleigh: Grand Lodge of North Carolina, 1975.

Peers, Douglas. "'The Habitual Nobility of Being': British Officers and the Social Construction of the Bengal Army in the Early Nineteenth Century." *Modern Asian Studies* 25 (1991): 545–69.

Penlington, Norman. *Canada and Imperialism, 1896–1899*. Toronto: University of Toronto Press, 1965.

Penman, A. T. "Freemasonry in South Africa." *Ars Quatuor Coronatorum* 80 (1967): 280–86.

Philp, Mark. "The Fragmented Ideology of Reform." In *The French Revolution and British Popular Politics*, edited by Mark Philp, 50–77. Cambridge: Cambridge University Press, 1991.

Pick, Fred, and Norman Knight. *The Pocket History of Freemasonry*. London: Frederick Muller, 1983.

Pocock, J. G. A. "British History: A Plea for a New Subject." *Journal of Modern History* 47 (1975): 601–21.

———. "The Limits and Divisions of British History: In Search of an Unknown Subject." *American Historical Review* 87 (1982): 311–36.

Pollock, John. *Kitchener: Architect of Victory, Artisan of Peace*. New York: Carroll & Graf, 2001.

Porter, Bernard. *The Lion's Share: A Short History of British Imperialism, 1850–1983*. London: Longman, 1984.

Porter, Roy. *The Creation of the Modern World*. New York: W. W. Norton & Co., 2001.

Power, Michael. "Religion and Community." In *The Capital Years: Niagara-on-the-Lake, 1792–1796*, edited by Richard Merritt, Nancy Butler, and Michael Power, 103–30. Toronto: Dundurn Press, 1991.

Power, Thomas. *Land, Politics and Society in Eighteenth-Century Tipperary*. Oxford: Oxford University Press, 1993.

Prescott, Andrew. "The Study of Freemasonry as a New Academic Discipline." In *Vrijmetselarij in Nederland: Een kennismaking met de wetenschappelijke studi van een 'geheim' genootschap*, edited by A. Kroon, 5–31. Leiden: OVN, 2003.

———. "The Unlawful Societies Act of 1799." In *The Social Impact of Freemasonry in the Modern Western World*, edited by M. D. J. Scanlan, 116–34. London: Canonbury Masonic Research Centre, 2002.

Read, D. B. *The Life and Times of Gen. John Graves Simcoe*. Toronto: G. Virtue, 1890.

Reese, Trevor R. *The History of the Royal Commonwealth Society*. Oxford: Oxford University Press, 1968.

Révauger, Cécile. *Noirs et Franc-maçons aux Etats-Unis*. Paris: EDIMAF, 2003.

———. "Women Barred from Masonic 'Work': A British Phenomenon." In *The Invisible Woman: Aspects of Women's Work in Eighteenth-Century Britain*, edited by Isabelle Baudino, Jacques Carre, and Cécile Révauger, 117–30. London: Ashgate, 2005.

———, ed. "Franc-Maçonnerie et Politiques au Siècle des Lumières: Europe-Amériques." *Lumières* 7, no. 1 (2006).

Rich, Paul J. *Chains of Empire: English Public Schools, Masonic Cabalism, Historical Causality, and Imperial Clubdom*. London: Regency, 1991.

———. *Elixir of Empire: The English Public Schools, Ritualism, Freemasonry, and Imperialism*. London: Regency, 1989.

Rich, Paul J., and David Merchant. "Inventing Tradition and Freemasonry: The Craft and

the Arabs." In *Freemasonry on Both Sides of the Atlantic*, edited by R. William Weisberger, 657–66. Boulder, Colo.: Easter European Monographs, 2002.

Riddell, William Renwick. *The Life of John Graves Simcoe, First Lieutenant-Governor of the
Province of Upper Canada 1792–6*. Toronto: McClelland and Stewart, 1926.

Ridley, Jasper. *The Freemasons*. London: Robinson, 2000.

Roberts, J. M. "Freemasonry: Possibilities of a Neglected Topic." *English Historical Review*
84 (1969): 323–55.

Robertson, John R. *History of Freemasonry in Canada*. Toronto: The Hunter, Rose Co.,
1899.

Robertson, Roland. *Globalization: Social Theory and Global Culture*. London: Sage, 1992.

Robinson, Ronald. "Non-European Foundations of European Imperialism: Sketch for a
Theory of Collaboration." In *Studies in the Theory of Imperialism*, edited by Roger
Owen and Bob Sutcliffe, 118–40. London: Longman, 1972.

Roper, Michael, and John Tosh, eds. *Manful Assertions: Masculinities in Britain since 1800*.
London: Routledge, 1991.

Rose, Sonya. *Limited Livelihoods: Gender and Class in Nineteenth-Century England*. Berkeley: University of California Press, 1992.

Ross, Robert. *Status and Respectability in the Cape Colony 1750–1870: A Tragedy of Manners*.
Cambridge: Cambridge University Press, 1999.

Royal Colonial Institute Lodge No. 3556. *History, 1912–1962*. Privately published, 1962.

Russell, Peter, ed. *Nationalism in Canada*. Toronto: McGraw-Hill, 1966.

Rutherford, Jonathan. *Forever England: Reflections on Masculinity and Empire*. London:
Lawrence & Wishart, 1997.

Sadler, Henry. *Masonic Facts and Fictions Comprising A New Theory of the Origin of the
"Antient" Grand Lodge*. 1887; reprint, Wellingborough: Aquarian Press, 1985.

Samson, Jane. "Are You What You Believe? Some Thoughts on *Ornamentalism* and Religion." *Journal of Colonialism and Colonial History* 3 (2002). <http://muse.jhu.edu.lp.
hscl.ufl.edu/journals/journal _ of _ colonialism _ and _ colonial _
history/toc/cch3.1.html>. 4 November 2005.

Samuel, Raphael. "British Dimensions: Four Nations History." *History Workshop Journal*
40 (1995): 3–22.

Saul, J. Beamish. *Historical Sketch of the Lodge of Antiquity*. Montreal: n.p., 1903.

Saunders, Christopher, and Iain R. Smith. "Southern Africa, 1795–1910." In *The Oxford
History of the British Empire*, vol. 3, *The Nineteenth Century*, edited by Andrew Porter,
597–623. Oxford: Oxford University Press, 1999.

Scanlan, M. D. J., ed. *The Social Impact of Freemasonry in the Modern Western World*.
London: Canonbury Masonic Research Centre, 2002.

Schlereth, Thomas. *The Cosmopolitan Ideal in Enlightenment Thought: Its Form and Function in the Ideas of Franklin, Hume, and Voltaire, 1694–1790*. Notre Dame, Ind.: University of Notre Dame Press, 1977.

Schoenbrun, David. *Triumph in Paris: The Exploits of Benjamin Franklin*. New York:
Harper & Row, 1976.

Scott, Duncan Campbell. *John Graves Simcoe*. Toronto: Morang & Co., 1906.

Sedgwick, Eve Kosofsky. *Between Men: English Literature and Male Homosocial Desire*. New York: Columbia University Press, 1985.

Sesquicentennial History of St. George's Lodge. Schenectady, N.Y.: Schenectady Union-Star Press, 1924.

Sheppard, Osborne, ed. *A Concise History of Freemasonry in Canada*. Hamilton: Osborne Sheppard, 1924.

Sheppard, Ray. "Details of Lodge's [sic] Issued to Foot Regiments of the British Army, 1732–1932." [available at FHL]

Shoemaker, Robert. *Gender in English Society, 1650–1850: The Emergence of Separate Spheres*. Harlow: Longman, 1998.

Sidhwa, Rustam Sohrabji. *District Grand Lodge of Pakistan, 1869–1969*. Lahore: District Grand Lodge, 1969.

Sinha, Mrinalini. "Britishness, Clubbability, and the Colonial Public Sphere: The Genealogy of an Imperial Institution in Colonial India." *Journal of British Studies* 40 (October 2001): 489–521.

———. *Colonial Masculinity: The "Manly Englishman" and the "Effeminate Bengali" in the Late Nineteenth Century*. Manchester: Manchester University Press, 1995.

Smith, Douglas. *Working the Rough Stone: Freemasonry and Society in Eighteenth-Century Russia*. Dekalb: Northern Illinois University Press, 1999.

Smith, Faith. *Creole Recitations: John Jacob Thomas and Colonial Formation in the Late Nineteenth-Century Caribbean*. Charlottesville: University of Virginia Press, 2002.

Smith, Woodruff. *Consumption and the Making of Respectability, 1600–1800*. London: Routledge, 2002.

Smyth, Frederick. "The Master-Mason-At-Arms: A Short Study of Freemasonry in the Armed Forces." *Ars Quatuor Coronatorum* 104 (1991): 222–36.

Smyth, Jim. "Freemasonry and the United Irishmen." In *The United Irishmen: Republicanism, Radicalism and Rebellion*, edited by David Dickson, Daire Keogh, and Kevin Whelan, 167–75. Dublin: Lilliput, 1993.

South African Freemasonry: Some Historical Jottings. Cape Town: Cape Times Ltd., 1987.

Srodes, James. *Franklin: The Essential Founding Father*. Washington, D.C.: Regnery, 2002.

Stacey, C. P. *Canada and the British Army, 1846–1871*. Toronto: University of Toronto Press, 1963.

Stemper, William. "Conflicts and Development in Eighteenth-Century Freemasonry: The American Context." *Ars Quatuor Coronatorum* 104 (1991): 198–205.

Stevenson, David. "James Anderson (1679–1739): Man and Mason." In *Freemasonry on Both Sides of the Atlantic*, edited by R. William Weisberg, 199–242. Boulder, Colo.: Eastern European Monographs, 2002.

———. *The Origins of Freemasonry: Scotland's Century, 1590–1710*. Cambridge: Cambridge University Press, 1988.

Stewart, A. T. Q. *A Deeper Silence: The Hidden Roots of the United Irish Movement*. London: Faber and Faber, 1993.

Szechi, Daniel. *The Jacobites: Britain and Europe, 1688–1788*. Manchester: Manchester University Press, 1994.

Tadmor, Naomi. "The Concept of the Household-Family in Eighteenth-Century England." *Past and Present* 151 (1996): 111–40.

Talman, James J. "Early Freemasonry in Ontario." *Papers of the Canadian Masonic Research Association* 1 (1986): 371–79.

Tatsch, J. Hugo. *Freemasonry in the Thirteen Colonies*. New York: Macoy Publishing, 1929.

Thomas, Evan. *John Paul Jones: Sailor, Hero, Father of the American Navy*. New York: Simon and Schuster, 2003.

Thompson, Andrew. *Imperial Britain: The Empire in British Politics*. Harlow: Longman, 2000.

Thompson, F. M. L. *The Rise of Respectable Society: A Social History of Victorian Britain, 1830–1900*. London: Fontana, 1988.

Thorne, Susan. *Congregational Missions and the Making of an Imperial Culture in Nineteenth-Century England*. Stanford: Stanford University Press, 1999.

Tosh, John. *A Man's Place: Masculinity and the Middle-Class Home in Victorian England*. New Haven: Yale University Press, 1999.

———. *Manliness and Masculinities in Nineteenth-Century Britain: Essays on Gender, Family, and Empire*. New York: Pearson Longman, 2005.

———. "The Old Adam and the New Man: Emerging Themes in the History of English Masculinities, 1750–1850." In *English Masculinities, 1660–1800*, edited by Tim Hitchcock and Michele Cohen, 217–38. London: Longman, 1999.

———. "What Should Historians Do with Masculinity? Reflections on Nineteenth-century Britain." *History Workshop Journal* 38 (1994): 179–202.

Tosh, John, and Michael Roper, eds. *Manful Assertions: Masculinities in Britain since 1800*. London: Routledge, 1991.

Treloar, William Purdie. *Wilkes and the City*. London: J. Murray, 1917.

Turnbull, Paul. "A Forgotten Cosmogony: William Hull's *Remarks on the . . . Aboriginal Natives*." *Australian Historical Studies* 24 (October 1990): 207–20.

Vamplew, Wray, ed. *Australians, Historical Statistics*. Broadway, N.S.W.: Fairfax, Syme & Weldon Associates, 1987.

Vickery, Amanda. "Golden Age to Separate Spheres? A Review of the Categories and Chronology of English Women's History." *Historical Journal* 36 (1993): 383–414.

Voorhis, Harold. *Freemasonry in Bermuda*. New York: n.p., 1962.

———. "Negro Masonry in the United States." In *Gould's History of Freemasonry Throughout the World*, vol. 4, edited by Dudley Wright, 364–68. New York: Charles Scribner's Sons, 1936.

Walker, G. E. "250 Years of Freemasonry in India." *Ars Quatuor Coronatorum* 92 (1979): 172–90.

Wallace, Elizabeth Kowaleski. "The Needs of Strangers: Friendly Societies in Late Eighteenth-Century England." *Eighteenth-Century Life* 24 (Fall 2000): 53–72.

Washbrook, D. A. "India, 1818–1860: The Two Faces of Colonialism." In *The Oxford*

History of the British Empire, vol. 3, *The Nineteenth Century*, edited by Andrew Porter, 395–421. Oxford: Oxford University Press, 1999.

Weisberger, R. William. *Speculative Freemasonry and the Enlightenment: A Study of the Craft in London, Paris, Prague, and Vienna*. New York: Columbia University Press, 1993.

———, ed. *Freemasonry on Both Sides of the Atlantic: Essays Concerning the Craft in the British Isles, Europe, the United States, and Mexico*. Boulder: Eastern European Monographs, 2002.

Wesley, Charles H. *Prince Hall: Life and Legacy*. Washington, D.C.: United Supreme Council, Southern Jurisdiction, 1983.

Whelan, Kevin. *The Tree of Liberty: Radicalism, Catholicism and the Construction of Irish Identity, 1760–1830*. South Bend, Ind.: University of Notre Dame Press, 2000.

White, Richard. *The Middle Ground: Indians, Empires, and Republics in the Great Lakes Region, 1650–1815*. New York: Cambridge University Press, 1991.

Whytehead, T. B. "Women in Freemasonry." In *Occasional Papers on the History of Freemasonry. Reprinted from the Freemason's Chronicle*. London: W. W. Morgan, 1882.

Williams, W. J. "Masonic Personalia, 1723–39." *Ars Quatuor Coronatorum* 40 (1928): 31–42, 127–37, 230–39.

Wilson, Angus. *The Strange Ride of Rudyard Kipling: His Life and Works*. London: Secker and Warburg, 1977.

Wilson, Brian G. "Patronage and Power: The Early Political Culture of the Niagara Peninsula." In *The Capital Years: Niagara-on-the-Lake, 1792–1796*, edited by Richard Merritt and Nancy Butler, 45–66. Toronto: Dundurn Press, 1991.

Wilson, David A. *United Irishmen, United States: Immigrant Radicals in the Early Republic*. Ithaca: Cornell University Press, 1998.

Wilson, Kathleen. "Empire, Gender, and Modernity." In *The Oxford History of the British Empire Companion Series Gender and Empire*, edited by Philippa Levine, 14–45. Oxford: Oxford University Press, 2004.

———. *The Island Race: Englishness, Empire and Gender in the Eighteenth Century*. London: Routledge, 2003.

———. *The Sense of the People: Politics, Culture and Imperialism in England, 1715–1785*. Cambridge: Cambridge University Press, 1998.

Windholz, Anne M. "An Emigrant and a Gentleman: Imperial Masculinity, British Magazines, and the Colony that Got Away." *Victorian Studies* 42 (1999): 631–58.

Woodham-Smith, Cecil. *Queen Victoria: From Her Birth to the Death of the Prince Consort*. New York: Knopf, 1972.

Wright, Dudley, ed. *Gould's History of Freemasonry Throughout the World*. 6 vols. New York: Charles Scribner's Sons, 1936.

York, Neil. "Freemasons and the American Revolution." *The Historian* 55 (1993): 315–30.

Zeller, Suzanne. *Inventing Canada: Early Victorian Science and the Idea of a Transcontinental Nation*. Toronto: University of Toronto Press, 1987.

INDEX

D'Urban, Benjamin (governor of Cape Colony), 196, 202
Durham, 1st Earl of (John George Lambton, governor of Canada, English Pro Grand Master, 1839–40), 176, 201
Dutch lodges, 36, 77, 85, 88–89, 97–98, 193–95, 197–99, 285
Dutt, Prosonno Coomar, 228–32

East India Company. See Merchants
Education: of orphans, 62, 75, 175, 190; of Indians, 174, 223–24, 225; at Cape, 194–95, 248. See also Benevolence; Punjab Masonic Institution; Royal Masonic Institution for Girls
Edward Augustus (1739-1767). See York, Duke of
Edward Augustus (1767-1820). See Kent, Duke of
Edward VII, King (English Grand Master, 1874–1901): as Prince of Wales, 253, 255, 256–58, 260, 269, 270, 271, 280; Indian tour of, 257–58
Egalitarianism, 15, 29, 70, 72–73, 82, 88–89, 115, 122, 176, 209, 233, 237–38, 297, 313 (n. 19)
Egypt, 260, 266; Cairo, 285
Elites: metropolitan, 28, 103–4; colonial, 53–55, 84, 115, 117–19, 163–75, 178, 189, 194–95, 201–2, 221, 237, 258–62, 264–67. See also Class; Collaboration; Royal family
Elphinstone, 1st Baron of (John Elphinstone, governor of Madras), 175, 201
Emancipists, 169, 186–93, 218
English-speaking Freemasonry. See Fraternalism
Europe, 31, 77, 128, 125; lodges of adoption in, 89; first lodges in, 106, 108; Jacobitism in, 106–7; Latin Masonry, 288–89
Exclusivity, 64, 73, 184, 238–39, 326

(n. 25); in tension with inclusive ideology, 6, 19–20, 176–77, 192–93, 215–17, 220, 227–28, 281, 283–84, 286, 306 (n. 48); masculine, 209–10; and Prince Hall Masons, 217, 235; and Hindus, 222, 228–29, 233–34. See also Anti-Catholicism; Protestantism

Family: Freemasonry as, 16; Mason's duty to, 17, 61–63, 94–96; as metaphor, 17–18, 204–6, 210, 215, 221, 234, 237, 239, 267, 271, 279, 293, 306 (n. 42); model, 71, 204–10; hierarchies within, 238–39
Family of man. See Brotherhood, universal
Fees and dues, 24, 39, 45, 59, 81, 86, 104, 145, 150, 155, 211; used to exclude candidates, 176, 184–85, 192
Florida, 38
Foreign Freemasons, 8, 36, 55, 74, 85–87, 193–95
France, 77, 84–85, 107–8, 120–21, 128, 138, 208; women Freemasons in, 89, 91–92; Paris, 107, 114. See also Grand Orient
Franklin, Benjamin, 83–85, 114
Fraternalism, 17–20; and empire, 3–4, 17, 22, 51–63, 268, 280–81, 283–84; significance of women to, 22, 53, 55–57, 60–63; conditions that fostered, 67; relationship to cosmopolitanism, 98; and United Irishmen, 102, 122–23; and George Washington, 115; English-speaking, 287, 289–91, 294; Anglo-Saxon, 287–88, 291–94, 340 (n. 4). See also Brotherhood, universal; Egalitarianism; Love, brotherly
Frederick Lewis. See Wales, Prince of
Free blacks: in Cape, 198–99; debate over admission of, 217–20
French lodges, 76, 77, 89, 97–98, 107, 138, 197, 314 (n. 27); in Indian Ocean region, 85–87, 91–92, 172
Funerals, 56, 63, 134, 168, 195

CPSIA information can be obtained
at www.ICGtesting.com
Printed in the USA
LVOW11s1942280917
550421LV00004B/315/P